THE LANGUAGE OF LITERATURE

THE *InterActive*
READER™ PLUS
with Additional Support

McDougal Littell
A HOUGHTON MIFFLIN COMPANY
Evanston, Illinois • Boston • Dallas

Reading Consultant, *The InterActive Reader™ Plus*

Sharon Sicinski-Skeans, Ph.D. Assistant Professor of Reading, University of Houston-Clear Lake; former K-12 Language Arts Program Director, Spring Independent School District, Houston, Texas
The reading consultant guided the conceptual development of the *InterActive Reader*. She participated in the development of prototype materials, the planning and writing of lessons, and the review of completed materials.

Senior Consultants, *The Language of Literature*

Arthur N. Applebee Professor of Education, State University of New York at Albany; Director, National Research Center on English Learning and Achievements; Senior Fellow, Center for Writing and Literacy

Andrea B. Bermúdez Professor of Studies in Language and Culture; Director, Research Center for Language and Culture; Chair, Foundations and Professional Studies, University of Houston-Clear Lake

Sheridan Blau Senior Lecturer in English and Education and former Director of Composition, University of California at Santa Barbara; Director, South Coast Writing Project; Director, Literature Institute for Teachers; Past President, National Council of Teachers of English

Rebekah Caplan Coordinator, English Language Arts K-12, Oakland Unified School District, Oakland, California; Teacher-Consultant, Bay Area Writing Project, University of California at Berkeley; served on the California State English Assessment Development Team for Language Arts

Peter Elbow Professor of English, University of Massachusetts at Amherst; Fellow, Bard Center for Writing and Thinking

Susan Hynds Professor and Director of English Education, Syracuse University, Syracuse, New York

Judith A. Langer Professor of Education, State University of New York at Albany; Director, National Research Center on English Learning and Achievements; Director, Albany Institute for Research on Education

James Marshall Professor of English and English Education, University of Iowa, Iowa City

Acknowledgments can be found on page 494.

11 12 13 -PBO- 08 07

Table of Contents

Academic and Informational Reading 401

Introducing *The InterActive Reader™ Plu*

The InterActive Reader™ Plus is a new kind of literature book. As you will see, this book helps you become an active reader. It is a book to mark on, to write in, and to make your own. You can use it in class *and* take it home.

An Easy-to-Carry Literature Text

This book won't weigh you down—it can fit as comfortably in your hand as it can in your backpack. Yet it contains works by such important authors as . . .

Edgar Allan Poe's classic tale of terror "The Masque of the Red Death"

William Faulkner's unforgettable story "A Rose for Emily"

Four memorable poems by **Emily Dickinson,** one of America's greatest poets

Martin Luther King, Jr.'s eloquent "Letter from Birmingham Jail"

You will read these selections and other great literature—plays, poems, stories, and nonfiction. In addition, you will learn how to understand the texts you use in classes, on tests, and in the real world, and you will study and practice specific strategies for taking standardized tests.

Help for Reading

The InterActive Reader™ Plus helps you understand many challenging works of literature. Here's how.

Before-You-Read Activities A prereading page helps you make connections to your everyday life and gives you a key to understanding the selection.

Preview A preview of every selection tells you what to expect.

Reading Tips Reading tips give useful help throughout.

Focus Each longer piece is broken into smaller 'bites' or sections. A focus at the beginning of each section tells you what to look for.

Pause and Reflect At the end of each section, a quick question or two helps you check your understanding.

Read Aloud Specific passages are marked for you to read aloud. You will use your voice and ears to interpret literature.

Reread This feature directs you to passages where a lot of action, change, or meaning is packed in a few lines.

Mark It Up This feature invites you to mark your own notes and questions right on the page.

Vocabulary Support

Words to Know Important new words are underlined. Their definitions appear in a Words to Know section at the bottom of any page where they occur in the selection. You will work with these words in the Words to Know SkillBuilder pages.

Personal Word List As you read, you will want to add some words from the selections to your own vocabulary. Write these words in your Personal Word List on page 476.

SkillBuilder Pages

After each literary selection, you will find these SkillBuilder pages:

  Active Reading SkillBuilder.
  Literary Analysis SkillBuilder.
  Words to Know SkillBuilder (for most selections).

These pages will help you practice and apply important skills.

The InterActive Reader™ Plus with Additional Support

The InterActive Reader™ Plus with Additional Support provides all of the literature selections and all of the features from the *InterActive Reader™ Plus*. Special additional features include:

Section summaries A brief summary helps get you started with each section or chunk of the text.

More About . . . These notes provide key background information about specific elements of the text such as historical events, scientific concepts, or political situations needed for understanding the selection.

What Does It Mean? These brief notes clearly explain any confusing words, phrases, references, or other constructions.

Reader Success Strategy These notes give useful and fun tips and strategies for comprehending the selection.

Reading Check These questions at key points in the text help you clarify what is happening in the selection.

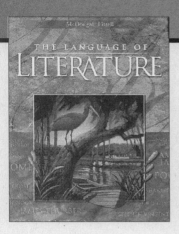

Links to *The Language of Literature*

If you are using McDougal Littell's *The Language of Literature,* you will find *The InterActive Reader™ Plus* to be a perfect companion. The literary selections in the reader can all be found in that book. *The InterActive Reader™ Plus* lets you read certain core selections from *The Language of Literature* more slowly and in greater depth.

Read on to learn more!

Academic and Informational Reading

Here is a special collection of real world examples to help you read every kind of informational material, from textbooks to technical directions. The strategies you learn will help you on tests, in other classes, and in the world outside of school. You will find strategies for the following:

Analyzing Text Features This section will help you read many different types of magazine articles and textbooks. You will learn how titles, subtitles, lists, graphics, many different kinds of visuals, and other special features work in magazines and textbooks. After studying this section you will be ready to read even the most complex material.

Understanding Visuals Tables, charts, graphs, maps, and diagrams all require special reading skills. As you learn the common elements of various visual texts, you will learn to read these materials with accuracy and skill.

Recognizing Text Structures Informational texts can be organized in many different ways. In this section you will study the following structures and learn about special key words that will help you identify the organizational patterns:

- Main idea and supporting details
- Problem and solution
- Sequence
- Cause and Effect
- Comparison and Contrast
- Argument

Reading in the Content Areas You will learn special strategies for reading social studies, science, and mathematics texts.

Reading Beyond the Classroom In this section you will encounter applications, schedules, technical directions, product information, Web pages, and other readings. Learning to analyze these texts will help you in your everyday life and on some standardized tests.

Test Preparation Strategies

In this section, you will find strategies and practice to help you succeed on many different kinds of standardized tests. After closely studying a variety of test formats through annotated examples, you will have an opportunity to practice each format on your own. Additional support will help you think through your answers. You will find strategies for the following:

Successful Test Taking This section provides many suggestions for preparing for and taking tests. The information ranges from analyzing test questions to tips for answering multiple-choice and open-ended test questions.

Reading Tests: Long Selections You will learn how to analyze the structure of a lengthy reading and prepare to answer the comprehension questions that follow it.

Reading Tests: Short Selections These selections may be a paragraph of text, a poem, a chart or graph, or some other item. You will practice the special range of comprehension skills required for these pieces.

Functional Reading These real-world texts present special challenges. You will learn about the various test formats that use applications, product labels, technical directions, Web pages, and more.

Revising and Editing Tests These materials test your under-standing of English grammar and usage. You may encounter capitalization and punctuation questions. Sometimes the focus is on usage questions such as verb tenses or pronoun agreement issues. You will become familiar with these formats through the guided practice in this section.

Writing Tests Writing prompts and sample student essays will help you understand how to analyze a prompt and what ele-ments make a successful written response. Scoring rubrics and a prompt for practice will prepare you for the writing tests you will take.

User's Guide

The *InterActive Reader™ Plus* has an easy-to-follow organization, illustrated by these sample pages from *Of Plymouth Plantation*.

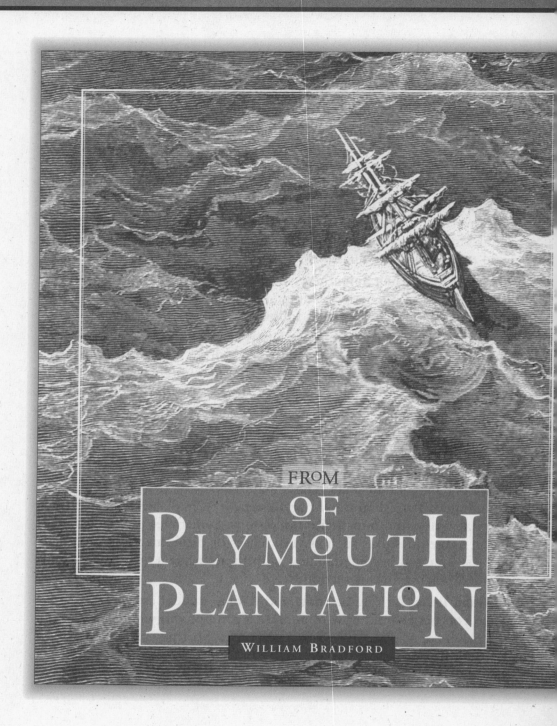

FROM

OF PLYMOUTH PLANTATION

WILLIAM BRADFORD

Before You Read

Connect to Your Life

If you were to go to a new place, such as a desert island, what would you need to survive? How would you get what you needed?

WHAT I NEED TO SURVIVE	HOW I WOULD GET IT
fuel for cooking and heat	gather twigs and branches to make a fire

Key to the Chronicle

WHAT YOU NEED TO KNOW During the 1500s and 1600s in England, a group of people wanted to separate themselves from the Church of England. The Pilgrims, as they are known today, fled from England because they were not allowed to practice their religious beliefs. The Pilgrims went first to Holland and then to America, settling in Plymouth in what is now Massachusetts. Survival in America was difficult, and nearly half of the Plymouth colonists died during the first winter.

Connect to Your Life

These activities help you see connections between your own life and what happens in the selection.

Key to the Selection

This section provides a "key" to help you unlock the selection so that you can understand and enjoy it. One of these four kinds of keys will appear:

- **What You Need to Know**— important background information.

- **What's the Big Idea?**—an introduction to key words or concepts in the selection.

- **What Do You Think?**— a preview of an important quotation from the selection.

- **What to Listen For**— a chance to examine the sound and rhythm of a piece.

And there's more

User's Guide *continued*

Reading Tips

1 These practical strategies will help you gain more from your reading.

PREVIEW

2 This feature tells you what the selection is about, so that you'll know what to expect.

FOCUS

3 Every literary work is broken into sections. Each section is introduced by a Focus that tells you what to look for as you read.

MARK IT UP

4 This feature often appears in the Focus. It may ask you to underline or circle key passages in the text or to take notes in the margin as you read.

As the chronicle begins . . .

5 This feature provides a brief summary to help you get started with each section of the text.

CHRONICLE

1 **Reading Tips**
A **chronicle** is a work of **nonfiction**, a historical account of important events. William Bradford actually witnessed the events he describes in this firsthand account.

Bradford wrote this chronicle more than 300 years ago. Some of the sentences are long, and some of the words may look strange. Try these strategies to help your understanding:

- Use the heading for each section as a guide to the content.
- Read at a steady pace and just keep moving. Try to take in big chunks of meaning. Look for main ideas and don't get lost in the details.

As the chronicle begins . . .

5
- The Pilgrims, who are devoted to God, have taken a long and difficult journey over the ocean.
- The Pilgrims face many hardships as they try to make a home in a new land.

FROM OF PLYMOUTH PLANTATION
WILLIAM BRADFORD

2 **PREVIEW** These excerpts tell about the Pilgrims' survival in America in the early 1600s. William Bradford, the first governor of Plymouth colony, describes the Pilgrims' many hardships, their strength of character, and their faith in God. He also explains how some Native Americans helped the colonists to survive.

3 **FOCUS**
Bradford describes the Pilgrims' arrival at Cape Cod in November of 1620. The Pilgrims faced the frightening wilderness of an unknown world.

4 **MARK IT UP** As you read, circle any details that help you understand the Pilgrims' situation. An example is highlighted.

THEIR SAFE ARRIVAL AT CAPE COD

But to omit other things (that I may be brief) after long beating at sea they[1] fell with that land which is called Cape Cod; the which being made and certainly known to be it, they were not a little joyful. . . .

Being thus arrived in a good harbor, and brought safe to land, they fell upon their knees and blessed the God of Heaven who had brought them over the vast and furious ocean, and delivered them from all the perils and miseries thereof, again to set their feet on the firm and stable earth, their proper element. . . .

But here I cannot but stay and make a pause, and stand half amazed at this poor people's present condition; and so I

---

1. **they:** Bradford refers to the Pilgrims in the third person even though he is one of them.

think will the reader, too, when he well considers the same. Being thus passed the vast ocean, and a sea of troubles before in their preparation (as may be remembered by that which went before), they had now no friends to welcome them nor [20] inns to entertain or refresh their weatherbeaten bodies; no houses or much less towns to repair to, to seek for succor.[2] It is recorded in Scripture as a mercy to the Apostle and his shipwrecked company, that the barbarians showed them no small kindness in refreshing them,[3] but these savage barbarians, when they met with them (as after will appear) were readier to fill their sides full of arrows than otherwise. And for the season it was winter, and they that know the winters of that country know them to be sharp and violent, and subject to cruel and fierce storms, dangerous to travel to [30] known places, much more to search an unknown coast. Besides, what could they see but a hideous and <u>desolate</u> wilderness, full of wild beasts and wild men—and what multitudes there might be of them they knew not. Neither could they, as it were, go up to the top of Pisgah[4] to view from this wilderness a more goodly country to feed their hopes; for which way soever they turned their eyes (save upward to the heavens) they could have little <u>solace</u> or content in respect of any outward objects. For summer being done, all things stand upon them with a weatherbeaten face, [40] and the whole country, full of woods and thickets, represented a wild and savage <u>hue</u>. If they looked behind them, there was the mighty ocean which they had passed and was now as a main bar and gulf to separate them from all the civil parts of the world. . . .

[10] *Pause* & *Reflect*

---

2. **succor** (sŭk′ər): help; relief.

3. **It is . . . refreshing them:** a reference to the biblical account of the courteous reception of Paul and his companions by the inhabitants of Malta (Acts 27:41–28:2).

4. **Pisgah** (pĭz′gə): the mountain from whose peak Moses saw the Promised Land (Deuteronomy 34:1–4).

[6] WORDS TO KNOW **desolate** (dĕs′ə-lĭt) *adj.* without inhabitants; barren
solace (sŏl′ĭs) *n.* comfort in sorrow or distress
hue (hyōō) *n.* appearance; color

---

[7] ✎ MARK IT UP WORD POWER

Mark words that you'd like to add to your **Personal Word List.** After reading, you can record the words and their meanings beginning on page 476.

☆ **Reader Success Strategy**

[8] As you read this section, fill in the following web with some of the hardships the Pilgrims faced.

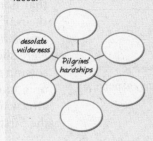

desolate wilderness

Pilgrims' hardships

✔ **Reading Check**

[9] How did the Pilgrims feel about the new world?

Pause & *Reflect*

[11] Imagine you are one of the Pilgrims who have just set foot on land. What do you think is the greatest challenge that awaits you and the other Pilgrims in the New World? **(Evaluate)**

_____

_____

_____

_____

Of Plymouth Plantation **5**

[6] WORDS TO KNOW Important **Words to Know** are underlined in each selection. Definitions are given at the bottom of the page.

✎ MARK IT UP WORD POWER

[7] This feature will remind you to mark words that you'd like to add to your **Personal Word List.** After reading, you can look up the definitions and record information about each word. The Personal Word List begins on page 476.

☆ **Reader Success Strategy**

[8] This feature gives useful and fun tips and strategies for comprehension.

✔ **Reading Check**

[9] These questions help you clarify what is happening in the selection.

Pause & *Reflect*

[10] Whenever you see these words in a selection, stop reading. Go to the side column and answer the questions. Then move ahead to the next Focus and continue your reading.

[11] These questions appear at the end of every section. They provide a follow-up to the Focus activity that begins each section, and they give you a quick way to check your understanding.

And there's more

Student Model

These pages show you how one student made use of *The InterActive Reader™ Plus*.

Pause & Reflect

✎ MARK IT UP **1.** What did the Pilgrims take from the Indians' houses? Circle the items mentioned on page 6. Star the item that kept the Pilgrims from starving. **(Clarify)**

2. What did the Pilgrims do to drive off the attacking Indians? **(Cause and Effect)**

They ran at them and shot at them.

✔ Reading Check

How did the Pilgrims respond to the Indians' arrows?

of their rendezvous[9] but were commanded not to shoot till they could take full aim at them. And the other two charged again with all speed, for there were only four had arms there, and defended the barricado, which was first assaulted. The cry of the Indians was dreadful, especially when they [the Indians] saw their men [the English] run out of the rendezvous toward the shallop to recover their arms, the Indians wheeling about upon them. But some running out with coats of mail on, and cutlasses[10] in their hands, they [the English] soon got their arms and let fly amongst them [the Indians] and quickly stopped their violence. . . .

Thus it pleased God to vanquish their enemies and give them deliverance; and by His special providence so to dispose that not any one of them were either hurt or hit, though their arrows came close by them and on every side [of] them; and sundry of their coats, which hung up in the barricado, were shot through and through. Afterwards they gave God solemn thanks and praise for their deliverance, and gathered up a bundle of their arrows and sent them into England afterward by the master of the ship, and called that place the First Encounter. . . .

Pause & Reflect

Note how this student used the following symbols:

✓ marks a place where something is made clear or understandable

? marks where something is not understood or is confusing

! marks a surprising or interesting place in the text

Also notice how two words are circled, *providence* and *sundry*. These are words that the student marked for her Personal Word List.

FOCUS
Read to find out about the Pilgrims' first winter at Cape Cod.

THE STARVING TIME

But that which was most sad and lamentable was, that in two or three months' time half of their company died, especially in January and February, being the depth of winter, and wanting houses and other comforts; being infected with the scurvy[11] and other diseases which this long voyage and their inaccommodate condition had brought upon them. So as there died some times two or three of a day in the foresaid time, that of 100 and odd persons, scarce fifty

___

9. **rendezvous** (rän′dā-vōō′): a gathering place; here used to denote the Pilgrims' encampment.

10. **coats of mail . . . and cutlasses:** armor made of joined metal links, and short curved swords.

11. **scurvy** (skûr′vē): a disease caused by lack of vitamin C.

WORDS
TO
KNOW   **vanquish** (văng′kwĭsh) *v.* to defeat in battle

remained. And of these, in the time of most distress, there was but six or seven sound persons who to their great
150 commendations, be it spoken, spared no pains night nor day, but with abundance of toil and hazard of their own health fetched them wood, made them fires, dressed them meat, made their beds, washed their loathsome clothes, clothed and unclothed them. . . . In a word, did all the homely and necessary offices for them which dainty and queasy stomachs cannot endure to hear named; and all this willingly and cheerfully, without any grudging in the least, showing herein their true love unto their friends and brethren; a rare example and worthy to be remembered. Two of these seven were Mr.
160 William Brewster, their reverend Elder, and Myles Standish, their Captain and military commander, unto whom myself and many others were much beholden in our low and sick condition. And yet the Lord so upheld these persons as in this general calamity they were not at all infected either with sickness or lameness. . . .

 Pause & Reflect

FOCUS
Read to find out about the relationship that develops between the Pilgrims and the Indians.

170 **MARK IT UP** As you read, underline details that show what the Pilgrims learn from their Indian friends.

INDIAN RELATIONS

All this while the Indians came skulking about them, and would sometimes show themselves aloof off, but when any approached near them, they would run away; and once they [the Indians] stole away their [the colonists'] tools where they had been at work and were gone to dinner. But about the 16th of March, a certain Indian came boldly amongst them and spoke to them in broken English, which they could well understand but marveled at it. At length they understood by discourse with him, that he was not of these parts, but belonged to the eastern parts where some English ships came to fish, with whom he was acquainted and could name sundry of them by their names,
180 amongst whom he had got his language. He became profitable to them in acquainting them with many things concerning the state of the country in the east parts where he lived, which was

✔ Reading Check
How do the healthy Pilgrims feel about caring for the sick?

 Pause & Reflect

MARK IT UP Why do almost half of the Pilgrims die the first winter? Write the answer below. Then circle details on page 8 that support your answer. **(Cause and Effect)**

They died of diseases. They also died because it was so cold.

As the chronicle continues . . .
- The Pilgrims meet the Indian named Samoset.
- Massasoit and Squanto visit the Pilgrims.
- The Pilgrims and the Indians come to an agreement.

 Why did they take the tools?

☆ Reader Success Strategy
On a separate piece of paper, make a brief outline to keep track of the major events in this section of the chronicle.

WORDS
TO
KNOW

aloof (ə-lōōf′) *adj.* distant

THE LANGUAGE OF LITERATURE

THE *InterActive*
READER™ PLUS
with Additional Support

FROM

OF
PLYMOUTH
PLANTATION

WILLIAM BRADFORD

Before You Read

Connect to Your Life

If you were to go to a new place, such as a desert island, what would you need to survive? How would you get what you needed?

WHAT I NEED TO SURVIVE	HOW I WOULD GET IT
fuel for cooking and heat	gather twigs and branches to make a fire

Key to the Chronicle

WHAT YOU NEED TO KNOW During the 1500s and 1600s in England, a group of people wanted to separate themselves from the Church of England. The Pilgrims, as they are known today, fled from England because they were not allowed to practice their religious beliefs. The Pilgrims went first to Holland and then to America, settling in Plymouth in what is now Massachusetts. Survival in America was difficult, and nearly half of the Plymouth colonists died during the first winter.

Reading Tips

A **chronicle** is a work of **nonfiction,** a historical account of important events. William Bradford actually witnessed the events he describes in this firsthand account.

Bradford wrote this chronicle more than 300 years ago. Some of the sentences are long, and some of the words may look strange. Try these strategies to help your understanding:

- Use the heading for each section as a guide to the content.
- Read at a steady pace and just keep moving. Try to take in big chunks of meaning. Look for main ideas and don't get lost in the details.

As the chronicle begins . . .

- The Pilgrims, who are devoted to God, have taken a long and difficult journey over the ocean.
- The Pilgrims face many hardships as they try to make a home in a new land.

FROM
OF PLYMOUTH PLANTATION

WILLIAM BRADFORD

PREVIEW These excerpts tell about the Pilgrims' survival in America in the early 1600s. William Bradford, the first governor of Plymouth colony, describes the Pilgrims' many hardships, their strength of character, and their faith in God. He also explains how some Native Americans helped the colonists to survive.

> **FOCUS**
> Bradford describes the Pilgrims' arrival at Cape Cod in November of 1620. The Pilgrims faced the frightening wilderness of an unknown world.
>
> ✏️ **MARK IT UP** As you read, circle any details that help you understand the Pilgrims' situation. An example is highlighted.

10

THEIR SAFE ARRIVAL AT CAPE COD

But to omit other things (that I may be brief) after long beating at sea they[1] fell with that land which is called Cape Cod; the which being made and certainly known to be it, they were not a little joyful. . . .

Being thus arrived in a good harbor, and brought safe to land, they fell upon their knees and blessed the God of Heaven who had brought them over the vast and furious ocean, and delivered them from all the perils and miseries thereof, again to set their feet on the firm and stable earth, their proper element. . . .

But here I cannot but stay and make a pause, and stand half amazed at this poor people's present condition; and so I

---

1. **they:** Bradford refers to the Pilgrims in the third person even though he is one of them.

think will the reader, too, when he well considers the same. Being thus passed the vast ocean, and a sea of troubles before in their preparation (as may be remembered by that which went before), they had now no friends to welcome them nor inns to entertain or refresh their weatherbeaten bodies; no houses or much less towns to repair to, to seek for succor.[2] It is recorded in Scripture as a mercy to the Apostle and his shipwrecked company, that the barbarians showed them no small kindness in refreshing them,[3] but these savage barbarians, when they met with them (as after will appear) were readier to fill their sides full of arrows than otherwise. And for the season it was winter, and they that know the winters of that country know them to be sharp and violent, and subject to cruel and fierce storms, dangerous to travel to known places, much more to search an unknown coast. Besides, what could they see but a hideous and <u>desolate</u> wilderness, full of wild beasts and wild men—and what multitudes there might be of them they knew not. Neither could they, as it were, go up to the top of Pisgah[4] to view from this wilderness a more goodly country to feed their hopes; for which way soever they turned their eyes (save upward to the heavens) they could have little <u>solace</u> or content in respect of any outward objects. For summer being done, all things stand upon them with a weatherbeaten face, and the whole country, full of woods and thickets, represented a wild and savage <u>hue</u>. If they looked behind them, there was the mighty ocean which they had passed and was now as a main bar and gulf to separate them from all the civil parts of the world. . . .

Pause & Reflect

---

2. **succor** (sŭk′ər): help; relief.

3. **It is . . . refreshing them:** a reference to the biblical account of the courteous reception of Paul and his companions by the inhabitants of Malta (Acts 27:41–28:2).

4. **Pisgah** (pĭz′gə): the mountain from whose peak Moses saw the Promised Land (Deuteronomy 34:1–4).

WORDS **desolate** (dĕs′ə-lĭt) *adj.* without inhabitants; barren
TO   **solace** (sŏl′ĭs) *n.* comfort in sorrow or distress
KNOW   **hue** (hyōō) *n.* appearance; color

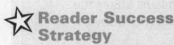

MARK IT UP WORD POWER

Mark words that you'd like to add to your **Personal Word List**. After reading, you can record the words and their meanings beginning on page 476.

Reader Success Strategy

As you read this section, fill in the following web with some of the hardships the Pilgrims faced.

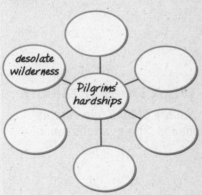

desolate wilderness

Pilgrims' hardships

Reading Check

How did the Pilgrims feel about the new world?

Pause & Reflect

Imagine you are one of the Pilgrims who have just set foot on land. What do you think is the greatest challenge that awaits you and the other Pilgrims in the New World? **(Evaluate)**

_____
_____
_____
_____

As the chronicle continues . . .

- The Pilgrims mend their boat and set out to search for a place to settle.

- They find some of the Indians' houses and take supplies while the Indians are away.

- The Indians attack the Pilgrims with arrows.

What Does It Mean?

Sundry of their implements means "their various tools."

✔ Reading Check

Reread the boxed paragraph. According to Bradford, how has God helped the Pilgrims?

FOCUS

After the Pilgrims landed, they discovered food and supplies in the deserted houses of Indians. Later, the Pilgrims were attacked. Read to find out about their first experiences on shore.

50

THE FIRST ENCOUNTER

Being thus arrived at Cape Cod the 11th of November, and necessity calling them to look out a place for habitation (as well as the master's and mariners' importunity); they having brought a large shallop[5] with them out of England, stowed in quarters in the ship, they now got her out and set their carpenters to work to trim her up; but being much bruised and shattered in the ship with foul weather, they saw she would be long in mending. Whereupon a few of them tendered themselves to go by land and discover those nearest places, whilst the shallop was in mending; . . .

After this, the shallop being got ready, they set out again for the better discovery of this place, and the master of the ship desired to go himself. So there went some thirty men but found it to be no harbor for ships but only for boats. There was also found two of their [the Indians'] houses covered with mats, and sundry of their implements in them, but the people were run away and could not be seen. Also there was found more of their corn and of their beans of various colors; the corn and beans they [the English] brought away, purposing to give them [the Indians] full satisfaction when they should meet with any of them as, about some six months afterward they did, to their good content.[6]

60

70

And here is to be noted a special providence of God, and a great mercy to this poor people, that here they got seed to plant them corn the next year, or else they might have starved, for they had none nor any likelihood to get any till the season had been past, as the sequel did manifest. Neither is it likely they had had this, if the first voyage had not been made, for the ground was now all covered with snow and hard frozen; but the Lord is never wanting unto His in their greatest needs; let His holy name have all the praise.

The month of November being spent in these affairs, and

---

5. **shallop** (shăl'əp): an open boat usually used in shallow waters.

6. **purposing . . . content:** intending to repay the Nauset Indians whose corn and beans they took, as they in fact did, to the Indians' satisfaction, six months later.

WORDS TO KNOW

providence (prŏv'ĭ-dəns) *n.* an instance of divine care or guidance

80 much foul weather falling in, the 6th of December they sent out their shallop again with ten of their principal men and some seamen, upon further discovery, intending to circulate that deep bay of Cape Cod. The weather was very cold and it froze so hard as the spray of the sea lighting on their coats, they were as if they had been glazed. . . . [The next night they landed and] made them a barricado[7] as usually they did every night, with logs, stakes, and thick pine boughs, the height of a man, leaving it open to leeward,[8] partly to shelter them from the cold and wind (making their fire in the middle and lying 90 round about it) and partly to defend them from any sudden assaults of the savages, if they should surround them; so being very weary, they betook them to rest. But about midnight they heard a hideous and great cry, and their <u>sentinel</u> called "Arm! arm!" So they bestirred them and stood to their arms and shot off a couple of muskets, and then the noise ceased. They concluded it was a company of wolves or such like wild beasts, for one of the seamen told them he had often heard such a noise in Newfoundland.

So they rested till about five of the clock in the morning; for 100 the tide, and their purpose to go from thence, made them be stirring betimes. So after prayer they prepared for breakfast, and it being day dawning it was thought best to be carrying things down to the boat. But some said it was not best to carry the arms down, others said they would be the readier, for they had lapped them up in their coats from the dew; but some three or four would not carry theirs till they went themselves. Yet as it fell out, the water being not high enough, they laid them down on the bank side and came up to breakfast.

But presently, all on the sudden, they heard a great and 110 strange cry, which they knew to be the same voices they heard in the night, though they varied their notes; and one of their company being abroad came running in and cried, "Men, Indians! Indians!" And withal, their arrows came flying amongst them. Their men ran with all speed to recover their arms, as by the good providence of God they did. In the meantime, of those that were there ready, two muskets were discharged at them, and two more stood ready in the entrance

---

7. **barricado** (băr´ĭ-kā´dō): a barrier for defense.

8. **to leeward** (lē´wərd): on the side sheltered from the wind.

WORDS
TO
KNOW   **sentinel** (sĕn´tə-nəl) *n.* a guard

Reader Success Strategy

To help organize the sequence of events in your mind, make a time line like the one below to record the actions of the Pilgrims that lead up to their encounter with the Indians.

November 11 Arrived at Cape Cod

 READ ALOUD Lines 109–115

Notice how this passage reflects the Puritan devotion to God.

Of Plymouth Plantation 7

Pause & Reflect

 MARK IT UP **1.** What did the Pilgrims take from the Indians' houses? Circle the items mentioned on page 6. Star the item that kept the Pilgrims from starving. **(Clarify)**

2. What did the Pilgrims do to drive off the attacking Indians? **(Cause and Effect)**

_____

_____

_____

_____

✔ Reading Check

How did the Pilgrims respond to the Indians' arrows?

As the chronicle continues . . .

- Many of the Pilgrims die.
- Those who are healthy care for the sick.

⭐ Reader Success Strategy

Use a ruler to help you read slowly and carefully. As you read, notice what happens to the Pilgrims and how they respond.

of their rendezvous[9] but were commanded not to shoot till they could take full aim at them. And the other two charged again with all speed, for there were only four had arms there, and defended the barricado, which was first assaulted. The cry of the Indians was dreadful, especially when they [the Indians] saw their men [the English] run out of the rendezvous toward the shallop to recover their arms, the Indians wheeling about upon them. But some running out with coats of mail on, and cutlasses[10] in their hands, they [the English] soon got their arms and let fly amongst them [the Indians] and quickly stopped their violence. . . .

Thus it pleased God to <u>vanquish</u> their enemies and give them deliverance; and by His special providence so to dispose that not any one of them were either hurt or hit, though their arrows came close by them and on every side [of] them; and sundry of their coats, which hung up in the barricado, were shot through and through. Afterwards they gave God solemn thanks and praise for their deliverance, and gathered up a bundle of their arrows and sent them into England afterward by the master of the ship, and called that place the First Encounter. . . .

Pause & Reflect

FOCUS
Read to find out about the Pilgrims' first winter at Cape Cod.

THE STARVING TIME

But that which was most sad and lamentable was, that in two or three months' time half of their company died, especially in January and February, being the depth of winter, and wanting houses and other comforts; being infected with the scurvy[11] and other diseases which this long voyage and their inaccommodate condition had brought upon them. So as there died some times two or three of a day in the foresaid time, that of 100 and odd persons, scarce fifty

---

9. **rendezvous** (rän′dā-vōō′): a gathering place; here used to denote the Pilgrims' encampment.

10. **coats of mail . . . and cutlasses:** armor made of joined metal links, and short curved swords.

11. **scurvy** (skûr′vē): a disease caused by lack of vitamin C.

WORDS
TO
KNOW    **vanquish** (văng′kwĭsh) v. to defeat in battle

remained. And of these, in the time of most distress, there was
but six or seven sound persons who to their great
commendations, be it spoken, spared no pains night nor day,
but with abundance of toil and hazard of their own health
fetched them wood, made them fires, dressed them meat,
made their beds, washed their loathsome clothes, clothed and
unclothed them. . . . In a word, did all the homely and
necessary offices for them which dainty and queasy stomachs
cannot endure to hear named; and all this willingly and
cheerfully, without any grudging in the least, showing herein
their true love unto their friends and brethren; a rare example
and worthy to be remembered. Two of these seven were Mr.
William Brewster, their reverend Elder, and Myles Standish,
their Captain and military commander, unto whom myself and
many others were much beholden in our low and sick
condition. And yet the Lord so upheld these persons as in this
general calamity they were not at all infected either with
sickness or lameness. . . .

Pause & Reflect

FOCUS
Read to find out about
the relationship that
develops between the
Pilgrims and the
Indians.

MARK IT UP As you
read, underline details
that show what the
Pilgrims learn from
their Indian friends.

INDIAN RELATIONS

All this while the Indians came skulking
about them, and would sometimes show
themselves <u>aloof</u> off, but when any
approached near them, they would run
away; and once they [the Indians] stole
away their [the colonists'] tools where
they had been at work and were gone to
dinner. But about the 16th of March, a
certain Indian came boldly amongst them and spoke to them
in broken English, which they could well understand but
marveled at it. At length they understood by discourse with
him, that he was not of these parts, but belonged to the eastern
parts where some English ships came to fish, with whom he
was acquainted and could name sundry of them by their names,
amongst whom he had got his language. He became profitable
to them in acquainting them with many things concerning the
state of the country in the east parts where he lived, which was

Reading Check
How do the healthy Pilgrims
feel about caring for the sick?

Pause & Reflect
MARK IT UP Why do
almost half of the Pilgrims
die the first winter? Write the
answer below. Then circle
details on page 8 that support
your answer. **(Cause and
Effect)**

_____

_____

_____

_____

**As the chronicle
continues . . .**
• The Pilgrims meet the Indian
named Samoset.
• Massasoit and Squanto visit
the Pilgrims.
• The Pilgrims and the Indians
come to an agreement.

**Reader Success
Strategy**
On a separate piece of paper,
make a brief outline to keep
track of the major events in this
section of the chronicle.

WORDS
TO
KNOW   **aloof** (ə-lo͞of′) *adj.* distant

In what ways did Samoset help
the Pilgrims?

More About . . .

(SQUANTO) Squanto was cap-
tured by the explorer Captain
Thomas Hunt in 1615. Squanto
and other Native Americans
were sold into slavery in Spain.
After escaping and spending
two years in England, Squanto
returned to North America. He
taught the Pilgrims how to grow
and cook corn and advised
them in their relations with
the Indians.

Pause & Reflect

READ ALOUD Read aloud
the terms in the peace treaty
between the Pilgrims and
Massasoit's people (the boxed
passage). Then cross out the
one phrase below that does
not apply to the treaty. **(Infer)**

promotes safety

discourages theft

sets up an alliance

protects the Indian languages

---

afterwards profitable unto them; as also of the people here, of
their names, number and strength, of their situation and
distance from this place, and who was chief amongst them.
His name was Samoset. He told them also of another Indian
whose name was (Squanto,) a native of this place, who had
been in England and could speak better English than himself.

Being, after some time of entertainment and gifts dismissed,
190　a while after he came again, and five more with him, and they
brought again all the tools that were stolen away before, and
made way for the coming of their great Sachem,[12] called
Massasoit. Who, about four or five days after, came with the
chief of his friends and other attendance, with the aforesaid
Squanto. With whom, after friendly entertainment and some
gifts given him, they made a peace with him (which hath now
continued this 24 years) in these terms:

> 1. That neither he nor any of his should injure or do hurt
> to any of their people.
> 200　2. That if any of his did hurt to any of theirs, he should
> send the offender, that they might punish him.
> 3. That if anything were taken away from any of theirs, he
> should cause it to be restored; and they should do the like to his.
> 4. If any did unjustly war against him, they would aid him;
> if any did war against them, he should aid them.
> 5. He should send to his neighbors confederates to certify
> them of this, that they might not wrong them, but might be
> likewise comprised in the conditions of peace.[13]
> 6. That when their men came to them, they should leave
> 210　their bows and arrows behind them.

After these things he returned to his place called Sowams,[14]
some 40 miles from this place, but Squanto continued with them
and was their interpreter and was a special instrument sent of
God for their good beyond their expectation. He directed them
how to set their corn, where to take fish, and to procure other
commodities, and was also their pilot to bring them to
unknown places for their profit, and never left them till he died.

Pause & Reflect

---

12. **Sachem** (sā′chəm): chief.
13. **He should . . . peace:** Massasoit was to inform other tribes about the
    compact so that they might also keep peace with the Pilgrims.
14. **Sowams** (sō′ämz): near the site of present-day Barrington, Rhode Island.

WORDS TO KNOW	
	procure (prō-kyŏŏr′) *v.* to get by special effort; obtain
	commodity (kə-mŏd′ĭ-tē) *n.* something useful; an article of commerce

FOCUS
Read to find out how
the Pilgrims prepare for
their second winter
in America.

FIRST THANKSGIVING

They began now to gather in the small harvest they had, and to fit up their houses and dwellings against winter, being all well recovered in health and strength and had all things in good plenty. For as some were thus employed in affairs abroad, others were exercised in fishing, about cod and bass and other fish, of which they took good store, of which every family had their portion. All the summer there was no want; and now began to come in store of fowl, as winter approached, of which this place did abound when they came first (but afterward decreased by degrees). And besides waterfowl there was great store of wild turkeys, of which they took many, besides venison, etc. Besides they had about a peck[15] a meal a week to a person, or now since harvest, Indian corn to that proportion. Which made many afterwards write so largely of their plenty here to their friends in England, which were not <u>feigned</u> but true reports.

Pause & Reflect

---

15. **peck:** a unit of measurement equal to eight dry quarts.

WORDS
TO
KNOW   **feigned** (fānd) *adj.* not real; pretended

As the chronicle ends . . .

- The Pilgrims gather in the harvest and prepare for winter.
- The families share their food with each other.
- The Pilgrims write home to England about their plenty in the new land.

What Does It Mean?

The highlighted passage means that the Pilgrims are storing food and preparing their homes to withstand the winter snow and bitter cold.

Pause & Reflect

MARK IT UP **1.** Circle the types of food that the Pilgrims store for the winter. **(Clarify)**

2. What do you think of the Pilgrims after reading these excerpts from *Of Plymouth Plantation?* **(Connect)**

_____

_____

_____

_____

CHALLENGE

At the beginning of this selection, Bradford says that the Pilgrims "fell upon their knees and blessed the God of Heaven who had brought them over the vast and furious ocean." Mark other passages in which Bradford mentions God. Then imagine that these passages were not included in the **chronicle.** How would your impression of the Pilgrims be different? **(Evaluate)**

Active Reading SkillBuilder

Summarizing

Summarizing means condensing a work into fewer words, restating only the main ideas and important details. Summarizing a complex selection, like the historical narrative from *Of Plymouth Plantation,* helps readers clarify their understanding of key information. In the chart below write a one- or two-sentence summary of each section listed. An example is shown.

Section	Summary
Their Safe Arrival at Cape Cod	*After reaching land, the Pilgrims thanked God. With no friends to help them, the Pilgrims faced the wilderness in the dead of winter.*
The First Encounter	
The Starving Time	
Indian Relations	
First Thanksgiving	

Literary Analysis SkillBuilder

Primary Sources

Primary sources are written or created by people who observed or participated in a historical event. Primary sources include letters, wills, diaries, tape recordings, photographs, speeches, and eyewitness accounts. Primary sources often reveal the writer's or speaker's personal opinions, beliefs, motives, assumptions—or preconceived ideas—and biases. Fill in the following chart to analyze *Of Plymouth Plantation* as a primary source. An example is shown.

Source	*Of Plymouth Plantation*
Purpose (reason for writing)	*to show how the Pilgrims survived in the new world*
Point of View (perspective from which events are told)	
Assumptions (preconceived ideas)	
Biases (personal prejudices)	

Words to Know SkillBuilder

Words to Know

aloof	desolate	hue	providence	solace
commodity	feigned	procure	sentinel	vanquish

A. Fill in each set of blanks with the correct word from the word list.

1. This is what the admirals and generals on *our* side
   hope to do to admirals and generals on *their* side.

   _ _ _ _ _ _ ☐ _

2. If you close your eyes, you'll miss this completely,
   because your other senses won't help.

   _ _ ☐

3. This is like *get* or *obtain* but suggests that the getting
   is not easy.

   ☐ _ _ _ _ _ _

4. If *our* admirals and generals succeed in their efforts,
   their admirals and generals may need this.

   _ _ _ ☐ _ _ _

5. This might be anything from a big, impressive
   miracle to a small, still voice inside.

   _ ☐ _ _ _ _ _ _ _ _

6. Although this can mean "emotionally distant,"
   Bradford uses it to mean just "far away."

   ☐ _ _ _ _

7. This could be a car, a shirt, a steel beam,
   a bushel of corn, or—yech!—a pork belly.

   _ _ _ _ _ _ _ _ ☐ _

8. When an employee calls in sick and then goes
   fishing, he or she has this kind of sickness.

   _ _ ☐ _ _ _ _ _

9. The Dead Sea, abandoned houses,
   ghost towns, and the moon are all this.

   _ _ ☐ _ _ _ ☐ _

10. You might see this at the White House, Buckingham
    Palace, or outside your kid brother's fort.

    ☐ _ _ _ _ _ _ _

Complete the following sentence with the word that the boxed letters spell out.

In England, the 41 Puritans on the *Mayflower* were known as _____.

B. Imagine that you are a Pilgrim at Plymouth in 1621. Write about the first fall
harvest as you might describe it in a letter to a friend back in England. Use at least
four of the Words to Know in your description.

from # Sinners

in the Hands of an Angry God

JONATHAN EDWARDS

Before You Read

Connect to Your Life

The author of this sermon uses fear to persuade his listeners. Do you think that is an effective strategy? What are the benefits and drawbacks of using fear to get results? Write your responses in the chart below.

BENEFITS	DRAWBACKS

Key to the Sermon

WHAT YOU NEED TO KNOW The Puritans came to colonial America in the 1600s for religious freedom. About a hundred years later, some of the Puritans began to feel that the community had lost its religious feeling. To bring back the religious fervor of the previous century, leaders such as Jonathan Edwards led the Great Awakening. The Great Awakening was a religious revival in New England that lasted from 1734 to 1750. Edwards delivered the sermon "Sinners in the Hands of an Angry God" to inspire people to rediscover and recommit themselves to their religious beliefs.

from Sinners
in the Hands of an Angry God

JONATHAN EDWARDS

PREVIEW "Sinners in the Hands of an Angry God" is a **sermon** about the punishment in store for the wicked after death. Jonathan Edwards, a Puritan minister, preached this sermon in 1741. He wanted his listeners to turn to God and save their souls. As this excerpt shows, he used the power of words to trigger a basic emotion—fear.

SERMON

Reading Tips

When reading this **sermon:**

- Remember that you don't need to understand every word in a sentence to understand the overall meaning.

- When you come to a long sentence, use the verbs to help you follow the action.

- Use the author's images to visualize his descriptions.

FOCUS

Edwards divides his listeners into two groups: those who have accepted Christ in their hearts and those who have not ("the unconverted," or unchanged). God is angry at the unconverted. Read to find out what God has planned for them.

We find it easy to tread on and crush a worm that we see crawling on the earth; so it is easy for us to cut or singe a slender thread that any thing hangs by; thus easy is it for God when he pleases to cast his enemies down to hell. . . .

They[1] are now the objects of that very same *anger* and <u>wrath</u> of God, that is expressed in the torments of hell. And the reason why they do not go down to hell at each moment, is not because God, in whose power they are, is not then very angry with them; as angry as he is with many miserable creatures now tormented in hell, who there feel and bear the fierceness of his wrath. Yea, God is a great deal more angry with great numbers

As the sermon begins . . .

- Edwards describes God's power and anger.

- Edwards explains why God is angry.

More About . . .

PURITAN BELIEFS The Puritans believed that people are basically sinful and that obeying God is necessary to avoid being punished in hell. These beliefs would have made this speech especially powerful to those Puritans who heard it.

---

1. **they:** Earlier in the sermon, Edwards refers to "unconverted men." They are people who have not been "born again," meaning that they have not accepted Christ.

WORDS
TO
KNOW
wrath (răth) *n.* fierce anger, or punishment resulting from such anger

that are now on earth; yea, doubtless, with many that are now
in this congregation,[2] who it may be are at ease, than he is
with many of those who are now in the flames of hell.

So that it is not because God is unmindful of their wickedness,
and does not resent it, that he does not let loose his hand and
cut them off. God is not altogether such an one as themselves,
though they may imagine him to be so. The wrath of God
burns against them, their damnation does not slumber; the pit
is prepared, the fire is made ready, the furnace is now hot,
ready to receive them; the flames do now rage and glow. The
glittering sword is whet,[3] and held over them, and the pit hath
opened its mouth under them. . . .

Unconverted men walk over the pit of hell on a rotten
covering, and there are innumerable places in this covering so
weak that they will not bear their weight, and these places are
not seen. The arrows of death fly unseen at noonday; the
sharpest sight cannot discern them. God has so many different
unsearchable ways of taking wicked men out of the world and
sending them to hell, that there is nothing to make it appear,
that God had need to be at the expense of a miracle, or go out
of the ordinary course of his providence, to destroy any wicked
man, at any moment. . . .

Pause & Reflect

So that, thus it is that natural men[4] are
held in the hand of God, over the pit of
hell; they have deserved the fiery pit, and
are already sentenced to it; and God is
dreadfully provoked, his anger is as great
towards them as to those that are
actually suffering the executions of the
fierceness of his wrath in hell; and they
have done nothing in the least to <u>appease</u>
or abate that anger, neither is God in the
least bound by any promise to hold them up one moment; the
devil is waiting for them, hell is gaping for them, the flames

---

2. **this congregation:** the Puritans listening to Edwards.
3. **whet:** sharpened.
4. **natural men:** people who have not been "born again."

Pause & Reflect

1. God is angry at the wicked in hell. He is even more angry at the unconverted. What does he have planned for these people? **(Main Idea)**

_____

_____

_____

_____

MARK IT UP **2.** Imagine you are in the audience, listening to Edwards's description of hell. In the boxed passage on this page, circle the words and phrases that might make you afraid. **(Emotional/Loaded Language)**

As the sermon continues . . .

• Edwards tells the people that God is offended by sinners and can destroy them at will.

• He explains that the punishment of God is everlasting.

What Does It Mean?
Abate means "lessen."

FOCUS
Read to find out more about the terrible danger that sinners (here, called "natural men") are in.

MARK IT UP As you read, circle the details that help you understand this danger. An example is highlighted.

WORDS
TO
KNOW

appease (ə-pēz′) *v.* to bring peace, quiet, or calm to; soothe

50 gather and flash about them, and would fain[5] lay hold on them, and swallow them up; the fire pent up in their own hearts is struggling to break out: and they have no interest in any Mediator,[6] there are no means within reach that can be any security to them. In short, they have no refuge, nothing to take hold of. . . .

The bow of God's wrath is bent, and the arrow made ready on the string, and justice bends the arrow at your heart, and strains the bow, and it is nothing but the mere pleasure of God, and that of an angry God, without any promise or obligation at all, that **60** keeps the arrow one moment from being made drunk with your blood. Thus all you that never passed under a great change of heart, by the mighty power of the Spirit of God upon your souls; all you that were never born again, and made new creatures, and raised from being dead in sin, to a state of new, and before altogether unexperienced light and life, are in the hands of an angry God. However you may have reformed your life in many things, and may have had religious affections,[7] and may keep up a form of religion in your families and closets,[8] and in the house of God, it is nothing but his mere pleasure that keeps you from **70** being this moment swallowed up in everlasting destruction. . . .

The God that holds you over the pit of hell, much as one holds a spider, or some <u>loathsome</u> insect over the fire, <u>abhors</u> you, and is dreadfully provoked: his wrath towards you burns like fire; he looks upon you as worthy of nothing else, but to be cast into the fire; he is of purer eyes than to bear to have you in his sight; you are ten thousand times more <u>abominable</u> in his eyes, than the most hateful venomous serpent is in ours. You have offended him infinitely more than ever a stubborn rebel did his prince; and yet it is nothing but his hand that holds you from falling into the fire **80** every moment. It is to be <u>ascribed</u> to nothing else, that you did not go to hell the last night; that you was suffered[9] to awake again in this world, after you closed your eyes to sleep. And there is no other reason to be given, why you have not dropped into hell since you arose in the morning, but that God's hand has held you

---

5. **fain:** rather.
6. **Mediator:** Christ, who mediates, or helps bring about, salvation.
7. **affections:** feelings or emotions.
8. **closets:** private rooms for meditation.
9. **suffered:** permitted.

WORDS TO KNOW	**loathsome** (lōth′səm) *adj.* arousing great dislike
	abhor (ăb-hôr′) *v.* to regard with disgust
	abominable (ə-bŏm′ə-nə-bəl) *adj.* thoroughly detestable
	ascribe (ə-skrīb′) *v.* to attribute to a specified cause or source

✎ **MARK IT UP** WORD POWER

Mark words that you'd like to add to your **Personal Word List.** After reading, you can record the words and their meanings beginning on page 476.

📖 **READ ALOUD** Lines 71–77

Read aloud the boxed sentences on this page. How would you describe the way God views sinners? **(Infer)**

_____

_____

_____

_____

✔ **Reading Check**

According to Edwards, why aren't all of the sinners already in hell?

up. There is no other reason to be given why you have not gone to hell, since you have sat here in the house of God, provoking his pure eyes by your sinful wicked manner of attending his solemn worship. Yea, there is nothing else that is to be given as a reason why you do not this very moment drop down into hell.

90   O sinner! Consider the fearful danger you are in: it is a great furnace of wrath, a wide and bottomless pit, full of the fire of wrath, that you are held over in the hand of that God, whose wrath is provoked and incensed as much against you, as against many of the damned in hell. You hang by a slender thread, with the flames of divine wrath flashing about it, and ready every moment to singe it, and burn it asunder;[10] and you have no interest in any Mediator, and nothing to lay hold of to save yourself, nothing to keep off the flames of wrath, nothing of your own, nothing that you ever have done, nothing that you

100 can do, to induce God to spare you one moment. . . .

It is *everlasting* wrath. It would be dreadful to suffer this fierceness and wrath of Almighty God one moment; but you must suffer it to all eternity. There will be no end to this exquisite[11] horrible misery. When you look forward, you shall see a long forever, a boundless duration before you, which will swallow up your thoughts, and amaze your soul; and you will absolutely despair of ever having any deliverance, any end, any mitigation, any rest at all. You will know certainly that you must wear out long ages, millions of millions of ages, in wrestling

110 and conflicting with this almighty merciless vengeance; and then when you have so done, when so many ages have actually been spent by you in this manner, you will know that all is but a point to what remains. So that your punishment will indeed be infinite. Oh, who can express what the state of a soul in such circumstances is! All that we can possibly say about it, gives but a very feeble, faint representation of it; it is inexpressible and inconceivable: For "who knows the power of God's anger?"[12]

How dreadful is the state of those that are daily and hourly in the danger of this great wrath and infinite misery! But this is

120 the dismal case of every soul in this congregation that has not been born again, however moral and strict, sober and religious, they may otherwise be. . . .

Pause & *Reflect*

---

10. **asunder** (ə-sŭn′dər): into separate parts or pieces.

11. **exquisite** (ĕk′skwĭ-zĭt): sharply intense.

12. **"who knows . . . anger?":** a reference to Psalm 90:11, "Who knoweth the power of thine anger?"

Reader Success Strategy

As you read Edwards's description of God's punishment for sinners, try to visualize the scene. Then draw a sketch of this scene.

What Does It Mean?

The highlighted words mean that a sinner will not be saved from punishment, and the suffering will not become less harsh.

Pause & *Reflect*

1. Review the details you circled as you read. Then write a sentence to **summarize** the danger facing sinners.

_____

_____

_____

_____

2. Circle the four words below that are true to Edwards's idea of God. **(Clarify)**

calm	furious
stern	loving
disgusted	tender
frightening	forgetful

130

And now you have an extraordinary opportunity, a day wherein Christ has thrown the door of mercy wide open, and stands in the door calling and crying with a loud voice to poor sinners; a day wherein many are flocking to him, and pressing into the kingdom of God. Many are daily coming[13] from the east, west, north, and south; many that were very lately in the same miserable condition that you are in, are now in a happy state, with their hearts filled with love to him who has loved them, and washed them from their sins in his own blood, and rejoicing in hope of the glory of God. How awful is it to be left behind at such a day! To see so many others feasting, while you are pining and perishing! To see so many rejoicing and singing for joy of heart, while you have cause to mourn for sorrow of

140 heart, and howl for vexation of spirit! How can you rest one moment in such a condition? . . .

Therefore, let every one that is out of Christ, now awake and fly from the wrath to come. . . .

Pause **&** *Reflect*

As the sermon ends . . .

- Edwards describes the glory that awaits the sinner who repents.
- He invites sinners to enter God's kingdom as soon as possible.

Pause **&** *Reflect*

1. What does Christ do for sinners? **(Main Idea)**

_____

_____

_____

_____

2. Reread the last sentence of Edwards's sermon. Then restate his idea in your own words. **(Paraphrase)**

_____

_____

_____

_____

✔ **Reading Check**

How do sinners who repent and recommit to their religious beliefs feel?

CHALLENGE

Circle or highlight examples of powerful **images** in this sermon. What makes these images so powerful? How do they help Edwards accomplish his purpose? **(Evaluate)**

---

13. **Many . . . coming:** Edwards is referring to the hundreds of people who were being converted during the Great Awakening. The Great Awakening was a religious movement during the years 1734 to 1750. Edwards was one of the leaders.

Active Reading SkillBuilder

Analyzing Emotional Language

Persuasive writing often contains **loaded language**—words or phrases with strong connotations, or emotional associations. As you read this sermon, use the chart to list three examples of specific words, phrases, and images that Edwards uses to achieve the greatest emotional effect. Then describe the emotional impact that this loaded language might have had on his audience.

Example	Emotional Impact
1. *The furnace is now hot.*	*terror, guilt*
2.	
3.	

Literary Analysis SkillBuilder

Persuasive Writing

The goal of **persuasive writing** is to convince readers to adopt a particular opinion or perform a certain action. Persuasive writing uses both logical and emotional appeals. Emotional appeals sometimes contain very little factual information. Instead, they rely on highly charged language that triggers intense feelings. On the diagram that follows, record three examples of emotional appeals that you find in Edwards's sermon.

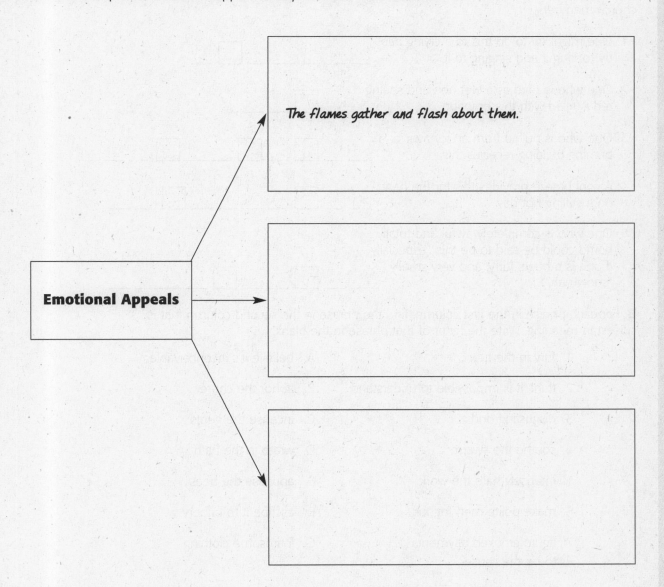

The flames gather and flash about them.

Emotional Appeals

Follow Up: Discuss whether Edwards's use of emotional appeals is justified, considering that his goal is to frighten people away from hell.

Words to Know SkillBuilder

Words to Know

abhor	appease	deliverance	inconceivable	mitigation
abominable	ascribe	incense	loathsome	wrath

A. Fill in each set of blanks with the correct word from the word list. The boxed letters will spell out something that Edwards claims is not automatically given to church members.

1. One might try to do this to a crying baby by rocking it and singing to it.
   __ __ __ __ __ ☐ __

2. One who is mad as a wet hen and seeing red is filled with this emotion.
   __ __ ☐ __ __

3. One who is pulled from an icy river or a burning building receives this.
   __ __ ☐ __ ☐ __ __ ☐ __ __ __

4. A cool breeze provides this for the heat on a stifling hot day.
   __ __ ☐ __ __ __ __ ☐ __ __

5. One who is completely awful and totally horrid could be said to be this (especially if one is a huge, furry, and very smelly "snowman").
   __ __ ☐ __ __ ☐ __ __ __ __

B. For each phrase in the first column, find the phrase in the second column that is closest in meaning. Write the letter of that phrase in the blank.

1. fury in the tub

2. think it is impossible to understand

3. disgusting duds

4. soothe the swarm

5. intensely hate the work

6. make polite men furious

7. figure crooked payments to be the cause

A. believe it's inconceivable

B. abhor the chore

C. incense the gents

D. wrath in the bath

E. appease the bees

F. ascribe it to bribery

G. loathsome clothing

C. How do your own views compare to Edwards's? Write a brief description of the agreement or disagreement between your views and his, using at least **five** of the Words to Know.

The CRUCIBLE

ARTHUR MILLER

Before You Read

Connect to Your Life

Have you ever been accused of something you did not do? What happened? How did it make you feel? Use the chart below to record your thoughts.

WHAT HAPPENED	HOW I FELT

Key to the Drama

WHAT YOU NEED TO KNOW *The Crucible,* a play written by Arthur Miller, is based on the witch trials that took place in the Puritan community of Salem, Massachusetts, in 1692. Panic and hysteria erupted in Salem when young girls accused people of witchcraft. During the Salem witch trials, many innocent people were sentenced to death. They were convicted on the basis of *spectral evidence.* Spectral evidence was the testimony of a church member who claimed to have seen a person's spirit performing witchcraft. Even people who were admired were suspected of being witches. Nineteen men and women were hanged. In addition, a man who was over eighty years old was crushed to death with heavy stones because he would not agree to a trial. Seventeen others died in prison. These tragic events had devastating consequences for the community of Salem.

from

The CRUCIBLE

ARTHUR MILLER

PREVIEW This lesson includes the opening scenes in Act One of *The Crucible,* one of the most powerful plays of this century. The play is about the fear of witchcraft that gripped Salem, Massachusetts, in 1692. Many innocent people were tried as witches, or agents of the devil. Those who were accused of witchcraft faced a painful choice. They could tell a lie to save their lives, or they could tell the truth and die for honor.

Cast of Characters (order of appearance)

Reverend Samuel Parris	**Giles Corey**
Betty Parris	**Reverend John Hale**
Tituba	**Francis Nurse**
Abigail Williams	**Ezekiel Cheever**
John Proctor	**Marshal Herrick**
Elizabeth Proctor	**Judge Hathorne**
Susanna Walcott	**Martha Corey**
Mrs. Ann Putnam	**Deputy Governor Danforth**
Thomas Putnam	**Girls of Salem**
Mercy Lewis	**Sarah Good**
Mary Warren	
Rebecca Nurse	

Reading Tips

Like most plays, the script of this **drama** includes **stage directions** and **dialogue.** Stage directions are the playwright's instructions to the director, the actors, and the stage crew. **Dialogue** is conversation between the characters. *The Crucible* also includes comments by the author. These commentaries look like "mini-essays." The author uses them to inform his readers about the Puritans. He sometimes uses them to share his views about American society in the 1950s.

• Treat the author's commentaries as nonfiction. Look for **main ideas.** Don't let the details bog you down.

• When you read **dialogue,** read some of the lines aloud—by yourself or with a partner. Try to imagine yourself saying these lines on stage. What words would you stress? What body movements would you use?

- Reverend Parris is introduced.
- The author describes the strictness of Puritan beliefs.

What Does It Mean?
Here, *overture* means "an introduction."

What Does It Mean?
In history he cut a villainous path means that Reverend Parris did many evil deeds during his lifetime.

Reading Check
How would you describe Reverend Parris? List three or four phrases that describe him.

MARK IT UP KEEP TRACK
As you read, you can use these marks to keep track of your understanding.
✔ ..... I understand.
? ..... I don't understand this.
! ..... Interesting or surprising idea

FOCUS
The play opens on a spring morning in 1692. Reverend Parris is kneeling beside the bed of his sick daughter. After briefly describing Reverend Parris, the author explains what Puritan life was like.
MARK IT UP As you read, circle any details that help you understand Puritan life. An example is highlighted on page 29.

Act One: An Overture

(A small upper bedroom in the home of Reverend Samuel Parris, Salem, Massachusetts, in the spring of the year 1692.) (There is a narrow window at the left. Through its leaded panes the morning sunlight streams. A candle still burns near the bed, which is at the right. A chest, a chair, and a small table are the other furnishings. At the back a door opens on the landing of the stairway to the ground floor. The room gives off an air of clean spareness. The roof rafters are exposed, and the wood colors are raw and unmellowed.)

10 *(As the curtain rises, Reverend Parris is discovered kneeling beside the bed, evidently in prayer. His daughter, Betty Parris, aged ten, is lying on the bed, inert.)*

At the time of these events Parris was in his middle forties. In history he cut a villainous path, and there is very little good to be said for him. He believed he was being persecuted wherever he went, despite his best efforts to win people and God to his side. In meeting, he felt insulted if someone rose to shut the door without first asking his permission. He was a widower with no interest in children, or talent with them. He

20 regarded them as young adults, and until this strange crisis he, like the rest of Salem, never conceived that the children were anything but thankful for being permitted to walk straight, eyes slightly lowered, arms at the sides, and mouths shut until bidden to speak.

His house stood in the "town"—but we today would hardly call it a village. The meeting house[1] was nearby, and from this point outward—toward the bay or inland—there were a few small-windowed, dark houses snuggling against the raw Massachusetts winter. Salem had been established

30 hardly forty years before. To the European world the whole

---

1. **meeting house:** the most important building in a Puritan community, used both for worship and for meetings.

province was a barbaric frontier inhabited by a sect of <u>fanatics</u> who, nevertheless, were shipping out products of slowly increasing quantity and value.

No one can really know what their lives were like. They had no novelists—and would not have permitted anyone to read a novel if one were handy. Their creed forbade anything resembling a theater or "vain enjoyment." They did not celebrate Christmas, and a holiday from work meant only that they must concentrate even more upon prayer.

40 Which is not to say that nothing broke into this strict and somber way of life. When a new farmhouse was built, friends assembled to "raise the roof," and there would be special foods cooked and probably some potent cider passed around. There was a good supply of ne'er-do-wells in Salem, who dallied at the shovelboard[2] in Bridget Bishop's tavern. Probably more than the creed, hard work kept the morals of the place from spoiling, for the people were forced to fight the land like heroes for every grain of corn, and no man had very much time for fooling around.

50 That there were some jokers, however, is indicated by the practice of appointing a two-man patrol whose duty was to "walk forth in the time of God's worship to take notice of such as either lye about the meeting house, without attending to the word and ordinances, or that lye at home or in the fields without giving good account thereof, and to take the names of such persons, and to present them to the magistrates, whereby they may be accordingly proceeded against." This <u>predilection</u> for minding other people's business was time-honored among the people of Salem, and it undoubtedly created many of the

60 suspicions which were to feed the coming madness. It was also, in my opinion, one of the things that a John Proctor would rebel against, for the time of the armed camp had almost passed, and since the country was reasonably—although not wholly—safe, the old disciplines were beginning to rankle. But, as in all such matters, the issue was not clear-cut, for danger was still a possibility, and in unity still lay the best promise of safety.

Pause & Reflect

---

2. **shovelboard:** a game in which a coin or disc is shoved across a board by hand.

WORDS TO KNOW

fanatic (fə-nặt'ĭk) *n.* a person possessed by an excessive and irrational zeal, especially for a religious or political cause

predilection (prĕd'l-ĕk'shən) *n.* a personal preference

☆ **Reader Success Strategy**

As you read, make a word web like the one below to write down what the Puritans and their lives were like.

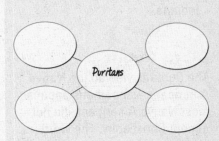

✔ **Reading Check**

According to the author, what keeps the Puritans from losing their morals?

What Does It Mean?

Rankle means "to cause anger or irritation."

Pause & Reflect

1. How does Reverend Parris feel about children? **(Clarify)**

_____

_____

_____

_____

✐ MARK IT UP **2.** Review the details you circled as you read. In your opinion, what are the most interesting or unusual details about Puritan life? Star those details. **(Make Judgments)**

As the drama continues...

- The author describes the Puritans' feelings about the wilderness.
- The Puritans were unable to convert more than a few Indians.

More About...

The Puritans viewed the Native Americans as (heathens) because most Native Americans did not accept Christianity. The word *heathen* as it is used here refers to someone who does not believe in God or the Bible. *Heathen* is a negative term suggesting that a person or a group of people is uncivilized or savage.

What Does It Mean?

Here, *parochial* means "narrow-minded."

Pause & Reflect

Which of the following phrases are true to the Puritans' view of the forest? Circle or check two of them. **(Clarify)**

a source of peace and beauty

a place of mystery and fear

the home of the Devil

a place for worshipping God

FOCUS
The Puritan settlement was close to the forest. Read to find out how the Puritans viewed the forest.

The edge of the wilderness was close by. The American continent stretched endlessly west, and it was full of mystery for them. It stood, dark and threatening, over their shoulders
70 night and day, for out of it Indian tribes marauded[3] from time to time, and Reverend Parris had parishioners who had lost relatives to these (heathen.)

The (parochial) snobbery of these people was partly responsible for their failure to convert the Indians. Probably they also preferred to take land from heathens rather than from fellow Christians. At any rate, very few Indians were converted, and the Salem folk believed that the virgin forest was the Devil's last preserve, his home base and the citadel of his final stand. To the best of their knowledge the
80 American forest was the last place on earth that was not paying homage to God.

For these reasons, among others, they carried about an air of innate resistance, even of persecution. Their fathers had, of course, been persecuted in England. So now they and their church found it necessary to deny any other sect its freedom, lest their New Jerusalem[4] be defiled and corrupted by wrong ways and deceitful ideas.

They believed, in short, that they held in their steady hands the candle that would light the world. We have inherited this
90 belief, and it has helped and hurt us. It helped them with the discipline it gave them. They were a dedicated folk, by and large, and they had to be to survive the life they had chosen or been born into in this country.

Pause & Reflect

---

3. **marauded** (mə-rôd'ĭd): attacked and raided.

4. **New Jerusalem:** in Christianity, a heavenly city and the last resting place of the souls saved by Jesus. It was considered the ideal city, and Puritans modeled their communities after it.

FOCUS

Read to find out how the Puritans were able to survive in Massachusetts and how their society changed over time.

The proof of their belief's value to them may be taken from the opposite character of the first Jamestown settlement, farther south, in Virginia. The Englishmen who landed there were motivated mainly by a hunt for profit. They had thought to pick off the wealth of the new country and then return rich to England. They were a band of individualists, and a much

100 more ingratiating[5] group than the Massachusetts men. But Virginia destroyed them. Massachusetts tried to kill off the Puritans, but they combined; they set up a communal society which, in the beginning, was little more than an armed camp with an autocratic and very devoted leadership. It was, however, an autocracy[6] by consent, for they were united from top to bottom by a commonly held ideology[7] whose perpetuation was the reason and justification for all their sufferings. So their self-denial, their purposefulness, their suspicion of all vain pursuits, their hardhanded justice, were

110 altogether perfect instruments for the conquest of this space so antagonistic to man.

But the people of Salem in 1692 were not quite the dedicated folk that arrived on the Mayflower. A vast differentiation had taken place, and in their own time a revolution had unseated the royal government and substituted a junta[8] which was at this moment in power. The times, to their eyes, must have been out of joint, and to the common folk must have seemed as insoluble and complicated as do ours today. It is not hard to

120 see how easily many could have been led to believe that the time of confusion had been brought upon them by deep and darkling forces. No hint of such speculation appears on the court record, but social disorder in any age breeds such mystical suspicions, and when, as in Salem, wonders are brought forth from below the social surface, it is too much to expect people to hold back very long from laying on the victims with all the force of their frustrations.

---

5. **ingratiating** (ĭn-grā′shē-ā′tĭng): pleasing.

6. **autocracy** (ô-tŏk′rə-sē): a government by one person.

7. **ideology** (ī′dē-ŏl′ə-jē): political beliefs.

8. **junta** (hŏŏn′tə): a Spanish term meaning a small, elite ruling council; in this case the group that led England's Glorious Revolution of 1688–1689.

As the drama continues...

• The author compares the Puritans to the settlers of Jamestown, Virginia.

• The Puritans of Salem begin to panic and become suspicious of each other.

JOT IT DOWN Lines 101–104

Reread the boxed sentence. What helped the Puritans to survive in Massachusetts? **(Cause and Effect)**

_____

_____

_____

_____

What Does It Mean?

Differentiation means "a change" or "a difference."

What Does It Mean?

Here, *insoluble* means "having no solution."

Reading Check

✔ **Reading Check**

What is the purpose of a theocracy?

What Does It Mean?

Ideology means "a system of beliefs." *Ideological enemies* refers to anyone or anything that might threaten the Puritan belief system and community.

Pause & Reflect

As Puritan society changed over time, many Puritans feared that the cause of social problems was "deep and darkling forces." What do these forces refer to? Circle the correct answer below. **(Clarify)**

greedy citizens

supernatural powers of evil

Indian warriors

British spies

As the drama continues...

- Many Puritans use the witch-hunt to confess their sins in public.

- Some Puritans accuse others of witchcraft out of revenge.

- People use the witch-hunt to justify their own hatred of others, or desire for their property.

☆ **Reader Success Strategy**

As you read, highlight words that are unfamiliar. Reread sentences to look for clues that might help you figure out the meaning of a word.

The Salem tragedy, which is about to begin in these pages, developed from a paradox.[9] It is a paradox in whose grip we still live, and there is no prospect yet that we will discover its
130 resolution. Simply, it was this: for good purposes, even high purposes, the people of Salem developed a theocracy,[10] a combine of state and religious power whose function was to keep the community together, and to prevent any kind of disunity that might open it to destruction by material or ideological enemies. It was forged for a necessary purpose and accomplished that purpose. But all organization is and must be grounded on the idea of exclusion and prohibition, just as two objects cannot occupy the same space. Evidently the time came in New England when the repressions of order were
140 heavier than seemed warranted by the dangers against which the order was organized. The witch-hunt was a perverse manifestation of the panic which set in among all classes when the balance began to turn toward greater individual freedom.

When one rises above the individual villainy displayed, one can only pity them all, just as we shall be pitied someday. It is still impossible for man to organize his social life without repressions, and the balance has yet to be struck between order and freedom.

Pause & Reflect

FOCUS

By searching for witches, the people of Salem hoped to root out evil. Read to find out how some Puritans used the witch-hunt for their own advantage.

The witch-hunt was not, however, a mere repression. It was
150 also, and as importantly, a long overdue opportunity for everyone so inclined to express publicly his guilt and sins, under the cover of accusations against the victims. It suddenly became possible—and patriotic and holy—for a man to say that Martha Corey had come into his bedroom at night, and

---

9. **paradox:** a seemingly contradictory statement that is in fact true.

10. **theocracy** (thē-ŏk′rə-sē): a government ruled by religious authority.

that, while his wife was sleeping at his side, Martha laid herself down on his chest and "nearly suffocated him." Of course it was her spirit only, but his satisfaction at confessing himself was no lighter than if it had been Martha herself. One could not ordinarily speak such things in public.

Long-held hatreds of neighbors could now be openly expressed, and vengeance taken, despite the Bible's charitable injunctions.[11] Land-lust which had been expressed before by constant bickering over boundaries and deeds, could now be elevated to the arena of morality; one could cry witch against one's neighbor and feel perfectly justified in the bargain. Old scores could be settled on a plane of heavenly combat between Lucifer and the Lord; suspicions and the envy of the miserable toward the happy could and did burst out in the general revenge.

Pause & Reflect

FOCUS
Reverend Parris is worried about his sick daughter, Betty. He tries to find out from Abigail, his niece, what she, Betty, and the other girls did in the forest the previous night.
MARK IT UP As you read, circle details that help you understand what the girls did.

(Reverend Parris *is praying now, and, though we cannot hear his words, a sense of his confusion hangs about him. He mumbles, then seems about to weep; then he weeps, then prays again; but his daughter does not stir on the bed.*)
(*The door opens, and his Negro slave enters.* Tituba *is in her forties.* Parris *brought her with him from Barbados,*[12] *where he spent some years as a merchant before entering the ministry. She enters as one does who can no longer bear to be barred from the sight of her beloved, but she is also very frightened because her*

---

11. **injunctions** (ĭn-jŭngk′shənz): commands; orders.
12. **Barbados** (bär-bā′dōs′): an island in the West Indies under British rule until 1966.

What Does It Mean?
Charitable means "full of love and goodwill toward others."
Injunction means "order" or "command." The Puritans acted out of hatred and revenge, even though the Bible commands believers to act with love and goodwill.

Pause & Reflect
Based on what you have learned about the witch-hunt, what do you **predict** will happen in this play?

_____
_____
_____

As the drama continues...
• Reverend Parris prays for his sick daughter.
• He and the doctor look for the cause of the illness.
• Reverend Parris asks Abigail what she and Betty did in the forest.

☆ **Reader Success Strategy**

Read this section aloud with a partner or in a small group. Look at stage directions for clues about the emotions of the characters.

slave sense has warned her that, as always, trouble in this house eventually lands on her back.)

Tituba (*already taking a step backward*). My Betty be hearty soon?

Parris. Out of here!

Tituba (*backing to the door*). My Betty not goin' die . . .

Parris (*scrambling to his feet in a fury*). Out of my sight! (*She is gone.*) Out of my—(*He is overcome with sobs. He clamps his teeth against them and closes the door and leans against it, exhausted.*) Oh, my God! God help me! (*Quaking with fear, mumbling to himself through his sobs, he goes to the bed and gently takes Betty's hand.*) Betty. Child. Dear child. Will you wake, will you open up your eyes! Betty, little one . . .

(*He is bending to kneel again when his niece,* Abigail Williams, *seventeen, enters—a strikingly beautiful girl, an orphan, with an endless capacity for dissembling.*[13] *Now she is all worry and apprehension and propriety.*)

Abigail. Uncle? (*He looks to her.*) Susanna Walcott's here from Doctor Griggs.

Parris. Oh? Let her come, let her come.

Abigail (*leaning out the door to call to Susanna, who is down the hall a few steps*). Come in, Susanna.

(Susanna Walcott, *a little younger than* Abigail, *a nervous, hurried girl, enters.*)

Parris (*eagerly*). What does the doctor say, child?

Susanna (*craning around Parris to get a look at Betty*). He bid me come and tell you, reverend sir, that he cannot discover no medicine for it in his books.

Parris. Then he must search on.

Susanna. Aye, sir, he have been searchin' his books since he left you, sir. But he bid me tell you, that you might look to unnatural things for the cause of it.

Parris (*his eyes going wide*). No—no. There be no unnatural cause here. Tell him I have sent for Reverend Hale of Beverly, and Mr. Hale will surely confirm that. Let him look to medicine and put out all thought of unnatural causes here. There be none.

What Does It Mean?

Unnatural things refers to unusual or extraordinary causes for illness.

☑ **Reading Check**

Why has Reverend Parris sent for Reverend Hale?

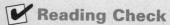

13. **dissembling:** disguising the truth about something.

Susanna. Aye, sir. He bid me tell you. (*She turns to go.*)

Abigail. Speak nothin' of it in the village, Susanna.

Parris. Go directly home and speak nothing of unnatural causes.

Susanna. Aye, sir. I pray for her. (*She goes out.*)

Abigail. Uncle, the rumor of witchcraft is all about; I think you'd best go down and deny it yourself. The parlor's packed with people, sir. I'll sit with her.

Parris (*pressed, turns on her*). And what shall I say to them? That my daughter and my niece I discovered dancing like heathen in the forest?

Abigail. Uncle, we did dance; let you tell them I confessed it—and I'll be whipped if I must be. But they're speakin' of witchcraft. Betty's not witched.

Parris. Abigail, I cannot go before the congregation when I know you have not opened with me. What did you do with her in the forest?

Abigail. We did dance, uncle, and when you leaped out of the bush so suddenly, Betty was frightened and then she fainted. And there's the whole of it.

Parris. Child, sit you down.

Abigail (*quavering, as she sits*). I would never hurt Betty. I love her dearly.

Parris. Now look you, child, your punishment will come in its time. But if you trafficked with[14] spirits in the forest I must know it now, for surely my enemies will, and they will ruin me with it.

Abigail. But we never conjured spirits.

Parris. Then why can she not move herself since midnight? This child is desperate! (*Abigail lowers her eyes.*) It must come out—my enemies will bring it out. Let me know what you done there. Abigail, do you understand that I have many enemies?

Abigail. I have heard of it, uncle.

Parris. There is a faction that is sworn to drive me from my pulpit. Do you understand that?

---

14. **trafficked with:** met.

from **The Crucible** **35**

Reader Success Strategy

As you read about Abigail in this section, notice the stage directions. Write a sentence or two telling what these stage directions suggest about Abigail.

What Does It Mean?

When Parris tells Abigail, "I know you have not opened with me," he means that she has not been completely open and honest with him.

READ ALOUD Lines 244–253

Do you think Parris is worried more about his daughter or about what other people think of him? (**Draw Conclusions**)

_____

_____

_____

What Does It Mean?

Faction means "a group of people united by a common cause or goal."

Abigail. I think so, sir.

Parris. Now then, in the midst of such disruption, my own household is discovered to be the very center of some obscene practice. Abominations[15] are done in the forest—

Abigail. It were sport, uncle!

Parris (*pointing at Betty*). You call this sport? (*She lowers her eyes. He pleads*). Abigail, if you know something that may help the doctor, for God's sake tell it to me. (*She is silent.*) I saw Tituba waving her arms over the fire when I came on you. Why was she doing that? And I heard a screeching and gibberish coming from her mouth. She were swaying like a dumb beast over that fire!

Abigail. She always sings her Barbados songs, and we dance.

Parris. I cannot blink what I saw, Abigail, for my enemies will not blink it. I saw a dress lying on the grass.

Abigail (*innocently*). A dress?

Parris (*it is very hard to say*). Aye, a dress. And I thought I saw—someone naked running through the trees!

Abigail (*in terror*). No one was naked! You mistake yourself, uncle!

Parris (*with anger*). I saw it! (*He moves from her. Then, resolved*). Now tell me true, Abigail. And I pray you feel the weight of truth upon you, for now my ministry's at stake, my ministry and perhaps your cousin's life. Whatever abomination you have done, give me all of it now, for I dare not be taken unaware when I go before them down there.

Abigail. There is nothin' more. I swear it, uncle.

Pause & Reflect

---

15. **abominations:** dreadful and evil things.

What Does It Mean?
Here, *blink* means "ignore."

Reading Check
What was Tituba doing in the forest?

Pause & Reflect

1. What is the matter with Betty? **(Clarify)**

_____

_____

_____

_____

2. Review the details you circled as you read. What do you know so far about what the girls did in the forest? **(Draw Conclusions)**

_____

_____

_____

_____

FOCUS

Parris questions Abigail about her reputation and mentions her former employer, Goody Proctor. Read to find out how Abigail feels about Goody Proctor.

Parris (*studies her, then nods, half convinced*). Abigail, I have fought here three long years to bend these stiff-necked people to me, and now, just now when some good respect is rising for me in the parish, you compromise my very character. I have given you a home, child, I have put clothes upon your back—now give me upright answer. Your name in the town—it is entirely white, is it not?

Abigail (*with an edge of resentment*). Why, I am sure it is, sir. There be no blush about my name.[16]

Parris (*to the point*). Abigail, is there any other cause than you have told me, for your being discharged from Goody[17] Proctor's service? I have heard it said, and I tell you as I heard it, that she comes so rarely to the church this year for she will not sit so close to something soiled. What signified that remark?

Abigail. She hates me, uncle, she must, for I would not be her slave. It's a bitter woman, a lying, cold, sniveling woman, and I will not work for such a woman!

Parris. She may be. And yet it has troubled me that you are now seven month out of their house, and in all this time no other family has ever called for your service.

Abigail. They want slaves, not such as I. Let them send to Barbados for that. I will not black my face for any of them! (*With ill-concealed resentment at him.*) Do you begrudge my bed, uncle?

Parris. No—no.

Abigail (*in a temper*). My name is good in the village! I will not have it said my name is soiled! Goody Proctor is a gossiping liar!

Pause & Reflect

---

16. **There be . . . my name:** there is nothing wrong with my reputation.
17. **Goody:** short for Goodwife, the Puritan equivalent of Mrs.

As the drama continues...
- Reverend Parris is worried about his reputation.
- He questions Abigail about her work for Goody Proctor.

What Does It Mean?
Stiff-necked means "stubborn."

More About...
GOODY One way in which the Puritans recognized social class was through titles. A member of the highest class was addressed as "Master" or "Mistress." A member of the middle class was called "Goodman" or "Goodwife." Servants were called by their first names. *Goodman* and *Goodwife* are like *Mr.* and *Mrs.* today. *Goodwife* was often shortened to Goody.

Pause & Reflect

1. What does Parris fear will happen if his enemies find out about the girls' misdeeds in the forest? (**Cause and Effect**)

_____
_____
_____
_____

MARK IT UP 2. Circle the two words below that describe Abigail's feelings about Goody Proctor. (**Evaluate**)

angry

grateful

resentful

respectful

from **The Crucible** 37

What Does It Mean?

Deference means "respect for a superior or an elder."

☆ Reader Success Strategy

As you read, picture the characters as they might act on stage. What expressions are on their faces? Do you think they make eye contact with each other? What body movements might they use to express their feelings?

✔ Reading Check

What does Goody Putnam believe is the cause of Betty's illness?

FOCUS

Mrs. Putnam and then her husband, Thomas, enter Betty's room. Read to find out what has happened to their daughter and how Thomas feels about Reverend Parris.

320

(*Enter* Mrs. Ann Putnam. *She is a twisted soul of forty-five, a death-ridden woman, haunted by dreams.*)

Parris (*as soon as the door begins to open*). No—no, I cannot have anyone. (*He sees her, and a certain deference springs into him, although his worry remains.*) Why, Goody Putnam, come in.

Mrs. Putnam (*full of breath, shiny-eyed*). It is a marvel. It is surely a stroke of hell upon you.

Parris. No, Goody Putnam, it is—

Mrs. Putnam (*glancing at* Betty). How high did she fly, how high?

330

Parris. No, no, she never flew—

Mrs. Putnam (*very pleased with it*). Why, it's sure she did. Mr. Collins saw her goin' over Ingersoll's barn, and come down light as bird, he says!

Parris. Now, look you, Goody Putnam, she never—(*Enter* Thomas Putnam, *a well-to-do, hardhanded landowner, near fifty.*) Oh, good morning, Mr. Putnam.

Putnam. It is a providence[18] the thing is out now! It is a providence. (*He goes directly to the bed.*)

340

Parris. What's out, sir, what's—?

(Mrs. Putnam *goes to the bed.*)

Putnam (*looking down at* Betty). Why, her eyes is closed! Look you, Ann.

Mrs. Putnam. Why, that's strange. (*To* Parris). Ours is open.

Parris (*shocked*). Your Ruth is sick?

Mrs. Putnam (*with vicious certainty*). I'd not call it sick; the Devil's touch is heavier than sick. It's death, y'know, it's death drivin' into them, forked and hoofed.

350

Parris. Oh, pray not! Why, how does Ruth ail?

18. providence (prŏv′ĭ-dəns): sign of good fortune.

Mrs. Putnam. She ails as she must—she never waked this morning, but her eyes open and she walks, and hears naught, sees naught, and cannot eat. Her soul is taken, surely.

(*Parris is struck.*)

Putnam (*as though for further details*). They say you've sent for Reverend Hale of Beverly?

Parris (*with dwindling conviction now*). A precaution only. He has much experience in all demonic arts, and I—

Mrs. Putnam. He has indeed; and found a witch in Beverly last year, and let you remember that.

Parris. Now, Goody Ann, they only thought that were a witch, and I am certain there be no element of witchcraft here.

Putnam. No witchcraft! Now look you, Mr. Parris—

Parris. Thomas, Thomas, I pray you, leap not to witchcraft. I know that you—you least of all, Thomas, would ever wish so disastrous a charge laid upon me. We cannot leap to witchcraft. They will howl me out of Salem for such corruption in my house.

A word about Thomas Putnam. He was a man with many grievances, at least one of which appears justified. Some time before, his wife's brother-in-law, James Bayley, had been turned down as minister of Salem. Bayley had all the qualifications, and a two-thirds vote into the bargain, but a faction stopped his acceptance, for reasons that are not clear.

Thomas Putnam was the eldest son of the richest man in the village. He had fought the Indians at Narragansett, and was deeply interested in parish affairs. He undoubtedly felt it poor payment that the village should so blatantly disregard his candidate for one of its more important offices, especially since he regarded himself as the intellectual superior of most of the people around him.

His vindictive[19] nature was demonstrated long before the witchcraft began. Another former Salem minister, George Burroughs, had had to borrow money to pay for his wife's funeral, and, since the parish was remiss in his salary, he was

---

19. **vindictive:** vengeful; eager to get even when wronged.

What Does It Mean?
Naught means "nothing."

Reading Check
What is Ruth Putnam's condition?

Reading Check
What does the author mean when he says that Thomas Putnam "was a man with many grievances"?

JOT IT DOWN Lines 374–385

Reread the boxed passage. How do you think Mr. Putnam feels about Reverend Parris? **(Infer)**

_____

_____

_____

_____

What Does It Mean?
Remiss in his salary means that the parish didn't pay him the salary he was promised.

Why do Putnam and his brother
have George Burroughs jailed?

[390] soon bankrupt. Thomas and his brother John had Burroughs
jailed for debts the man did not owe. The incident is
important only in that Burroughs succeeded in becoming
minister where Bayley, Thomas Putnam's brother-in-law, had
been rejected; the motif of resentment is clear here. Thomas
Putnam felt that his own name and the honor of his family
had been smirched[20] by the village, and he meant to right
matters however he could.

Another reason to believe him a deeply embittered man was
his attempt to break his father's will, which left a
[400] <u>disproportionate</u> amount to a stepbrother. As with every other
public cause in which he tried to force his way, he failed in
this.

So it is not surprising to find that so many accusations
against people are in the handwriting of Thomas Putnam, or
that his name is so often found as a witness corroborating the
supernatural testimony, or that his daughter led the crying-out
at the most opportune junctures of the trials, especially
when—But we'll speak of that when we come to it.

Pause ❷ Reflect

What is your opinion of Mr.
and Mrs. Putnam? Give your
reasons. **(Evaluate)**

_____

_____

_____

_____

As the drama continues...

• The Putnams insist that witchcraft is behind the illnesses of
both Betty and Ruth.

• Mercy Lewis and Mary
Warren are introduced.

FOCUS
The Putnams are convinced that a witch is
responsible for recent events. Read to
learn more about what the girls did in the
forest.
MARK IT UP As you read, underline details
that reveal more about what happened.

Putnam (*at the moment he is intent upon getting* Parris,
[410] *for whom he has only contempt, to move toward the
abyss*). Mr. Parris, I have taken your part in all contention here, and I would continue; but I cannot if
you hold back in this. There are hurtful, vengeful
spirits layin' hands on these children.

_____

20. **smirched:** soiled; reduced in value.

WORDS
TO
KNOW

disproportionate (dĭs′prə-pôr′shə-nĭt) *adj.* out of
proportion; of an unequal size or amount

Parris. But, Thomas, you cannot—

Putnam. Ann! Tell Mr. Parris what you have done.

Mrs. Putnam. Reverend Parris, I have laid seven babies
unbaptized in the earth. Believe me, sir, you never saw
more hearty babies born. And yet, each would wither
in my arms the very night of their birth. I have spoke
nothin', but my heart has clamored intimations.[21] And
now, this year, my Ruth, my only—I see her turning
strange. A secret child she has become this year, and
shrivels like a sucking mouth were pullin' on her life
too. And so I thought to send her to your Tituba—

Parris. To Tituba! What may Tituba—?

Mrs. Putnam. Tituba knows how to speak to the dead,
Mr. Parris.

Parris. Goody Ann, it is a formidable sin to conjure up
the dead!

Mrs. Putnam. I take it on my soul, but who else may
surely tell us what person murdered my babies?

Parris (*horrified*). Woman!

Mrs. Putnam. They were murdered, Mr. Parris! And
mark this proof! Mark it! Last night my Ruth were
ever so close to their little spirits; I know it, sir. For
how else is she struck dumb now except some
power of darkness would stop her mouth? It is a
marvelous sign, Mr. Parris!

Putnam. Don't you understand it, sir? There is a mur-
dering witch among us, bound to keep herself in the
dark. (Parris *turns to* Betty, *a frantic terror rising in
him.*) Let your enemies make of it what they will,
you cannot blink it more.

Parris (*to* Abigail). Then you were conjuring spirits last
night.

Abigail (*whispering*). Not I, sir—Tituba and Ruth.

Parris (*turns now, with new fear, and goes to* Betty,
looks down at her, and then, gazing off). Oh,
Abigail, what proper payment for my charity! Now
I am undone.[22]

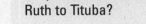

Reading Check

Why does Mrs. Putnam send
Ruth to Tituba?

What Does It Mean?

Formidable means "terrible."

---

21. **clamored intimations** (klăm´ərd ĭn´tə-mā´shəns): nagging suspicions.

22. **undone:** ruined.

Putnam. You are not undone! Let you take hold here. Wait for no one to charge you—declare it yourself. You have discovered witchcraft—

Parris. In my house? In my house, Thomas? They will topple me with this! They will make of it a— (*Enter* Mercy Lewis, *the Putnams' servant, a fat, sly, merciless girl of eighteen.*)

Mercy. Your pardons. I only thought to see how Betty is.

Putnam. Why aren't you home? Who's with Ruth?

Mercy. Her grandma come. She's improved a little, I think—she give a powerful sneeze before.

Mrs. Putnam. Ah, there's a sign of life!

Mercy. I'd fear no more, Goody Putnam. It were a grand sneeze; another like it will shake her wits together, I'm sure. (*She goes to the bed to look.*)

Parris. Will you leave me now, Thomas? I would pray a while alone.

Abigail. Uncle, you've prayed since midnight. Why do you not go down and—

Parris. No—no. (*To* Putnam). I have no answer for that crowd. I'll wait till Mr. Hale arrives. (*To get* Mrs. Putnam *to leave.*) If you will, Goody Ann . . .

Putnam. Now look you, sir. Let you strike out against the Devil, and the village will bless you for it! Come down, speak to them—pray with them. They're thirsting for your word, Mister! Surely you'll pray with them.

Parris (*swayed*). I'll lead them in a psalm, but let you say nothing of witchcraft yet. I will not discuss it. The cause is yet unknown. I have had enough contention since I came; I want no more.

Mrs. Putnam. Mercy, you go home to Ruth, d'y'hear?

Mercy. Aye, mum.

(Mrs. Putnam *goes out.*)

Parris (*to* Abigail). If she starts for the window, cry for me at once.

Abigail. I will, uncle.

☑ **Reading Check**

What does Putnam urge Parris to do?

What Does It Mean?

Contention means "fighting" or "disagreements."

☑ **Reading Check**

What does Parris mean when he tells Abigail, "If she starts for the window, cry for me at once"?

Parris (*to* Putnam). There is a terrible power in her arms today. (*He goes out with* Putnam.)

Abigail (*with hushed trepidation*).[23] How is Ruth sick?

Mercy. It's weirdish, I know not—she seems to walk like a dead one since last night.

Abigail (*turns at once and goes to* Betty, *and now, with fear in her voice*). Betty? (Betty *doesn't move. She shakes her.*) Now stop this! Betty! Sit up now!

(Betty *doesn't stir.* Mercy *comes over.*)

Mercy. Have you tried beatin' her? I gave Ruth a good one and it waked her for a minute. Here, let me have her.

Abigail (*holding* Mercy *back*). No, he'll be comin' up. Listen, now; if they be questioning us, tell them we danced—I told him as much already.

Mercy. Aye. And what more?

Abigail. He knows Tituba conjured Ruth's sisters to come out of the grave.

Mercy. And what more?

Abigail. He saw you naked.

Mercy (*clapping her hands together with a frightened laugh*). Oh, Jesus!

(*Enter* Mary Warren, *breathless. She is seventeen, a <u>subservient</u>, naive, lonely girl.*)

Mary Warren. What'll we do? The village is out! I just come from the farm; the whole country's talkin' witchcraft! They'll be callin' us witches, Abby!

Mercy (*pointing and looking at* Mary Warren). She means to tell, I know it.

Mary Warren. Abby, we've got to tell. Witchery's a hangin' error, a hangin' like they done in Boston two year ago! We must tell the truth, Abby! You'll only be whipped for dancin', and the other things!

Abigail. Oh, we'll be whipped!

---

23. **trepidation** (trĕp´ĭ-dā´shən): alarm or dread.

✔ **Reading Check**

What does Mercy want to do to wake Betty up?

⭐ **Reader Success Strategy**

As you read, notice in what ways Mary Warren is different from Abigail and Mercy. Fill in the following chart noting Mary Warren's traits and contrasting them to those of Abigail and Mercy.

Mary Warren	
Abigail	
Mercy	

What Does It Mean?

Hangin' error means "a sin punishable by hanging."

Reading Check

What finally causes Betty to wake up?

Reading Check

Why does Betty run to the window?

Mary Warren. I never done none of it, Abby. I only looked!

Mercy (*moving menacingly toward* Mary). Oh, you're a great one for lookin', aren't you, Mary Warren? What a grand peeping courage you have!

(Betty, *on the bed, whimpers.* Abigail *turns to her at once.*)

Abigail. Betty? (*She goes to* Betty.) Now, Betty, dear, wake up now. It's Abigail. (*She sits* Betty *up and furiously shakes her.*) I'll beat you, Betty! (Betty *whimpers.*) My, you seem improving. I talked to your papa and I told him everything. So there's nothing to—

Betty (*darts off the bed, frightened of* Abigail, *and flattens herself against the wall*). I want my mama!

Abigail (*with alarm, as she cautiously approaches* Betty). What ails you, Betty? Your mama's dead and buried.

Betty. I'll fly to Mama. Let me fly! (*She raises her arms as though to fly, and streaks for the window, gets one leg out.*)

Abigail (*pulling her away from the window*). I told him everything; he knows now, he knows everything we—

Betty. You drank blood, Abby! You didn't tell him that!

Abigail. Betty, you never say that again! You will never—

Betty. You did, you did! You drank a charm to kill John Proctor's wife! You drank a charm to kill Goody Proctor!

Abigail (*smashes her across the face*). Shut it! Now shut it!

Betty (*collapsing on the bed*). Mama, Mama! (*She dissolves into sobs.*)

Abigail. Now look you. All of you. We danced. And Tituba conjured Ruth Putnam's dead sisters. And that is all. And mark this. Let either of you breathe a word, or the edge of a word, about the other things, and I will come to you in the black of some terrible night and I will bring a pointy reckoning that will shudder you.[24] And you know I can do it; I saw Indians smash my dear parents' heads on the pillow next to mine, and I have seen some reddish work done at night, and I can make you wish you had never seen the sun go down! (*She goes to* Betty *and roughly sits her up.*) Now, you—sit up and stop this! (*But* Betty *collapses in her hands and lies inert on the bed.*)

Mary Warren (*with hysterical fright*). What's got her? (Abigail *stares in fright at* Betty.) Abby, she's going to die! It's a sin to conjure, and we—

Abigail (*starting for* Mary). I say shut it, Mary Warren! (*Enter* John Proctor. *On seeing him,* Mary Warren *leaps in fright.*)

Pause & Reflect

> **FOCUS**
> Read to find out about Abigail's relationship with John Proctor.
> **MARK IT UP** As you read, underline phrases in the dialogue and the stage directions that help you understand how they feel about each other.

Proctor was a farmer in his middle thirties. He need not have been a partisan of any faction in the town, but there is evidence to suggest that he had a sharp and biting way with hypocrites.[25] He was the kind of man—powerful of body, even-tempered, and not easily led—who cannot refuse support to partisans without drawing their deepest resentment. In Proctor's presence a fool felt his foolishness instantly—and a Proctor is always marked for calumny[26] therefore.

But as we shall see, the steady manner he displays does not spring from an untroubled soul. He is a sinner, a sinner not

---

24. **bring . . . shudder you:** inflict a terrifying punishment on you.

25. **hypocrites** (hĭp′ə-krĭts′): people who pretend to be what they are not.

26. **calumny** (kăl′əm-nē): slander; lies about someone.

What Does It Mean?
Reddish work refers to "bloody, violent acts."

 Reading Check
Why is Abigail threatening the other girls?

Pause & Reflect
Review the details you underlined as you read. What would you say was the worst thing the girls did in the forest? (**Evaluate**)

_____

_____

_____

_____

As the drama continues . . .
• The author pauses to describe John Proctor and his relationship with Abigail.

What Does It Mean?
A *partisan* is a member of a group with certain goals or beliefs.

only against the moral fashion of the time, but against his own vision of decent conduct. These people had no ritual for the washing away of sins. It is another trait we inherited from them, and it has helped to discipline us as well as to breed hypocrisy among us. Proctor, respected and even feared in Salem, has come to regard himself as a kind of fraud. But no hint of this has yet appeared on the surface, and as he enters from the crowded parlor below it is a man in his prime we see, with a quiet confidence and an unexpressed, hidden force. Mary Warren, his servant, can barely speak for embarrassment and fear.

Mary Warren. Oh! I'm just going home, Mr. Proctor.

Proctor. Be you foolish, Mary Warren? Be you deaf? I forbid you leave the house, did I not? Why shall I pay you? I am looking for you more often than my cows!

Mary Warren. I only come to see the great doings in the world.

Proctor. I'll show you a great doin' on your arse one of these days. Now get you home; my wife is waitin' with your work! (*Trying to retain a shred of dignity, she goes slowly out.*)

Mercy Lewis (*both afraid of him and strangely titillated*). I'd best be off. I have my Ruth to watch. Good morning, Mr. Proctor.

(Mercy *sidles out. Since* Proctor's *entrance,* Abigail *has stood as though on tiptoe, absorbing his presence, wide-eyed. He glances at her, then goes to* Betty *on the bed.*)

Abigail. Gah! I'd almost forgot how strong you are, John Proctor!

Proctor (*looking at* Abigail *now, the faintest suggestion of a knowing smile on his face*). What's this mischief here?

Abigail (*with a nervous laugh*). Oh, she's only gone silly somehow.

Proctor. The road past my house is a pilgrimage[27] to Salem all morning. The town's mumblin witchcraft.

⭐ **Reader Success Strategy**

Before moving on, reread the author's description of John Proctor. Try to predict how he might respond to the accusations of witchcraft. As you read, note John Proctor's actions and whether your prediction comes true.

✔️ **Reading Check**

How is Mary Warren associated with John Proctor?

What Does It Mean?

A *pilgrimage* is "a journey to a religious or sacred place." The use of the term is ironic here because the townspeople are going in search of witchcraft instead of something holy.

---

27. **pilgrimage:** a journey to a religious shrine, often made in groups.

Abigail. Oh, posh! (*Winningly she comes a little closer, with a confidential, wicked air.*) We were dancin' in the woods last night, and my uncle leaped in on us. She took fright, is all.

Proctor (*his smile widening*). Ah, you're wicked yet, aren't y'! (*A trill of expectant laughter escapes her, and she dares come closer, feverishly looking into his eyes.*) You'll be clapped in the (stocks) before you're twenty.

(*He takes a step to go, and she springs into his path.*)

Abigail. Give me a word, John. A soft word. (*Her concentrated desire destroys his smile.*)

Proctor. No, no, Abby. That's done with.

Abigail (*tauntingly*). You come five mile to see a silly girl fly? I know you better.

Proctor (*setting her firmly out of his path*). I come to see what mischief your uncle's brewin' now. (*With final emphasis.*) Put it out of mind, Abby.

Abigail (*grasping his hand before he can release her*). John—I am waitin' for you every night.

Proctor. Abby, I never give you hope to wait for me.

Abigail (*now beginning to anger—she can't believe it*). I have something better than hope, I think!

Proctor. Abby, you'll put it out of mind. I'll not be comin' for you more.

Abigail. You're surely sportin' with me.

Proctor. You know me better.

Abigail. I know how you clutched my back behind your house and sweated like a stallion whenever I come near! Or did I dream that? It's she put me out, you cannot pretend it were you. I saw your face when she put me out, and you loved me then and you do now!

Proctor. Abby, that's a wild thing to say—

Abigail. A wild thing may say wild things. But not so wild, I think. I have seen you since she put me out; I have seen you nights.

Proctor. I have hardly stepped off my farm this seven-month.

More About . . .

(STOCKS) *Stocks,* or "stockades," were used to punish people in public. The stocks consisted of a wooden frame with holes in which the feet and hands could be locked. Offenders would be locked in the stocks in a public place for all to see. The punishment served as an example and a warning to others.

READ ALOUD Lines 640–644

What does Abigail imply is Proctor's real reason for coming to Salem? **(Infer)**

_____

_____

_____

What Does It Mean?
This seven-month means "in the last seven months."

✔ **Reading Check**
How does John Proctor respond to Abigail's hopes?

What Does It Mean?

Abigail is referring here to the coldness of winter. She is saying that Proctor is not cold like winter, but is instead warm and passionate.

⭐ **Reader Success Strategy**

John Proctor and Abigail seem to view their relationship differently. As you read, use two different-colored markers to underline words and phrases that reveal how each feels about the relationship.

Abigail. I have a sense for heat, John, and yours has drawn me to my window, and I have seen you looking up, burning in your loneliness. Do you tell me you've never looked up at my window?

670 **Proctor.** I may have looked up.

Abigail (*now softening*). And you must. You are no wintry man. I know you, John. I know you. (*She is weeping.*) I cannot sleep for dreamin'; I cannot dream but I wake and walk about the house as though I'd find you comin' through some door. (*She clutches him desperately*).

Proctor (*gently pressing her from him, with great sympathy but firmly*). Child—

Abigail (*with a flash of anger*). How do you call me 680 child!

Proctor. Abby, I may think of you softly from time to time. But I will cut off my hand before I'll ever reach for you again. Wipe it out of mind. We never touched, Abby.

Abigail. Aye, but we did.

Proctor. Aye, but we did not.

Abigail (*with a bitter anger*). Oh, I marvel how such a strong man may let such a sickly wife be—

Proctor (*angered—at himself as well*). You'll speak 690 nothin' of Elizabeth!

Abigail. She is blackening my name in the village! She is telling lies about me! She is a cold, sniveling woman, and you bend to her! Let her turn you like a—

Proctor (*shaking her*). Do you look for whippin'?

(*A psalm is heard being sung below.*)

Abigail (*in tears*). I look for John Proctor that took me from my sleep and put knowledge in my heart! I never knew what pretense Salem was, I never knew 700 the lying lessons I was taught by all these Christian women and their covenanted[27] men! And now you bid me tear the light out of my eyes? I will not, I

---

27. **covenanted** (kŭv'ə-nən'tĭd): in Puritan religious practice, the men of a congregation would make an agreement, or a covenant, to govern the community.

cannot! You loved me, John Proctor, and whatever sin it is, you love me yet! (*He turns abruptly to go out. She rushes to him.*) John, pity me, pity me!

Pause & Reflect

FOCUS
Find out what Betty does that alarms the people in the parlor.

(*The words "going up to Jesus" are heard in the psalm, and* Betty *claps her ears suddenly and whines loudly.*)

Abigail. Betty? (*She hurries to Betty, who is now sitting up and screaming.* Proctor *goes to Betty as* Abigail *is trying to pull her hands down, calling* "Betty!")

Proctor (*growing unnerved*). What's she doing? Girl, what ails you? Stop that wailing!

(*The singing has stopped in the midst of this, and now* Parris *rushes in.*)

Parris. What happened? What are you doing to her? Betty! (*He rushes to the bed, crying,* "Betty, Betty!" Mrs. Putnam *enters, feverish with curiosity, and with her* Thomas Putnam *and* Mercy Lewis. Parris, *at the bed, keeps lightly slapping* Betty's *face, while she moans and tries to get up.*)

Abigail. She heard you singin' and suddenly she's up and screamin'.

Mrs. Putnam. The psalm! The psalm! She cannot bear to hear the Lord's name!

Parris. No. God forbid. Mercy, run to the doctor! Tell him what's happened here! (Mercy Lewis *rushes out.*)

Mrs. Putnam. Mark it for a sign, mark it!

(Rebecca Nurse, *seventy-two, enters. She is white-haired, leaning upon her walking-stick.*)

Putnam (*pointing at the whimpering* Betty). That is a notorious sign of witchcraft afoot, Goody Nurse, a prodigious²⁹ sign!

---

29. **prodigious** (prə-dĭj′əs): extraordinary.

Pause & Reflect
What happened between Abigail and John Proctor when she worked in the Proctor home? **(Infer)**

_____

_____

_____

_____

As the drama ends...

* Betty alarms the people in the parlor.
* Reverend Parris rushes in to see what has happened.
* Rebecca Nurse comforts Betty.

More About...

PSALMS *Psalms* is one of the books of the Bible. It contains many poems that praise God and ask for God's help and guidance. Many religious people recite psalms when facing a difficult situation, such as the illness of a loved one.

✔**Reading Check**
Why do people think Betty covers her ears?

Exude means "to display in abundance."

1. What does Betty do that alarms those in the parlor below? **(Clarify)**

   _____

   _____

2. How do Parris and the Putnams interpret her action? **(Infer)**

   _____

   _____

   _____

3. What do you think will happen to Betty, Abigail, and the other girls later in this act? **(Predict)**

   _____

   _____

   _____

   _____

CHALLENGE

Think about the **conflicts,** or problems, that the author has set in motion so far in this play. Remember that in an **external conflict,** a character struggles against nature, society, or other characters. An **internal conflict** is a struggle between opposing forces *within* a character. What external and internal conflicts can you identify in the play? Mark the lines using two different-colored pens that give evidence of these conflicts. Which type of conflict do you think is most important as the play goes on? **(Evaluate)**

Mrs. Putnam. My mother told me that! When they cannot bear to hear the name of—

Parris (*trembling*). Rebecca, Rebecca, go to her, we're lost. She suddenly cannot bear to hear the Lord's— (Giles Corey, *eighty-three, enters. He is knotted with muscle, canny, inquisitive, and still powerful.*)

Rebecca. There is hard sickness here, Giles Corey, so please to keep the quiet.

Giles. I've not said a word. No one here can testify I've said a word. Is she going to fly again? I hear she flies.

Putnam. Man, be quiet now!
(*Everything is quiet. Rebecca walks across the room to the bed. Gentleness exudes from her. Betty is quietly whimpering, eyes shut. Rebecca simply stands over the child, who gradually quiets.*)

Active Reading SkillBuilder

Using a Graphic Organizer

A **graphic organizer** is a visual representation of information in a text. Graphic organizers include charts, diagrams, and time lines. Using a graphic organizer when reading can help the reader keep track of details and relationships. As you read *The Crucible,* fill in the chart below. Write one of John Proctor's character traits and the evidence that reveals this trait. The evidence may be from his actions, from his dialogue, or from the stage directions. An example is shown.

John Proctor

Trait: *self-doubt*	Trait:
Evidence: *still attracted to Abigail, but wants to forget her*	Evidence:

Follow Up: Create a similar chart for Abigail Williams, and fill it in as you continue to read the play.

Literary Analysis SkillBuilder

Stage Directions

The **stage directions** of a play are instructions for the director, actors, and stage crew. Stage directions may describe the props, scenery, costumes, and sound effects used during a performance and tell how characters look, move, speak, and feel. In *The Crucible* Arthur Miller also provides commentaries about the Puritans and American society. Fill in the chart below. In the first column list three details from the stage directions that help you imagine an important character in the play. In the second column, list three insights about Puritan life that Miller conveys in his commentaries. An example of each has been provided.

Character Details	Insights About Puritan Life
John Proctor has a quiet confidence.	*Puritans liked to mind other people's business.*

Words to Know SkillBuilder

Words to Know

arbitrate*	disproportionate	iniquity*	subservient
ascertain*	fanatic	predilection	

A. Decide which Word to Know best completes each sentence below. Write the word on the blank line on the right. Some words may be used more than once.

An atmosphere of fear can exist when a (1) ruthlessly pursues his or her goal.

(1) _____

Mistreating those who are helpless is a special kind of (2).

(2) _____

People who feel that they have no power sometimes assume a (3) attitude.

(3) _____

Victims who have suffered serious financial losses may have to spend a (4) amount of money to resolve their situation.

(4) _____

Outside observers who do not know if attacks are valid may find the truth hard to (5).

(5) _____

Some people take their cases to court, where a judge will (6) and try to determine the truth.

(6) _____

Generally, people respect justice and have a strong (7) for following the law.

(7) _____

Respect for the law sometimes deters even someone who is overzealous, such as a (8).

(8) _____

B. Find the Word to Know that best matches each clue below. Write the word in the blank.

1. inclined that way _____

2. the need to know _____

3. witch hunt person _____

4. more than it should be _____

5. settling an argument _____

6. worthy of punishment or shame _____

7. working hard without power or authority

* These words appear later in Act One of *The Crucible.* You can use a dictionary to check the definitions. The words are also defined in the lesson for *The Crucible,* found in ***The Language of Literature.***

SPEECH *in the*

VIRGINIA CONVENTION

PATRICK HENRY

Before You Read

Connect to Your Life

Have you ever tried to persuade someone about something? What
arguments did you use? Describe a time when you tried to persuade
someone and list your arguments.

What did you want to persuade someone to think or do?

_____

_____

Arguments

1. _____

2. _____

3. _____

4. _____

Key to the Speech

WHAT YOU NEED TO KNOW The second Virginia Convention was held in
Richmond, Virginia, in March 1775. It lasted one week and was attended
by important patriots such as George Washington and Thomas Jefferson.
The speech that follows was written and delivered by Patrick Henry, a
member of the delegation. He tried to convince members of the need for
armed resistance against the British.

Reading Tips

In this **persuasive speech**, Patrick Henry uses emotional and forceful language to try to convince his listeners to go to war with Great Britain. Some of the words and sentences may be difficult at first.

- As you read, imagine that you are a delegate at the Virginia Convention listening to Patrick Henry.

- Break up long, complicated sentences into smaller sections.

- Use the information in the Guide for Reading to help you with unfamiliar words and difficult passages.

SPEECH *in the*

VIRGINIA CONVENTION

PATRICK HENRY

PREVIEW In 1775, American colonists were divided about their relationship to Great Britain. Some were still hoping to work out disagreements and remain British subjects. Others, like the fiery Virginian Patrick Henry, believed that the only choice left was to go to war with Britain. In this speech to his fellow Virginia patriots, Henry makes a stirring plea for his cause.

As the speech begins . . .

- Patrick Henry addresses the delegates to the Virginia Convention.

- He acknowledges that there are differing opinions among the delegates.

- He explains why he feels it necessary to voice his ideas so forcefully.

FOCUS
Henry believes that the colonies are facing a critical moment in their struggle with Great Britain.
MARK IT UP Underline at least two statements that show Henry's view of the situation. An example is highlighted.

March 23, 1775

Mr. President: No man thinks more highly than I do of the patriotism, as well as abilities, of the very worthy gentlemen who have just addressed the House. But different men often see the same subject in different lights; and, therefore, I hope that it will not be thought disrespectful to those gentlemen, if, entertaining as I do

10 opinions of a character very opposite to theirs, I shall speak forth my sentiments freely and without reserve. This is no time for ceremony. The question before the House is one of awful moment to this country. For my own part I consider it as nothing less than a question of freedom or slavery; and in proportion to the magnitude of the subject ought to be the freedom of the debate. It is only in this way that we can hope to arrive at truth, and fulfill the great responsibility which we

Use this guide for help with unfamiliar words
and difficult passages.

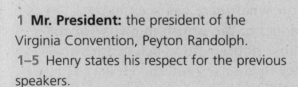

⭐ **Reader Success Strategy**

Use a ruler to help you read slowly and
carefully. Pay attention to the reasons
Henry gives for presenting his opinion.

More About . . .

THE AMERICAN COLONISTS Fewer than
three million people lived in the American
colonies at the time of the Revolutionary
War. Although the Colonial forces were
outnumbered by British troops, they had
outstanding leaders, such as George
Washington. They also felt they had a just
cause for which to fight. These factors
gave the colonists a critical advantage.

1 Mr. President: the president of the
Virginia Convention, Peyton Randolph.
1–5 Henry states his respect for the previous
speakers.

✏️ **MARK IT UP** WORD POWER

Mark words that you'd like to add to your
Personal Word List. After reading, you
can record the words and their meanings
beginning on page 476.

9 entertaining: holding in mind.

12 The question before the House: The
Virginia Convention must decide whether or
not to prepare for war against Great Britain;
awful moment: great importance.

hold to God and our country. Should I keep back my opinions at such a time, through fear of giving offense, I should consider myself as guilty of treason towards my country, and of an act of disloyalty towards the majesty of heaven, which I revere above all earthly kings.

Mr. President, it is natural to man to indulge in the illusions of hope. We are apt to shut our eyes against a painful truth, and listen to the song of that siren, till she transforms us into beasts. Is this the part of wise men, engaged in a great and arduous struggle for liberty? Are we disposed to be of the number of those who, having eyes, see not, and having ears, hear not, the things which so nearly concern their temporal salvation? For my part, whatever anguish of spirit it may cost, I am willing to know the whole truth—to know the worst and to provide for it.

Pause & Reflect

FOCUS
Henry explains why he thinks there is no hope for improving relations with Britain. As you read, look for the main reasons he gives for his position.

I have but one lamp by which my feet are guided; and that is the lamp of experience. I know of no way of judging of the future but by the past. And judging by the past, I wish to know what there has been in the conduct of the British ministry for the last ten years, to justify those hopes with which gentlemen have been pleased to solace themselves and the House? Is it that insidious smile with which our petition has been lately received? Trust it not, sir; it will prove a snare to your feet. Suffer not yourselves to be betrayed with a kiss.

Ask yourselves how this gracious reception of our petition comports with these warlike preparations which cover our waters and darken our land. Are fleets and armies necessary to a work of love and reconciliation? Have we shown ourselves so unwilling to be reconciled that force must be called in to win back our love? Let us not deceive ourselves, sir. These are the implements of war and subjugation—the last arguments to which kings resort. I ask gentlemen, sir,

WORDS
TO
KNOW

insidious (ĭn-sĭd′ē-əs) *adj.* treacherous
subjugation (sŭb′jə-gā′shən) *n.* control by conquering

25–26 song . . . beasts: an allusion, or reference, to Homer's *Odyssey*. The sirens' tempting song lured sailors to their deaths. The goddess Circe lured men to her island and then magically turned them into pigs. Henry compares "the illusions of hope" to these dangerous mythical creatures.

28–29 having eyes . . . hear not: an allusion to a biblical passage (Ezekiel 12:2) that describes stubborn people who won't pay attention to important messages they receive.

30 temporal: worldly.

41 solace (sŏl'ĭs)**:** comfort.

43 snare: trap.

44 betrayed with a kiss: a biblical reference to the Apostle Judas, who betrayed Jesus. When soldiers came to arrest Jesus, Judas identified him by kissing him. Like Judas, the British government might betray the American colonists with friendly words that hide evil intentions.

What Does It Mean?

Treason means "to betray a trust," especially of a government or a country.

Pause & Reflect

1. Look at the statements you underlined. How serious is the situation of the colonies in the eyes of Patrick Henry? **(Infer)**

   _____

   _____

   _____

2. In lines 23–32, Henry warns his listeners against the "illusions of hope," or false hopes. What does he prefer instead, whatever the cost? **(Clarify)**

   _____

   _____

   _____

As the speech continues . . .

- Henry reminds the delegates of the efforts they have already made to prevent war.
- He explains the consequences of failing to act against the British.

✔ Reading Check

How did the British respond to the requests of the patriots?

what means this <u>martial</u> array, if its purpose be not to force us to submission? Can gentlemen assign any other possible motives for it? Has Great Britain any enemy, in this quarter of the world, to call for all this accumulation of navies and armies? No, sir, she has none. They are meant for us; they can be meant for no other. They are sent over to bind and rivet upon us those chains which the British ministry have been so long forging.

And what have we to oppose to them? Shall we try argument? Sir, we have been trying that for the last ten years. Have we anything new to offer on the subject? Nothing. We have held the subject up in every light of which it is capable; but it has been all in vain. Shall we resort to entreaty and humble supplication? What terms shall we find which have not been already exhausted? Let us not, I beseech you, sir, deceive ourselves longer.

Sir, we have done everything that could be done to avert the storm which is now coming on. We have petitioned; we have remonstrated; we have supplicated; we have prostrated ourselves before the throne, and have implored its interposition to arrest the <u>tyrannical</u> hands of the ministry and Parliament. Our petitions have been slighted; our remonstrances have produced additional violence and insult; our supplications have been disregarded; and we have been <u>spurned</u>, with contempt, from the foot of the throne. In vain, after these things, may we indulge the fond hope of peace and reconciliation. There is no longer any room for hope.

Pause & Reflect

FOCUS

Henry now focuses on convincing the Virginia patriots to go to war with Great Britain.

MARK IT UP Underline three of Henry's most powerful statements.

If we wish to be free—if we mean to preserve inviolate those inestimable privileges for which we have been so long contending—if we mean not basely to abandon the noble struggle in which we have been so long engaged, and which we have pledged ourselves never to abandon until the glorious object of our contest shall

WORDS	**martial** (mär′shəl) *adj.* warlike
TO	**tyrannical** (tĭ-răn′ĭ-kəl) *adj.* harsh; oppressive
KNOW	**spurn** (spûrn) *v.* to reject scornfully

61–67 Notice how Henry uses rhetorical questions—questions that don't need answers—to point out the arguments of his opponents.

65 **entreaty** (ĕn-trē′tē): earnest request; plea

66 **supplication** (sŭp′lĭ-kā′shən): the act of asking for something humbly or earnestly.

71 **remonstrated** (rĭ-mŏn′strā-tĭd): objected.

72–74 **implored its interposition . . . of the ministry and Parliament:** the colonists asked for help to stop the tyranny of the British government.

81 **inviolate** (ĭn-vī′ə-lĭt): not harmed; intact; **inestimable** (ĭn-ĕs′tə-mə-bəl): extremely valuable.

84 **basely** (bās′lē): dishonorably.

What Does It Mean?

Force us to submission means that Great Britain is trying to make the colonists give in, or yield, to the British.

Reader Success Strategy

Reread this section carefully. Make a list of what the Americans have already done to keep peace with the British.

MARK IT UP **Reread Lines 74–77**

The colonists took action to avoid "the storm which is now coming on" (line 70). Circle the words that describe how Great Britain has responded. **(Clarify)**

Pause & Reflect

1. Circle two words below that describe methods the colonists used to protest Great Britain's treatment of them: **(Clarify)**

   violence   petition

   argument   war

MARK IT UP 2. Henry gets the attention of his audience by asking many questions in his speech. Mark four questions that Henry asks. **(Rhetorical Questions/ Persuasion)**

As the speech ends . . .

• Henry argues that war is winnable.

• He inspires the group with cries for freedom.

be obtained, we must fight! I repeat it, sir, we must fight! An appeal to arms and to the God of Hosts is all that is left us!

They tell us, sir, that we are weak—unable to cope with so <u>formidable</u> an <u>adversary</u>. But when shall we be stronger? Will it be the next week, or the next year? Will it be when we are totally disarmed, and when a British guard shall be stationed in every house? Shall we gather strength by <u>irresolution</u> and inaction? Shall we acquire the means of effectual resistance, by lying supinely on our backs, and hugging the delusive phantom of hope, until our enemies shall have bound us hand and foot?

Sir, we are not weak, if we make a proper use of those means which the God of nature hath placed in our power. Three millions of people, armed in the holy cause of liberty, and in such a country as that which we possess, are <u>invincible</u> by any force which our enemy can send against us. Besides, sir, we shall not fight our battles alone. There is a just God who presides over the destinies of nations, and who will raise up friends to fight our battles for us. The battle, sir, is not to the strong alone; it is to the <u>vigilant</u>, the active, the brave. Besides, sir, we have no election. If we were base enough to desire it, it is now too late to retire from the contest. There is no retreat but in submission and slavery! Our chains are forged! Their clanking may be heard on the plains of Boston! The war is inevitable—and let it come! I repeat it, sir, let it come!

It is in vain, sir, to extenuate the matter. Gentlemen may cry, "Peace! peace!"—but there is no peace. The war is actually begun! The next gale that sweeps from the north will bring to our ears the clash of resounding arms! Our brethren are already in the field! Why stand we here idle? What is it that gentlemen wish? What would they have? Is life so dear, or peace so sweet, as to be purchased at the price of chains and slavery? Forbid it, Almighty God! I know not what course others may take; but as for me, give me liberty, or give me death!

Pause & Reflect

62

88–89 Henry has reached the climax, or emotional high point, of his speech—his call to arms.

105–106 battle . . . strong alone: an allusion, or reference, to Ecclesiastes 9:11— "the race is not to the swift, nor the battle to the strong."
107 election: choice.

112 extenuate (ĭk-stĕn′yōō-āt′): to lessen the seriousness of, especially by providing partial excuses.
114 the next gale . . . north: Some colonists in Massachusetts had already shown open resistance to the British and were on the brink of war.

✔ Reading Check

What is Henry trying to convince his listeners to do?

Pause & Reflect

1. Reread the statements you underlined. What do you think Henry sounded like and looked like when he was delivering the final part of his speech? **(Visualize)**

_____

_____

_____

_____

2. If you were a Virginian hearing Henry's speech, would you vote to go to war with Britain? *Yes/No,* because _____

_____

_____

_____.

(Connect)

✏ CHALLENGE

Henry gave this speech to **persuade,** or convince, others to act according to his opinion. In this speech, Henry presents ideas, such as freedom from slavery, that make his arguments strong. What other ideas does Henry use to convince his listeners? **(Persuasive Techniques)**

Active Reading SkillBuilder

Rhetorical Questions and Persuasion

A **rhetorical question** is a question to which no answer is expected because the answer is obvious. Writers often use rhetorical questions in persuasive writing to emphasize a point or create an emotional effect. As you read this speech, write in each block of the diagram below one rhetorical question that Henry uses to convince his audience to prepare for war with the British. Under each question, indicate what you think is the primary purpose of the question—emphasis or emotional effect. One box is filled in for you.

Question: *"Is this the part of wise men, engaged in a great and arduous struggle for liberty?"*

Purpose: *emphasize a point*

Question:

Purpose:

Preparing for War

Question:

Purpose:

Question:

Purpose:

Literary Analysis SkillBuilder

Allusion

An **allusion** is an indirect reference to a person, place, event, or literary work with which the author believes the reader will be familiar. By using allusions, writers draw on associations already in the reader's mind. On the chart below, list allusions from Henry's speech. Then identify the origin of each—according to the notes in the Guide for Reading—and describe the meaning that each allusion suggests to you. One example is given.

Allusion	Origin	Meaning
1. "listen to the song of that siren, till she transforms us into beasts"	Homer's *Odyssey*	If we let ourselves be deceived by false hopes, we may lose our freedom.
2.		
3.		
4.		

Follow Up: Which of the allusions that you listed on your chart do you think is most effective in the speech? Why?

Words to Know SkillBuilder

Words to Know

adversary	insidious	irresolution	spurn	tyrannical
formidable	invincible	martial	subjugation	vigilant

A. Decide which word from the word list belongs in each numbered blank. Then write the word on the blank line on the right.

My husband's a bully. He's as (1) as a dictator, and nobody can do a thing about it because he's so darn big. Oh, some brave souls have tried, but his size makes him pretty doggone (2) . I'm not saying nobody could defeat him. I'm not saying the big oaf is (3) , but it wouldn't be easy. He's always cutting the tops off candles with his sword and knocking chimneys off houses with karate kicks and generally practicing all his (4) skills.

One day this kid named Jack comes to the door. I'm afraid to let him in, seeing as how my husband's so mean, but I don't want to leave him standing out there either. My (5) about what to do keeps me hemming and hawing, but then I hear Mr. Big Shot coming, so I hustle the kid into a closet to hide him.

Well, in stomps Jumbo and gives a sniff. He prides himself on being observant and (6) for any sign of danger. Like everybody in town is hatching some (7) plot to overthrow him. Nobody could even lift him. Anyway, he starts carrying on about smelling the blood of an Englishman and how he's going to grind his bones to make bread. Give me a break. He can't make a TV dinner.

"Take a load off," I say, throwing a dozen hams on the table. "Sit down and eat." But he pushes the hams away, which is the first time I have ever seen Mr. Fee-Fi-Fo-Fum (8) anything edible, and tells me to get the chicken that lays the golden eggs.

"Ha!" I say. "You've got this territory subdued, conquered, and crushed. But I am not under your (9) . Get the chicken yourself."

I hate that bird. We can't eat the eggs, and fowls don't belong in the house. We're giants, not slobs, for Pete's sake! Anyway, Mr. Huge finally eats his dinner and nods off. The kid hops out and grabs the chicken. I tip him a wink and off he goes. Then Mr. Sears Tower wakes up and blunders out after him.

"Hey," I yell. "Pick on an (10) your own size!" Of course, he ignores me. I don't know what happens to the kid. I guess nobody does. But, here's the good part. *The Big Guy never comes back!* Me? I'm packing for Florida!

(1) _____

(2) _____

(3) _____

(4) _____

(5) _____

(6) _____

(7) _____

(8) _____

(9) _____

(10) _____

B. Take the position of someone whose views oppose those of Patrick Henry. How might such a person respond to Henry's speech? Write a paragraph or two from such an opposing speech, using at least **five** of the Words to Know.

What Is an American?

Michel-Guillaume Jean de Crèvecoeur

Before You Read

Connect to Your Life

What words or phrases come to mind when you hear the word *America*?
Use the word web below to write down your ideas.

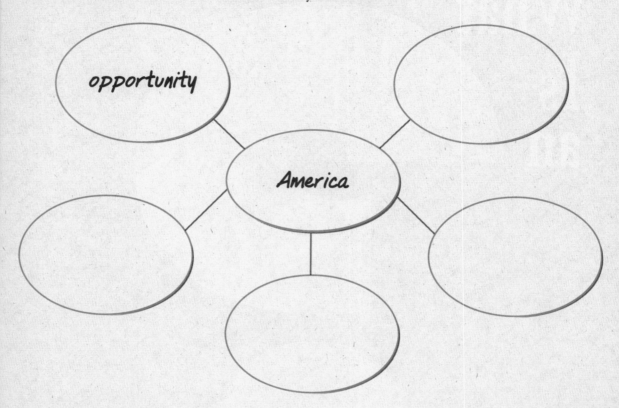

Key to the Essay

WHAT DO YOU THINK de Crèvecoeur means when he says that in America,
people "of all nations are melted into a new race of men"? Use the word
melted to help you unlock the meaning of the phrase. Write your ideas
below.

_____

_____

_____

_____

_____

What Is an American?

Michel-Guillaume Jean de Crèvecoeur[1]

PREVIEW "What Is an American?" is part of an **essay** first published in 1782. It was written by a French immigrant to America. He described how immigrants improved their lives after settling in this country. He also created a famous definition of an American.

FOCUS

In this part, the author contrasts the immigrants' old life in Europe with their new one in America.

MARK IT UP As you read, circle any details that help you understand what the immigrants to America leave behind in Europe. An example is highlighted.

10

ESSAY

Reading Tips

In this **essay,** the author states his **opinions** about European immigrants. He argues that they are better off in America than they were in Europe.

- As you read, notice how conditions in Europe **contrast** to those in America.

- Look for **details** that tell how these conditions differ.

More About . . .

IMMIGRANTS Most of the immigrants who came to America in the 1700s were poor Europeans. They owned no land and had few political rights. Moving to America gave them a chance to have a better life.

As the essay begins . . .

- Crèvecoeur describes what life was like for many people in Europe in the 1700s.

- He explains why Europeans want to come to America and what kind of life they hope to find there.

What Does It Mean?

A *wretch* is a person who is miserable, unhappy, or in great misfortune.

In this great American asylum,[2] the poor of Europe have by some means met together, and in consequence of various causes; to what purpose should they ask one another, what countrymen they are? Alas, two-thirds of them had no country. Can a wretch who wanders about, who works and starves, whose life is a continual scene of sore affliction or pinching penury[3]—can that man call England or any other kingdom his country? A country that had no bread for him, whose fields procured him no harvest, who met with

---

1. **Michel-Guillaume Jean de Crèvecoeur** (mē-shĕl′ gē-yōm′ zhän də-krĕv-kœr′)
2. **asylum** (ə-sī′ləm): a shelter.
3. **penury** (pĕn′yə-rē): extreme poverty.

nothing but the frowns of the rich, the severity of the laws, with jails and punishments, who owned not a single foot of the extensive surface of this planet? No! urged by a variety of motives, here they came. Everything has tended to regenerate them: new laws, a new mode of living, a new social system. Here they are become men; in Europe they were as so many useless plants, wanting vegetative mold[4] and refreshing showers; they withered and were mowed down by want, hunger, and war. But now, by the power of transplantation, like all other plants, they have taken root and flourished! Formerly they were not numbered in any civil list of their country, except in those of the poor; here they rank as citizens. . . .

Pause & Reflect

As the essay ends . . .

- Crèvecoeur explains how immigrants become Americans and why they should love America better than the countries from which they came.

- He explains that hard work is rewarded in America.

What Does It Mean?

Mixture of blood refers to people of different countries and cultures marrying and having children.

☆ Reader Success Strategy

Which of the following would be the best title for this section of the essay? Circle one.

Europeans Are Poor

Hard Work Will Help You Succeed

The American Is a New Man

FOCUS
Read to find out how de Crèvecoeur defines an American.

What attachment can a poor European emigrant have for a country where he had nothing? The knowledge of the language, the love of a few <u>kindred</u> as poor as himself were the only cords that tied him. His country is now that which gives him land, bread, protection, and consequence.[5] _Ubi panis ibi patria_ [where my bread is earned, there is my country] is the motto of all emigrants. What then is the American, this new man? He is either a European or the descendant of a European; hence that strange mixture of blood which you will find in no other country. I could point out to you a man whose grandfather was an Englishman, whose wife was Dutch, whose son married a French woman, and whose present four sons have now four wives of different nations. _He_ is an American who, leaving behind him all his ancient prejudices and manners, receives new ones from the new mode of life he has embraced, the new government he obeys, and the new

---

4. **vegetative mold:** loose, crumbly soil that is rich in nutrients and helps plants to grow.

5. **consequence:** importance.

WORDS
TO
KNOW

kindred (kĭn′drĭd) _n._ relatives or family

rank he holds. He becomes an American by being received in the broad lap of our great alma mater.[6]

Here individuals of all nations are melted into a new race of men, whose labors and posterity will one day cause great change in the world. Americans are the western pilgrims who are carrying along with them that great mass of arts, sciences, **50** vigor, and industry[7] which began long since in the east; they will finish the great circle. The Americans were once scattered all over Europe; here they are incorporated into one of the finest systems of population which has ever appeared, and which will hereafter become distinct by the power of the different climates they inhabit. The American ought, therefore, to love this country much better than that wherein either he or his forefathers were born. Here the rewards of his industry follow with equal steps the progress of his labor; his labor is founded on the basis of nature, self-interest. Can it want a **60** stronger <u>allurement</u>? Wives and children, who before in vain demanded of him a morsel of bread, now, fat and frolicsome, gladly help their father to clear those fields whence exuberant crops are to arise to feed and to clothe them all, without any part being claimed, either by a <u>despotic</u> prince, a rich abbot,[8] or a mighty lord. Here, religion demands but little of him; a small voluntary salary to the minister, and gratitude to God. Can he refuse these?

The American is a new man, who acts upon new principles; he must, therefore, entertain new ideas and form new **70** opinions. From involuntary idleness, <u>servile</u> dependence, penury, and useless labor he has passed to toils of a very different nature, rewarded by ample <u>subsistence</u>. This is an American.

Pause **&** *Reflect*

---

6. **alma mater** (ăl′mə mä′tər): A Latin phrase that literally means "nourishing mother."

7. **industry**: energetic devotion to a task or endeavor; diligence.

8. **abbot** (ăb′ət): the head of a monastery.

WORDS TO KNOW	**allurement** (ə-lŏor′mənt) *n.* attraction; enticement **despotic** (dĭ-spŏt′ĭk) *adj.* like a dictator **servile** (sur′vəl) *adj.* humbly submissive; slavish **subsistence** (səb-sĭs′təns) *n.* livelihood

✔ **Reading Check**

According to de Crèvecoeur, what is the definition of an American?

Pause **&** *Reflect*

De Crèvecoeur defines an American. Which of the following phrases fit his definition? Circle or check three of them. **(Clarify/Infer)**

belongs to a new race

has little freedom

lives in poverty

owns land

has new ideas

pays high taxes

CHALLENGE

De Crèvecoeur uses a compare-and-contrast structure to give his view of America. Using this structure helps the author draw conclusions about why poor Europeans might want to come to America. Circle or highlight words and phrases that describe these conclusions that the author has drawn. **(Author's Perspective)**

Active Reading SkillBuilder

Analyzing Contrast

"What Is an American?" is structured as a series of contrasts: de Crèvecoeur contrasts America and Americans with Europe and Europeans. To **contrast** two things is to state or show how they are dissimilar. As you read de Crèvecoeur's essay, complete the chart by noting the contrasts he makes. The first two contrasts have been noted for you.

Category	Europe/European	America/American
Government	*"despotic prince"*	*a new government*
Work	*no incentive to work hard*	*rewarded for working hard*
Quality of Life		
Ethnic Background		
Religion		

Literary Analysis SkillBuilder

Theme

The **theme** of a literary work is the central idea the writer wishes to share with the reader. This idea may be a lesson about life or about people and their actions. Sometimes writers state the theme directly. Often, however, the reader must infer the central message. Review the contrasts between Americans and Europeans that you have already identified. Then use the categories on the diagram to list de Crèvecoeur's ideas about Americans. An example is shown.

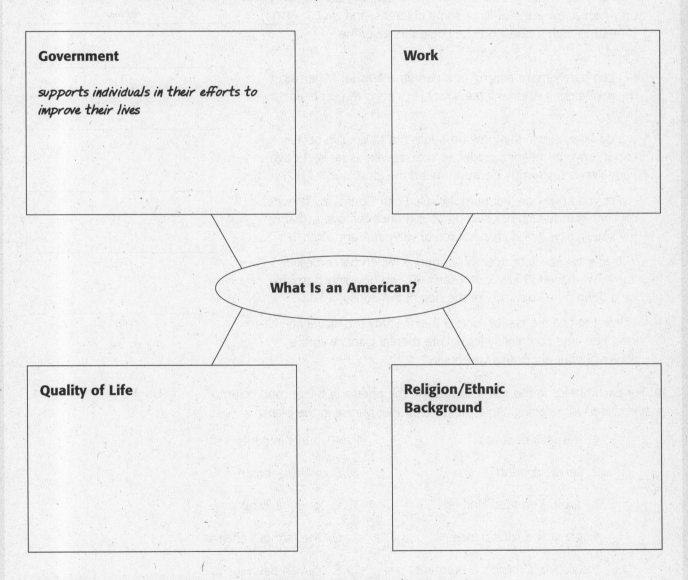

Government

supports individuals in their efforts to improve their lives

Work

What Is an American?

Quality of Life

Religion/Ethnic Background

Follow Up: Draw on the ideas you listed to write a statement that expresses de Crèvecoeur's theme. Share your statement with your classmates.

Words to Know SkillBuilder

Words to Know

allurement   despotic   kindred   servile   subsistence

A. Each of the following sentences suggests a word in the word list. The word itself is hidden in the sentence. Underline the hidden word and then write it on the line. An example, using another word from the story, has been done for you.

Example: My sister built an agricultural empire, starting only with a few acres of land, some chickens, and a calf. Arm Ernestine with a hoe, and she could take over the world.   *farmer*

I can barely make a living as a part-time teacher. When I get my paychecks, I wonder if the salary for subs is ten cents an hour!   (1) _____

I do every single thing my boss tells me to do. I've never known anyone meaner, cruder, or coarser. Vile as he is, though, I am always respectful, because I need the job.   (2) _____

For good nutrition, eat pumpkin. Dr. Edith Gourd, my father's cousin's granddaughter's second cousin once removed (that is, my sister), says it is a great source of vitamin A and fiber.   (3) _____

Dad's the absolute ruler in our house. When he comes home, we have to hide Spot. I can't tell you how much trouble we'd be in if he knew we let the dog in the house!   (4) _____

Want to snare a genius, date a brain? Study the dictionary! It's safe, free, and completely legal. Lure mental giants with the power of your enormous vocabulary!   (5) _____

B. For each phrase in the first column, find the phrase in the second column that is closest in meaning. Write the letter of that phrase in the blank.

_____   1. despotic deputies   A. aunts in pants

_____   2. servile conduct   B. a bossy posse

_____   3. sportily dressed kindred   C. giving a living

_____   4. granting a subsistence   D. the farmer's charm

_____   5. Old MacDonald's allurement E. slavish behavior

C. Does de Crèvecoeur's description of America seem appealing to you? Use at least **three** of the Words to Know in your answer.

FROM

Self-Reliance

Ralph Waldo Emerson

Before You Read

Connect to Your Life

Have you ever refused to go along with a group of friends? Perhaps you had a different opinion or were uncomfortable doing something everyone else wanted to do. Think of such a time. How did others react? Record your thoughts below.

A time when I did not go along with the crowd: _____

_____

How others reacted: _____

_____

_____

_____

Key to the Essay

WHAT YOU NEED TO KNOW Emerson was a leader of the movement in the early 1800s called Transcendentalism. Part of transcendental thinking includes a focus on the importance of the individual. Transcendentalists advocate self-reliance, believing that each individual must depend on his or her own judgment and experience as a guide for living.

Reading Tips

Sprinkled throughout this essay are short statements of general truth or wisdom called **aphorisms**. One way to get the main points of what Emerson is saying is to look for these kinds of statements.

- Identify the sentences that sound like aphorisms to you. They will usually be fairly short.

- Restate the **main idea** of each aphorism in your own words.

FROM
Self-Reliance
Ralph Waldo Emerson

PREVIEW Ralph Waldo Emerson was a well-known writer and lecturer in the United States in the 19th century. He believed strongly in the need for every person to develop his or her potential as an individual. Emerson's essay "Self-Reliance" is a collection of his thoughts on the importance of the individual and the need to think independently.

As the essay begins . . .

- Emerson describes his belief in the importance of the individual.

- He outlines steps for becoming self-reliant and explains why people should become self-reliant.

What Does It Mean?

Imitation is suicide means that people should avoid copying what others do and think. Imitating others destroys a person's uniqueness and individuality.

> **FOCUS**
> In these paragraphs, Emerson explains what he means by an independent, or self-reliant, person.
> **MARK IT UP** Underline the passages that you think contain the **main ideas** in these paragraphs. An example is highlighted.

There is a time in every man's education when he arrives at the conviction that envy is ignorance; that imitation is suicide; that he must take himself for better for worse as his portion; that though the wide universe is full of good, no kernel of nourishing corn can come to him but through his toil <u>bestowed</u> on that plot of ground which is given to him to till. . . .

Trust thyself: every heart vibrates to that iron string. Accept the place the divine providence has found for you, the society of your contemporaries, the connection of events. Great men have always done so, and confided themselves childlike to the genius of their age, betraying their perception that the absolutely trustworthy was seated at their heart, working through their hands, <u>predominating</u> in all their being. . .

Whoso would be a man, must be a <u>nonconformist</u>. He who

WORDS
TO
KNOW

bestowed (bĭ-stōd') *adj.* applied; used **bestow** *v.*
predominating (prĭ-dŏm'ə-nāt'ing) *adj.* having controlling power or influence **predominate** *v.*
nonconformist (nŏn'kən-fôr'mĭst) *n.* one who does not follow generally accepted beliefs, customs, or practices

Use this guide for help with unfamiliar words
and difficult passages.

> ✎ **MARK IT UP** WORD POWER
>
> Mark words that you'd like to add to your
> **Personal Word List.** After reading, you can
> record the words and their meanings
> beginning on page 432.

11 iron string: the divine nature that is part
of every person; self-knowledge.

12 the divine providence: God.

13–17 great men . . . being: Great men
have always recognized and made the most
of the particular strengths and unique
characteristics of the time period they were
born into. By doing so, they show their
understanding that God **(the absolutely
trustworthy)** is within them, working
through them and controlling all parts of their
lives.

What Does It Mean?

Contemporaries means "people who are
about the same age or who live in the
same period of time."

> ✎ **MARK IT UP** Reread Lines 11–18
>
> Star one sentence that is an aphorism.

would gather immortal palms must not be hindered by the name of goodness, but must explore if it be goodness. Nothing is at last sacred but the integrity of your own mind. <u>Absolve</u> you to yourself, and you shall have the suffrage of the world. I remember an answer which when quite young I was prompted to make to a valued adviser who was wont to importune me with the dear old doctrines of the church. On my saying, "What have I to do with the sacredness of traditions, if I live wholly from within?" my friend suggested—"But these impulses may be from below, not from above." I replied, "They do not seem to me to be such; but if I am the Devil's child, I will live then from the Devil." No law can be sacred to me but that of my nature. Good and bad are but names very readily transferable to that or this; the only right is what is after my constitution; the only wrong what is against it. . . .

What I must do is all that concerns me, not what the people think. This rule, equally arduous in actual and in intellectual life, may serve for the whole distinction between greatness and meanness. It is the harder because you will always find those who think they know what is your duty better than you know it. It is easy in the world to live after the world's opinion; it is easy in solitude to live after our own; but the great man is he who in the midst of the crowd keeps with perfect sweetness the independence of solitude. . . .

Pause ● Reflect

FOCUS

In this section, Emerson talks about obstacles facing the person who is trying to be self-reliant.
MARK IT UP Underline one obstacle that is created by other people and one that comes from within an individual.

For nonconformity the world whips you with its displeasure. And therefore a man must know how to estimate a sour face. The by-standers look askance on him in the public street or in the friend's parlor. If this <u>aversion</u> had its origin in contempt and resistance like his own he might well go home with a sad countenance; but

WORDS
TO
KNOW

absolve (əb-zŏlv′) v. to clear of guilt or blame
aversion (ə-vûr′zhən) n. a strong dislike

80

19 immortal palms: everlasting triumph and honor. In ancient times, people carried palm leaves as a symbol of victory, success, or joy.

22 suffrage: approval; support.

24 wont to importune me: accustomed to trouble me.

33 after my constitution: goes along with my physical and mental nature.

37 meanness: the state of being inferior in quality, character, or value.

39–42 Emerson says it is easy to go along with popular opinion when you are with other people. It is also easy to follow your own ideas when you are alone. A great person, however, remains independent even in a crowd.

43–48 Emerson notes that those who are nonconformists will meet with negative reactions from other people.

47 askance (ə-skăns′)**:** with disapproval, suspicion, or distrust.

Reading Check

How does Emerson describe a great person?

Reader Success Strategy

Emerson's writing includes words and phrases not commonly used today. His sentences are also long and complex. Break up longer sentences into parts and summarize the main idea.

Pause & Reflect

Look at the passages you underlined as you read. Two of Emerson's main ideas about self-reliance are

_____

_____

_____

and _____

_____

_____

_____.

(Main Idea)

As the essay ends . . .

• Emerson explains that sometimes it is difficult to become self-reliant.

• Emerson encourages his readers by referring to great thinkers in history.

the sour faces of the multitude, like their sweet faces, have no deep cause, but are put on and off as the wind blows and a newspaper directs. . . .

The other terror that scares us from self-trust is our consistency; a reverence for our past act or word because the eyes of others have no other data for computing our orbit than our past acts, and we are loth to disappoint them. . . .

A foolish consistency is the hobgoblin of little minds, adored by little statesmen and philosophers and divines. With consistency a great soul has simply nothing to do. He may as well concern himself with his shadow on the wall. Speak what you think now in hard words and to-morrow speak what to-morrow thinks in hard words again, though it contradict every thing you said today.—"Ah, so you shall be sure to be misunderstood."— Is it so bad then to be misunderstood? Pythagoras was misunderstood, and Socrates, and Jesus, and Luther, and Copernicus, and Galileo, and Newton, and every pure and wise spirit that ever took flesh. To be great is to be misunderstood.

Pause & Reflect

58 **loth** (lōth): unwilling; reluctant.
59 **hobgoblin:** a source of fear or dread. Notice that Emerson does not criticize all consistency, only "foolish" consistency that does not allow for change or progress.
60 **divines:** religious leaders.

67–70 **Pythagoras . . . Newton:** great thinkers whose new theories and viewpoints caused controversy.

What Does It Mean?

Emerson uses the words *sour faces* to describe the public's negative feelings toward those who choose not to conform to societal norms and beliefs. The wind is compared to the public's views, which change depending on the views of outside authorities such as newspapers. Emerson infers that the public thinks neither deeply nor independently.

Pause & Reflect

1. Look back at the two obstacles that you underlined as you read. The obstacles are

_____

_____

and_____

_____ .

(Clarify)

2. Emerson states that great thinkers may change their minds and seem to contradict themselves as they develop new ideas. According to Emerson, is such willingness to change a good or a bad trait? *Good/Bad,* because_____

_____

_____ .

(Infer)

CHALLENGE

Based on this essay, does Emerson think it would be easy or difficult for most people to become self-reliant? Mark passages that give you clues about his view.
(Author's Perspective)

Active Reading SkillBuilder

Summarizing

To **summarize** a piece of writing is to state its main ideas briefly in one's own words, omitting less important details. Read the first paragraph in this essay, and then use the diagram below to record two important phrases or statements. Then write a sentence of your own to express the main idea of each statement you identified. The diagram has been started for you.

Paragraph 1	
Important Phrases and Statements	**Main Idea**
"imitation is suicide"	If you always imitate others, you will kill your own personality.

Follow Up: Use similar diagrams to identify and restate the main ideas of each paragraph in Emerson's essay. Then pull your sentences together to create a single summary.

Literary Analysis SkillBuilder

Aphorism

An **aphorism** is a brief statement, usually one sentence long, that expresses a general principle or truth about life. An example is Benjamin Franklin's aphorism "Honesty is the best policy." Using the diagram below, identify two aphorisms that you find in Emerson's essay. Then summarize the general principle or truth that he reveals in each one. An example is given.

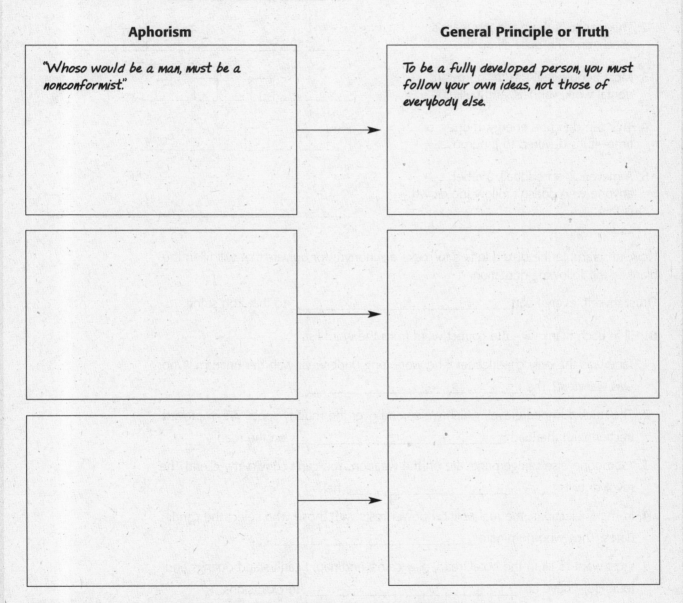

Aphorism	General Principle or Truth
"Whoso would be a man, must be a nonconformist."	To be a fully developed person, you must follow your own ideas, not those of everybody else.

Follow Up: Discuss with groups of classmates the similarities and differences among the ideas that Emerson expresses in his aphorisms.

Words to Know SkillBuilder

Words to Know

absolve   aversion   bestowed   nonconformist   predominate

A. Fill in each set of blanks with the correct word from the word list.

1. This is what accused people hope an
alibi will do for them.

___ ___ ___ ___ ___ □ □

2. The leader of the pack, the team's
coach, and the boss all do this.

___ ___ ___ ___ ___ ___ ___ □ ___ ___

3. Most people feel this for or toward
dental work, vandals, and bullies.

___ ___ ___ □ ___ □ ___ ___

4. This can describe energy, money, or
time—if it's devoted to a purpose.

□ ___ ___ □ ___ ___ ___ ___

5. A maverick, an oddball, a rebel . . .
anyone who doesn't follow the crowd
is this.

___ ___ ___ ___ ___ ___ ___ ___ ___ ___ □

___

Now, unscramble the boxed letters to make a synonym for quivers that will fill in the blank in the following quotation.

"Trust thyself: every heart _____ to that iron string."

B. Fill in each blank with the correct word from the word list.

1. Jane was the only cheerleader who wore long underwear with her uniform. Who
was warmest? The _____ .

2. The truck dumped gravel, which we spread over the muddy spots. We improved
traction with the load _____ on the road.

3. "Someone else's fingerprints are on the weapon. You can't convict my client! The
revolver will _____ her!"

4. In many elections, the real political power rests with those who select the candidates. They who nominate _____ .

5. I just want to sit in the hotel, read, play cards, and nap. I can't stand outings and
tours, for I have an _____ to excursions.

C. A maxim is a concise rule of conduct. Write a maxim that reflects Emerson's phi-
losophy, using at least **one** of the Words to Know.

from

Civil Disobedience

Henry David Thoreau

Before You Read

Connect to Your Life

Many people protest ideas or situations that seem unfair or wrong. What are some of the ways in which people can protest peacefully against injustices in society? Write your ideas in the word web below.

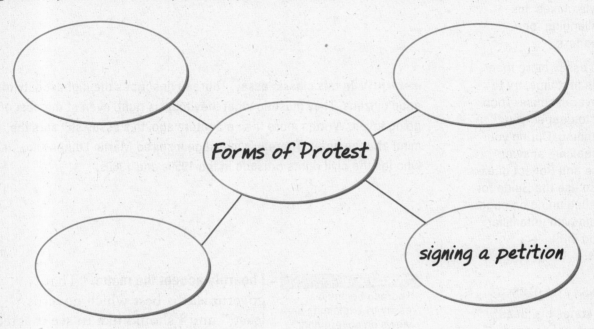

Forms of Protest

signing a petition

Key to the Essay

WHAT'S THE BIG IDEA? Is there something about society that you think is unfair or that you would like to change? How would such a change make society better? Use the chart below to record your ideas.

WHAT I WOULD LIKE TO CHANGE	HOW THE CHANGE WOULD IMPROVE SOCIETY

Reading Tips

An **essay** is a short work of **nonfiction** in which a writer presents his or her personal views. Thoreau published this essay in 1847. At that time, writers typically used long sentences and paragraphs. Such a style makes this essay challenging for modern readers.

- Read the essay more than once. The first time, try to get the overall sense. Then reread it to deepen your understanding. During your second reading, answer the Pause and Reflect questions. Also use the Guide for Reading, beginning on page 91, for help with unfamiliar words and difficult passages.

As the essay begins…

- Thoreau states his ideas about what makes good government.
- Thoreau asks for a better government.

from

Civil Disobedience

Henry David Thoreau

PREVIEW In this classic **essay**, Thoreau describes the highest duty of good citizens. They must do what they think is right, even at the cost of going to jail. Written more than a century ago, this essay still stirs the mind and the heart. Thoreau's message inspired Martin Luther King, Jr., who led the civil rights crusade in the 1950s and 1960s.

> **FOCUS**
> Thoreau begins his essay by explaining his views on government. Read to find out whether he favors more government or less.

I heartily accept the motto, "That government is best which governs least;" and I should like to see it acted up to more rapidly and systematically. Carried out, it finally amounts to this, which also I believe,—"That government is best which governs not at all;" and when men are prepared for it, that will be the kind of government which they will have.

Government is at best but an expedient; but most governments are usually, and all governments are sometimes, <u>inexpedient</u>. The objections which have been brought against a standing army, and they are many and weighty, and deserve to prevail, may also at last be brought against a standing government. The standing army is only an arm of the standing government. The government itself, which is only the mode which the people have chosen to execute their will, is equally liable to be abused and perverted before the people can act

WORDS
TO
KNOW

inexpedient (ĭn′ĭk-spē′dē-ənt) *adj.* not useful for achieving a goal

Use this guide for help with unfamiliar words and difficult passages.

More About . . .

CIVIL DISOBEDIENCE The term *civil disobedience* means protesting without violence. In this essay, Thoreau favors the nonviolent protest of unjust government policies, even if that protest results in going to jail.

 Reader Success Strategy

After you read each section of the essay, go back and reread long sentences aloud. Try breaking long sentences into smaller sections. Often, a comma will set off a section of a sentence.

> ✎ MARK IT UP **KEEP TRACK**
>
> As you read, you can use these marks to keep track of your understanding.
>
> ✔ ..... I understand.
>
> ? ..... I don't understand this.
>
> ! ..... Interesting or surprising idea

6–7 "That government . . . not at all": Thoreau is saying that it is best to have no government at all. Someday, people will need no government to make laws and enforce them.

9 expedient (ĭk-spē′dē-ənt): a means to an end.

13 standing army: a peace-time army, or one in place even though the nation is not at war. When Thoreau was writing, the United States did not have a standing army.

18 perverted: turned away from what is right.

> ✎ MARK IT UP **WORD POWER**
>
> Mark words that you'd like to add to your **Personal Word List.** After reading, you can record the words and their meanings beginning on page 476.

through it. Witness the present (Mexican war,) the work of comparatively a few individuals using the standing government as their tool; for, in the outset, the people would not have consented to this measure. . . .

But, to speak practically and as a citizen, unlike those who call themselves no-government men, I ask for, not at once no government, but *at once* a better government. Let every man make known what kind of government would command his respect, and that will be one step toward obtaining it.

Pause & Reflect

FOCUS
Thoreau wanted to limit the power of the majority so that individuals could follow their conscience. Read to find out why the individual conscience is so important to him.

After all, the practical reason why, when the power is once in the hands of the people, a majority are permitted, and for a long period continue, to rule is not because they are most likely to be in the right, nor because this seems fairest to the minority, but because they are physically the strongest. But a government in which the majority rule in all cases cannot be based on justice, even as far as men understand it. Can there not be a government in which majorities do not virtually decide right and wrong, but conscience?—in which majorities decide only those questions to which the rule of expediency is applicable? Must the citizen ever for a moment, or in the least degree, resign his conscience to the legislator? Why has every man a conscience, then? I think that we should be men first, and subjects afterward. It is not desirable to cultivate a respect for the law, so much as for the right. The only obligation which I have a right to assume is to do at any time what I think right. It is truly enough said, that a corporation has no conscience; but a corporation of <u>conscientious</u> men is a corporation *with* a conscience. Law never made men a whit more just; and, by means of their respect for it, even the well-disposed are daily made the agents of injustice.

WORDS
TO
KNOW

conscientious (kŏn'shē-ĕn'shəs) *adj.* guided by conscience; honest

19 the present Mexican war: the war between the United States and Mexico in 1846–1848. Thoreau strongly opposed this war.

More About . . .

THE U.S.–  During Thoreau's time, many Americans believed that the United States should expand until it reached from coast to coast. President James Polk tried to buy the territories that are now California, Arizona, and New Mexico. When Mexico refused to sell, Polk prepared to fight. Thoreau viewed the war as an unjust cause.

Pause & Reflect

MARK IT UP Thoreau favors (circle one) *more/less* government. Circle details on page 90 that support your answer. **(Infer)**

28–37 Thoreau points out that a government based on the rule of the majority is based on power, not justice. The majority rule because they are the strongest class.

As the essay continues . . .

• Thoreau explains why the majority is able to rule.

• He explains the difference between being ruled by law and being ruled by one's conscience.

41–42 Must the citizen . . . legislator: To Thoreau, the answer to this question is "No." In other words, the citizen must always follow his or her conscience; **resign:** give up.

47 corporation: group.

49–51 Thoreau says that people can commit injustices by having too much respect for the law; **a whit:** the least bit.

✓ Reading Check

What is the only obligation, or duty, that Thoreau feels he has?

A common and natural result of an undue respect for law is, that you may see a file of soldiers, colonel, captain, corporal, privates, powder-monkeys, and all, marching in admirable order over hill and dale to the wars, against their wills, ay, against their common sense and consciences, which makes it very steep marching indeed, and produces a palpitation of the heart. They have no doubt that it is a damnable business in which they are concerned; they are all peaceably inclined. Now, what are they? Men at all? or small movable forts and magazines, at the service of some <u>unscrupulous</u> man in power? Visit the Navy-Yard, and behold a marine, such a man as an American government can make, or such as it can make a man with its black arts—a mere shadow and reminiscence of humanity, a man laid out alive and standing, and already, as one may say, buried under arms with funeral accompaniments, though it may be,—

> "Not a drum was heard, not a funeral note,
> As his corse to the rampart we hurried;
> Not a soldier discharged his farewell shot
> O'er the grave where our hero we buried."

Pause **&** *Reflect*

FOCUS

Thoreau describes three ways that citizens can serve the state: with their bodies, with their heads, and with their consciences.

MARK IT UP As you read, circle details that explain these three ways. An example is highlighted.

The mass of men serve the state thus, not as men mainly, but as machines, with their bodies. They are the standing army, and the militia, jailers, constables, *posse comitatus*, etc. In most cases there is no free exercise whatever of the judgment or of the moral sense; but they put themselves on a level with wood and earth and stones; and wooden men can perhaps be manufactured that will serve the purpose as well. Such command no more respect than men of

WORDS
TO
KNOW

unscrupulous (ŭn-skroo′pyə-ləs) *adj.* without principles; dishonorable

54 powder-monkeys: boys with the job of carrying gunpowder to artillery crews.

57 palpitation (păl′pĭ-tā′shən)**:** irregular, rapid beating.

61 magazines: places where ammunition is stored.

64 black arts: witchcraft.

65 a man . . . standing: a man who is dead as a human being because he does not obey his conscience.

68–71 "Not a drum . . . we buried": the opening lines of "The Burial of Sir John Moore After Corunna" by the Irish poet Charles Wolfe.

72 The mass of men: most people; **the state:** the nation or the government.

76 *posse comitatus* (pŏs′ē kŏm′ĭ-tŏt′əs) *Latin:* power of the county—a term used to refer to the group of people that can be called on by a sheriff to help enforce the law.

 Reading Check

Why does Thoreau criticize soldiers?

 Reader Success Strategy

One way in which Thoreau makes his point is by comparing people to things, such as when he likens soldiers to "movable forts." Use a marker to highlight sentences or phrases in which Thoreau compares people to things.

Pause & Reflect

1. Underline the phrase below that completes the following sentence correctly: According to Thoreau, his highest duty as a citizen is to _____ . **(Infer)**

follow majority rule

do what he thinks is right

obey the law

READ ALOUD 2. Read aloud the boxed sentence on page 94. The soldiers marching off to war respect (circle one) *the law/their consciences* more than anything else. **(Main Idea)**

As the essay continues . . .

- Thoreau distinguishes between the different ways a person can serve his or her government.

- He believes that the noblest way to serve the government is with one's conscience.

straw or a lump of dirt. They have the same sort of worth only as horses and dogs. Yet such as these even are commonly esteemed good citizens. Others—as most legislators, politicians, lawyers, ministers, and office-holders—serve the state chiefly with their heads; and, as they rarely make any moral distinctions, they are as likely to serve the Devil, without *intending* it, as God. A very few—as heroes, patriots, martyrs, reformers in the great sense, and *men*—serve the state with their consciences also, and so necessarily resist it for the most part; and they are commonly treated as enemies by it. . . .

Pause **&** *Reflect*

FOCUS

The government does not value reformers. Read to find out how the government treats reformers and how citizens should respond to unjust laws.

Unjust laws exist: shall we be content to obey them, or shall we <u>endeavor</u> to amend them, and obey them until we have succeeded or shall we transgress them at once? Men generally, under such a government as this, think that they ought to wait until they have persuaded the majority to alter them. They think that, if they should resist, the remedy would be worse than the evil. But it is the fault of the government itself that the remedy *is* worse than the evil. *It* makes it worse. Why is it not more apt to anticipate and provide for reform? Why does it not cherish its wise minority? Why does it cry and resist before it is hurt? Why does it not encourage its citizens to be on the alert to point out its faults, and *do* better than it would have them? Why does it always crucify Christ, and excommunicate Copernicus and Luther, and pronounce Washington and Franklin rebels? . . .

If the injustice is part of the necessary friction of the machine of government, let it go, let it go: perchance it will wear smooth, —certainly the machine will wear out. If the injustice

WORDS
TO
KNOW

endeavor (ĕn-dĕv′ər) *v.* to make an earnest effort; strive

90–93 Notice that those who serve the state in the highest way challenge or oppose it if their consciences tell them to do so.

97 transgress: to act in violation of the law.

110 Copernicus (kō-pûr′nə-kəs) **and Luther:** Nicolaus Copernicus (1473–1543), a Polish astronomer, theorized that the sun rather than the earth is the center of our planetary system. Martin Luther (1483–1546), a German theologian, was a leader in the Protestant Reformation. Both men were excommunicated (barred from participation in religious rites) by the Roman Catholic Church.

112–114 Thoreau compares injustice within government to friction in the workings of a machine. Both are often unavoidable byproducts of the workings of a complex system.

Pause & Reflect

1. Review the details you circled as you read. Thoreau favors serving the state with your (circle one) *body/mind/conscience* because

_____

_____

_____

_____.

(Main Idea)

2. Imagine you are Thoreau. Which one of the following groups would you say is serving the state in the best way? Circle or check your answer. **(Evaluate)**

police officers who arrest dangerous criminals

students who protest against an unfair law

judges who sentence lawbreakers to jail

As the essay continues...

• Thoreau points out that government resists reform, or change for the better.

• He comments on injustice in government.

⭐ Reader Success Strategy

Rhetorical questions are questions to which an answer is not expected. Highlight the rhetorical questions Thoreau poses in this section. Think about the point he is trying to make by using these types of questions.

READ ALOUD Lines 103–111

Read aloud the boxed passage on page 96. Then write a sentence to **summarize** how the government treats those who resist injustice.

_____

_____

_____

has a spring, or a pulley, or a rope, or a crank, exclusively for itself, then perhaps you may consider whether the remedy will not be worse than the evil; but if it is of such a nature that it requires you to be the agent of injustice to another, then, I say, break the law. Let your life be a counter-friction to stop the machine. What I have to do is to see, at any rate, that I do not lend myself to the wrong which I condemn. . . .

Pause & Reflect

FOCUS

A citizen can protest government policy by not paying taxes. Thoreau believes that citizens should be willing to go to jail to protest unjust policies. Read to find out why he believes such extremes are needed.

I meet this American government, or its representative, the state government, directly, and face to face, once a year— no more—in the person of its (tax-gatherer;) this is the only mode in which a man situated as I am necessarily meets it; and it then says distinctly, Recognize me; and the simplest, most effectual, and, in the present posture of affairs, the indispensablest mode of treating with it on this head, of expressing your little satisfaction with and love for it, is to deny it then. My civil neighbor, the tax-gatherer, is the very man I have to deal with,—for it is, after all, with men and not with parchment that I quarrel,—and he has voluntarily chosen to be an agent of the government. How shall he ever know well what he is and does as an officer of the government, or as a man, until he is obliged to consider whether he shall treat me, his neighbor, for whom he has respect, as a neighbor and well-disposed man, or as a maniac and disturber of the peace, and see if he can get over this obstruction to his neighborliness without a ruder and more impetuous thought or speech corresponding with his action. I know this well, that if one thousand, if one hundred, if ten men whom I could name,—if ten *honest* men only,—ay, if *one* HONEST man, in this State of Massachusetts, *ceasing to hold slaves,* were actually to withdraw from this copartnership, and be locked up in the county jail therefor, it would be the abolition of slavery in America. For it matters not how small

130–131 **posture of affairs:** situation.

143 **impetuous:** filled with sudden emotion.
144–151 Thoreau says that the opponents of slavery should break the law and go to jail. Although most people in Thoreau's time did not act on his suggestion, civil rights leaders more than one hundred years later, in the 1960s, staged protests and went to jail to oppose unjust segregation laws and practices.

Pause & Reflect

MARK IT UP **1.** Thoreau says that if a certain condition applies, a citizen should break the law. Underline the words at the top of page 98 that identify that condition. **(Clarify)**

2. In Thoreau's time it was legal to own slaves. Can you think of other examples of laws that allow injustice? Name one example below and explain the injustice. **(Connect)**

_____

_____

_____

As the essay continues...

• Thoreau explains why he does not pay taxes.

• He believes that prison can be a house of honor.

• Thoreau encourages protests without violence.

More About...

TAXES The American government collects taxes from all U.S. citizens. Taxes are monies used to pay for government programs, roads, and schools, among other things. Today we do not have tax-gatherers who come to our doors. Rather, Americans send taxes to the Internal Revenue Service and to their respective state governments every year on April 15. It is illegal not to pay taxes.

What Does It Mean?

The word *indispensable* means "absolutely necessary" or "essential." *Indispensablest,* then, means "the most necessary." The most common form of this expression is "most indispensable."

Reader Success Strategy

Find the long sentences in this section. As you read them, write down the main idea of each sentence.

from Civil Disobedience **99**

the beginning may seem to be: what is once well done is done forever. But we love better to talk about it: that we say is our mission. Reform keeps many scores of newspapers in its service, but not one man. . . .

Under a government which imprisons any unjustly, the true place for a just man is also a prison. The proper place today, the only place which Massachusetts has provided for her freer and less desponding spirits, is in her prisons, to be put out and locked out of the State by her own act, as they have already put themselves out by their principles. It is there that the fugitive slave, and the Mexican prisoner on parole, and the Indian come to plead the wrongs of his race should find them; on that separate, but more free and honorable ground, where the State places those who are not *with* her, but *against* her,— the only house in a slave State in which a free man can abide with honor. If any think that their influence would be lost there, and their voices no longer afflict the ear of the State, that they would not be as an enemy within its walls, they do not know by how much truth is stronger than error, nor how much more eloquently and effectively he can combat injustice who has experienced a little in his own person. Cast your whole vote, not a strip of paper merely, but your whole influence. A minority is powerless while it conforms to the majority; it is not even a minority then; but it is irresistible when it clogs by its whole weight. If the alternative is to keep all just men in prison, or give up war and slavery, the State will not hesitate which to choose. If a thousand men were not to pay their tax bills this year, that would not be a violent and bloody measure, as it would be to pay them, and enable the State to commit violence and shed innocent blood. This is, in fact, the definition of a peaceable revolution, if any such is possible. If the tax-gatherer, or any other public officer, asks me, as one has done, "But what shall I do?" my answer is, "If you really wish to do anything, resign your office." When the subject has refused allegiance, and the officer has resigned his office, then the revolution is accomplished. But even suppose blood should flow. Is there not a sort of blood shed when the conscience is wounded? Through this wound a man's real manhood and immortality flow out, and he bleeds to an everlasting death. I see this blood flowing now. . . .

Pause & *Reflect*

152–153 Many newspapers print editorials calling for reform. No one, however, has the courage to go to jail for the sake of justice; **score:** 20.

157 desponding: discouraging.

159–165 Thoreau was opposed to the government because it allowed slavery in the South and waged war against Mexico in the West. By not paying his taxes, Thoreau denied the government some of the revenue it needed to exist. The punishment for refusing to pay taxes was imprisonment. To Thoreau's way of thinking, however, a prison was not a place of shame. Instead, it was a place of honor set aside for those brave enough to act on their consciences.

171–174 A minority is powerless when it goes along with the majority. However, a minority can have great influence when it opposes the majority.

176–179 If a thousand . . . innocent blood. If a thousand men refused to pay taxes, such action would not be violent. Those who pay taxes to support a war, however, are guilty of violence.

☑ **Reading Check**

What does Thoreau suggest is the best way to change unjust policies?

Pause & **Reflect**

1. Thoreau says that he denies the government through its representative. Who is that representative? **(Clarify)**

_____

_____

✎ MARK IT UP **2.** What would happen to slavery if even one honest person were to go to jail as a form of protest? Circle the sentence on page 98 that tells the answer. **(Cause and Effect)**

3. Reread the boxed sentence on page 100. How would you state Thoreau's idea in your own words? **(Paraphrase)**

_____

_____

_____

4. Which two phrases below are true to Thoreau's views of a "peaceable revolution"? Circle or check them. **(Infer)**

involves breaking the law

never causes bloodshed

is led by the majority

is based on conscience

190

200

210

220

FOCUS

Read to find out about Thoreau's experience in jail.

MARK IT UP As you read, circle details that help you understand his attitude toward this experience.

I have paid no poll-tax for six years. I was put into a jail once on this account, for one night; and, as I stood considering the walls of solid stone, two or three feet thick, the door of wood and iron, a foot thick, and the iron grating which strained the light, I could not help being struck with the foolishness of that institution which treated me as if I were mere flesh and blood and bones, to be locked up. I wondered that it should have <u>concluded</u> at length that this was the best use it could put me to, and had never thought to avail itself of my services in some way. I saw that, if there was a wall of stone between me and my townsmen, there was a still more difficult one to climb or break through before they could get to be as free as I was. I did not for a moment feel confined, and the walls seemed a great waste of stone and mortar. I felt as if I alone of all my townsmen had paid my tax. They plainly did not know how to treat me, but behaved like persons who are underbred. In every threat and in every compliment there was a <u>blunder</u>; for they thought that my chief desire was to stand the other side of that stone wall. I could not but smile to see how industriously they locked the door on my <u>meditations</u>, which followed them out again without let or hindrance, and *they* were really all that was dangerous. As they could not reach me, they had resolved to punish my body; just as boys, if they cannot come at some person against whom they have a spite, will abuse his dog. I saw that the State was half-witted, that it was timid as a lone woman with her silver spoons, and that it did not know its friends from its foes, and I lost all my remaining respect for it, and pitied it.

Thus the State never intentionally <u>confronts</u> a man's sense, intellectual or moral, but only his body, his senses. It is not armed with superior wit or honesty, but with superior physical strength. I was not born to be forced. I will breathe

WORDS TO KNOW	**conclude** (kən-klōōd′) *v.* to arrive at a judgment or decision
	blunder (blŭn′dər) *n.* a mistake
	meditation (mĕd′ĭ-tā′shən) *n.* a thought or reflection
	confront (kən-frŭnt′) *v.* to come up against; meet face to face

190 poll tax: a tax that one had to pay in order to vote.

209 underbred: ill-mannered.

211–215 I could not . . . that was dangerous: To Thoreau, his townspeople are fools. They locked him in jail to punish him. All they punished, however, was his body. They could not lock up their real enemies— Thoreau's mind and his conscience; **without let or hindrance** (hĭn′drəns): without encountering obstacles.

217 spite: grudge.

As the essay ends . . .

- Thoreau tells of his time in jail and his feelings about his experience.
- Others do not know how to react to him.
- Thoreau will not let government force him to do anything.

 Reading Check

Why has Thoreau refused to pay his taxes?

 **READ ALOUD** **Lines 202–207**

Notice the contradiction in these lines. Thoreau in jail is truly free. The townsmen outside the jail are not.

What Does It Mean?

Hindrance means "something that delays, blocks, or prevents action."

 **Reading Check**

Why does Thoreau lose all respect for the State?

after my own fashion. Let us see who is the strongest. What force has a <u>multitude</u>? They only can force me who obey a higher law than I. They force me to become like themselves. I do not hear of *men* being *forced* to live this way or that by masses of men. What sort of life were that to live? When I meet a government which says to me, "Your money or your life," why should I be in haste to give it my money? It may be in a great strait, and not know what to do: I cannot help that. It must help itself; do as I do. It is not worth the while to snivel about it. I am not responsible for the successful working of the machinery of society. I am not the son of the engineer. I perceive that, when an acorn and a chestnut fall side by side, the one does not remain inert to make way for the other, but both obey their own laws, and spring and grow and <u>flourish</u> as best they can, till one, perchance, overshadows and destroys the other. If a plant cannot live according to its nature, it dies; and so a man.

Pause & Reflect

WORDS
TO
KNOW

multitude (mŭl′tĭ-tōōd′) *n.* a great number of people
flourish (flûr′ĭsh) *v.* to thrive

227–228 They only can force me who obey a higher law than I: Thoreau says that only those on a higher spiritual level can make him want to be like them.

235 snivel: whine or complain.

236 machinery of society: the government.

237 an acorn and a chestnut: An acorn is the fruit of an oak tree; a chestnut is the nut from a chestnut tree.

238 inert: unable to act.

Pause & Reflect

1. Thoreau was put in jail because _____

_____ .

(Clarify)

2. Review the details you circled as you read. Then write a sentence to **summarize** Thoreau's feelings about his experience in jail. **(Main Idea)**

_____

_____

_____

READ ALOUD **3.** Read aloud the boxed sentences on page 104. Both the acorn and the chestnut obey the laws of nature. They fall to the ground, where each tries to take root, grow, and develop into a tree. What does this example suggest about Thoreau himself? **(Infer)**

_____

_____

_____

_____

CHALLENGE

In this essay, Thoreau uses **aphorisms**—brief statements that each express a truth about life. Why do you think Thoreau uses aphorisms in this **persuasive essay? In your own words, rewrite the following aphorisms.**

1. "That government is best which governs not at all;" (lines 6–8)
2. "Law never made men a whit more just;" (lines 49–50)
3. "If a plant cannot live according to its nature, it dies; and so a man." (lines 241–242)

Active Reading SkillBuilder

Strategies for Reading Essays

To get the most from this essay, use these **strategies for reading essays:** Keep in mind the historical context, continue reading even if a sentence is unclear, read the entire selection more than once, and keep track of the main ideas and supporting details. As you read, use the following chart to explore one of Thoreau's main ideas— how citizens serve the state. Identify the three ways indicated by Thoreau, then give examples of each. Circle the way that Thoreau believes is the best way. One example is given.

Ways to Serve the State

1. *with the body*	2.	3.
soldiers		

Literary Analysis SkillBuilder

Essay

An **essay** is a short work of nonfiction that deals with a single subject. The purpose of an essay may be to express ideas and feelings, to analyze, to inform, to entertain, or, as in the case of "Civil Disobedience," to persuade. Even when they discuss serious ideas, essays are often informal and highly personal. On the chart below, identify three passages in this essay in which Thoreau refers to himself—identifying his personal opinions or recounting personal experiences. Mark with an X the scale for each passage to show the degree to which Thoreau's personal opinions or experiences influence your acceptance of his arguments.

1. Passage:_____

   _____

   Very Influential |—|—|—|—|—|—|—|—|—|—| Not Influential

2. Passage:_____

   _____

   Very Influential |—|—|—|—|—|—|—|—|—|—| Not Influential

3. Passage:_____

   _____

   Very Influential |—|—|—|—|—|—|—|—|—|—| Not Influential

Follow Up: Discuss what effect omitting these passages would have on the essay.

Words to Know SkillBuilder

Words to Know

blunder	confront	endeavor	inexpedient	multitude
conclude	conscientious	flourish	meditation	unscrupulous

A. For each phrase in the first column, find the phrase in the second column that is closest in meaning. Write the letter of that phrase in the blank.

_____ 1. corrupt boss   A. a conscientious multitude

_____ 2. useless way to proceed   B. an unscrupulous manager

_____ 3. think it through   C. concede it's a blunder

_____ 4. many honest people   D. an inexpedient plan

_____ 5. admit a mistake   E. learn through meditation

B. Circle the word in each group that is a synonym for the capitalized word.

1. **inexpedient**	unnecessary	improper	useful	impractical
2. **meditation**	thinking	memory	peace	nature
3. **endeavor**	plan	regulate	attempt	promote
4. **flourish**	accomplish	predict	thrive	accept
5. **conscientious**	able	honest	careless	useful
6. **multitude**	meeting	reunion	crowd	conference
7. **unscrupulous**	unusual	disjointed	upset	dishonorable
8. **conclude**	decide	predict	reverse	alter
9. **confront**	manage	oppose	disappear	disagree
10. **blunder**	choice	decision	mistake	confusion

C. Write a letter to a representative in Congress suggesting one way the government might be improved. Use at least **four** Words to Know in the letter.

WALT WHITMAN

I Hear America Singing

I Sit and Look Out

Song of Myself

Before You Read

Connect to Your Life

If America could sing, what would its song be about? List your ideas below.

freedom

people of different backgrounds

Key to the Poems

WHAT DO YOU THINK? In "Song of Myself," the speaker celebrates himself as an ordinary man.

I celebrate myself, and sing myself . . .

If you were writing a poem celebrating yourself, what information would you include? Use the word web below to write down your ideas.

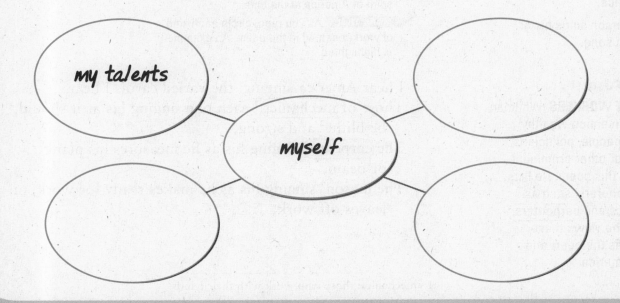

Reading Tips

Whitman wrote **free verse**, or poetry without regular patterns of rhyme and meter. His free verse rolls along like a song, echoing the rhythms of music and everyday speech.

• As you read each poem, keep moving and let the **images** form pictures in your imagination. Let the lines sweep you along. Note that each new line begins with a capital letter. Words that spill over from a line are indented.

• Read the poems once or twice for their overall sense. Then reread each poem to deepen your understanding. After you reread each poem, answer the Pause and Reflect questions.

• Also use the Guide for Reading, beginning on page 115, as you reread "I Sit and Look Out" and the excerpts from "Song of Myself."

As the poem begins . . .

• The speaker talks about different kinds of workers in America.

• Each person sings his or her own song.

More About . . .

TYPES OF WORKERS Whitman does not mention wealthy businesspeople, politicians, doctors, or other prominent people in this poem. He lists manual laborers, such as mechanics and carpenters, because he views these workers as the heart and soul of America.

PREVIEW As a poet, Walt Whitman was a rebel. In 1855 he published *Leaves of Grass*. This collection of 12 poems broke new ground in content and style. Whitman treated subjects that often shocked his readers. He also made his own rhythms, rejecting typical verse forms and techniques. A spokesman for all that was American, he created a new poetry for a new age.

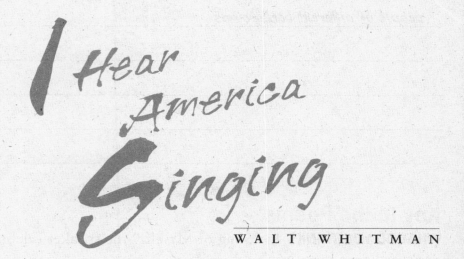

I Hear America Singing

WALT WHITMAN

FOCUS

This poem is one sentence long. The speaker names different kinds of workers, singing joyously. These workers reflect the spirit of America at the time.

MARK IT UP As you read, circle each kind of worker named in the poem. An example is highlighted.

I hear America singing, the varied carols I hear,
Those of mechanics,[1] each one singing his as it should
   be blithe[2] and strong,
The carpenter singing his as he measures his plank
   or beam,
The mason[3] singing his as he makes ready for work, or
   leaves off work,

---

1. **mechanics:** those who work with their hands.
2. **blithe** (blīth): carefree and lighthearted.
3. **mason:** one who works with bricks or stone.

⑤ The boatman singing what belongs to him in his boat,
    the deckhand singing on the steamboat deck,
The shoemaker singing as he sits on his bench, the
    hatter singing as he stands,
The wood-cutter's song, the ploughboy's on his way in
    the morning, or at noon intermission or at sundown,
The delicious singing of the mother, or of the young
    wife at work, or of the girl sewing or washing,
Each singing what belongs to him or her and to
    none else,
⑩ The day what belongs to the day—at night the party of
    young fellows, robust,[4] friendly,
Singing with open mouths their strong melodious songs.

Pause **&** *Reflect*

What Does It Mean?

In line 9, the speaker is saying that everyone is an individual, like no other person.

☆ **Reader Success Strategy**

Poems often contain repeated elements and patterns. Nearly every line of this poem starts by naming a type of worker. Look for repetition and patterns as you read the poems to help you understand what the speaker is saying.

Pause **&** *Reflect*

1. Review the kinds of workers you circled as you read. How do these workers feel about their work? **(Infer)**

  _____

  _____

  _____

  _____

2. What does the workers' singing suggest about America? **(Draw Conclusions)**

  _____

  _____

  _____

  _____

---

4. **robust** (rō-bŭst'): full of health and strength.

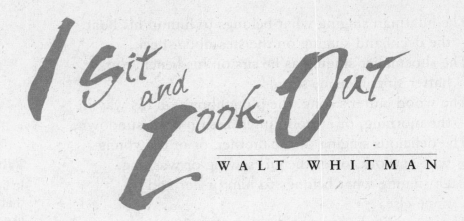

I Sit and Look Out

WALT WHITMAN

FOCUS

Like the previous poem, this one is a single sentence in length. This time, though, the speaker describes the sorrows of life. Read to find out about these sorrows and the speaker's response to them.

I sit and look out upon all the sorrows of the world,
    and upon all oppression and shame,
I hear secret convulsive sobs from young men at
    anguish with themselves, remorseful after deeds done,
I see in low life the mother misused by her children,
    dying, neglected, gaunt, desperate,
I see the wife misused by her husband, I see the
    treacherous seducer of young women,
5 I mark the ranklings of jealousy and unrequited love
    attempted to be hid, I see these sights on the earth,
I see the workings of battle, pestilence, tyranny, I see
    martyrs and prisoners,
I observe a famine at sea, I observe the sailors casting
    lots who shall be kill'd to preserve the lives of the rest,
I observe the slights and degradations cast by arrogant persons
    upon laborers, the poor, and upon negroes, and the like;
All these—all the meanness and agony without end I
    sitting look out upon,
10 See, hear, and am silent.

Pause **&** **Reflect**

Use this guide for help with unfamiliar words and difficult passages.

1 oppression: cruel or unjust use of power. The first line states a general theme: "all the sorrows of the world." The speaker then gives examples of these sorrows.

2–5 In these lines, the speaker describes personal sorrows.

2 convulsive: intense and uncontrolled; **anguish:** extreme mental pain; **remorseful:** guilty.

3 low life: the life of the lower classes; **gaunt:** thin and bony.

4 seducer: a person who leads someone away from proper conduct.

5 ranklings: bitter feelings or resentments; **unrequited:** not returned.

6–8 In these lines the speaker lists social evils.

7 casting lots: deciding by means of a random choice of objects (as in drawing straws). The sailors draw lots to decide who will be thrown overboard so that the rest of them might live. There is not enough food to keep all the sailors alive.

8 degradations: insults; **arrogant:** very proud.

As the poem begins...

• The speaker gives examples of the sorrows of life.

• He has a response to all the misery.

What Does It Mean?
Treacherous means "likely to betray trust."

✔ Reading Check
Who are the "arrogant persons," and how do they treat others?

Pause & Reflect

MARK IT UP **1.** Reread lines 2–5. Underline three of the personal sorrows that the speaker observes. **(Clarify)**

2. List at least three of the social problems the speaker notices in lines 6–8. (Line 6 begins with the words "I see the workings.") **(Clarify)**

_____
_____
_____
_____

READ ALOUD **3.** Read aloud lines 9–10. In those lines the speaker describes his response to all this misery. Why do you think he responds in this way? **(Infer)**

_____
_____
_____
_____

from

Song of Myself

WALT WHITMAN

FOCUS

Epic poems celebrate heroes of the past.
The speaker of this poem celebrates an
ordinary man—himself. Read to find out
about his larger-than-life personality.

1

I celebrate myself, and sing myself,
And what I assume you shall assume,
For every atom belonging to me as good belongs to you.

I loaf and invite my soul,
5   I lean and loaf at my ease observing a spear of
       summer grass.

My tongue, every atom of my blood, form'd from this
      soil, this air,
Born here of parents born here from parents the same,
      and their parents the same,
I, now thirty seven years old in perfect health begin,
Hoping to cease not till death.

10   Creeds and schools in abeyance,
Retiring back a while sufficed at what they are, but never
      forgotten,
I harbor for good or bad, I permit to speak at every
      hazard,
Nature without check with original energy.

Pause & Reflect

Read through section one for a general overview. Then, go back and reread the section, focusing on one sentence at a time. Restate each sentence in your own words.

As the poem begins . . .

• The speaker is happy about being who he is.

• He speaks of himself in relation to the natural world.

1–3 The speaker relates to the reader from the beginning of the poem. He wants the reader to accept him as a spokesman for all.

5 a spear of summer grass: a blade or leaf of grass.

6–7 The speaker describes himself as a product of the soil and air of the United States.

Pause & Reflect

1. Circle or check three phrases below that are true of the speaker. **(Infer)**

   is self-confident

   considers others his equal

   celebrates the wisdom of books

   praises city life

   enjoys good health

2. Reread the boxed line on page 116. How would you restate this idea in your own words? **(Paraphrase)**

   _____

   _____

   _____

10 Creeds . . . in abeyance: The speaker says that for now he will set aside time-honored beliefs and ways of thinking.

11 sufficed at: satisfied with.

12–13 The speaker says that he will take in **(harbor for)** good or bad experiences. He will allow Nature to speak freely and forcefully through him.

✎ MARK IT UP   3. Which lines on page 116 suggest that the speaker is united with Nature? Circle these lines. **(Evaluate)**

FOCUS

Throughout Section 6, the speaker uses
comparisons to suggest what the grass
means to him. Each of these comparisons
is highlighted. Read to find out what these
comparisons suggest about the grass.

6

A child said *What is the grass?* fetching it to me with
full hands,

How could I answer the child? I do not know what it
is any more than he.

I guess it must be the flag of my disposition, out of
hopeful green stuff woven.

Or I guess it is the handkerchief of the Lord,
A scented gift and remembrancer designedly dropt,
Bearing the owner's name someway in the corners, that
we may see and remark, and say *Whose?*

Or I guess the grass is itself a child, the produced babe
of the vegetation.

Or I guess it is a uniform hieroglyphic,

And it means, Sprouting alike in broad zones and
narrow zones,
Growing among black folks as among white,
Kanuck, Tuckahoe, Congressman, Cuff, I give them the
same, I receive them the same.

Pause **&** *Reflect*

- In this section, the speaker talks about what grass means to him.

16 The speaker says that the grass is the sign **(flag)** of his usual mood **(disposition)**. The green color reminds the speaker that he usually looks on the bright side of things.

17–19 The speaker says that the grass is the token **(handkerchief)** that God **(the Lord)** uses to get people's attention. A lady's perfumed **(scented)** handkerchief has her name or initials inscribed in one of its corners. The lady purposely drops this token of affection **(remembrancer designedly dropt)** to get someone to notice her. Similarly, the fragrance and freshness of the grass make people aware of God, who created it.

20 The speaker says that the grass is a child that the natural world **(the vegetation)** has given birth to **(produced)**.

21 The speaker says that the grass is a picture or symbol that represents something **(hieroglyphic)**. This picture looks the same wherever it is found **(uniform)**.

24 Kanuck, Tuckahoe, . . . Cuff: slang terms for various groups of people. A Kanuck (now spelled Canuck) is a Canadian, especially a French Canadian. A Tuckahoe is someone from the coast of Virginia. A Cuff is an African American.

Pause & Reflect

1. What does a child ask the speaker to define? **(Clarify)**

_____

_____

MARK IT UP 2. Review the highlighted comparisons on page 118. Star the one you find most interesting and then tell why. **(Evaluate)**

_____

_____

_____

_____

READ ALOUD 3. Read aloud the boxed passage on page 118. At the end of line 24, the speaker imagines that the grass says, "I receive them [all humans] the same." What does this sentence mean? **(Infer)**

_____

_____

_____

_____

FOCUS

Read to find out the connection between the grass and the dead.

25 And now it seems to me the beautiful uncut hair of graves.
Tenderly will I use you curling grass,

It may be you transpire from the breasts of young men,
It may be if I had known them I would have loved them,
It may be you are from old people, or from offspring
taken soon out of their mothers' laps,
30 And here you are the mothers' laps.

This grass is very dark to be from the white heads of
old mothers,
Darker than the colorless beards of old men,
Dark to come from under the faint red roofs of mouths.

O I perceive after all so many uttering tongues,
35 And I perceive they do not come from the roofs of
mouths for nothing.

Pause & Reflect

FOCUS

The speaker tries to put into words the message about dead people that the grass reveals. Read to find out this message.

I wish I could translate the hints about the dead young
men and women,
And the hints about old men and mothers, and the
offspring taken soon out of their laps.

What do you think has become of the young and old men?
And what do you think has become of the women and
children?
40 They are alive and well somewhere,
The smallest sprout shows there is really no death,

25–29 The speaker says that the grass is "the beautiful uncut hair of graves." These lines suggest the cycle of decay and new growth. After death, the human body breaks down into basic chemical elements. These elements eventually become part of the soil and help form the grass.

27 transpire: emerge; ooze out.

29 offspring: babies.

34–35 The speaker compares the grass to "uttering tongues." Each blade of grass is like a tongue revealing **(uttering)** a message. These lines extend the idea of the life cycle in lines 25–29. The elements once were part of the "roofs of mouths" of those buried in the soil. These same elements now are part of the grass that grows on their graves.

41 sprout: young plant growth, such as a bud or shoot.

As the poem continues...

• The speaker makes a connection between the grass and those who are dead as part of the cycle of nature.

Pause & Reflect

READ ALOUD **1.** Read aloud the boxed passage on page 120. List the dead people the speaker imagines buried beneath the grass. **(Clarify)**

_____

_____

_____

3. Reread lines 34–35 and the accompanying note in the Guide for Reading. The blades of grass are compared to "so many uttering tongues." What message about death might they reveal to the speaker? **(Draw Conclusions)**

_____

_____

_____

_____

As the poem continues...

• The speaker makes a statement about death in general.

What Does It Mean?

Hints here refers again to the grass that is growing over people's graves. The _smallest sprouts_ of that grass support Whitman's belief that the dead don't really die, but become part of the cycle of nature and life.

And if ever there was it led forward life, and does not
    wait at the end to arrest it,
And ceas'd the moment life appear'd.

All goes onward and outward, nothing collapses,

45   And to die is different from what any one supposed,
    and luckier.

Pause & Reflect

FOCUS

In the final section, the speaker suggests
what will happen to him.
MARK IT UP As you read, circle details
that help you understand what will become
of him.

52

The spotted hawk swoops by and accuses me, he
    complains of my gab and my loitering.

I too am not a bit tamed, I too am untranslatable,
I sound my barbaric yawp over the roofs of the world.

The last scud of day holds back for me,

50   It flings my likeness after the rest and true as any on
    the shadow'd wilds,
It coaxes me to the vapor and the dusk.

I depart as air, I shake my white locks at the
    runaway sun,
I effuse my flesh in eddies, and drift it in lacy jags.

Pause & Reflect

1. How would you restate line 41 on page 120 in your own words? **(Paraphrase)**

_____

_____

_____

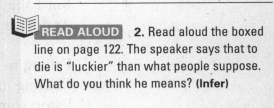

READ ALOUD **2.** Read aloud the boxed line on page 122. The speaker says that to die is "luckier" than what people suppose. What do you think he means? **(Infer)**

_____

_____

As the poem ends . . .

• The speaker explains that he is part of nature.

★ Reader Success Strategy

As you read this section, highlight phrases that show the speaker's union with nature.

What Does It Mean?

Gab means "chatting." *Loitering* means "hanging around for no reason."

48 barbaric yawp: A yawp is a sharp cry. This phrase may refer to Whitman's own poetry.
49 scud: wind-driven clouds.

52–58 The speaker describes his future physical changes.
52 locks: strands of hair.
53 effuse (ĭ-fyo͞os): pour out;
eddies: currents, as of air or water.

What Does It Mean?

I effuse my flesh in eddies means "my body is dissolving; I am becoming one with the elements."

I bequeath myself to the dirt to grow from the grass
    I love,
55 If you want me again look for me under your
    boot-soles.

You will hardly know who I am or what I mean,
But I shall be good health to you nevertheless,
And filter and fibre your blood.

Failing to fetch me at first keep encouraged,
60 Missing me one place search another,
I stop somewhere waiting for you.

Pause & Reflect

54 bequeath (bĭ-kwēth): leave (property) to another by a last will.

58 filter and fibre: clean and toughen.

59 The speaker may mean that if at first you don't get or understand his poetry **(fetch me)**, don't give up **(keep encouraged).**

What Does It Mean?

Here, *missing* means "not finding."

Pause & Reflect

1. The speaker compares himself to a hawk in three ways (lines 47–48 on page 122). Describe one of these comparisons. **(Compare and Contrast)**

_____

_____

_____

_____

MARK IT UP **2.** Review the details you circled as you read. Star the ones that suggest that the speaker will become one with nature. **(Evaluate)**

3. At the end of the poem, the speaker says he's "waiting for you." What do you think he means? **(Infer)**

_____

_____

_____

CHALLENGE

"Song of Myself" begins with the word *I* and ends with the word *you*. The poem creates a special relationship between the **speaker** ("I") and the reader ("you"). Go back through the poem and mark the lines that help you understand this relationship. How would you describe it? **(Analyze)**

Active Reading SkillBuilder

Strategies for Reading Free Verse

Free verse is poetry without regular patterns of rhyme and meter. To better appreciate the rhythm—as well as the ideas—that Whitman creates in his free verse, use these **strategies for reading free verse:** Read the poems aloud; notice where Whitman uses the devices of catalog, repetition, and parallelism; appreciate the sweep of his images and ideas; build a mental image of the speaker. Then record your thoughts and impressions on the spider map below. Two examples are given.

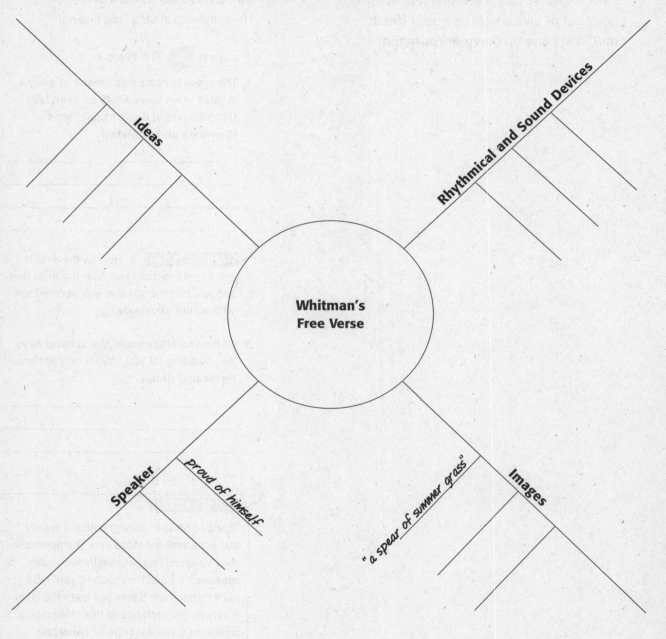

Ideas

Rhythmical and Sound Devices

Whitman's Free Verse

Speaker

proud of himself

"a spear of summer grass"

Images

Literary Analysis SkillBuilder

Free Verse

Free verse is poetry without regular patterns of rhyme and meter. Lines in free verse often flow more naturally than do rhymed, metrical lines and therefore sound more like human speech. Although free verse lacks meter, it does exhibit a variety of rhythmical devices such as **repetition,** or recurring words, phrases, or lines; **parallelism,** or related ideas phrased in similar ways; and **catalog,** or lists of people, things, or attributes. Record on the chart below two examples of each of these devices found in "Song of Myself." An example of each device has been given.

Repetition	Parallelism	Catalog
"born here of parents born here from parents" (line 7)	this soil, this air (line 6)	Kenuck, Tuckahoe, Congressman, Cuff (line 24)

The Masque of the Red Death

Edgar Allan Poe

Before You Read

Connect to Your Life

People face their fears in many different ways. What are some of the ways in which people deal with fear? Use the word web below to record your ideas.

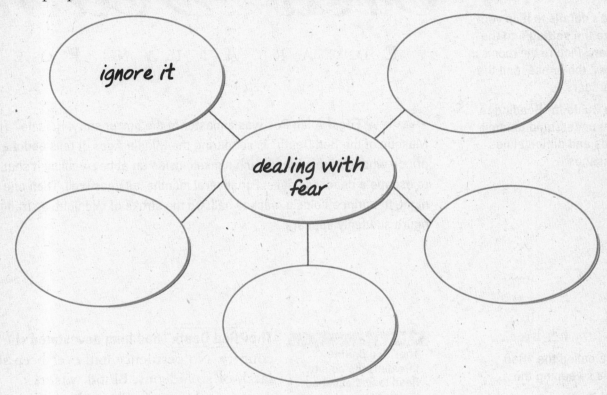

Key to the Story

WHAT YOU NEED TO KNOW The title of this story contains a play on words. A *masquerade*, or a masked ball, is a party at which people wear costumes. *Masque* is a shortened form of the word *masquerade*. The word *masque* also means "a disguise." Read the story to find out who or what is disguised.

Reading Tips

In his **short stories**, Poe creates an eerie world beyond everyday life. When you read a Poe story, let your imagination run wild. Feel the terror of the unknown.

- Use Poe's **details** to help you **visualize** the **setting** and the **characters.** Picture the rooms in the abbey, the prince, and the masqueraders.

- Use the Guide for Reading to help you understand unfamiliar words and difficult lines and passages.

As the story begins . . .

- A plague called the "Red Death" is sweeping the country.

- The symptoms of the disease are described.

- The main character, Prince Prospero, tries to escape the Red Death.

More About . . .

The Red Death is a plague. A *plague* is a deadly disease that spreads through a community. At the time this story takes place, there was little knowledge about how diseases spread, and antibiotics hadn't been invented yet.

The Masque of the Red Death

EDGAR ALLAN POE

PREVIEW Edgar Allan Poe was a master of the horror story. His tale "The Masque of the Red Death" is set during the Middle Ages. It tells about a prince who locks his friends and himself inside an abbey, walling it shut, to escape a deadly disease. For several months, all goes well. Then one night, the prince holds a masked ball. On the stroke of midnight, a strange figure suddenly appears.

FOCUS
The "Red Death" threatens the country. Read to find out about the disease and what Prospero does to try to escape it.

MARK IT UP As you read, circle details that help you understand how life outside Prospero's abbey is different from life inside. An example is highlighted on page 132.

The "Red Death" had long devastated the country. No pestilence had ever been so fatal, or so hideous. Blood was its Avatar and its seal—the redness and horror of blood. There were sharp pains, and sudden dizziness, and then profuse bleeding at the pores, with dissolution. The scarlet stains upon the body, and especially upon the face of the victim, were the pest ban which shut him out from the aid and from the sympathy of his fellow men. And the whole seizure, progress, and termination of the disease were the incidents of half an hour.

But the Prince Prospero was happy and <u>dauntless</u> and <u>sagacious</u>. When his dominions were half depopulated, he

WORDS
TO
KNOW

dauntless (dônt'lĭs) *adj.* fearless
sagacious (sə-gā'shəs) *adj.* wise

GUIDE FOR READING

Use this guide for help with unfamiliar words and difficult passages.

1 **devastated** (dĕv′ə-stā′tĭd): laid waste to.
2 **pestilence** (pĕs′tə-ləns): a very destructive infectious disease.
4 **Avatar** (ăv′ə-tär′): an appearance in physical form of an unseen force.

8 **dissolution:** death.

10 **pest ban:** a proclamation announcing that a person is sick with the plague.

MARK IT UP WORD POWER

Mark words that you'd like to add to your **Personal Word List**. After reading, you can record the words and their meanings beginning on page 476.

★ **Reader Success Strategy**

To help establish a setting in the past, Poe uses archaic language, or language that is characteristic of an earlier time. As you read, try to restate difficult sentences in your own words. Look for context clues to help you figure out the meanings of words.

What Does It Mean?

His dominions were half depopulated means that half of the people in Prospero's country had died from the plague.

More About . . .

PLAGUE SYMPTOMS During the fourteenth century, the bubonic plague swept through Europe. It killed a quarter to a third of the population. People suffering from the plague had high fever, vomiting, pain, and swellings that oozed blood. They usually died within three to five days. Poe's story may have been inspired by this outbreak.

JOT IT DOWN Reread Lines 8–12

Why do people show no pity for the victims of the Red Death? **(Clarify)**

_____

_____

_____

summoned to his presence a thousand hale and lighthearted friends from among the knights and dames of his court, and with these retired to the deep seclusion of one of his castellated abbeys. This was an extensive and magnificent structure, the creation of the prince's own eccentric yet august taste. A strong and lofty wall girded it in. This wall had gates of iron. The <u>courtiers</u>, having entered, brought furnaces and massy hammers and welded the bolts. They resolved to leave means neither of ingress or egress to the sudden impulses of despair or of frenzy from within. The abbey was amply provisioned. With such precautions the courtiers might bid defiance to <u>contagion</u>. The external world could take care of itself. In the meantime it was folly to grieve, or to think. The prince had provided all the appliances of pleasure. There were buffoons, there were improvisatori, there were ballet-dancers, there were musicians, there was Beauty, there was wine. All these and security were within. Without was the "Red Death."

Pause & Reflect

FOCUS
Read to find out about the seven rooms in which Prince Prospero holds the masked ball. Pay close attention to what is different about the black room.

It was toward the close of the fifth or sixth month of his seclusion, and while the pestilence raged most furiously abroad, that the Prince Prospero entertained his thousand friends at a masked ball of the most unusual magnificence.

It was a voluptuous scene, that masquerade. But first let me tell of the rooms in which it was held. There were seven— an imperial suite. In many palaces, however, such suites form a long and straight vista, while the folding doors slide back nearly to the walls on either hand, so that the view of the whole extent is scarcely impeded. Here the case was very different; as might have been expected from the duke's love of the *bizarre*. The apartments were so irregularly disposed that the vision embraced but little more than one at a time. There was a sharp turn at every twenty or thirty yards, and at each turn a novel effect. To the right and left, in the middle of each

WORDS
TO
KNOW

courtier (kôr′tē-ər) *n.* a member of a royal court
contagion (kən-tā′jən) *n.* the spreading of disease

20 castellated abbey (kăs′tə-lā′tĭd ăb′ē): a fortified building formerly used as, or built to resemble, a monastery.

25 ingress (ĭn′grĕs′) **or egress** (ē′grĕs′): entry or exit.

26–33 Inside the abbey, Prospero tries to create a world filled with amusements.

27 provisioned: provided with supplies.

31 improvisatori (ĭm-prŏv′ĭ-zə-tôr′ē): poets who recite verses that they make up as they go along.

41 voluptuous (və-lŭp′cho͞o-əs): appealing to the senses; luxurious.

47 The duke and Prince Prospero are the same person.

51 novel: strikingly new, unusual, or different.

What Does It Mean?
Bid defiance to contagion means "fight the spread of disease."

Pause & Reflect
What does Prince Prospero do to try to escape this disease? **(Infer)**

_____

_____

_____

_____

As the story continues . . .
- Prospero and his friends have been in the abbey for about six months.
- Prospero plans a masked ball to entertain his guests.
- The abbey has seven rooms, each decorated in a different color.

What Does It Mean?
Bizarre means "strikingly odd or unconventional."

wall, a tall and narrow Gothic window looked out upon a closed corridor which pursued the windings of the suite. These windows were of stained glass whose color varied in accordance with the prevailing hue of the decorations of the chamber into which it opened. That at the eastern extremity was hung, for example, in blue—and vividly blue were its windows. The second chamber was purple in its ornaments and tapestries, and here the panes were purple. The third was green throughout, and so were the casements. The fourth was furnished and lighted with orange—the fifth with white—the sixth with violet. The seventh apartment was closely shrouded in black velvet tapestries that hung all over the ceiling and down the walls, falling in heavy folds upon a carpet of the same material and hue. But in this chamber only, the color of the windows failed to correspond with the decorations. The panes here were scarlet—a deep blood color. Now in no one of the seven apartments were there any lamp or candelabrum amid the profusion of golden ornaments that lay scattered to and fro or depended from the roof. There was no light of any kind emanating from lamp or candle within the suite of chambers. But in the corridors that followed the suite, there stood, opposite to each window, a heavy tripod, bearing a brazier of fire that projected its rays through the tinted glass and so glaringly illumined the room. And thus were produced a multitude of gaudy and fantastic appearances. But in the western or black chamber the effect of the firelight that streamed upon the dark hangings through the blood-tinted panes, was ghastly in the extreme, and produced so wild a look upon the countenances of those who entered, that there were few of the company bold enough to set foot within its precincts at all.

It was in this apartment, also, that there stood against the western wall a gigantic clock of ebony. Its pendulum swung to and fro with a dull, heavy, monotonous clang; and when the minute hand made the circuit of the face, and the hour was to be stricken, there came from the brazen lungs of the clock a sound which was clear and loud and deep and exceedingly musical, but of so peculiar a note and emphasis that, at each lapse of an hour, the musicians of the orchestra were constrained to pause, momentarily, in their performance, to hearken to the sound; and thus the waltzers perforce ceased their evolutions; and there was a brief

59 tapestries: woven cloths hung on walls.

60 casements: windows.

74 brazier (brā′zhər)**:** metal pan for holding a fire.

80 countenances (koun′tə-nən-səz)**:** faces.

84 ebony (ĕb′ə-nē)**:** a hard, very dark wood.

87 brazen: brass.

93 evolutions: intricate patterns of movement.

JOT IT DOWN   **Reread Lines 56–65**

Fill in the chart below by listing the missing colors. One is shown. **(Clarify)**

Rooms in the abbey

			4th		6th	
1st **blue**	2nd	3rd		5th		7th

eastern   western

READ ALOUD **Lines 62–67**

What makes the black room different from the six other rooms? **(Compare and Contrast)**

_____

_____

_____

_____

What Does It Mean?

Here, *depended* means "hung."

Reading Check

How do the partygoers feel about the seventh room?

What Does It Mean?

The clock is used as a symbol. It represents time running out as death approaches.

disconcert of the whole gay company; and, while the chimes of the clock yet rang, it was observed that the giddiest turned pale, and the more aged and sedate passed their hands over their brows as if in confused reverie or meditation. But when the echoes had fully ceased, a light laughter at once <u>pervaded</u> the assembly; the musicians looked at each other and smiled as if at their own nervousness and folly, and made whispering vows, each to the other, that the next chiming of the clock should produce in them no similar emotion; and then, after the lapse of sixty minutes (which embrace three thousand and six hundred seconds of the Time that flies), there came yet another chiming of the clock, and then were the same disconcert and tremulousness and meditation as before.

Pause & Reflect

FOCUS
Read to find out about the guests' costumes and behavior at the masked ball.

But in spite of these things, it was a gay and magnificent revel. The tastes of the duke were peculiar. He had a fine eye for colors and effects. He disregarded the *decora* of mere fashion. His plans were bold and fiery, and his conceptions glowed with barbaric luster. There are some who would have thought him mad. His followers felt that he was not. It was necessary to hear and see and touch him to be *sure* that he was not.

He had directed, in great part, the movable embellishments of the seven chambers, upon occasion of this great *fête*; and it was his own guiding taste which had given character to the masqueraders. Be sure they were <u>grotesque</u>. There were much glare and glitter and piquancy and phantasm—much of what has been seen since in *Hernani*. There were arabesque figures with unsuited limbs and appointments. There were delirious fancies such as the madman fashions. There was much of the beautiful, much of the wanton, much of the *bizarre*, something of the terrible, and not a little of that which might have excited disgust. To and fro in the seven chambers there

WORDS
TO
KNOW
pervade (pər-vād´) *v.* to spread throughout
grotesque (grō-těsk´) *adj.* having a bizarre, fantastic appearance

94 disconcert: confusion.

97 reverie: daydreaming.

108 revel: a celebration.

111 *decora:* fine things.

114 mad: insane.

116–138 Notice the comparison of the masqueraders to dreams, phantasms, and a madman's fancies.
116 movable embellishments: furnishings and decorations.
120 phantasm (făn'tăz'əm): a shifting appearance.
121 *Hernani* (ĕr'nä-nē): a play by Victor Hugo, first staged in 1830, known for its use of color and spectacle; **arabesque** (ăr'ə-bĕsk'): characterized by complicated decorations.

Pause & Reflect

MARK IT UP **1.** What happens whenever the ebony clock chimes? Write the answer below. Then circle details on pages 134 and 136 that led you to your answer. **(Cause and Effect)**

_____
_____
_____
_____

2. What do you think might occur in the black room? **(Predict)**

_____
_____
_____
_____

As the story continues . . .

• Prospero has decorated the rooms for the masquerade according to his own tastes.

• He has designed strange and grotesque costumes for his guests.

• As the evening progresses, none of the guests will enter the seventh room.

 **Reader Success Strategy**

Work with a partner to paraphrase the highlighted lines.

stalked, in fact, a multitude of dreams. And these—the dreams—writhed in and about, taking hue from the rooms, and causing the wild music of the orchestra to seem as the echo of their steps. And, anon, there strikes the ebony clock which stands in the hall of velvet. And then, for a moment, all is still, and all is silent save the voice of the clock. The dreams are stiff-frozen as they stand. But the echoes of the chime die away—they have endured but an instant—and a light, half-subdued laughter floats after them as they depart. And now again the music swells, and the dreams live, and writhe to and fro more merrily than ever, taking hue from the many-tinted windows through which stream the rays of the tripods. But to the chamber which lies most westwardly of the seven, there are now none of the maskers who venture; for the night is waning away; and there flows a ruddier light through the blood-colored panes; and the blackness of the sable drapery appalls; and to him whose foot falls upon the sable carpet, there comes from the near clock of ebony a muffled peal more solemnly emphatic than any which reaches *their* ears who indulge in the more remote gaieties of the other apartments.

Pause **&** *Reflect*

FOCUS

At midnight a masked figure suddenly appears at the ball. Read to find out about this figure and Prospero's reaction to it.

◢ MARK IT UP As you read, circle any details that help you picture this figure.

But these other apartments were densely crowded, and in them beat feverishly the heart of life. And the revel went whirlingly on, until at length there commenced the sounding of midnight upon the clock. And then the music ceased, as I have told; and the evolutions of the waltzes were quieted; and there was an uneasy cessation of all things as before. But now there were twelve strokes to be sounded by the bell of the clock; and thus it happened, perhaps, that more of thought crept, with more of time, into the meditations of the thoughtful among those who reveled. And thus, too, it happened, perhaps, that before the last echoes of the last chime had utterly sunk into silence, there were many individuals in the crowd who had found leisure to become aware of the presence of a masked figure which had arrested the attention of no single individual

127 The **dreams** are not literal dreams. The guests wear costumes so fantastic that they look as though they have stepped out of a dream.

128 writhed (rīthd)**:** made twisting or turning movements.

138-146 The dancers avoid the black room because the combination of red and black in the room and the loud chiming of the clock frightens them; **appalls:** fills with dread.

What Does It Mean?
Waning away means "gradually decreasing and passing away."

Pause & Reflect

1. Prospero's followers believe that he *is/is not* insane. (Clarify)

2. Would you like to be a guest at Prospero's masked ball? *Yes/No,* because _____ _____ _____ _____.

(Connect)

As the story continues . . .
- The clock strikes midnight.
- A masked figure suddenly appears at the party.
- The guests and Prospero are astonished at the masked figure's costume.

☆ Reader Success Strategy

Authors use word choice and description to create mood and build suspense. As you read this section, highlight words and phrases that Poe uses to build suspense.

before. And the rumor of this new presence having spread itself whisperingly around, there arose at length from the whole company a buzz, or murmur, expressive of disapprobation and surprise—then, finally of terror, of horror, and of disgust.

In an assembly of phantasms such as I have painted, it may well be supposed that no ordinary appearance could have excited such sensation. In truth the masquerade <u>license</u> of the night was nearly unlimited; but the figure in question had out-Heroded Herod, and gone beyond the bounds of even the prince's indefinite decorum. There are chords in the hearts of the most reckless which cannot be touched without emotion. Even with the utterly lost, to whom life and death are equally jests, there are matters of which no jest can be made. The whole company, indeed, seemed now deeply to feel that in the costume and bearing of the stranger neither wit nor propriety existed. The figure was tall and gaunt, and shrouded from head to foot in the habiliments of the grave. The mask which concealed the visage was made so nearly to resemble the countenance of a stiffened corpse that the closest scrutiny must have difficulty in detecting the cheat. And yet all this might have been endured, if not approved, by the mad revellers around. But the mummer had gone so far as to assume the type of the Red Death. His vesture was dabbed in *blood*—and his broad brow, with all the features of the face, was besprinkled with the scarlet horror.

When the eyes of Prince Prospero fell upon this spectral image (which with a slow and solemn movement, as if more fully to sustain its *role*, stalked to and fro among the waltzers), he was seen to be convulsed, in the first moment with a strong shudder either of terror or distaste; but, in the next, his brow reddened with rage.

"Who dares?" he demanded hoarsely of the courtiers who stood near him—"who dares insult us with this blasphemous mockery? Seize him and unmask him—that we may know whom we have to hang at sunrise, from the battlements!"

Pause & Reflect

WORDS TO KNOW

license (līʹsəns) *n.* a lack of restrictions on behavior; freedom

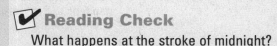

Reading Check

What happens at the stroke of midnight?

174 out-Heroded Herod: been more extreme than the biblical king Herod, who ordered the deaths of all male babies up to two years old in an effort to kill the infant Jesus. This expression is used in Shakespeare's *Hamlet*.

182 habiliments (hə-bĭl'ə-mənts): clothing.
183 visage (vĭz'ĭj): face.

Reading Check

How is the masked figure dressed?

Pause & Reflect

1. Review the details you circled as you read. What makes the masked figure so horrible? **(Infer)**

_____

_____

_____

_____

187 mummer: a person dressed for a masquerade.

MARK IT UP 2. How does Prospero react to the masked figure? Cross out the word below that does *not* describe his reaction. Then underline any details on page 140 that led you to the answer. **(Clarify)**

frightened

angry

sympathetic

disgusted

198 blasphemous (blăs'fə-məs): mocking something holy.

It was in the eastern or blue chamber in which stood the Prince Prospero as he uttered these words. They rang throughout the seven rooms loudly and clearly—for the prince was a bold and robust man, and the music had become hushed at the waving of his hand.

It was in the blue room where stood the prince, with a group of pale courtiers by his side. At first, as he spoke, there was a slight rushing movement of this group in the direction of the intruder, who at the moment was also near at hand, and now, with deliberate and stately step, made closer approach to the speaker. But from a certain nameless awe with which the mad assumptions of the mummer had inspired the whole party, there were found none who put forth a hand to seize him; so that, unimpeded, he passed within a yard of the prince's person; and, while the vast assembly, as if with one impulse, shrank from the centers of the rooms to the walls, he made his way uninterruptedly, but with the same solemn and measured step which had distinguished him from the first, through the blue chamber to the purple—through the purple to the green—through the green to the orange—through this again to the white—and even thence to the violet, ere a decided movement had been made to arrest him. It was then, however, that the Prince Prospero, maddening with rage and the shame of his own momentary cowardice, rushed hurriedly through the six chambers while none followed him on account of a deadly terror that had seized upon all. He bore aloft a drawn dagger, and had approached, in rapid <u>impetuosity</u>, to within three or four feet of the retreating figure, when the latter, having attained the extremity of the velvet apartment, turned suddenly and confronted his pursuer. There was a sharp cry— and the dagger dropped gleaming upon the sable carpet, upon which, instantly afterwards, fell prostrate in death the Prince Prospero. Then, summoning the wild courage of despair, a throng of the revellers at once threw themselves into the

WORDS
TO
KNOW

impetuosity (ĭm-pĕch′ŏo-ŏs′ĭ-tē) *n.* unthinking action

206 robust (rō-bŭst′)**:** full of health and strength.

212–225 The masked figure walks through the rooms with great dignity and no haste.

236–242 When a group of revellers rip off the figure's costume, there is nothing underneath.

As the story ends . . .

- The masked figure makes his way through each of the rooms.
- Prospero hesitates and then pursues him in rage.
- The guests rip off the figure's costume.

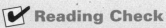 **JOT IT DOWN**   **Reread Lines 213–225**

Why do you think the masked figure is allowed to walk the length of the rooms uninterrupted? **(Infer)**

_____

_____

_____

_____

What Does It Mean?

Unimpeded means "without interference." The masked figure is not stopped by any of the guests.

Reading Check

What does Prospero do as the masked figure makes his way through the rooms?

black apartment, and seizing the mummer, whose tall figure stood erect and motionless within the shadow of the ebony clock, gasped in unutterable horror at finding the grave-cerements and corpselike mask, which they handled with so violent a rudeness, <u>untenanted</u> by any <u>tangible</u> form.

And now was acknowledged the presence of the Red Death. He had come like a thief in the night. And one by one dropped the revellers in the blood-bedewed halls of their revel, and died each in the despairing posture of his fall. And the life of the ebony clock went out with that of the last of the gay. And the flames of the tripods expired. And Darkness and Decay and the Red Death held illimitable dominion over all.

Pause & Reflect

untenanted (ŭn-tĕn′ən-tĭd) *adj.* not occupied
tangible (tăn′jə-bəl) *adj.* able to be touched or felt

241 cerements (sĕr'ə-mənts): cloth wrappings for the dead.

249 illimitable dominion (ĭ-lĭm'ĭ-tə-bəl də-mĭn'yən): unlimited power.

✔ Reading Check

Who is the mysterious figure, and what happens when he appears?

Pause **&** Reflect

1. Describe Prospero's death. **(Clarify)**

_____

_____

_____

_____

READ ALOUD   **2.** Read aloud the boxed sentence on page 144. Then restate its idea in your own words. **(Paraphrase)**

_____

_____

_____

_____

CHALLENGE

Irony is the contrast between what is expected and what actually exists or happens. For example, Prospero, who tries to escape the Red Death, actually rushes toward it at his own party. Highlight other examples of irony in this story. You may also consider the prince's name (to *prosper* means "to have material success.") **(Analyze)**

Active Reading SkillBuilder

Clarifying Meaning

In "The Masque of the Red Death," Poe uses unusual, old-fashioned vocabulary to help reinforce the story's setting in the past. The following strategies can help **clarify** the meanings of particular words and passages: use the Guide for Reading notes; reread difficult passages carefully, then **paraphrase** them (state them in your own words); **summarize** difficult passages; use **context clues** (clues found in the surrounding phrases) to figure out the meanings of unfamiliar words. Use these strategies while reading the story. Record on the chart below any difficult words and passages, questions about them, and possible meanings for each word or passage. An example is given.

Difficult Words and Passages	Questions	Possible Meanings
The courtiers might bid defiance to contagion.	What does "bid defiance" mean?	The courtiers thought they were safe from the disease.

Literary Analysis SkillBuilder

Allegory

"The Masque of the Red Death" can be read as an **allegory,** a literary work in which the characters, objects, and events represent abstract qualities, such as kindness or greed. An allegory has a second level of meaning in addition to its literal meaning. Some allegories are intended to teach moral lessons. Use the chart below to analyze allegorical elements in Poe's story. Give a possible meaning for the listed elements and explain how Poe uses each one to convey a moral lesson.

Person, Object, Event	Possible Meaning	Possible Moral of Story
The prince	*selfishness*	*Selfish people in the end destroy themselves.*
The abbey		
The series of seven rooms		
The clock		
The stranger		

Follow Up: Compare your chart with that of a partner; defend your interpretations of allegorical elements in Poe's story.

Words to Know SkillBuilder

Words to Know

contagion	dauntless	impetuosity	pervade	tangible
courtier	grotesque	license	sagacious	untenanted

A. Fill in each set of blanks with the correct word from the word list. The boxed letters will spell out what the Red Death turned out to be.

1. Children sometimes act as if this has been granted to them when their teacher is replaced by a substitute.

   __ □ __ __ __ __ __

2. This is what you are if a visit to the dentist, noises in the night, and an algebra exam fail to bother you.

   __ __ __ □ __ __ __ __ __

3. This is one who spends time bowing, attending royal banquets, and saying "Your Highness."

   __ __ __ __ __ __ □ __ __

4. This describes some high-fashion items and many things possessed by people with truly horrible taste.

   __ __ __ __ __ __ □ __ __ __

5. This describes someone who knows that a stitch in time saves nine and too many cooks spoil the broth.

   __ __ __ __ __ □ __ __ __ __

6. This is what vaccines prevent and what we try to limit by covering our mouths when we cough.

   __ __ __ __ __ □ __ __ __

7. This could cause you to jump into a lake to save a drowning child or to dye your hair green on a dare.

   __ __ □ __ __ __ __ __ __ __ __

8. This could describe an abandoned house, a dead body, or a hive after the bees have vacated it.

   __ __ __ __ __ □ __ __ __ __

9. This describes a wedding ring but not the words "I do," or a piece of apple pie but not the taste.

   __ __ __ __ __ __ □ □ __

10. Solids cannot do this to the spaces they occupy, but sounds, moods, and gases can.

    __ □ __ __ __ __ __

B. Write the invitation that Prince Prospero sent out to a thousand of his subjects when he got his clever idea. Use at least **four** of the Words to Know.

Dr. Heidegger's Experiment

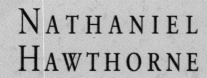

NATHANIEL
HAWTHORNE

Before You Read

Connect to Your Life

What kinds of things do people do to stay young? How do they try to slow the effects of getting older? Fill in the word web below with your ideas.

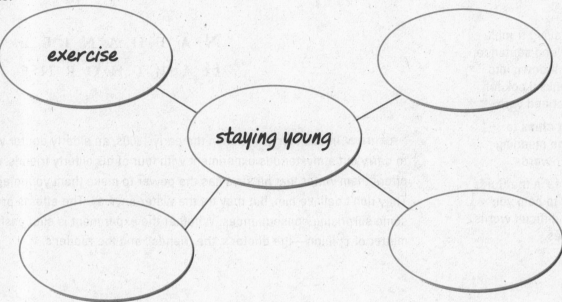

Key to the Story

WHAT'S THE BIG IDEA? Younger people sometimes wish to be older. Older people sometimes wish to be younger. In "Dr. Heidegger's Experiment," the characters drink magical water to make them young again. Why do you think an older person might want to be young again? Why might a younger person want to be older? Write your responses below.

An older person might want to be younger because

_____.

A younger person might want to be older because

_____.

Dr. Heidegger's Experiment

NATHANIEL HAWTHORNE

PREVIEW In this story, written in the early 1800s, an elderly doctor wants to carry out a mysterious experiment with four of his elderly friends. He offers them water that he says has the power to make them young again. They don't believe him, but they try the water anyway. The effects produce some surprising consequences. Whether the experiment is successful is a matter of opinion—the doctor's, the friends', and the reader's.

As the story begins . . .

- Dr. Heidegger, an elderly doctor, is preparing to conduct an experiment.

- Dr. Heidegger has invited four elderly friends to his study.

What Does It Mean?

Melancholy means "sad."

MARK IT UP KEEP TRACK

As you read, you can use these marks to keep track of your understanding.

✔ ..... I understand.

? ..... I don't understand this.

! ..... Interesting or surprising idea

FOCUS

The first part of the story introduces Dr. Heidegger and his four friends. It also describes the doctor's study.

MARK IT UP As you read, underline details that describe what each of the four friends has wasted or lost. An example is highlighted.

⑩

That very singular man, old Dr. Heidegger, once invited four <u>venerable</u> friends to meet him in his study. There were three white-bearded gentlemen, Mr. Medbourne, Colonel Killigrew, and Mr. Gascoigne, and a withered gentlewoman, whose name was the Widow Wycherly. They were all melancholy old creatures, who had been unfortunate in life, and whose greatest misfortune it was, that they were not long ago in their graves. Mr. Medbourne, in the vigor of his age, had been a prosperous merchant, but had lost his all by a frantic speculation, and was now little better than a mendicant. Colonel Killigrew had wasted his best years, and his health and substance, in the pursuit of sinful pleasures, which had

WORDS
TO
KNOW

venerable (vĕn′ər-ə-bəl) *adj.* worthy of respect because of age, dignity, or character

Use this guide for help with unfamiliar words and difficult passages.

★ Reader Success Strategy

The language of "Dr. Heidegger's Experiment" is rather formal, so you may find it helpful to read some sentences aloud. As you read a sentence aloud, imagine that you are telling the story. How would you phrase the sentence in your own words?

6 Gascoigne: (găs-coin').

10–11 whose . . . graves: The most unfortunate aspect of their lives was that they were not already dead.

14 speculation: risky business deals; **mendicant** (měn'dĭ-kənt): beggar.

MARK IT UP WORD POWER

Mark words that you'd like to add to your **Personal Word List.** After reading, you can record the words and their meanings beginning on page 476.

What Does It Mean?

Wasted his best years means that Colonel Killigrew had misspent the most active years of his life.

given birth to a brood of pains, such as the gout, and divers other torments of soul and body. Mr. Gascoigne was a ruined politician, a man of evil fame, or at least had been so, till time had buried him from the knowledge of the present generation, and made him obscure instead of infamous. As for the Widow Wycherly, tradition tells us that she was a great beauty in her day; but, for a long while past, she had lived in deep seclusion, on account of certain scandalous stories, which had prejudiced the gentry of the town against her. It is a circumstance worth mentioning, that each of these three old gentlemen, Mr. Medbourne, Colonel Killigrew, and Mr. Gascoigne, were early lovers of the Widow Wycherly, and had once been on the point of cutting each other's throats for her sake. And, before proceeding farther, I will merely hint, that Dr. Heidegger and all his four guests were sometimes thought to be a little beside themselves; as is not unfrequently the case with old people, when worried either by present troubles or woeful recollections.

"My dear old friends," said Dr. Heidegger, motioning them to be seated, "I am desirous of your assistance in one of those little experiments with which I amuse myself here in my study."

If all stories were true, Dr. Heidegger's study must have been a very curious place. It was a dim, old-fashioned chamber, festooned with cobwebs, and besprinkled with antique dust. Around the walls stood several oaken bookcases, the lower shelves of which were filled with rows of gigantic folios, and black-letter quartos, and the upper with little parchment covered duodecimos. Over the central bookcase was a bronze bust of Hippocrates, with which, according to some authorities, Dr. Heidegger was accustomed to hold consultations, in all difficult cases of his practice. In the obscurest corner of the room stood a tall and narrow oaken closet, with its door ajar, within which doubtfully appeared a skeleton. Between two of the book-cases hung a looking-glass, presenting its high and dusty plate within a tarnished gilt frame. Among many wonderful stories related of this mirror, it was fabled that the spirits of all the doctor's deceased patients dwelt within its verge, and would stare him in the face whenever he looked thitherward. The opposite side of the chamber was ornamented with the full length portrait of a young lady, arrayed in the faded magnificence of silk, satin, and brocade, and with a visage as faded as her

17 gout (gout): a painful disease of the joints, once thought to be caused by eating too much rich food.

21 obscure instead of infamous (ĭn'fə-məs): little known rather than well-known for wickedness.

25 gentry: respectable or socially high-ranking people.

32 beside themselves: upset; not rational.

40 festooned: decorated in draping curves.

43–44 folios . . . quartos . . . duodecimos: books of different sizes.
45 Hippocrates (hǐ-pŏk'rə-tēz'): a Greek physician, considered to be the father of medicine.

50–55 This is no ordinary mirror. People say that Dr. Heidegger can see in the glass the ghosts of patients who have died.

54 verge: border.
55 thitherward: in that direction.

58 visage (vĭz'ĭj): face.

 Reading Check

The four guests have several things in common. Name two of them.

 JOT IT DOWN   Reread Lines 26–30

What relationship did the four guests have in their youth? **(Clarify)**

_____

_____

_____

What Does It Mean?

A *bust* is a sculpture of a person's head, shoulders, and upper chest.

 Reading Check

How does Dr. Heidegger behave toward the bust of Hippocrates?

What Does It Mean?

Obscurest means "darkest" or "most hidden."

⭐ **Reader Success Strategy**

Draw a sketch of Dr. Heidegger's study based on the description in this section.

dress. Above half a century ago, Dr. Heidegger had been on the point of marriage with this young lady; but, being affected with some slight disorder, she had swallowed one of her lover's prescriptions, and died on the bridal evening.

The greatest curiosity of the study remains to be mentioned: it was a ponderous folio volume, bound in black leather, with massive silver clasps. There were no letters on the back, and nobody could tell the title of the book. But it was well known to be a book of magic; and once, when a chambermaid had lifted it, merely to brush away the dust, the skeleton had rattled in its closet, the picture of the young lady had stepped one foot upon the floor, and several ghastly faces had peeped forth from the mirror; while the brazen head of Hippocrates frowned, and said—"Forbear!"

Such was Dr. Heidegger's study. On the summer afternoon of our tale, a small round table, as black as ebony, stood in the center of the room, sustaining a cut-glass vase, of beautiful form and elaborate workmanship. The sunshine came through the window, between the heavy festoons of two faded damask curtains, and fell directly across this vase; so that a mild splendor was reflected from it on the ashen visages of the five old people who sat around. Four champagne glasses were also on the table.

Pause & Reflect

FOCUS
Dr. Heidegger demonstrates the experiment he wants to carry out with his friends. He will try to make an old dried-up rose bloom again. As you read, look for magical elements in the demonstration.

"My dear old friends," repeated Dr. Heidegger, "may I reckon on your aid in performing an exceedingly curious experiment?"

Now Dr. Heidegger was a very strange old gentleman, whose eccentricity had become the nucleus for a thousand fantastic stories. Some of these fables, to my shame be it spoken, might possibly be traced back to mine own veracious self; and if any passages of the present tale

64 ponderous folio volume: a large book. The magical effects of this book are described later in this paragraph.

72 forbear: stop; cease.

78 damask (dăm′əsk)**:** A patterned cloth.

89–94 The narrator admits to having told fables, or untrue stories, about Dr. Heidegger in the past.

92 veracious (və-rā′shəs)**:** truthful.

 Reading Check

What happened to the chambermaid once when she lifted Dr. Heidegger's book of magic?

Pause & Reflect

1. Review the details that you underlined as you read. For each of the four guests, write one word or phrase that describes what that character has lost or wasted. **(Clarify)**

   Mr. Medbourne: _____

   Colonel Killigrew: _____

   Mr. Gascoigne: _____

   Widow Wycherly: _____

2. Why has Dr. Heidegger invited his friends to his study? **(Clarify)**

   _____

   _____

   _____

   _____

As the story continues . . .

- Dr. Heidegger describes the experiment to his guests.

- He demonstrates the experiment using a dried rose.

- He invites his guests to take part in the experiment but warns them to be cautious.

should startle the reader's faith, I must be content to bear the <u>stigma</u> of a fiction-monger.

When the doctor's four guests heard him talk of his proposed experiment, they anticipated nothing more wonderful than the murder of a mouse in an air-pump, or the examination of a cobweb by the microscope, or some similar nonsense, with which he was constantly in the habit of pestering his intimates. But without waiting for a reply, Dr. Heidegger hobbled across the chamber, and returned with the same ponderous folio, bound in black leather, which common report affirmed to be a book of magic. Undoing the silver clasps, he opened the volume, and took from among its black-letter pages a rose, or what was once a rose, though now the green leaves and crimson petals had assumed one brownish hue, and the ancient flower seemed ready to crumble to dust in the doctor's hands.

"This rose," said Dr. Heidegger, with a sigh, "this same withered and crumbling flower, blossomed five-and-fifty years ago. It was given me by Sylvia Ward, whose portrait hangs yonder; and I meant to wear it in my bosom at our wedding. Five-and-fifty years it has been treasured between the leaves of this old volume. Now, would you deem it possible that this rose of half a century could ever bloom again?"

"Nonsense!" said the Widow Wycherly, with a peevish toss of her head. "You might as well ask whether an old woman's wrinkled face could ever bloom again."

"See!" answered Dr. Heidegger.

He uncovered the vase, and threw the faded rose into the water which it contained. At first, it lay lightly on the surface of the fluid, appearing to imbibe none of its moisture. Soon, however, a singular change began to be visible. The crushed and dried petals stirred, and assumed a deepening tinge of crimson, as if the flower were reviving from a death-like slumber; the slender stalk and twigs of foliage became green; and there was the rose of half a century, looking as fresh as when Sylvia Ward had first given it to her lover. It was scarcely full-blown; for some of its delicate red leaves curled modestly around its moist bosom, within which two or three dewdrops were sparkling.

WORDS
TO
KNOW

stigma (stĭg′mə) *n.* a mark of disgrace

94 fiction-monger: liar.

95–100 The guests are used to being called in to watch Dr. Heidegger's experiments. They expect nothing unusual.

> **✎ ▸MARK IT UP**   **Reread Lines 109–114**
>
> Who gave Dr. Heidegger the rose and how old is it? Circle words in the boxed passage that tell the answers. **(Clarify)**

116 peevish: irritable.

122 imbibe: absorb.

> **✎ JOT IT DOWN**   **Reread Lines 122–131**
>
> What happens to the rose? **(Summarize)**
>
> _____
>
> _____
>
> _____

129 full-blown: completely open.

"That is certainly a very pretty deception," said the doctor's friends; carelessly, however, for they had witnessed greater miracles at a conjurer's show: "pray how was it effected?"

"Did you never hear of the (Fountain of Youth,)" asked Dr. Heidegger, "which Ponce De Leon, the Spanish adventurer, went in search of, two or three centuries ago?"

"But did Ponce De Leon ever find it?" said the Widow Wycherly.

"No," answered Dr. Heidegger, "for he never sought it in the right place. The famous Fountain of Youth, if I am rightly informed, is situated in the southern part of the Floridian peninsula, not far from Lake Macaco. Its source is overshadowed by several gigantic magnolias, which, though numberless centuries old, have been kept as fresh as violets, by the virtues of this wonderful water. An acquaintance of mine, knowing my curiosity in such matters, has sent me what you see in the vase."

"Ahem!" said Colonel Killigrew, who believed not a word of the doctor's story: "and what may be the effect of this fluid on the human frame?"

"You shall judge for yourself, my dear colonel," replied Dr. Heidegger; "and all of you, my respected friends, are welcome to so much of this admirable fluid, as may restore to you the bloom of youth. For my own part, having had much trouble in growing old, I am in no hurry to grow young again. With your permission, therefore, I will merely watch the progress of the experiment."

While he spoke, Dr. Heidegger had been filling the four champagne glasses with the water of the Fountain of Youth. It was apparently impregnated with an effervescent gas, for little bubbles were continually ascending from the depths of the glasses, and bursting in silvery spray at the surface. As the liquor diffused a pleasant perfume, the old people doubted not that it possessed cordial and comfortable properties; and, though utter skeptics as to its rejuvenescent power, they were inclined to swallow it at once. But Dr. Heidegger besought them to stay a moment.

"Before you drink, my respectable old friends," said he, "it would be well that, with the experience of a life-time to direct you, you should draw up a few general rules for your guidance, in passing a second time through the perils of

134 conjurer's: magician's.

137 Ponce De Leon (pŏns′ də lē-ōn′)**:**
Spanish explorer who went to Florida in
1513.

162 was apparently . . . gas: seemed to
have a bubbling gas dissolved in it.

166 cordial (kôr′jəl)**:** stimulating.
167 rejuvenescent (rǐ-jōō′və-něs′ənt)**:**
producing renewed youth.
168–169 besought them to stay: begged
them to wait.
170–176 Dr. Heidegger warns his friends
against making the same mistakes they made
in their youth. He fully expects them to
regain their youth.

✔ **Reading Check**

What do the guests think of Dr. Heidegger's
demonstration with the rose?

More About . . .

(THE FOUNTAIN OF YOUTH) In the 1500s,
the Spanish explorer Ponce de Leon
searched all over Florida for the Fountain
of Youth. Some people believed that water
from the Fountain of Youth would make
those who drank it young again.

🖉 **JOT IT DOWN**   **Reread Lines 142–149**

Where did the water for Dr. Heidegger's
experiment come from? **(Clarify)**

_____

_____

⭐ **Reader Success
Strategy**

A narrator's comments and descriptions
can create a mood or influence the reader's opinion about characters and events.
As you read, highlight the narrator's words
that help to create a mood or to influence
the reader.

🖉 **JOT IT DOWN**   **Reread Lines 156–158**

Why doesn't Dr. Heidegger want to drink the
water himself? **(Infer)**

_____

_____

✔ **Reading Check**

Why are the guests willing to drink the
water that Dr. Heidegger offers them?

youth. Think what a sin and shame it would be, if, with your peculiar advantages, you should not become patterns of virtue and wisdom to all the young people of the age!"

The doctor's four venerable friends made him no answer, except by a feeble and <u>tremulous</u> laugh; so very ridiculous was the idea, that, knowing how closely repentance treads behind the steps of error, they should ever go astray again.

"Drink, then," said the doctor, bowing: "I rejoice that I have so well selected the subjects of my experiment."

Pause & Reflect

FOCUS

The four guests are about to drink the magical water. Read on to see if your prediction on page 163 was correct.

MARK IT UP Underline details that show how each guest acts after drinking the water.

With palsied hands, they raised the glasses to their lips. The liquor, if it really possessed such virtues as Dr. Heidegger imputed to it, could not have been bestowed on four human beings who needed it more woefully. They looked as if they had never known what youth or pleasure was, but had been the offspring of Nature's dotage, and always the gray, <u>decrepit</u>, sapless, miserable creatures, who now sat stooping round the doctor's table, without life enough in their souls or bodies to be animated even by the prospect of growing young again. They drank off the water, and replaced their glasses on the table.

Assuredly there was an almost immediate improvement in the aspect of the party, not unlike what might have been produced by a glass of generous wine, together with a sudden glow of cheerful sunshine, brightening over all their visages at once. There was a healthful suffusion on their cheeks, instead of the ashen hue that had made them look so corpselike. They gazed at one another, and fancied that some magic power had really begun to smooth away the deep and sad inscriptions which Father Time had been so long engraving on their brows. The Widow Wycherly adjusted her cap, for she felt almost like a woman again.

WORDS TO KNOW

tremulous (trĕm′yə-ləs) *adj.* marked by trembling, quivering, or shaking

decrepit (dĭ-krĕp′ĭt) *adj.* weakened, worn out, or broken down by old age or hard use

177–180 At this point, the four friends are certain that they would never repeat the errors of their past.

183 palsied: trembling.

186 imputed: attributed; credited.

191 dotage (dō'tĭj)**:** feebleness due to old age.

198 aspect: appearance.

201 healthful suffusion: rosy glow of health.

203–206 fancied . . . power: The narrator does not tell you whether the changes are really happening or are just in the characters' minds.

Pause **&** *Reflect*

1. What do you think will happen when the guests drink the water? **(Predict)**

_____

_____

_____

_____

2. If you were one of the guests, would you join in the experiment? Give your reasons. **(Connect)**

_____

_____

_____

As the story continues . . .

- The guests drink the magical water.
- They ask Dr. Heidegger for more.
- They rejoice in their newfound youth.

✓ Reading Check

What is the "immediate improvement" that happens to the guests after they drink the water?

"Give us more of this wondrous water!" cried they, eagerly. "We are younger—but we are still too old! Quick!— give us more!"

"Patience, patience!" quoth Dr. Heidegger, who sat watching the experiment, with philosophic coolness. "You have been a long time growing old. Surely, you might be content to grow young in half an hour! But the water is at your service."

Again he filled their glasses with the liquor of youth, enough of which still remained in the vase to turn half the old people in the city to the age of their own grand-children. While the bubbles were yet sparkling on the brim, the doctor's four guests snatched their glasses from the table, and swallowed the contents at a single gulp. Was it delusion? Even while the draught was passing down their throats, it seemed to have wrought a change on their whole systems. Their eyes grew clear and bright; a dark shade deepened among their silvery locks; they sat around the table, three gentlemen of middle age, and a woman, hardly beyond her buxom prime.

"My dear widow, you are charming!" cried Colonel Killigrew, whose eyes had been fixed upon her face, while the shadows of age were flitting from it like darkness from the crimson day-break.

The fair widow knew, of old, that Colonel Killigrew's compliments were not always measured by sober truth; so she started up and ran to the mirror, still dreading that the ugly visage of an old woman would meet her gaze. Meanwhile, the three gentlemen behaved in such a manner, as proved that the water of the Fountain of Youth possessed some intoxicating qualities; unless, indeed, their exhilaration of spirits were merely a lightsome dizziness, caused by the sudden removal of the weight of years. Mr. Gascoigne's mind seemed to run on political topics, but whether relating to the past, present, or future, could not easily be determined, since the same ideas and phrases have been in vogue these fifty years. Now he rattled forth full-throated sentences about patriotism, national glory, and the people's right; now he muttered some

WORDS
TO
KNOW

exhilaration (ĭg-zĭl'ə-rā'shən) *n.* a lively delight

READ ALOUD Reread Lines 208–221

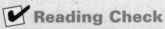

As you read this passage aloud, try to express the excitement and impatience of the guests.

221 delusion: trick; deception.
222 draught (drăft)**:** the amount taken in a single act of drinking.

Reading Check
What do the guests do when they begin to feel young?

What Does It Mean?
In vogue means "popular" or "in fashion."

perilous stuff or other, in a sly and doubtful whisper, so cautiously that even his own conscience could scarcely catch the secret; and now, again, he spoke in measured accents, and a deeply <u>deferential</u> tone, as if a royal ear were listening to his well-turned periods. Colonel Killigrew all this time had been trolling forth a jolly bottle-song, and ringing his glass in symphony with the chorus, while his eyes wandered towards the buxom figure of the Widow Wycherly. On the other side of the table, Mr. Medbourne was involved in a calculation of dollars and cents, with which was strangely intermingled a project for supplying the East Indies with ice, by harnessing a team of whales to the polar icebergs.

As for the Widow Wycherly, she stood before the mirror, curtseying and simpering to her own image, and greeting it as the friend whom she loved better than all the world beside. She thrust her face close to the glass, to see whether some long-remembered wrinkle or crow's-foot had indeed vanished. She examined whether the snow had so entirely melted from her hair, that the venerable cap could be safely thrown aside. At last, turning briskly away, she came with a sort of dancing step to the table.

"My dear old doctor," cried she, "pray favor me with another glass!"

"Certainly, my dear madam, certainly!" replied the complaisant doctor; "See! I have already filled the glasses."

There, in fact, stood the four glasses, brim full of this wonderful water, the delicate spray of which, as it effervesced from the surface, resembled the tremulous glitter of diamonds. It was now so nearly sunset, that the chamber had grown duskier than ever; but a mild and moon-like splendor gleamed from within the vase, and rested alike on the four guests, and on the doctor's venerable figure. He sat in a high-backed, elaborately-carved, oaken arm-chair, with a gray dignity of aspect that might have well befitted that very Father Time, whose power had never been <u>disputed</u>, save by this fortunate company. Even while quaffing the third draught of the Fountain of Youth, they were almost awed by the expression of his mysterious visage.

246 perilous stuff: dangerous information; Mr. Gascoigne's mind is moving so fast that he talks about all kinds of political subjects, including some secret ones.

259 simpering: smiling in a silly, self-conscious way.

270 complaisant (kəm-plā'sənt): willing to please.

277–283 Dr. Heidegger remains calm, though his guests are quite excited.

281 quaffing (kwŏf'ĭng): drinking heartily.

What Does It Mean?
Trolling forth a jolly bottle-song means "singing a merry drinking song."

✔ Reading Check
How does the Widow Wycherly act in front of the mirror?

READ ALOUD **Lines 271–277**

Listen for the repetition of *s, m,* and *n* sounds. Try to picture the scene that is described.

☆ Reader Success Strategy

The narrator compares Dr. Heidegger to Father Time. Think about why the narrator makes this comparison. In the following web, jot down a few phrases that you would use to describe Dr. Heidegger.

Dr. Heidegger

But, the next moment, the exhilarating gush of young life shot through their veins. They were now in the happy prime of youth. Age, with its miserable train of cares, and sorrows, and diseases, was remembered only as the trouble of a dream, from which they had joyously awoke. The fresh gloss of the soul, so early lost, and without which the world's successive scenes had been but a gallery of faded pictures, again threw its enchantment over all their prospects. They felt like new-created beings, in a new-created universe.

"We are young! We are young!" they cried, <u>exultingly</u>.

Youth, like the extremity of age, had <u>effaced</u> the strongly marked characteristics of middle life, and mutually assimilated them all. They were a group of merry youngsters, almost maddened with the exuberant frolicksomeness of their years. The most singular effect of their gayety was an impulse to mock the infirmity and decrepitude of which they had so lately been the victims. They laughed loudly at their old-fashioned attire, the wide-skirted coats and flapped waistcoats of the young men, and the ancient cap and gown of the blooming girl. One limped across the floor, like a gouty grandfather; one set a pair of spectacles astride of his nose, and pretended to pore over the black-letter pages of the book of magic; a third seated himself in an arm-chair, and strove to imitate the venerable dignity of Dr. Heidegger. Then all shouted mirthfully, and leaped about the room. The Widow Wycherly—if so fresh a damsel could be called a widow—tripped up to the doctor's chair, with a mischievous merriment in her rosy face.

"Doctor, you dear old soul," cried she, "get up and dance with me!" And then the four young people laughed louder than ever, to think what a queer figure the poor old doctor would cut.

"Pray excuse me," answered the doctor, quietly. "I am old and rheumatic, and my dancing days were over long ago. But either of these gay young gentlemen will be glad of so pretty a partner."

Pause & Reflect

WORDS
TO
KNOW

exultingly (ĭg-zŭl′tĭng-lē) *adv.* in a joyful and triumphant way
efface (ĭ-fās′) *v.* to rub or wipe out; erase

296 **assimilated:** absorbed.

297 **exuberant** (ĭg--zoo'bər-ənt)

frolicksomeness: joyous playfulness.

298–315 The four guests begin to make fun of old people, even mocking Dr. Heidegger.

308 **mirthfully:** joyfully.

317 **rheumatic** (roo-măt'ĭk): made stiff by a condition such as arthritis.

✔ **Reading Check**

What is the guests' attitude toward old age now?

What Does It Mean?

Infirmity means "frailty" or "illness."
Decrepitude means "the weakness of old age."

Pause **&** **Reflect**

1. In an **allegory,** people and objects represent certain qualities. Write the name of the character who might stand for each of the following qualities:

   living for pleasure _____

   political corruption _____

   pride about appearance _____

   love of money _____
   (Interpret Allegory)

2. Reread the boxed passage, lines 312–319. Compare the behavior of the four guests with the behavior of Dr. Heidegger.
   (Compare and Contrast)

   _____

   _____

   _____

   _____

320

FOCUS
Read to discover the final results of Dr. Heidegger's experiment.

"Dance with me, Clara!" cried Colonel Killigrew.

"No, no, I will be her partner!" shouted Mr. Gascoigne.

"She promised me her hand, fifty years ago!" exclaimed Mr. Medbourne.

They all gathered round her. One caught both her hands in his passionate grasp—another threw his arm about her waist—the third buried his hand among the glossy curls that clustered beneath the widow's cap. Blushing, panting, struggling, chiding, laughing, her warm breath fanning each of their faces by turns, she strove to disengage herself, yet still remained in their triple embrace. Never was there a livelier picture of youthful rivalship, with bewitching beauty for the prize. Yet, by a strange deception, owing to the duskiness of the chamber, and the antique dresses which they still wore, the tall mirror is said to have reflected the figures of the three old, gray, withered grand-sires, ridiculously contending for the skinny ugliness of a shrivelled grand-dam.

But they were young: their burning passions proved them so. Inflamed to madness by the coquetry of the girl-widow, who neither granted nor quite withheld her favors, the three rivals began to interchange threatening glances. Still keeping hold of the fair prize, they grappled fiercely at one another's throats. As they struggled to and fro, the table was overturned, and the vase dashed into a thousand fragments. The precious Water of Youth flowed in a bright stream across the floor, moistening the wings of a butterfly, which, grown old in the decline of summer, had alighted there to die. The insect fluttered lightly through the chamber, and settled on the snowy head of Dr. Heidegger.

"Come, come, gentlemen!—come, Madam Wycherly," exclaimed the doctor, "I really must protest against this riot."

They stood still, and shivered; for it seemed as if gray Time were calling them back from their sunny youth, far down into the chill and darksome vale of years. They looked at old Dr. Heidegger, who sat in his carved arm-chair, holding the rose of half a century, which he had rescued from among the fragments of the shattered vase. At the motion of his hand, the four rioters resumed their seats; the more readily, because their violent exertions had wearied them, youthful though they were.

331 strove to disengage herself: struggled to free herself.

337–338 grand-sires . . . grand-dam: old men . . . old woman.

340 coquetry (kō'kĭ-trē): flirtatious behavior.

355 vale: valley.

As the story ends . . .

- The narrator reveals the results of the experiment.
- Dr. Heidegger learns a lesson.

✔ Reading Check

Briefly describe the behavior of the guests now that they are young again.

JOT IT DOWN   **Reread Lines 334–338**

The narrator is unclear about whether the reflection is real or not. What does the image in the mirror reveal? **(Clarify)**

_____

_____

_____

_____

☆ Reader Success Strategy

An author sometimes tells a story to teach a lesson. As you read the end of the story, think of what lesson the author might be trying to teach the reader. (Notice how Dr. Heidegger's behavior is different from that of his guests.)

"My poor Sylvia's rose!" ejaculated Dr. Heidegger, holding it in the light of the sunset clouds: "it appears to be fading again."

And so it was. Even while the party were looking at it, the flower continued to shrivel up, till it became as dry and fragile as when the doctor had first thrown it into the vase. He shook off the few drops of moisture which clung to its petals.

370   "I love it as well thus, as in its dewy freshness," observed he, pressing the withered rose to his withered lips. While he spoke, the butterfly fluttered down from the doctor's snowy head, and fell upon the floor.

His guests shivered again. A strange chillness, whether of the body or spirit they could not tell, was creeping gradually over them all. They gazed at one another, and fancied that each fleeting moment snatched away a charm, and left a deepening furrow where none had been before. Was it an illusion? Had the changes of a life-time been crowded into so brief a space, and were they now four aged people, sitting

380   with their old friend, Dr. Heidegger?

"Are we grown old again, so soon!" cried they, dolefully.

In truth, they had. The Water of Youth possessed merely a virtue more <u>transient</u> than that of wine. The delirium which it created had effervesced away. Yes! they were old again. With a shuddering impulse, that showed her a woman still, the widow clasped her skinny hands before her face, and wished that the coffin-lid were over it, since it could be no longer beautiful.

"Yes, friends, ye are old again," said Dr. Heidegger; "and lo! the Water of Youth is all lavished on the ground. Well—I

390   bemoan it not; for if the fountain gushed at my very doorstep, I would not stoop to bathe my lips in it—no, though its delirium were for years instead of moments. Such is the lesson ye have taught me!"

But the doctor's four friends had taught no such lesson to themselves. They resolved forthwith to make a pilgrimage to Florida, and quaff at morning, noon, and night, from the Fountain of Youth.

Pause **& Reflect**

362 ejaculated: exclaimed.

369–370 Note that Dr. Heidegger still loves the rose, even though it is now old again.

383 delirium (dĭ-lîr′ē-əm)**:** a state of uncontrolled excitement or emotion.

389 lavished: wasted

✔ **Reading Check**

How does Dr. Heidegger feel about the rose when it begins to change?

What Does It Mean?

Bemoan it not means "am not sorry." Dr. Heidegger is not sorry that the water is gone.

Pause **&** *Reflect*

1. What do the four guests decide to do at the end of the story? **(Clarify)**

_____
_____
_____
_____

2. What lesson has Dr. Heidegger learned? **(Infer)**

_____
_____
_____
_____

✎ **CHALLENGE**

Several times the author seems to create uncertainty about whether the four guests really become young again. Do you think the changes are real or imaginary? Mark evidence from the story to support your opinion. Why do you think the author introduces the element of uncertainty? **(Draw Conclusions)**

Active Reading SkillBuilder

Interpreting Allegory

An **allegory** is a work of literature in which people, objects, and events represent general qualities, such as good and evil. Allegories are written not only to entertain but also to teach lessons. As you read "Dr. Heidegger's Experiment," complete the following chart by identifying a quality or idea that each guest in the story might represent. An example is given.

Character	What he or she loses or wastes	What happens when he or she is given a second youth	What he or she might represent
Mr. Medbourne	wealth	schemes to make money again	greed
Col. Killigrew			
Mr. Gascoigne			
Widow Wycherly			

Literary Analysis SkillBuilder

Foreshadowing

Foreshadowing is a writer's use of hints or clues to indicate events that will occur later in a story. It is a technique that builds suspense and arouses the reader's curiosity. For example, the eerie effects that occur when the chambermaid lifts the book of magic foreshadow the strange effects of drinking the water. Use the following diagram to record two other effective examples of foreshadowing that Hawthorne uses in "Dr. Heidegger's Experiment."

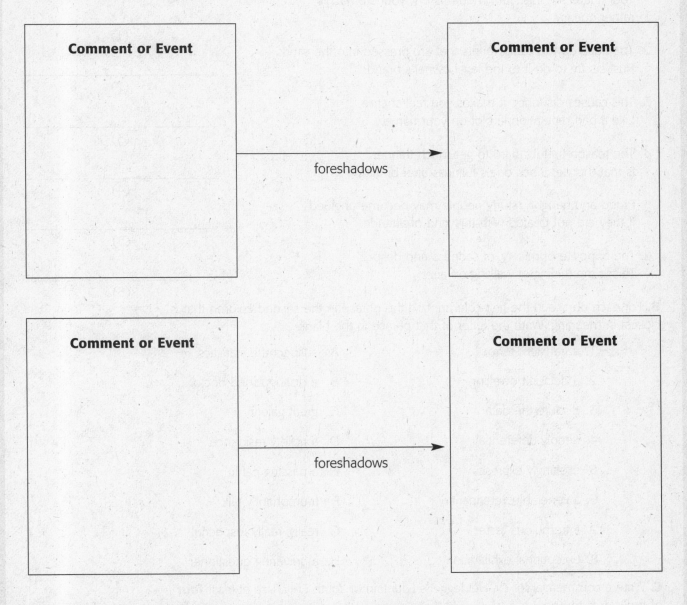

Comment or Event

Comment or Event

foreshadows

Comment or Event

Comment or Event

foreshadows

Follow Up: Explain whether foreshadowing added to or took away from your enjoyment of this story.

Words to Know SkillBuilder

Words to Know

decrepit	dispute	exhilaration	stigma	tremulous
deferential	efface	exultingly	transient	venerable

A. On each blank line, write the word from the word list that the rhyme describes.

1. If you have to speak in public and it makes you quite uneasy,
   Your knees are this, your mouth is dry, your stomach's
   rather queasy.

   _____ (1)

2. The tides do this to footprints that are pressed into the sand.
   Rustlers try to do it to the legal owner's brand.

   _____ (2)

3. This causes dishonor, it makes you feel shame,
   Like a bad reputation, a blot on your name.

   _____ (3)

4. The reason that it's hard to get much thinner
   Is that this describes one's fullness after dinner.

   _____ (4)

5. Proud and haughty, stuffy people may become unglued
   If they are not treated with this kind of attitude.

   _____ (5)

6. The opposite of misery, of sadness and despair,
   This is the feeling of walking on air.

   _____ (6)

B. For each phrase in the first column, find the phrase in the second column that is closest in meaning. Write the letter of that phrase in the blank.

1. a transient terror	A. suspect the statistics
2. a decrepit dwelling	B. a distinguished doctor
3. dispute the data	C. great gaiety
4. deeply deferential	D. a rickety residence
5. exultingly express	E. a passing panic
6. a venerable veterinarian	F. triumphantly talk
7. a tremulous tester	G. really, really respectful
8. exceptional exhilaration	H. a quivering questioner

C. Write a commercial for Dr. Heidegger's Fountain of Youth Elixir. Use at least **four** of the Words to Know.

A ROSE for EMILY

William Faulkner

Before You Read

Connect to Your Life

Think of the people in your neighborhood. Have you ever been curious
about them? What characteristics made you curious? Write a few sentences
or phrases to describe one person in your community who seems mysterious
or about whom you would like to know more.

_____

_____

_____

_____

_____

_____

Key to the Short Story

WHAT YOU NEED TO KNOW Faulkner modeled the setting and people in his
stories after his own hometown of Oxford, Mississippi. The narrator of
"A Rose for Emily" is part of the community and speaks for the entire
town. The narrator's values and those of the community reflect the
manners of Southern life at an earlier time.

A ROSE for EMILY

William Faulkner

PREVIEW This story is set in a town in Mississippi. The narrator, who speaks for the entire town, tells about Miss Emily Grierson. She was from an upper-class family. Proud and strong-willed, she cut herself off from the community. Years passed, and the town changed. Few people ever saw Miss Emily, and no one set foot inside her house. There was something mysterious about her and her house—especially about one of the rooms upstairs.

I

FOCUS

The narrator tells about Miss Emily's funeral and describes her house and street. The narrator also tells how a former mayor helped her.

MARK IT UP As you read, circle details that help you picture how her house and street have changed over the years. An example is highlighted.

When Miss Emily Grierson died, our whole town went to her funeral: the men through a sort of respectful affection for a fallen monument, the women mostly out of curiosity to see the inside of her house, which no one save an old manservant—a combined gardener and cook—had seen in at least ten years.

It was a big, squarish frame house that had once been white, decorated with cupolas and spires and scrolled balconies in the heavily lightsome style of the seventies,[1] set on what had once been our most select street. But garages and cotton gins[2] had

---

1. **the seventies:** the 1870s.
2. **cotton gins:** machines that separate the seeds and other small objects from the fibers of cotton.

SHORT STORY

Reading Tips

William Faulkner once stated, "There is no such thing as *was*—only *is*." This view of the past led him to tell stories in new ways, shuffling the order of events. In this story, for example, the **narrator** recalls events from Miss Emily's life, not in **sequence** but as memory might link them.

- Some sentences in this story are long. When you come upon them, look for the main clause and pick out the subject and the verb. That will take you to the heart of the sentence.

- You will also come upon poetic passages, rich with **figurative language.** Read them at your usual pace and mark them. After reading the story, reread these passages and examine the language.

As the story begins . . .

- Miss Emily Grierson is dead, and the whole town attended her funeral.

- The narrator describes Miss Emily's house and neighborhood.

- The narrator explains how Colonel Sartoris helped Miss Emily after her father's death.

✔ Reading Check

Why do all of the towns-people attend Miss Emily's funeral?

August means "marked by
dignity and grandeur."

Pause & Reflect

1. Review the details you circled
as you read. Miss Emily's street
has changed over the years.
Only her house is left. All
the other houses are gone,
replaced by _____

_____

and_____ .

(Clarify)

2. What does Colonel Sartoris do to
help Miss Emily after her father's
death? **(Cause and Effect)**

_____

_____

_____

_____

As the story continues . . .

• The community tries to force
Miss Emily to pay taxes.

• The narrator describes Miss
Emily's appearance.

☆ **Reader Success
Strategy**

The events of the story are not
told in the order in which they
happened. As you read, make a
time line to help you keep track
of the order of events.

encroached and obliterated even the august names of that
neighborhood; only Miss Emily's house was left, lifting its
stubborn and coquettish decay above the cotton wagons and
the gasoline pumps—an eyesore among eyesores. And now
Miss Emily had gone to join the representatives of those
20 august names where they lay in the cedar-bemused[3] cemetery
among the ranked and anonymous graves of Union and
Confederate soldiers who fell at the battle of Jefferson.

   Alive, Miss Emily had been a tradition, a duty, and a care;
a sort of hereditary obligation upon the town, dating from
that day in 1894 when Colonel Sartoris, the mayor—he who
fathered the edict that no Negro woman should appear on
the streets without an apron—remitted her taxes, the
dispensation dating from the death of her father on into
perpetuity.[4] Not that Miss Emily would have accepted charity.
30 Colonel Sartoris invented an involved tale to the effect that
Miss Emily's father had loaned money to the town, which the
town, as a matter of business, preferred this way of repaying.
Only a man of Colonel Sartoris' generation and thought
could have invented it, and only a woman could have
believed it.

Pause & Reflect

FOCUS
A committee of
aldermen visits Miss
Emily to force her to
pay her taxes. Read to
find out how she reacts
to them.

When the next generation, with its more
modern ideas, became mayors and
aldermen, this arrangement created
some little dissatisfaction. On the first
of the year they mailed her a tax notice.
February came, and there was no reply.
They wrote her a formal letter, asking
her to call at the sheriff's office at her convenience. A week

---

3. **cedar-bemused:** almost lost in cedar trees (literally, confused by cedars).

4. **remitted . . . perpetuity:** released her from paying taxes forever after the
time of her father's death.

WORDS
TO
KNOW

encroach (ĕn-krōch') *v.* to advance beyond original limits;
   intrude
obliterate (ə-blĭt'ə-rāt') *v.* to wipe out, leaving no trace
coquettish (kō-kĕt'ĭsh) *adj.* flirtatious
edict (ē'dĭkt') *n.* an order put out by a person in authority

later the mayor wrote her himself, offering to call or to send his car for her, and received in reply a note on paper of an archaic shape, in a thin, flowing calligraphy[5] in faded ink, to the effect that she no longer went out at all. The tax notice was also enclosed, without comment.

They called a special meeting of the Board of Aldermen. A deputation[6] waited upon her, knocked at the door through which no visitor had passed since she ceased giving china-painting lessons eight or ten years earlier. They were admitted by the old Negro into a dim hall from which a stairway mounted into still more shadow. It smelled of dust and disuse—a close, <u>dank</u> smell. The Negro led them into the parlor. It was furnished in heavy, leather-covered furniture. When the Negro opened the blinds of one window, they could see that the leather was cracked; and when they sat down, a faint dust rose sluggishly about their thighs, spinning with slow motes[7] in the single sun-ray. On a tarnished gilt easel before the fireplace stood a crayon portrait of Miss Emily's father.

They rose when she entered—a small, fat woman in black, with a thin gold chain descending to her waist and vanishing into her belt, leaning on an ebony cane with a tarnished gold head. Her skeleton was small and spare; perhaps that was why what would have been merely plumpness in another was obesity in her. She looked bloated, like a body long submerged in motionless water, and of that <u>pallid</u> hue. Her eyes, lost in the fatty ridges of her face, looked like two small pieces of coal pressed into a lump of dough as they moved from one face to another while the visitors stated their errand.

She did not ask them to sit. She just stood in the door and listened quietly until the spokesman came to a stumbling halt. Then they could hear the invisible watch ticking at the end of the gold chain.

Her voice was dry and cold. "I have no taxes in Jefferson. Colonel Sartoris explained it to me. Perhaps one of you can gain access to the city records and satisfy yourselves."

"But we have. We are the city authorities, Miss Emily. Didn't you get a notice from the sheriff, signed by him?"

---

5. **calligraphy:** beautiful handwriting.
6. **deputation:** a small group representing a larger one.
7. **motes:** specks.

WORDS TO KNOW
dank (dăngk) *adj.* unpleasantly damp; moist and chilly
pallid (păl'ĭd) *adj.* abnormally pale

A Rose for Emily 181

What Does It Mean?

An *alderman* is an elected official who represents a certain *part of a town or city. The Board of Aldermen* is the group of elected officials who manage the town or city's affairs.

Reading Check

How does Miss Emily's house look and smell?

READ ALOUD Lines 62–71

Read aloud the boxed passage. Then circle the two phrases below that are true of Miss Emily. **(Infer)**

is overweight

looks healthy

wears a bright dress

keeps her watch hidden

Pause & Reflect

MARK IT UP   1. The aldermen are shown into a dim hall
and then into the parlor. Circle
details on page 181 that help
you visualize these rooms.
(Visualize)

2. What is strange about Miss
Emily's order to "see Colonel
Sartoris"? **(Evaluate)**

_____

_____

_____

As the story continues . . .

- Miss Emily was deserted by
her sweetheart 30 years ago.

- About two years after her
father's death, neighbors complained about a smell coming
from her house.

What Does It Mean?

Vanquished means "defeated."
Miss Emily would not let the
aldermen force her to pay
taxes.

What Does It Mean?

Gross, teeming world refers
to the common and tasteless
people who the Griersons think
are too awful to associate with.

"I received a paper, yes," Miss Emily said. "Perhaps he
considers himself the sheriff . . . I have no taxes in Jefferson."

"But there is nothing on the books to show that, you see.
We must go by the—"

"See Colonel Sartoris. I have no taxes in Jefferson."

"But, Miss Emily—"

"See Colonel Sartoris." (Colonel Sartoris had been dead
almost ten years.) "I have no taxes in Jefferson. Tobe!" The
Negro appeared. "Show these gentlemen out."

Pause & Reflect

II

90 **FOCUS**
Read to find out about
the smell coming from
Miss Emily's house.

So she vanquished them, horse and foot,
just as she had vanquished their fathers
thirty years before about the smell. That
was two years after her father's death
and a short time after her sweetheart—
the one we believed would marry her—had deserted her. After
her father's death she went out very little; after her sweetheart
went away, people hardly saw her at all. A few of the ladies
had the <u>temerity</u> to call, but were not received, and the only
sign of life about the place was the Negro man—a young man
100 then—going in and out with a market basket.

"Just as if a man—any man— could keep a kitchen
properly," the ladies said; so they were not surprised when the
smell developed. It was another link between the gross,
teeming world and the high and mighty Griersons.

A neighbor, a woman, complained to the mayor, Judge
Stevens, eighty years old.

"But what will you have me do about it, madam?" he said.

"Why, send her word to stop it," the woman said. "Isn't
there a law?"

110 "I'm sure that won't be necessary," Judge Stevens said. "It's
probably just a snake or a rat that nigger[8] of hers killed in the
yard. I'll speak to him about it."

---

8. This character uses an offensive term. Faulkner helps create the setting of
this story by using language typical of certain people living in the South at
that time.

WORDS
TO   **temerity** (tə-mĕr′ĭ-tē) *n.* foolish boldness
KNOW

The next day he received two more complaints, one from a man who came in <u>diffident</u> deprecation.[9] "We really must do something about it, Judge. I'd be the last one in the world to bother Miss Emily, but we've got to do something." That night the Board of Aldermen met—three graybeards and one younger man, a member of the rising generation.

"It's simple enough," he said. "Send her word to have her place cleaned up. Give her a certain time to do it in, and if she don't . . ."

"Dammit, sir," Judge Stevens said, "will you accuse a lady to her face of smelling bad?"

So the next night, after midnight, four men crossed Miss Emily's lawn and slunk about the house like burglars, sniffing along the base of the brickwork and at the cellar openings while one of them performed a regular sowing motion with his hand out of a sack slung from his shoulder. They broke open the cellar door and sprinkled (lime) there, and in all the outbuildings. As they recrossed the lawn, a window that had been dark was lighted and Miss Emily sat in it, the light behind her, and her upright torso motionless as that of an idol. They crept quietly across the lawn and into the shadow of the locusts that lined the street. After a week or two the smell went away.

Pause & Reflect

FOCUS

Read to find out about Miss Emily's relationship with her father and her reaction to his death.

MARK IT UP As you read, underline any details that help you understand this relationship.

That was when people had begun to feel really sorry for her. People in our town, remembering how old lady Wyatt, her great-aunt, had gone completely crazy at last, believed that the Griersons held themselves a little too high for what they really were. None of the young men were quite good enough for Miss Emily and such. We had long thought of them as a tableau,[10] Miss Emily a slender figure in white in the

---

9. **deprecation:** disapproval.
10. **tableau** (tăb'lō'): dramatic scene or picture.

WORDS
TO
KNOW

diffident (dĭf'ĭ-dənt) *adj.* shy and timid; lacking self-confidence

More About . . .

(LIME) *Lime* is a calcium-based mineral. It is used to absorb bad odors and help decompose bodies.

Pause & Reflect

MARK IT UP **1.** Circle the sentence on page 182 that tells when the smell develops. **(Clarify)**

2. What steps do the aldermen take to deal with this problem? **(Summarize)**

_____

_____

_____

_____

As the story continues . . .

• Miss Emily's father was overbearing.

• Miss Emily was unable to accept her father's death.

More About . . .

HORSEWHIPS At the time of this story, a horsewhip was the preferred weapon of fathers who wanted to chase away their daughters' suitors. You learn from this image that Miss Emily's father was overly protective of her.

Pause & Reflect

1. Reread the boxed sentence on this page. How would you restate this idea in your own words? **(Paraphrase)**

_____

_____

_____

MARK IT UP **2.** What does Miss Emily tell the doctors and ministers who come for her father's body? Circle the sentence on this page that tells the answer. **(Clarify)**

As the story continues . . .

• Miss Emily is sick for a long time after her father's death.

• A Northern construction worker named Homer Barron comes to town.

• Miss Emily and Homer begin spending time together.

background, her father a spraddled silhouette in the foreground, his back to her and clutching a horsewhip, the two of them framed by the back-flung front door. So when she got to be thirty and was still single, we were not pleased exactly, but vindicated; even with insanity in the family she
150 wouldn't have turned down all of her chances if they had really materialized.

When her father died, it got about that the house was all that was left to her; and in a way, people were glad. At last they could pity Miss Emily. Being left alone, and a pauper, she had become humanized. Now she too would know the old thrill and the old despair of a penny more or less.

The day after his death all the ladies prepared to call at the house and offer condolence and aid, as is our custom. Miss Emily met them at the door, dressed as usual and with no trace
160 of grief on her face. She told them that her father was not dead. She did that for three days, with the ministers calling on her, and the doctors, trying to persuade her to let them dispose of the body. Just as they were about to resort to law and force, she broke down, and they buried her father quickly.

We did not say she was crazy then. We believed she had to do that. We remembered all the young men her father had driven away, and we knew that with nothing left, she would have to cling to that which had robbed her, as people will.

Pause & Reflect

III

FOCUS

170 After her father's death, Emily meets Homer Barron. Read to find out about their relationship.

MARK IT UP As you read, circle any details that help you form impressions of Homer Barron.

She was sick for a long time. When we saw her again, her hair was cut short, making her look like a girl, with a vague resemblance to those angels in colored church windows—sort of tragic and serene.

The town had just let the contracts for paving the sidewalks, and in the summer after her father's death they began the work. The construction company came with niggers and mules and machinery, and a
180 foreman named Homer Barron, a Yankee—a big, dark, ready

man, with a big voice and eyes lighter than his face. The little boys would follow in groups to hear him cuss the niggers, and the niggers singing in time to the rise and fall of picks. Pretty soon he knew everybody in town. Whenever you heard a lot of laughing anywhere about the square, Homer Barron would be in the center of the group. Presently we began to see him and Miss Emily on Sunday afternoons driving in the yellow-wheeled buggy and the matched team of bays from the livery stable.

190   At first we were glad that Miss Emily would have an interest, because the ladies all said, "Of course a Grierson would not think seriously of a Northerner, a day laborer." But there were still others, older people, who said that even grief could not cause a real lady to forget *noblesse oblige*[11]— without calling it *noblesse oblige*. They just said, "Poor Emily. Her kinsfolk should come to her." She had some kin in Alabama; but years ago her father had fallen out with them over the estate of old lady Wyatt, the crazy woman, and there was no communication between the two families. They had

200 not even been represented at the funeral.

And as soon as the old people said, "Poor Emily," the whispering began. "Do you suppose it's really so?" they said to one another. "Of course it is. What else could . . ." This behind their hands; rustling of craned[12] silk and satin behind jalousies[13] closed upon the sun of Sunday afternoon as the thin, swift clop-clop-clop of the matched team passed: "Poor Emily."

She carried her head high enough—even when we believed that she was fallen. It was as if she demanded more than ever

210 the recognition of her dignity as the last Grierson; as if it had wanted that touch of earthiness to reaffirm her imperviousness. Like when she bought the rat poison, the arsenic. That was over a year after they had begun to say "Poor Emily," and while the two female cousins were visiting her.

Pause & Reflect

---

11. *noblesse oblige* (nō-blĕs′ ō-blēzh′): the responsibility of people of high social position to behave in a noble fashion.

12. **craned:** stretched.

13. **jalousies** (jăl′ə-sēz): doors or windows containing overlapping slats that can be opened or closed.

What Does It Mean?
Presently means "soon."

☆ **Reader Success Strategy**

Make a word web with important facts about the Northerner, Homer Barron, who comes to work in Jefferson.

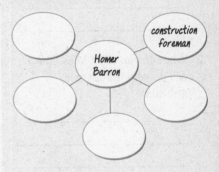

Pause & Reflect

1. Why do you think Emily began seeing Homer? **(Infer)**

_____
_____
_____
_____

📖 **READ ALOUD** 2. Read aloud the boxed sentences on this page. What do the older people think of Miss Emily's new boyfriend? **(Draw Conclusions)**

_____
_____
_____
_____

- Miss Emily refuses to tell the druggist why she wants to purchase poison.

Pause & Reflect

READ ALOUD 1. Read aloud the boxed passage on this page. Miss Emily refuses to tell the druggist why she wants to buy arsenic. Why does he sell it to her anyway? **(Infer)**

_____

_____

_____

2. What do you think Miss Emily will do with the arsenic? **(Predict)**

_____

_____

_____

_____

As the story continues . . .

- Everyone assumes that Miss Emily will kill herself.
- The townspeople see the last of Homer Barron.

☑ **Reading Check**

What had the townspeople assumed when Emily was first seen with Homer Barron?

FOCUS
Read to find out what Miss Emily buys from the druggist.

"I want some poison," she said to the druggist. She was over thirty then, still a slight woman, though thinner than usual, with cold, haughty black eyes in a face
220 the flesh of which was strained across the temples and about the eye-sockets as you imagine a lighthouse-keeper's face ought to look. "I want some poison," she said.

"Yes, Miss Emily. What kind? For rats and such? I'd recom—"

"I want the best you have. I don't care what kind."

The druggist named several. "They'll kill anything up to an elephant. But what you want is—"

"Arsenic," Miss Emily said. "Is that a good one?"

"Is . . . arsenic? Yes, ma'am. But what you want—"
230 "I want arsenic."

The druggist looked down at her. She looked back at him, erect, her face like a strained flag. "Why, of course," the druggist said. "If that's what you want. But the law requires you to tell what you are going to use it for."

Miss Emily just stared at him, her head tilted back in order to look him eye for eye, until he looked away and went and got the arsenic and wrapped it up. The Negro delivery boy brought her the package; the druggist didn't come back. When she opened the package at home there was written on the box,
240 under the skull and bones: "For rats."

Pause & Reflect

FOCUS
Read to find out more about Miss Emily and Homer Barron and the town's opinion of them.

So the next day we all said, "She will kill herself"; and we said it would be the best thing. When she had first begun to be seen with Homer Barron, we had said, "She will marry him." Then we said, "She will persuade him yet," because Homer himself had remarked—he liked men, and it was known that he drank with the younger men in the Elks' Club—that he was not a marrying man. Later we said, "Poor Emily" behind the
250 jalousies as they passed on Sunday afternoon in the glittering buggy, Miss Emily with her head high and Homer Barron

with his hat cocked and a cigar in his teeth, reins and whip in a yellow glove.

Then some of the ladies began to say that it was a (disgrace) to the town and a bad example to the young people. The men did not want to interfere, but at last the ladies forced the Baptist minister—Miss Emily's people were Episcopal—to call upon her. He would never <u>divulge</u> what happened during that interview, but he refused to go back again. The next Sunday they again drove about the streets, and the following day the minister's wife wrote to Miss Emily's relations in Alabama.

So she had blood-kin under her roof again and we sat back to watch developments. At first nothing happened. Then we were sure that they were to be married. We learned that Miss Emily had been to the jeweler's and ordered a man's toilet set in silver, with the letters H. B. on each piece. Two days later we learned that she had bought a complete outfit of men's clothing, including a nightshirt, and we said, "They are married." We were really glad. We were glad because the two female cousins were even more Grierson than Miss Emily had ever been.

So we were not surprised when Homer Barron—the streets had been finished some time since—was gone. We were a little disappointed that there was not a public blowing-off,[14] but we believed that he had gone on to prepare for Miss Emily's coming, or to give her a chance to get rid of the cousins. (By that time it was a cabal,[15] and we were all Miss Emily's allies to help <u>circumvent</u> the cousins.) Sure enough, after another week they departed. And, as we had expected all along, within three days Homer Barron was back in town. A neighbor saw the Negro man admit him at the kitchen door at dusk one evening.

And that was the last we saw of Homer Barron. And of Miss Emily for some time. The Negro man went in and out with the market basket, but the front door remained closed. Now and then we would see her at a window for a moment, as the men did that night when they sprinkled the lime, but for almost six months she did not appear on the streets. Then we knew that this was to be expected too; as if that quality of

---

14. **blowing-off:** celebration.

15. **cabal** (kə-băl'): a group united in a secret plot.

WORDS TO KNOW

divulge (dĭ-vŭlj') *v.* to make known something private

circumvent (sûr'kəm-věnt') *v.* to avoid or get around by clever maneuvering

More About . . .
SOUTHERN ATTITUDES At the time, Miss Emily's behavior would have been considered (disgraceful) because it was not considered proper for a woman to spend so much time with a man unless they were married.

What Does It Mean?
Blood-kin means "people who are related by ancestry, not by marriage."

 Reading Check
What does Miss Emily purchase? For whom does she purchase these items?

What Does It Mean?
The highlighted words refer to the fact that the cousins were more proud and snobbish—like the Grierson family—than Miss Emily was.

Pause & Reflect

Pause & Reflect

MARK IT UP After a time, the townspeople assume that Miss Emily and Homer Barron are married. Circle the two sentences on page 187 that tell why they think so. (**Cause and Effect**)

As the story continues . . .

- The townspeople do not see Miss Emily for a long time.
- Miss Emily teaches china-painting lessons for a few years.
- Miss Emily dies.

✔ **Reading Check**

Why does Miss Emily stop teaching china-painting?

What Does It Mean?

The highlighted phrase means that Miss Emily has become like a religious icon or statue on display.

FOCUS

Read to find out about Miss Emily's later years. **MARK IT UP** As you read, circle details that describe her appearance and actions.

When we next saw Miss Emily, she had grown fat and her hair was turning gray. During the next few years it grew grayer and grayer until it attained an even pepper-and-salt iron-gray, when it ceased turning. Up to the day of her death at seventy-four it was still that vigorous iron-gray, like the hair of an active man.

From that time on her front door remained closed, save for a 300 period of six or seven years, when she was about forty, during which she gave lessons in china-painting. She fitted up a studio in one of the downstairs rooms, where the daughters and granddaughters of Colonel Sartoris' contemporaries were sent to her with the same regularity and in the same spirit that they were sent to church on Sundays with a twenty-five-cent piece for the collection plate. Meanwhile her taxes had been remitted.

Then the newer generation became the backbone and the spirit of the town, and the painting pupils grew up and fell away and did not send their children to her with boxes of 310 color and <u>tedious</u> brushes and pictures cut from the ladies' magazines. The front door closed upon the last one and remained closed for good. When the town got free postal delivery, Miss Emily alone refused to let them fasten the metal numbers above her door and attach a mailbox to it. She would not listen to them.

Daily, monthly, yearly we watched the Negro grow grayer and more stooped, going in and out with the market basket. Each December we sent her a tax notice, which would be returned by the post office a week later, unclaimed. Now and 320 then we would see her in one of the downstairs windows—she had evidently shut up the top floor of the house—like the carven torso of an idol in a niche,[16] looking or not looking at

---

16. **niche** (nĭch): an indented space in a wall.

WORDS TO KNOW	**thwart** (thwôrt) *v.* to block or hinder; prevent the fulfillment of
	virulent (vîr′yə-lənt) *adj.* extremely poisonous or harmful
	tedious (tē′dē-əs) *adj.* boring because of dullness

us, we could never tell which. Thus she passed from generation to generation—dear, inescapable, impervious, tranquil, and perverse.

And so she died. Fell ill in the house filled with dust and shadows, with only a doddering Negro man to wait on her. We did not even know she was sick; we had long since given up trying to get any information from the Negro. He talked to no one, probably not even to her, for his voice had grown harsh and rusty, as if from disuse.

She died in one of the downstairs rooms, in a heavy walnut bed with a curtain, her gray head propped on a pillow yellow and moldy with age and lack of sunlight.

Pause & Reflect

V

FOCUS
Read to find out about Miss Emily's funeral and what the towns-people find in the locked room.
MARK IT UP As you read, circle any details that help you picture what is in this room.

The Negro met the first of the ladies at the front door and let them in, with their hushed, sibilant[17] voices and their quick, curious glances, and then he disappeared. He walked right through the house and out the back and was not seen again.

The two female cousins came at once. They held the funeral on the second day, with the town coming to look at Miss Emily beneath a mass of bought flowers, with the crayon face of her father musing <u>profoundly</u> above the bier[18] and the ladies sibilant and <u>macabre;</u> and the very old men—some in their brushed Confederate uniforms—on the porch and the lawn, talking of Miss Emily as if she had been a contemporary of theirs, believing that they had danced with her and courted her perhaps, confusing time with its mathematical progression, as the old do, to whom all the past is not a diminishing road but, instead, a huge meadow which no winter ever quite touches, divided from them now by the narrow bottle-neck of the most recent decade of years.

---

17. **sibilant** (sĭb′ə-lənt): making a hissing sound.
18. **bier** (bîr) a platform for a coffin.

WORDS
TO
KNOW

profoundly (prə-found′lē) *adv.* deeply; intensely

Pause & Reflect
Review the details you circled as you read. Then list two of Miss Emily's physical changes after Homer Barron disappears. **(Clarify)**

_____

_____

_____

_____

As the story ends . . .
• The narrator describes Miss Emily's funeral.
• Miss Emily's servant allows the ladies to come into the house.
• They make a shocking discovery.

☑ Reading Check
What happens to Miss Emily's servant after her death?

READ ALOUD Lines 346–354

This passage, which is part of a long sentence, is beautifully written and rich in figurative language. It suggests a view of the past that Miss Emily may have shared. Notice the rhythm Faulkner creates by using present participles—*talking, believing,* and *confusing.*

A Rose for Emily 189

Already we knew that there was one room in that region above stairs which no one had seen in forty years, and which would have to be forced. They waited until Miss Emily was decently in the ground before they opened it.

360 The violence of breaking down the door seemed to fill this room with pervading dust. A thin, acrid pall[19] as of the tomb seemed to lie everywhere upon this room decked and furnished as for a bridal:[20] upon the valance curtains of faded rose color, upon the rose-shaded lights, upon the dressing table, upon the delicate array of crystal and the man's toilet things backed with tarnished silver, silver so tarnished that the monogram was obscured. Among them lay a collar and tie, as if they had just been removed, which, lifted, left upon the surface a pale crescent in the dust. Upon a chair hung the suit, carefully folded; beneath it the two mute shoes and the 370 discarded socks.

The man himself lay in the bed.

For a long while we just stood there, looking down at the profound and fleshless grin. The body had apparently once lain in the attitude of an embrace, but now the long sleep that outlasts love, that conquers even the grimace of love, had cuckolded him.[21] What was left of him, rotted beneath what was left of the nightshirt, had become inextricable from the bed in which he lay; and upon him and upon the pillow beside him lay that even coating of the patient and 380 biding dust.

Then we noticed that in the second pillow was the indentation of a head. One of us lifted something from it, and leaning forward, that faint and invisible dust dry and acrid in the nostrils, we saw a long strand of iron-gray hair.

Pause & Reflect

---

19. **acrid pall** (ăk′rĭd pôl′): bitter-smelling covering.
20. **bridal:** wedding.
21. **cuckolded him:** made his wife or lover unfaithful to him.

What Does It Mean?
Inextricable means "unable to be removed."

Pause & Reflect

1. Review the details you circled as you read. Among the items in the room are "toilet things backed with . . . silver so tarnished that the monogram [the initials of a name] was obscured." Write the initials that are covered over. **(Infer)**

_____

_____

2. On the second pillow, a strand of hair is found. Whose hair is it? **(Infer)**

_____

_____

✎ CHALLENGE

The **narrator** uses the first-person plural pronoun *we* instead of speaking just for himself or herself. Mark passages that help you understand the relationship between the narrator, Miss Emily, and the town. Look for places where the narrator and the townspeople make important discoveries.

Active Reading SkillBuilder

Sequencing Events

Faulkner often shuffled the order of events in his stories by using flashbacks—scenes that interrupt the present action to describe events that took place at an earlier time. Sentences beginning with the words *when, after,* and *during* can help the reader follow Faulkner's unusual approach to **sequencing events.** After reading each part of the story, record on the lines below important events in Miss Emily's life. Write them in chronological order—the order in which they occurred in time. After reading the entire story, use the information you have recorded to complete the time line that has been started below. Examples are shown.

Part I ___taxes remitted___   ___receives tax notice___   ___confronts aldermen___   ___Emily's funeral___

Part II _____   _____   _____   _____

Part III _____   _____   _____   _____

Part IV _____   _____   _____   _____

Part V _____   _____   _____   _____

Miss Emily's Life

taxes remitted   funeral

Literary Analysis SkillBuilder

Characterization

Characterization refers to the techniques writers use to develop characters. A writer may reveal a character through physical description; the character's actions, words, and feelings; the actions, words, and feelings of other characters; or the narrator's direct comments about a character. Fill in the following diagram with at least three specific examples of characterization in the story that help you learn more about Miss Emily. An example is shown.

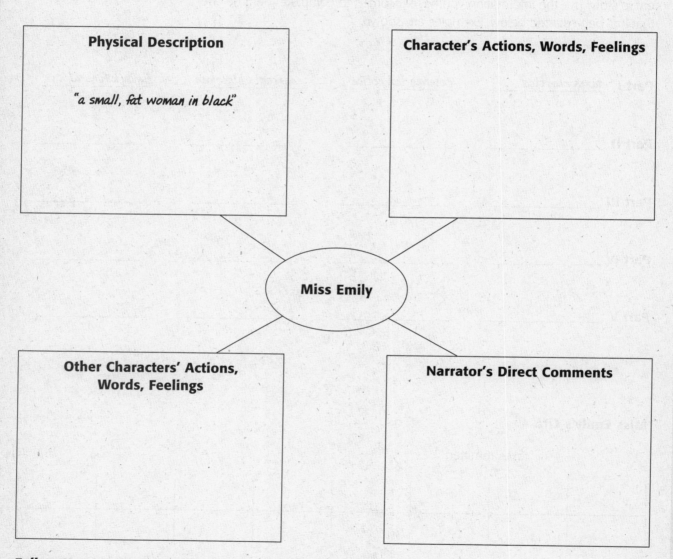

Physical Description

"a small, fat woman in black"

Character's Actions, Words, Feelings

Miss Emily

Other Characters' Actions, Words, Feelings

Narrator's Direct Comments

Follow Up: Compare your examples of characterization with those of your classmates. Then discuss which techniques Faulkner uses most effectively to reveal the character of Miss Emily.

Words to Know SkillBuilder

Words to Know

circumvent	diffident	encroach	pallid	temerity
coquettish	divulge	obliterate	profoundly	thwart
dank	edict	obscure	tedious	virulent

A. Decide which word from the word list belongs in each numbered blank. Then write the word on the blank line on the right. Use each word only once.

Resting at the edge of the forest, he heard the distant sounds of his pursuers. Their steady, lumbering progress showed their mindless determination to (1) his escape. He was afraid of the forest, (2) afraid, but the need to flee was deeper than that fear.

What had he done that was so terrible? Different as he was, he had liked these oddly shaped beings with their (3) skin the color of moonbeams and their small, glittering eyes. He had pitied them for the harshness of their rulers. Listening, unseen, to meetings of their high council, he had heard the secrets of their ruthless plans and then, foolishly, had the (4) to (5) those secrets.

He had done this only to help these creatures, and they had turned on him. Their unthinking obedience and their viciousness astounded him. Would he have been so brave if he had known how (6) the council's counterattack would be? It had issued an (7) that he was to be shot on sight. Now, hounded and persecuted, he had to get to the ship and the others.

The sun sent flirting glances, like those of a (8) maiden, through the hideous trees. Then the clouds and the horrible, flesh-colored leaves moved to (9) the light. Still, he waited in the dark, humid forest, its (10) air clinging to his face.

He didn't know whose land he was about to (11) upon, but trespassing did not concern him. It would take cleverness to (12) his pursuers. Had he managed to (13) his tracks, or did some small trace of them remain? If only he could find the ship!

Suddenly, there was a shuffling in the tall, stinging grass, and he whirled, weapon ready, only to see a tiny animal peeking out at him in a (14) way. Its bashfulness overcame its curiosity, and it hopped away. Relief left him almost faint. At just that moment, a hand grasped his shoulder—a glistening green hand, covered with scales. Three deep black eyes stared into his own.

"Here you are, Zanoz," said a voice like a saw. "At long last. It was beginning to get (15) waiting for you, and I do dislike being bored. Let's get out of here before the humans catch up with you."

(1) _____

(2) _____

(3) _____

(4) _____

(5) _____

(6) _____

(7) _____

(8) _____

(9) _____

(10) _____

(11) _____

(12) _____

(13) _____

(14) _____

(15) _____

B. Write a brief summary of "A Rose for Emily," using at least **six** of the Words to Know.

An Occurrence at Owl Creek Bridge

Ambrose Bierce

Before You Read

Connect to Your Life

Think of a time when you have been in a difficult or even dangerous situation. What were your thoughts and feelings at the time? Use the word web below to record your ideas.

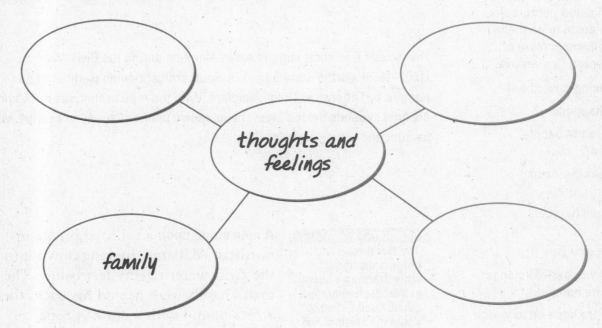

thoughts and feelings

family

Key to the Story

WHAT YOU NEED TO KNOW This story takes place in the South during the Civil War. The author, Ambrose Bierce, draws on firsthand knowledge of the war in writing the story. As a former soldier and a reporter, Bierce creates vivid descriptions of the setting of a hanging that is about to take place. This story is a fictional version of an actual hanging that occurred in 1862 during a bloody battle in Tennessee.

Reading Tips

The author of this **short story** served in the Civil War and later worked as a journalist. As you might expect, some paragraphs read like those in a news story.

There are some long sentences and complicated paragraphs. When you come upon them, ask yourself one or more of the five "reporter's questions":

- *Who* is being described?
- *What* is happening?
- *Where* are the people positioned?
- *When* does the event occur?
- *Why* does it happen?

As the story begins...

- A thirty-five-year-old man is about to be hanged.
- Soldiers are lined up to watch the execution.

☆ **Reader Success Strategy**

In this section, the narrator describes the scene in great detail. As you read, use a ruler to help you read slowly and deliberately. Pause after every few sentences to picture the scene in your mind before moving on.

AN OCCURRENCE AT OWL CREEK BRIDGE

Ambrose Bierce

PREVIEW This short story is set in Alabama during the Civil War (1861–1865). As the story begins, a Southern gentleman is about to be hanged by Federal, or Union, soldiers. With the rope around his neck and his final seconds ticking away, he suddenly thinks of a way to escape. Will he succeed?

I

FOCUS
The first three paragraphs of this story describe a scene in almost photographic detail. Read to find out about the soldiers and their prisoner.
MARK IT UP As you read, circle the details that suggest why the soldiers and the prisoner are on the bridge. An example is highlighted.

A man stood upon a railroad bridge in northern Alabama, looking down into the swift water twenty feet below. The man's hands were behind his back, the wrists bound with a cord. A rope closely encircled his neck. It was attached to a stout cross-timber above his head and the slack fell to the level of his knees. Some loose boards laid upon the sleepers[1] supporting the metals of the railway supplied a footing for him and his executioners—two private soldiers of the Federal army, directed by a sergeant who in civil life may have been a deputy sheriff. At a short remove upon the same temporary platform was an officer in the uniform of his rank, armed. He was a captain. A sentinel at each end of the bridge stood with his rifle in the position known as "support," that is to say, vertical in front of the left shoulder, the hammer resting on the forearm thrown straight across the chest—a formal and unnatural position, enforcing an erect carriage of the body. It did not appear to be the duty of these two men to know what was occurring at the center of

---

1. sleepers: railroad ties.

the bridge; they merely blockaded the two ends of the foot planking that traversed it.

Beyond one of the sentinels nobody was in sight; the railroad ran straight away into a forest for a hundred yards, then, curving, was lost to view. Doubtless there was an outpost farther along. The other bank of the stream was open ground—a gentle acclivity[2] topped with a stockade of vertical tree trunks, loopholed for rifles, with a single embrasure[3] through which protruded the muzzle of a brass cannon commanding the bridge. Midway of the slope between bridge and fort were the spectators—a single company of infantry in line, at "parade rest," the butts of the rifles on the ground, the barrels inclining slightly backward against the right shoulder, the hands crossed upon the stock. A lieutenant stood at the right of the line, the point of his sword upon the ground, his left hand resting upon his right. Excepting the group of four at the center of the bridge, not a man moved. The company faced the bridge, staring stonily, motionless. The sentinels, facing the banks of the stream, might have been statues to adorn the bridge. The captain stood with folded arms, silent, observing the work of his <u>subordinates</u>, but making no sign. Death is a dignitary who when he comes announced is to be received with formal manifestations of respect, even by those most familiar with him. In the code of military etiquette silence and fixity are forms of deference.[4]

The man who was engaged in being hanged was apparently about thirty-five years of age. He was a civilian, if one might judge from his habit, which was that of a planter.[5] His features were good—a straight nose, firm mouth, broad forehead, from which his long, dark hair was combed straight back, falling behind his ears to the collar of his well-fitting frock-coat. He wore a mustache and pointed beard, but no whiskers; his eyes were large and dark gray, and had a kindly expression which one would hardly have expected in one whose neck was in the hemp. Evidently this was no vulgar assassin.

---

2. **acclivity** (ə-klĭv′ĭ-tē): an upward slope of ground.

3. **embrasure** (ĕm-brā′zhər): an opening with the sides slanting outward to increase the angle of fire of a gun.

4. **deference** (dĕf′ər-əns): courteous respect.

5. **planter:** the owner of a plantation.

WORDS
TO   **subordinate** (sə-bôr′dn-ĭt) *n.* one who is lower in rank
KNOW

What Does It Mean?
Parade rest describes the stance of soldiers between maneuvers during a ceremonial review, or parade.

What Does It Mean?
Here, death is personified, or given the human qualities of a *dignitary,* or a person of high rank or position.

MARK IT UP Lines 49–57

What details create a positive image of the prisoner? Underline these details. **(Evaluate)**

Pause & Reflect

Review the details you circled as you read. Why are the soldiers and the prisoner on the bridge? (Infer)

_____

_____

_____

_____

As the story continues . . .

• The prisoner is on the bridge, waiting to be hanged.

• What he is thinking and feeling in his final moments is revealed.

☆ Reader Success Strategy

As you read this section, make a list of the prisoner's thoughts before he is hanged.

What Does It Mean?

The highlighted text in lines 76–77 refers to the usual practice of covering the face or eyes of a person before execution.

What Does It Mean?

An *anvil* is an iron or steel block on which a blacksmith works metal.

Pause & Reflect

60 FOCUS

The prisoner is standing on the bridge with a noose around his neck. Read to find out about his thoughts and sensations.

The preparations being complete, the two private soldiers stepped aside and each drew away the plank upon which he had been standing. The sergeant turned to the captain, saluted and placed himself immediately behind that officer, who in turn moved apart one pace.

These movements left the condemned man and the sergeant standing on the two ends of the same plank, which spanned three of the cross-ties of the bridge. The end upon which the

70 civilian stood almost, but not quite, reached a fourth. This plank had been held in place by the weight of the captain; it was now held by that of the sergeant. At a signal from the former the latter would step aside, the plank would tilt and the condemned man go down between two ties. The arrangement commended itself to his judgment as simple and effective. His face had not been covered nor his eyes bandaged. He looked a moment at his "unsteadfast footing," then let his gaze wander to the swirling water of the stream racing madly beneath his feet. A piece of dancing driftwood

80 caught his attention and his eyes followed it down the current. How slowly it appeared to move! What a sluggish stream!

He closed his eyes in order to fix his last thoughts upon his wife and children. The water, touched to gold by the early sun, the brooding mists under the banks at some distance down the stream, the fort, the soldiers, the piece of drift—all had distracted him. And now he became conscious of a new disturbance. Striking through the thought of his dear ones was a sound which he could neither ignore nor understand, a sharp, distinct, metallic percussion like the stroke of a

90 blacksmith's hammer upon the anvil; it had the same ringing quality. He wondered what it was, and whether immeasurably distant or near by—it seemed both. Its recurrence was regular, but as slow as the tolling of a death knell.[6] He awaited each

---

6. **tolling of a death knell:** the slow, steady ringing of a bell at a funeral.

stroke with impatience and—he knew not why—
apprehension. The intervals of silence grew progressively
longer; the delays became maddening. With their greater
infrequency the sounds increased in strength and sharpness.
They hurt his ear like the thrust of a knife; he feared he would
shriek. What he heard was the ticking of his watch.

100   He unclosed his eyes and saw again the water below him.
"If I could free my hands," he thought, "I might throw off the
noose and spring into the stream. By diving I could <u>evade</u> the
bullets and, swimming vigorously, reach the bank, take to the
woods and get away home. My home, thank God, is as yet
outside their lines; my wife and little ones are still beyond the
invader's farthest advance."

As these thoughts, which have here to be set down in
words, were flashed into the doomed man's brain rather than
evolved from it the captain nodded to the sergeant. The
110 sergeant stepped aside.

Pause & Reflect

II

<img: FOCUS>
This section—a **flash-back**—interrupts the
action of the story to
describe earlier events.
Read to find out about
the prisoner, Peyton
Farquhar, before his
capture.
MARK IT UP As you
read, circle details that
help you learn about
his character.

120

Peyton Farquhar was a well-to-do planter,
of an old and highly respected Alabama
family. Being a slave owner and like
other slave owners a politician he was
naturally an original secessionist[7] and
ardently devoted to the Southern cause.
Circumstances of an imperious nature,
which it is unnecessary to relate here,
had prevented him from taking service
with the gallant army that had fought
the disastrous campaigns ending with
the fall of Corinth,[8] and he chafed under the inglorious

---

7. **secessionist** (sĭ-sĕsh′ə-nĭst): one who supported the withdrawal of Southern states from the Union.

8. **Corinth:** a town in Mississippi that was the site of a Civil War battle in 1862.

WORDS
TO
KNOW
    evade (ĭ-vād′) v. to escape or avoid

What Does It Mean?
Apprehension means "anxiety"
or "fear."

Pause & Reflect
MARK IT UP   **1.** What
sound tortures the prisoner as
he closes his eyes? Underline
the phrase at the top of this
page that answers the question.
(Clarify)

2. Why does the captain nod to the
sergeant? **(Infer)**

_____

_____

_____

_____

As the story continues . . .
• In a flashback, the narrator
tells of earlier events involving
the prisoner.
• He was a well-to-do planter, a
slave owner, and a supporter
of the South in the Civil War.

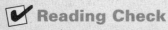
restraint, longing for the release of his energies, the larger life of the soldier, the opportunity for distinction. That opportunity, he felt, would come, as it comes to all in war time. Meanwhile he did what he could. No service was too humble for him to perform in aid of the South, no adventure too perilous for him to undertake if consistent with the character of a civilian who was at heart a soldier, and who in good faith and without too much qualification assented to at least a part of the frankly villainous dictum that all is fair in love and war.

One evening while Farquhar and his wife were sitting on a rustic bench near the entrance to his grounds, a gray-clad soldier rode up to the gate and asked for a drink of water. Mrs. Farquhar was only too happy to serve him with her own white hands. While she was fetching the water her husband approached the dusty horseman and inquired eagerly for news from the front.

"The Yanks are repairing the railroads," said the man, "and are getting ready for another advance. They have reached the Owl Creek bridge, put it in order and built a stockade on the north bank. The commandant has issued an order, which is posted everywhere, declaring that any civilian caught interfering with the railroad, its bridges, tunnels or trains will be <u>summarily</u> hanged. I saw the order."

"How far is it to the Owl Creek bridge?" Farquhar asked.

"About thirty miles."

"Is there no force on this side the creek?"

"Only a picket post[9] half a mile out, on the railroad, and a single sentinel at this end of the bridge."

"Suppose a man—a civilian and student of hanging—should elude the picket post and perhaps get the better of the sentinel," said Farquhar, smiling, "what could he accomplish?"

The soldier reflected. "I was there a month ago," he replied. "I observed that the flood of last winter had lodged a great quantity of driftwood against the wooden pier at this end of the bridge. It is now dry and would burn like tow."[10]

---

9. **picket post:** the camp of soldiers who are assigned to guard against a surprise attack.

10. **tow:** coarse, dry fiber.

The lady had now brought the water, which the soldier drank. He thanked her ceremoniously, bowed to her husband and rode away. An hour later, after nightfall, he repassed the plantation, going northward in the direction from which he had come. He was a Federal scout.

Pause & Reflect

Pause & Reflect

Why is it important that the man who stops for a drink is a Federal scout, not a Confederate soldier? **(Cause and Effect)**

_____

_____

_____

_____

III

FOCUS

Read to find out what happens to Farquhar shortly after he falls through the bridge.

MARK IT UP As you read, underline details that describe his sensations.

As Peyton Farquhar fell straight downward through the bridge he lost consciousness and was as one already dead. From this state he was awakened—ages later, it seemed to him—by the pain of a sharp pressure upon his throat, followed by a sense of suffocation. Keen, poignant[11] agonies seemed to shoot from his neck downward through every fiber of his body and limbs. These pains appeared to flash along well-defined lines of ramification[12] and to beat with an inconceivably rapid periodicity.[13] They seemed like streams of pulsating fire heating him to an intolerable temperature. As to his head, he was conscious of nothing but a feeling of fullness—of congestion. These sensations were unaccompanied by thought. The intellectual part of his nature was already effaced; he had power only to feel, and feeling was torment. He was conscious of motion. Encompassed in a luminous cloud, of which he was now merely the fiery heart, without material substance, he swung through unthinkable arcs of oscillation, like a vast pendulum. Then all at once, with terrible suddenness, the light about him shot upward with the noise of a loud plash; a frightful roaring was in his ears, and all was cold and dark. The power of thought was restored; he knew that the rope had broken and he had fallen into the stream. There was no additional strangulation; the noose about his neck was already suffocating him and kept the water from his lungs. To die of hanging at the bottom of a

---

11. **poignant** (poin′yənt): physically painful.

12. **flash . . . ramification:** spread out rapidly along branches from a central point.

13. **periodicity** (pĭr′ē-ə-dĭs′ĭ-tē): recurring at regular intervals.

As the story continues . . .

• Farquhar falls through the bridge.

• He awakens after landing in the stream.

• The narrator describes Farquhar's struggle and pain.

Reader Success Strategy

In this section, the narrator returns to the scene of the hanging. He uses sensory words to describe the physical sensations that Farquhar experiences. As you read, highlight the words that help you imagine what Farquhar is feeling.

Reader Success Strategy

Create a flow chart like the one below to summarize what happens to Farquhar after he drops through the bridge.

feels himself being strangled
the rope breaks

Reading Check

What makes Farquhar realize that he is trying to free his hands?

river!—the idea seemed to him <u>ludicrous</u>. He opened his eyes in the darkness and saw above him a gleam of light, but how distant, how <u>inaccessible</u>! He was still sinking, for the light became fainter and fainter until it was a mere glimmer. Then it began to grow and brighten, and he knew that he was rising toward the surface—knew it with reluctance, for he was now very comfortable. "To be hanged and drowned," he thought, "that is not so bad; but I do not wish to be shot. No; I will not be shot; that is not fair."

He was not conscious of an effort, but a sharp pain in his wrist <u>apprised</u> him that he was trying to free his hands. He gave the struggle his attention, as an idler might observe the feat of a juggler, without interest in the outcome. What splendid effort!—what magnificent, what superhuman strength! Ah, that was a fine endeavor! Bravo! The cord fell away; his arms parted and floated upward, the hands dimly seen on each side in the growing light. He watched them with a new interest as first one and then the other pounced upon the noose at his neck. They tore it away and thrust it fiercely aside, its undulations resembling those of a water-snake. "Put it back, put it back!" He thought he shouted these words to his hands, for the undoing of the noose had been succeeded by the direst pang that he had yet experienced. His neck ached horribly; his brain was on fire; his heart, which had been fluttering faintly, gave a great leap, trying to force itself out at his mouth. His whole body was racked and wrenched with an insupportable anguish![14] But his disobedient hands gave no heed to the command. They beat the water vigorously with quick, downward strokes, forcing him to the surface. He felt his head emerge; his eyes were blinded by the sunlight; his chest expanded convulsively, and with a supreme and crowning agony his lungs engulfed a great draught of air, which instantly he expelled in a shriek!

He was now in full possession of his physical senses. They were, indeed, <u>preternaturally</u> keen and alert. Something in the awful disturbance of his organic system had so exalted and

What Does It Mean?

Undulations are wavelike motions.

Reading Check

What does the narrator mean when he says that Farquhar "was now in full possession of his physical senses"?

---

14. **racked . . . anguish:** stretched and twisted with unendurable physical pain.

WORDS
TO
KNOW

ludicrous (loo′dĭ-krəs) *adj.* laughably absurd; ridiculous
inaccessible (ĭn′ăk-sĕs′ə-bəl) *adj.* not obtained easily, if at all; unreachable
apprise (ə-prīz′) *v.* to give notice to; inform
preternaturally (prē′tər-năch′ər-əl-ē) *adv.* more than naturally; extraordinarily

refined them that they made record of things never before
perceived. He felt the ripples upon his face and heard their
⟨230⟩ separate sounds as they struck. He looked at the forest on the
bank of the stream, saw the individual trees, the leaves and
the veining of each leaf—saw the very insects upon them: the
locusts, the brilliant-bodied flies, the gray spiders stretching
their webs from twig to twig. He noted the prismatic colors[15]
in all the dewdrops upon a million blades of grass. The
humming of the gnats that danced above the eddies of the
stream, the beating of the dragon-flies' wings, the strokes of
the water-spiders' legs, like oars which had lifted their boat—
all these made audible music. A fish slid along beneath his
⟨240⟩ eyes and he heard the rush of its body parting the water.

Pause & Reflect

FOCUS

Farquhar reaches the
surface of the water.
Read to find out what
happens as the
soldiers try to gun him
down.

MARK IT UP As you
read, list key events in
the margins.

He had come to the surface facing down
the stream; in a moment the visible
world seemed to wheel slowly round,
himself the pivotal point, and he saw
the bridge, the fort, the soldiers upon
the bridge, the captain, the sergeant, the
two privates, his executioners. They
were in silhouette against the blue sky.
They shouted and gesticulated,[16]
⟨250⟩ pointing at him. The captain had drawn his pistol, but did not
fire; the others were unarmed. Their movements were
grotesque and horrible, their forms gigantic.

Suddenly he heard a sharp report and something struck the
water smartly within a few inches of his head, spattering his
face with spray. He heard a second report, and saw one of the
sentinels with his rifle at his shoulder, a light cloud of blue
smoke rising from the muzzle. The man in the water saw the
eye of the man on the bridge gazing into his own through the
sights of the rifle. He observed that it was a gray eye and
⟨260⟩ remembered having read that gray eyes were keenest, and that
all famous marksmen had them. Nevertheless, this one
had missed.

---

15. **prismatic colors** (prĭz-măt′ĭk): basic colors produced by passing light
through a prism.

16. **gesticulated** (jĕ-stĭk′yə-lāt′ĭd): gestured with the hands.

Pause & Reflect

MARK IT UP 1. Review the
details you underlined as you
read. Then tell what happens to
Farquhar after he falls through
the bridge. (Summarize)

_____

_____

_____

_____

MARK IT UP 2. Reread the
boxed sentences on this page.
They suggest that Farquhar's
senses are amazingly sharp.
Underline details that show his
heightened sense of hearing.
(Supporting Details)

As the story continues . . .

• Farquhar reaches the water's
surface.

• The soldiers shoot at him as
he tries to get away.

• He escapes into the woods.

☑ Reading Check

What does Farquhar notice
about the man who tried to
shoot him?

The narrator describes many sounds in this section, giving the reader a sense of what Farquhar was hearing. As you read, highlight words and phrases that describe sounds. Try to imagine what Farquhar is hearing and what is happening.

What Does It Mean?

Ramrods were rods used to push ammunition down the barrels of the style of rifle in use at this time.

A counter-swirl had caught Farquhar and turned him half round; he was again looking into the forest on the bank opposite the fort. The sound of a clear, high voice in a monotonous singsong now rang out behind him and came across the water with a distinctness that pierced and subdued all other sounds, even the beating of the ripples in his ears. Although no soldier, he had frequented camps enough to know the dread significance of that deliberate, drawling, aspirated chant; the lieutenant on shore was taking a part in the morning's work. How coldly and pitilessly—with what an even, calm intonation, presaging,[17] and enforcing tranquillity in the men—with what accurately measured intervals fell those cruel words:

"Attention, company! . . . Shoulder arms! . . . Ready! . . . Aim! . . . Fire!"

Farquhar dived—dived as deeply as he could. The water roared in his ears like the voice of Niagara, yet he heard the dulled thunder of the volley and, rising again toward the surface, met shining bits of metal, singularly flattened, oscillating slowly downward. Some of them touched him on the face and hands, then fell away, continuing their descent. One lodged between his collar and neck; it was uncomfortably warm and he snatched it out.

As he rose to the surface, gasping for breath, he saw that he had been a long time under water; he was <u>perceptibly</u> farther down stream—nearer to safety. The soldiers had almost finished reloading; the metal ramrods flashed all at once in the sunshine as they were drawn from the barrels, turned in the air, and thrust into their sockets. The two sentinels fired again, independently and ineffectually.

The hunted man saw all this over his shoulder; he was now swimming vigorously with the current. His brain was as energetic as his arms and legs; he thought with the rapidity of lightning.

"The officer," he reasoned, "will not make that martinet's[18] error a second time. It is as easy to dodge a volley as a single

---

17. **presaging** (prĕs′ĭj-ĭng): predicting.
18. **martinet** (mär′tn-ĕt′): strict disciplinarian; one who demands that regulations be followed exactly.

WORDS TO KNOW · **perceptibly** (pər-sĕp′tə-blē) *adv.* in a way that can be perceived by the senses or the mind; noticeably

shot. He has probably already given the command to fire at will. God help me, I cannot dodge them all!"

An appalling plash within two yards of him was followed by a loud, rushing sound, *diminuendo,*[19] which seemed to travel back through the air to the fort and died in an explosion which stirred the very river to its deeps! A rising sheet of water curved over him, fell down upon him, blinded him, strangled him! The cannon had taken a hand in the game. As he shook his head free from the commotion of the smitten water he heard the deflected shot humming through the air ahead, and in an instant it was cracking and smashing the branches in the forest beyond.

"They will not do that again," he thought; "the next time they will use a charge of grape.[20] I must keep my eye upon the gun; the smoke will apprise me—the report arrives too late; it lags behind the missile. That is a good gun."

Suddenly he felt himself whirled round and round—spinning like a top. The water, the banks, the forests, the now distant bridge, fort and men—all were commingled and blurred. Objects were represented by their colors only; circular horizontal streaks of color—that was all he saw. He had been caught in a vortex[21] and was being whirled on with a velocity of advance and gyration that made him giddy and sick. In a few moments he was flung upon the gravel at the foot of the left bank of the stream—the southern bank—and behind a projecting point which concealed him from his enemies. The sudden arrest of his motion, the abrasion of one of his hands on the gravel, restored him, and he wept with delight. He dug his fingers into the sand, threw it over himself in handfuls and audibly blessed it. It looked like diamonds, rubies, emeralds; he could think of nothing beautiful which it did not resemble. The trees upon the bank were giant garden plants; he noted a definite order in their arrangement, inhaled the fragrance of their blooms. A strange, roseate light shone through the spaces among their trunks and the wind made in their branches the music of æolian harps.[22] He had no wish to perfect his escape—was content to remain in that

What Does It Mean?
Smitten means "having been attacked or struck."

 READ ALOUD Lines 315–325

Read aloud the boxed passage on this page. Then circle the word or phrase below that completes the following sentence correctly:

Farquhar finally escapes the soldiers mainly because of his

cleverness.

swimming skills.

luck.

(Draw Conclusions)

 Reading Check

Why does Farquhar think that the sand looks like diamonds, rubies, and emeralds?

---

19. *diminuendo* (dĭ-mĭn′yōō-ĕn′dō) *Italian:* gradually decreasing in loudness.
20. **grape:** short for *grapeshot,* a cluster of several small iron balls fired in one shot from a cannon.
21. **vortex:** a whirlpool or spinning water.
22. **music of æolian** (ē-ō′lē-ən) **harps:** heavenly music.

Review the list of key events that you wrote in the margin. Why are the soldiers unsuccessful in their attempts to shoot Farquhar? **(Cause and Effect)**

_____

_____

_____

_____

As the story ends...

• Farquhar travels through the forest.

• He finds a road that leads him to his home.

What Does It Mean?

Uncanny means "eerie" or "strange."

Reading Check

What is unusual about the road on which Farquhar travels?

enchanting spot until retaken.

A whiz and rattle of grapeshot among the branches high above his head roused him from his dream. The baffled cannoneer had fired him a random farewell. He sprang to his feet, rushed up the sloping bank, and plunged into the forest.

Pause & Reflect

FOCUS
Read to find out what finally happens to Farquhar.

All that day he traveled, laying his course by the rounding sun. The forest seemed <u>interminable</u>; nowhere did he discover a break in it, not even a woodman's road. He had not known that he lived in so wild a region. There was something uncanny in the revelation.

By night fall he was fatigued, footsore, famishing. The thought of his wife and children urged him on. At last he found a road which led him in what he knew to be the right direction. It was as wide and straight as a city street, yet it seemed untraveled. No fields bordered it, no dwelling anywhere. Not so much as the barking of a dog suggested human habitation. The black bodies of the trees formed a straight wall on both sides, terminating on the horizon in a point, like a diagram in a lesson in perspective. Overhead, as he looked up through this rift in the wood, shone great golden stars looking unfamiliar and grouped in strange constellations. He was sure they were arranged in some order which had a secret and malign[23] significance. The wood on either side was full of singular noises, among which—once, twice, and again, he distinctly heard whispers in an unknown tongue.

His neck was in pain and lifting his hand to it he found it horribly swollen. He knew that it had a circle of black where the rope had bruised it. His eyes felt congested; he could no longer close them. His tongue was swollen with thirst; he relieved its fever by thrusting it forward from between his teeth into the cold air. How softly the turf had carpeted the untraveled avenue—he could no longer feel the roadway beneath his feet!

---

23. **malign** (mə-līn′): evil; harmful; threatening harm or evil.

370 Doubtless, despite his suffering, he had fallen asleep while walking, for now he sees another scene—perhaps he has merely recovered from a delirium.[24] He stands at the gate of his own home. All is as he left it, and all bright and beautiful in the morning sunshine. He must have traveled the entire night. As he pushes open the gate and passes up the wide white walk, he sees a flutter of female garments; his wife, looking fresh and cool and sweet, steps down from the veranda to meet him. At the bottom of the steps she stands waiting, with a smile of <u>ineffable</u> joy, an attitude of matchless

380 grace and dignity. Ah, how beautiful she is! He springs forward with extended arms. As he is about to clasp her he feels a stunning blow upon the back of the neck; a blinding white light blazes all about him with a sound like the shock of a cannon—then all is darkness and silence!

Peyton Farquhar was dead; his body, with a broken neck, swung gently from side to side beneath the timbers of the Owl Creek bridge.

Pause & Reflect

✔ Reading Check
Briefly describe Farquhar's thoughts in this paragraph.

Pause & Reflect

✏ **MARK IT UP** 1. Reread the boxed sentences on page 206. What details make the surroundings look unreal? Circle these details. (**Analyze**)

2. What kills Farquhar? (**Infer**)

_____

_____

_____

_____

✏ **CHALLENGE**

Irony is a contrast between what is expected to happen and what actually occurs. Bierce's finest stories show the ironies of war. One irony in this story is that the prisoner is not a "vulgar assassin," but a well-bred gentleman. Mark another example of irony in this story. What makes your example ironic? (**Analyze**)

---

24. **delirium** (dĭ-lîr′ē-əm): a temporary state of extreme mental confusion, marked by hallucinations.

WORDS
TO
KNOW

ineffable (ĭn-ĕf′ə-bəl) *adj.* unable to be expressed in words

Active Reading SkillBuilder

Analyzing Structure

The **structure** of a work of literature is the arrangement of its parts. This story, for example, is arranged in three numbered sections. Each section signals a change in time. To help keep track of the sequence of events in the story and to clarify what happens, use the chart below to record your responses to the reading strategy questions. An example is shown.

Reading Strategy Questions	Answers
Section I Whose thoughts and feelings does the narrator relate?	*the thoughts and feelings of the condemned man*
What does the captain's nod mean?	
Section II When do these events occur and what do they explain?	
Section III Would these be the thoughts of a man on the brink of death?	
Can you account for the changes in the surroundings?	
What kills Farquhar?	

Literary Analysis SkillBuilder

Point of View

Point of view is the perspective from which events in a story are narrated. The first three paragraphs of this story are told from a **third-person omniscient,** or all-knowing, point of view. In the fourth paragraph, the perspective shifts to focus on Farquhar's personal thoughts and sensations. This focus on one person's inner life is called **third-person limited** point of view. Identify the point of view in sections II and III of the story. Indicate where the point of view shifts. An example is shown.

Section II

Point of View: *third person limited*

Where It Shifts:
Line:
Page

New Point of View:

Section III

Point of View:

Where It Shifts:
Line:
Page:

New Point of View:

Follow Up: Why do you think Bierce did not use a consistent point of view to tell this story?

Words to Know SkillBuilder

Words to Know

apprise	inaccessible	interminable	perceptibly	subordinate
evade	ineffable	ludicrous	preternaturally	summarily

A. Fill in each set of blanks with the correct word from the word list. The boxed letters will spell out a word that describes the forces Peyton Farquhar supports.

1. This describes Chicken Little's belief that the sky was falling or the idea of a cow jumping over the moon.

   _ _ _ _ ☐ _ ☐ _ _

2. This describes your emotion when you are speechless with dismay, happiness, or fear.

   _ ☐ _ _ ☐ _ _ _ _

3. This is what the pyramid builders hoped would describe the treasures hidden in the pharaohs' tombs.

   _ _ _ _ _ _ ☐ _ _ _

4. This is a private to a sergeant, a sergeant to a captain, and a captain to a colonel.

   _ _ _ _ _ _ ☐ _ _ _ _ ☐

5. This is how shocked you are when you gasp and how sleepy you are when you yawn.

   _ ☐ _ _ _ _ _ _ _ _

6. This is how people wed when they elope and how people execute prisoners when they lynch them.

   _ _ _ _ ☐ _ _ _ _

7. This describes the motion of the waves, the spinning of the Earth, and what a boring lecture seems to be.

   _ _ ☐ _ _ _ _ _ _ _ _ ☐

Write the word the boxed letters spell out. _____

B. Fill in each blank with the correct word from the word list.

1. Sleeping Beauty snoozed for a _____ long time.

2. People tend to give up if their goals seem _____.

3. Warning signs _____ the public of danger.

4. A gazelle's speed helps it _____ a pursuing lion.

5. A giggling person is _____ amused.

C. Write the report the captain might have submitted to his superior officer regarding the occurrence at Owl Creek Bridge. Use at least **four** of the Words to Know.

from LIFE ON THE Mississippi

MARK TWAIN

Before You Read

Connect to Your Life

Have you ever changed your mind about a place or an activity—such as a new job or a class—as you learned more about it? How did you feel at first? How did your feelings change as you gained more knowledge? Did you start something you didn't want to do, and then enjoy it? Or, were you looking forward to something that you ended up disliking? Use the chart below to write down your thoughts.

Place or activity: _____

_____

HOW I FELT AT FIRST	HOW MY FEELINGS CHANGED

Key to the Memoir

WHAT YOU NEED TO KNOW Until the late 1800s, steam-powered riverboats were essential for transportation on the Mississippi River. People traveled on riverboats and also used them to ship cargo. The Mississippi River is 2,350 miles long and flows through ten states, from Minnesota to Louisiana. Piloting riverboats required much knowledge and skill. People who wanted to become riverboat pilots first served as apprentices, learning by working with skilled pilots.

from LIFE ON THE Mississippi

MARK TWAIN

PREVIEW In this excerpt, Mark Twain recalls his on-the-job training as a riverboat pilot on the *Paul Jones.* The **setting** is the Mississippi River in 1856, when Twain was 21. He tells how a famous riverboat pilot, Mr. Bixby, taught him the art of steering a riverboat, even at night. He describes how his view of the river changed as he learned to look at it with a trained eye.

Reading Tips

A **memoir** is a form of **autobiographical writing** in which a person recalls actual events in his or her life.

• The first two sections are like brief stories. Read them as you would any other **narratives**. Pay close attention to what happens and when. Keep track of the **sequence** of events.

• The third section relies more on **description**. You may find it difficult because of its long sentences and many details. As you read, slow down your pace. Picture in your mind what the author describes.

A Cub-Pilot's Experience

FOCUS

Twain tells how he came to be a pilot in training on a riverboat. Read to find out how young Twain does his first day on the job.

MARK IT UP As you read, circle details that show his difficulty in steering the riverboat. An example is highlighted on page 214.

What with lying on the rocks four days at Louisville, and some other delays, the poor old *Paul Jones* fooled away about two weeks in making the voyage from Cincinnati to New Orleans. This gave me a chance to get acquainted with one of the pilots, and he taught me how to steer the boat, and thus made the fascination

10 of river life more potent than ever for me. . . .

I soon discovered two things. One was that a vessel would not be likely to sail for the mouth of the Amazon under ten or twelve years; and the other was that the nine or ten dollars still left in my pocket would not suffice for so impossible an exploration as I had planned, even if I could afford to wait for a ship. Therefore it followed that I must contrive a new career. The *Paul Jones* was now bound for St. Louis. I planned a siege against my pilot, and at the end of three hard days he surrendered. He agreed to teach me the Mississippi River from

20 New Orleans to St. Louis for five hundred dollars, payable out of the first wages I should receive after graduating. I entered upon the small enterprise of "learning" twelve or

As the memoir begins . . .

• Mark Twain, the narrator, begins a story about his experience on the Mississippi River when he was a young man.

• Twain convinces Mr. Bixby, pilot of the *Paul Jones,* to teach him how to pilot a riverboat.

• The job is more difficult than Twain expects.

What Does It Mean?
Potent means "powerful."

More About . . .

RIVERBOAT (PILOTS) Piloting a steamboat down the Mississippi River was a tricky job. One hazard was the river's powerful currents. Along the twisting river were hidden dangers, such as sandbars and sunken ships. Also, pilots had to navigate up-stream, against the current, as well as downstream, with the current.

What Does It Mean?

The verb *flay* can mean "to strip off the skin" or "to whip." Twain uses this figure of speech to describe the harsh-ness of Mr. Bixby's comments.

☆ Reader Success Strategy

As you read, compare and con-trast Twain's original perception of a riverboat pilot's job and the reality of the job. Use a chart like the one below.

Twain's Perceptions	Reality

thirteen hundred miles of the great Mississippi River with the easy confidence of my time of life. If I had really known what I was about to require of my faculties,[1] I should not have had the courage to begin. I supposed that all a (pilot) had to do was to keep his boat in the river, and I did not consider that that could be much of a trick, since it was so wide.

The boat backed out from New Orleans at four in the afternoon, and it was "our watch" until eight. Mr. Bixby, my chief, "straightened her up," plowed her along past the sterns of the other boats that lay at the Levee,[2] and then said, "Here, take her; shave those steamships as close as you'd peel an apple." I took the wheel, and my heartbeat fluttered up into the hundreds; for it seemed to me that we were about to scrape the side off every ship in the line, we were so close. I held my breath and began to claw the boat away from the danger; and I had my own opinion of the pilot who had known no better than to get us into such peril, but I was too wise to express it. In half a minute I had a wide margin of safety intervening between the *Paul Jones* and the ships; and within ten seconds more I was set aside in disgrace, and Mr. Bixby was going into danger again and flaying me alive with abuse of my cowardice. I was stung, but I was obliged to admire the easy confidence with which my chief loafed from side to side of his wheel, and trimmed the ships so closely that disaster seemed ceaselessly imminent.[3] When he had cooled a little he told me that the easy water was close ashore and the current outside, and therefore we must hug the bank, upstream, to get the benefit of the former, and stay well out, downstream, to take advantage of the latter. In my own mind I resolved to be a downstream pilot and leave the upstreaming to people dead to prudence.[4]

Now and then Mr. Bixby called my attention to certain things. Said he, "This is Six-Mile Point." I assented. It was pleasant enough information, but I could not see the bearing of it. I was not conscious that it was a matter of any interest to me. Another time he said, "This is Nine-Mile Point." Later he said, "This is Twelve-Mile Point." They were all about level with the water's edge; they all looked about alike to me;

---

1. **faculties:** abilities.
2. **Levee** (lĕv′ē): a landing place for boats on a river.
3. **imminent** (ĭm′ə-nənt): about to happen.
4. **dead to prudence:** lacking good judgment.

they were monotonously unpicturesque. I hoped Mr. Bixby would change the subject. But no; he would crowd up around a point, hugging the shore with affection, and then say: "The slack water ends here, abreast this bunch of China trees; now we cross over." So he crossed over. He gave me the wheel once or twice, but I had no luck. I either came near chipping off the edge of a sugar plantation, or I yawed[5] too far from shore, and so dropped back into disgrace again and got abused.

70   The watch was ended at last, and we took supper and went to bed. At midnight the glare of a lantern shone in my eyes, and the night watchman said, "Come, turn out!" And then he left. I could not understand this extraordinary procedure; so I presently gave up trying to, and dozed off to sleep. Pretty soon the watchman was back again, and this time he was gruff. I was annoyed. I said,

"What do you want to come bothering around here in the middle of the night for? Now, as like as not, I'll not get to sleep again to-night."

80   The watchman said, "Well, if this ain't good, I'm blessed."

> The "offwatch" was just turning in, and I heard some brutal laughter from them, and such remarks as "Hello, watchman! ain't the new cub turned out yet? He's delicate, likely. Give him some sugar in a rag, and send for the chambermaid to sing 'Rock-a-by Baby' to him."

About this time Mr. Bixby appeared on the scene. Something like a minute later I was climbing the pilothouse steps with some of my clothes on and the rest in my arms. Mr. Bixby was close behind, commenting. Here was something

90 fresh[6]—this thing of getting up in the middle of the night to go to work. It was a detail in piloting that had never occurred to me at all. I knew that boats ran all night, but somehow I had never happened to reflect that somebody had to get up out of a warm bed to run them. I began to fear that piloting was not quite so romantic as I had imagined it was; there was something very real and worklike about this new phase of it. . . .

Pause & Reflect

---

5. **yawed:** swerved.
6. **fresh:** new.

from **Life on the Mississippi**   215

What Does It Mean?
Monotonously unpicturesque means that each was as boring and uninteresting as the next.

☆ Reader Success Strategy
Review this section to become more familiar with the order of events. As you reread, make a simple time line. Note major events, and notice how Twain reacts to each event.

✔ Reading Check
Why is Twain surprised when the watchman wakes him up in the middle of the night?

Pause & Reflect
1. Review the details you circled as you read. What mistakes did Twain make in steering the riverboat? **(Draw Conclusions)**
_____
_____
_____
_____

READ ALOUD 2. Read aloud the boxed passage on this page. Then circle the phrase below that tells how the other crew members view young Twain. **(Infer)**

with affection

with mockery

with respect

As the memoir continues...

- Mr. Bixby pilots the riverboat at night.
- He becomes angry with Twain.
- Twain begins to keep a notebook.

⭐ Reader Success Strategy

Twain uses dialogue, or conversation, as well as descriptions to convey emotions. As you read, try to picture the scene in your mind. What are the attitudes of Twain and Mr. Bixby? How do you know?

What Does It Mean?

Dunderhead means "fool" or "idiot."

✔ Reading Check

Why does Mr. Bixby call Twain "the stupidest dunderhead I ever saw or ever heard of"?

FOCUS

Mr. Bixby steers the riverboat through the dark night. Read to find out why Mr. Bixby gets angry at young Twain and what happens as a result.

Mr. Bixby made for the shore and soon was scraping it, just the same as if it had been daylight. And not only that, but singing:

Father in heaven, the day is declining, etc.

It seemed to me that I had put my life in the keeping of a peculiarly reckless outcast. Presently he turned on me and said, "What's the name of the first point above New Orleans?"

I was gratified to be able to answer promptly, and I did. I said I didn't know.

"Don't *know*?"

This manner jolted me. I was down at the foot[7] again, in a moment. But I had to say just what I had said before.

"Well, you're a smart one!" said Mr. Bixby. "What's the name of the *next* point?"

Once more I didn't know.

"Well, this beats anything. Tell me the name of *any* point or place I told you."

I studied awhile and decided that I couldn't.

"Look here! What do you start out from, above Twelve-Mile Point, to cross over?"

"I—I—don't know."

"You—you—don't know?" mimicking my drawling manner of speech. "What *do* you know?"

"I—I—nothing, for certain."

"By the great Caesar's ghost, I believe you! You're the stupidest dunderhead I ever saw or ever heard of, so help me Moses! The idea of *you* being a pilot—you! Why, you don't know enough to pilot a cow down a lane."

Oh, but his wrath was up! He was a nervous man, and he shuffled from one side of his wheel to the other as if the floor was hot. He would boil awhile to himself, and then overflow and scald me again.

"Look here! What do you suppose I told you the names of those points for?"

I tremblingly considered a moment, and then the devil of temptation provoked me to say, "Well to—to—be entertaining, I thought."

---

7. **down at the foot:** at the bottom of the class.

This was a red rag to the bull. He raged and stormed so (he was crossing the river at the time) that I judged it made him blind, because he ran over the steering oar of a trading scow.[8] Of course the traders sent up a volley of red-hot profanity. Never was a man so grateful as Mr. Bixby was, because he was brimful, and here were subjects who could *talk back*. He threw open a window, thrust his head out, and such an irruption followed as I never had heard before. The fainter and farther away the scowmen's curses drifted, the higher Mr. Bixby lifted his voice and the weightier his adjectives grew. When he closed the window he was empty. You could have drawn a seine[9] through his system and not caught curses enough to disturb your mother with. Presently he said to me in the gentlest way, "My boy, you must get a little memorandum book; and every time I tell you a thing, put it down right away. There's only one way to be a pilot, and that is to get this entire river by heart. You have to know it just like A B C."

That was a dismal revelation to me, for my memory was never loaded with anything but blank cartridges. However, I did not feel discouraged long. I judged that it was best to make some allowances, for doubtless Mr. Bixby was "stretching."[10] . . .

By the time we had gone seven or eight hundred miles up the river, I had learned to be a tolerably plucky upstream steersman, in daylight; and before we reached St. Louis I had made a trifle of progress in night work, but only a trifle. I had a notebook that fairly bristled with the names of towns, "points," bars, islands, bends, reaches, etc.; but the information was to be found only in the notebook—none of it was in my head. It made my heart ache to think I had only got half of the river set down; for as our watch was four hours off and four hours on, day and night, there was a long four-hour gap in my book for every time I had slept since the voyage began. . . .

Pause & *Reflect*

8. **scow:** a flat-bottomed boat used chiefly to transport freight.

9. **seine** (sān): large fishing net.

10. **"stretching":** exaggerating.

What Does It Mean?
Here, *red rag* is a reference to the red-lined capes bullfighters use to get the bull to charge them.

What Does It Mean?
Brimful means "filled up." In this case, Mr. Bixby is filled with anger and ready to vent it on somebody.

What Does It Mean?
Plucky means "gutsy."

Pause & *Reflect*
What does young Twain jot down in his notebook? **(Clarify)**

_____

_____

_____

_____

As the memoir ends...

- Twain explains how the Mississippi River is like a book.
- He talks of what he has lost by learning how to pilot a steamboat.

READ ALOUD **Lines 178–188**

Twain says that the Mississippi River is more fascinating than a book. In this passage, Twain creates a rolling rhythm by repeating the word *never* and by using parallel word groups.

What Does It Mean?

Trifling means "least important" or "minor."

FOCUS

Twain compares the Mississippi River to a book. He then tells what he has gained and what he has lost by learning his trade.

MARK IT UP As you read, underline any details that help you understand what he has gained and what he has lost.

... **The face of the water,** in time, became a wonderful book—a book that was a dead language to the uneducated passenger, but which told its mind to me without reserve, delivering its most cherished secrets as clearly as if it uttered them with a voice. And it was not a book to be read once and thrown aside, for it had a new story to tell every day. Throughout the long twelve hundred miles there was never a page that was void of interest, never one that you could leave unread without loss, never one that you would want to skip, thinking you could find higher enjoyment in some other thing. There never was so wonderful a book written by man; never one whose interest was so absorbing, so unflagging, so sparklingly renewed with every reperusal.[11] The passenger who could not read it was charmed with a peculiar sort of faint dimple on its surface (on the rare occasions when he did not overlook it altogether); but to the pilot that was an *italicized* passage; indeed, it was more than that, it was a legend of the largest capitals,[12] with a string of shouting exclamation points at the end of it, for it meant that a wreck or a rock was buried there that could tear the life out of the strongest vessel that ever floated. It is the faintest and simplest expression the water ever makes, and the most hideous to a pilot's eye. In truth, the passenger who could not read this book saw nothing but all manner of pretty pictures in it, painted by the sun and shaded by the clouds, whereas to the trained eye these were not pictures at all, but the grimmest and most dead earnest of reading matter.

Now when I had mastered the language of this water, and had come to know every trifling feature that bordered the great river as familiarly as I knew the letters of the alphabet, I had made a valuable acquisition. But I had lost something, too. I had lost something which could never be restored to me while I lived. All the grace, the beauty, the poetry, had gone out of the majestic river! I still kept in mind a certain wonderful sunset which I witnessed when steamboating was new to me. A broad expanse of the river was turned to blood;

---

11. reperusal (rē'pə-rōō'zəl): rereading.
12. a legend of the largest capitals: an inscription in large capital letters.

in the middle distance the red hue brightened into gold, through which a solitary log came floating, black and conspicuous; in one place a long, slanting mark lay sparkling upon the water; in another the surface was broken by boiling, tumbling rings, that were as many-tinted as an opal; where the ruddy flush was faintest, was a smooth spot that was covered with graceful circles and radiating lines, ever so delicately traced; the shore on our left was densely wooded, and the somber shadow that fell from this forest was broken in one place by a long, ruffled trail that shone like silver; and high above the forest wall a clean-stemmed dead tree waved a single leafy bough that glowed like a flame in the unobstructed splendor that was flowing from the sun. There were graceful curves, reflected images, woody heights, soft distances; and over the whole scene, far and near, the dissolving lights drifted steadily, enriching it every passing moment with new marvels of coloring.

I stood like one bewitched. I drank it in, in a speechless rapture. The world was new to me, and I had never seen anything like this at home. But as I have said, a day came when I began to cease from noting the glories and the charms which the moon and the sun and the twilight wrought upon the river's face; another day came when I ceased altogether to note them. Then, if that sunset scene had been repeated, I should have looked upon it without rapture, and should have commented upon it, inwardly, after this fashion: "This sun means that we are going to have wind tomorrow; that floating log means that the river is rising, small thanks to it; that slanting mark on the water refers to a bluff reef[13] which is going to kill somebody's steamboat one of these nights, if it keeps on stretching out like that; those tumbling 'boils' show a dissolving bar and a changing channel there; the lines and circles in the slick water over yonder are a warning that that troublesome place is shoaling up[14] dangerously; that silver streak in the shadow of the forest is the 'break' from a new snag, and he has located himself in the very best place he could have found to fish for steamboats; that tall dead tree, with a single living branch, is not going to last long, and then how is a body ever going to get through this blind place at night without the friendly old landmark?"

---

13. **bluff reef:** an underwater ridge of rock.
14. **shoaling up:** becoming too shallow for safe navigation, because of a buildup of sand or silt in the riverbed.

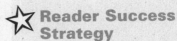
Reader Success Strategy

This section contains some very long sentences. As you read, break long sentences into smaller sections. Determine the main idea of each section before moving on to the next.

What Does It Mean?

Rapture means "overwhelming emotion."

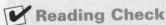 **Reading Check**

How does Twain view the sunset now that he is a skilled pilot?

Pause & **Reflect**

1. Review the details you underlined as you read. Then **summarize** what Twain feels he has lost by learning to pilot a steamboat.

_____

_____

_____

2. List one piece of useful information Twain learns from "reading" the river's appearance. **(Clarify)**

_____

_____

_____

📖 READ ALOUD   3. Read aloud the boxed sentences on this page. Then restate Twain's **main idea** in your own words. **(Paraphrase)**

_____

_____

_____

✏️ CHALLENGE

Twain compares Mr. Bixby's temper to boiling water: "He would boil awhile to himself, and then overflow and scald me again." Circle other examples of **figurative language** that refer to Mr. Bixby.

No, the romance and beauty were all gone from the river. All the value any feature of it had for me now was the amount of usefulness it could furnish toward compassing the safe piloting of a steamboat. Since those days, I have pitied doctors from my heart. What does the lovely flush in a beauty's cheek mean to a doctor but a "break" that ripples above some deadly disease? Are not all her visible charms sown thick with what are to him the signs and symbols of hidden decay? Does he ever see her beauty at all, or doesn't he simply view her professionally, and comment upon her unwholesome condition all to himself? And doesn't he sometimes wonder whether he has gained most or lost most by learning his trade?

260

Pause & **Reflect**

Active Reading SkillBuilder

Visualizing

When writers skillfully describe a scene or character, they help readers **visualize,** or form mental pictures of, whatever is being described. Readers can visualize what the Mississippi River looks like from Twain's precise details. When reading the selection, use the chart below to record three vivid details and comparisons that Twain uses to help you visualize the Mississippi. Examples are given.

Mississippi Descriptions	
Details	**Comparison**
Sunset turns river to blood. A single log floats in the middle distance.	Leafy bough glows like a flame.

Literary Analysis SkillBuilder

Description

Description is a process by which a writer creates a picture in words of a scene, an event, or a character. One descriptive device is **imagery**—descriptive words and phrases that re-create sensory experiences to help readers see, hear, smell, taste, or feel what is being described. Another descriptive device is the use of **analogies,** which show similarities between two dissimilar things. On the chart below, list two descriptive details from the selection. Identify each detail as an example of imagery or analogy, then record how it affects you as a reader. An example is shown.

Twain's Descriptions		
Detail	**Descriptive Device**	**Effect**
1 . . . began to claw the boat away from the danger.	imagery	It shows how slowly and painfully Twain steered his boat away from the others.

Follow Up: Which scene, event, or character do you picture most vividly as a result of Twain's description? Explain why.

A Wagner Matinee

Willa Cather

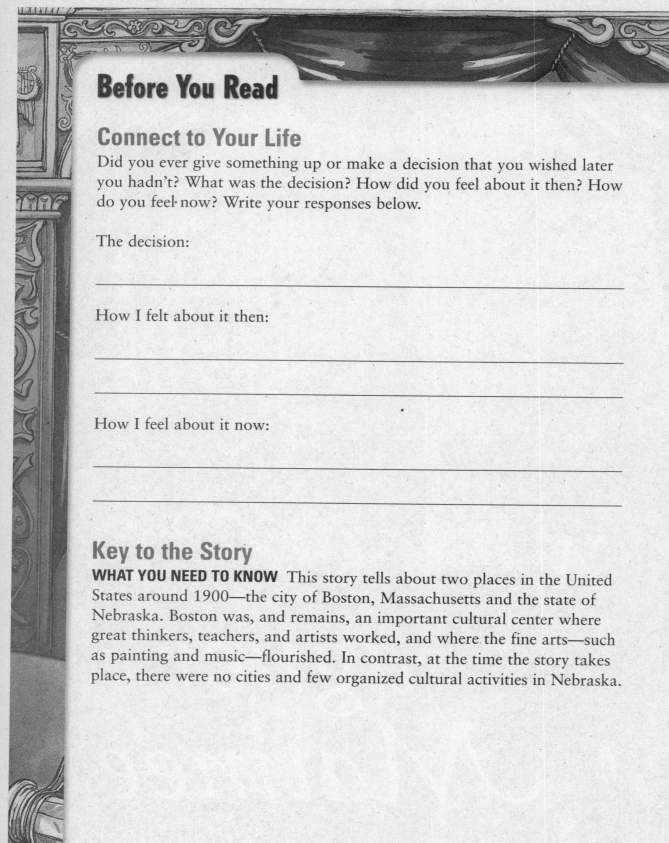

Before You Read

Connect to Your Life

Did you ever give something up or make a decision that you wished later
you hadn't? What was the decision? How did you feel about it then? How
do you feel now? Write your responses below.

The decision:

_____

How I felt about it then:

_____

_____

How I feel about it now:

_____

_____

Key to the Story

WHAT YOU NEED TO KNOW This story tells about two places in the United
States around 1900—the city of Boston, Massachusetts and the state of
Nebraska. Boston was, and remains, an important cultural center where
great thinkers, teachers, and artists worked, and where the fine arts—such
as painting and music—flourished. In contrast, at the time the story takes
place, there were no cities and few organized cultural activities in Nebraska.

A Wagner Matinee

Willa Cather

SHORT STORY

Reading Tips

In "A Wagner Matinee," the author includes scenes from the past as well as from the present time of the story. Watch for shifts between the present and the past **settings** as you read.

- Put a *T* in the margin every time the story shifts from the present to the past or from the past to the present.
- Circle the word, phrase, or sentence that indicates a time shift has occurred.

✎ **MARK IT UP** **KEEP TRACK**

As you read, you can use these marks to keep track of your understanding.

✔ ..... I understand.

? ..... I don't understand this.

! ..... Interesting or surprising idea

As the story begins . . .

- The narrator is expecting a visit from his aunt.
- He describes what Aunt Georgiana's life has been like since she moved with her husband from Boston to Nebraska.
- When she arrives, Aunt Georgiana's appearance is somewhat unusual.

✔ Reading Check

Why is Aunt Georgiana coming to Boston?

PREVIEW "A Wagner Matinee" is set in Boston in the 1890s. Wagner (väg′ nər) was a famous German composer. His music plays a key role in this story. The main character, the narrator's Aunt Georgiana, has lived most of her adult life on a poor farm on the Nebraska frontier. When she visits her nephew in Boston after being gone for 30 years, he makes plans to take her to an afternoon concert. The matinee is an ordinary event to most of the audience. It stirs complicated feelings in the quiet, care-worn woman, however.

FOCUS

In this section, you will be introduced to Aunt Georgiana and learn something about her. ✎ **MARK IT UP** As you read, circle details that give you some first impressions of Aunt Georgiana. An example is highlighted on page 226.

I received one morning a letter, written in pale ink on glassy, blue-lined notepaper, and bearing the postmark of a little Nebraska village. This communication, worn and rubbed, looking as though it had been carried for some days in a coat pocket that was none too clean, was from my Uncle Howard and informed me that his wife had been left a small legacy by a bachelor relative who had recently died, and that it would be necessary for her to go to Boston to attend to the settling of the estate. He requested me to meet her at the station and render her whatever services might be necessary. On examining the date indicated as that of her arrival, I found it no later than tomorrow. He had characteristically delayed writing until, had I been away from home for a day, I must have missed the good woman altogether.

What Does It Mean?
A *duster* was a long overcoat worn on the frontier to protect clothing from dust.

Reader Success Strategy
Once you have read this section, go back over it, looking for details about Aunt Georgiana. Then, write a brief summary of what you know about her so far.

What Does It Mean?
In the highlighted passage, the narrator is referring to the dangers of exploring. Many explorers lost fingers, toes, and ears to frostbite in the bitter cold of northern regions, or caught malaria and other tropical diseases in places like the Congo in Africa.

The name of my Aunt Georgiana called up not alone her own figure, at once pathetic and grotesque, but opened before my feet a gulf of recollection so wide and deep, that, as the letter dropped from my hand, I felt suddenly a stranger to all the present conditions of my existence, wholly ill at ease and out of place amid the familiar surroundings of my study. I became, in short, the gangling farmer-boy my aunt had known, scourged with chilblains[1] and bashfulness, my hands cracked and sore from the corn husking. I felt the knuckles of my thumb tentatively, as though they were raw again. I sat again before her parlor organ, fumbling the scales with my stiff, red hands, while she, beside me, made canvas mittens for the huskers.[2]

The next morning, after preparing my landlady somewhat, I set out for the station. When the train arrived I had some difficulty in finding my aunt. She was the last of the passengers to alight, and it was not until I got her into the carriage that she seemed really to recognize me. She had come all the way in a day coach; her linen duster had become black with soot and her black bonnet grey with dust during the journey. When we arrived at my boarding-house the landlady put her to bed at once and I did not see her again until the next morning.

Whatever shock Mrs. Springer experienced at my aunt's appearance, she considerately concealed. As for myself, I saw my aunt's misshapen figure with that feeling of awe and respect with which we behold explorers who have left their ears and fingers north of Franz-Josef-Land,[3] or their health somewhere along the Upper Congo.[4] My Aunt Georgiana had been a music teacher at the Boston Conservatory, somewhere back in the latter sixties. One summer, while visiting in the little village among the Green Mountains where her ancestors had dwelt for generations, she had kindled the callow fancy of

---

1. **chilblains:** painful swelling or sores on the feet or hands, caused by exposure to the cold.

2. **huskers:** farm workers who remove cornhusks by hand.

3. **Franz-Josef-Land:** a group of small, mostly ice-covered islands in the Arctic Ocean north of Russia.

4. **Upper Congo:** river in central Africa, now called the Zaire (zä-îr′) River.

WORDS TO KNOW

pathetic (pə-thĕt′ĭk) *adj.* arousing pity or compassion
callow (kăl′ō) *adj.* lacking adult maturity or experience; immature

the most idle and shiftless of all the village lads, and had conceived for this Howard Carpenter one of those extravagant passions which a handsome country boy of twenty-one sometimes inspires in an angular, spectacled woman of thirty. When she returned to her duties in Boston, Howard followed her, and the upshot of this <u>inexplicable</u> infatuation was that she eloped with him, eluding the <u>reproaches</u> of her family and the criticisms of her friends by going with him to the Nebraska frontier. Carpenter, who, of course, had no money, had taken a homestead in Red Willow County, fifty miles from the railroad. There they had measured off their quarter section themselves by driving across the prairie in a wagon, to the wheel of which they had tied a red cotton handkerchief, and counting off its revolutions. They built a dugout in the red hillside, one of those cave dwellings whose inmates so often reverted to primitive conditions. Their water they got from the lagoons where the buffalo drank, and their slender stock of provisions was always at the mercy of bands of roving Indians. For thirty years my aunt had not been further than fifty miles from the homestead.

But Mrs. Springer knew nothing of all this, and must have been considerably shocked at what was left of my kinswoman. Beneath the soiled linen duster which, on her arrival, was the most conspicuous feature of her costume, she wore a black stuff dress, whose ornamentation showed that she had surrendered herself unquestioningly into the hands of a country dressmaker. My poor aunt's figure, however, would have presented astonishing difficulties to any dressmaker. Originally stooped, her shoulders were now almost bent together over her sunken chest. She wore no stays, and her gown, which trailed unevenly behind, rose in a sort of peak over her abdomen. She wore ill-fitting false teeth, and her skin was as yellow as a Mongolian's from constant exposure to a pitiless wind and to the alkaline water which hardens the most transparent cuticle into a sort of flexible leather.

Pause & Reflect

✔ **Reading Check**
Why had the Carpenters gone to the Nebraska frontier?

More About . . .
HOMESTEADING Many Easterners headed west to start new lives in the 1800s. The government offered them parcels of land, referred to as home-steads, as an incentive to settle the western frontier. The homesteaders marked off the amount of land the government allowed them to have and then lived off that land. It was a difficult life filled with long hours of hard work.

What Does It Mean?
Stays refer to a corset, a close-fitting undergarment that is worn to shape the body. If Aunt Georgiana had worn a corset, her figure would have appeared less stooped.

Pause & Reflect

1. Two consequences of Aunt Georgiana's decision to marry Howard Carpenter are_____

_____

_____

and_____

_____.

(Clarify)

2. How does the narrator feel toward his aunt? **(Infer)**

_____

_____

_____

WORDS
TO
KNOW

inexplicable (ĭn-ĕkʹsplĭ-kə-bəl) *adj.* difficult or impossible to explain
reproach (rĭ-prōchʹ) *n.* an expression of blame or disapproval

As the story continues . . .

- The narrator tells about his life in Nebraska when he was young.
- At that time, his aunt taught him many things.
- He invites her to a concert featuring the music of Wagner.

Reading Check

Why do you think Aunt Georgiana took so much time to teach the narrator Latin, Shakespeare, and music?

What Does It Mean?

A *martyr* is someone who endures great suffering, especially for a cause. *Martyrdom* means "great suffering or affliction."

FOCUS

Read on to learn more about the narrator's life with his aunt in Nebraska. Find out what he is planning for her during her visit.

90

MARK IT UP Circle two passages that show how Aunt Georgiana treated the narrator when he was a boy.

I owed to this woman most of the good that ever came my way in my boyhood, and had a reverential affection for her. During the years when I was riding herd for my uncle, my aunt, after cooking the three meals—the first of which was ready at six o'clock in the morning— and putting the six children to bed, would often stand until midnight at her ironing-board with me at the kitchen table beside her, hearing me recite Latin declensions and conjugations,[5] gently shaking me when my drowsy head sank down over a page of irregular verbs. It was to her, at her 100 ironing or mending, that I read my first Shakespeare, and her old text-book on mythology was the first that ever came into my empty hands. She taught me my scales and exercises, too—on the little parlor organ, which her husband had bought her after fifteen years, during which she had not so much as seen any instrument, but an accordion that belonged to one of the Norwegian farmhands. She would sit beside me by the hour, darning and counting while I struggled with the "Joyous Farmer," but she seldom talked to me about music, and I understood why. She was a <u>pious</u> woman; she had the 110 consolations of religion and, to her at least, her martyrdom was not wholly <u>sordid</u>. Once when I had been doggedly beating out some easy passages from an old score of *Euryanthe*[6] I had found among her music books, she came up to me and, putting her hands over my eyes, gently drew my head back upon her shoulder, saying tremulously, "Don't love it so well, Clark, or it may be taken from you. Oh! dear boy, pray that whatever your sacrifice may be, it be not that."

When my aunt appeared on the morning after her arrival, she was still in a semi-somnambulant[7] state. She seemed not to 120 realize that she was in the city where she had spent her youth, the place longed for hungrily half a lifetime. She had been so

---

5. **Latin declensions and conjugations** (kŏn´jə-gā´shəns): Latin word endings and verb forms.

6. *Euryanthe* (yōō´rē-ăn´thē): an opera by the German composer Carl Maria von Weber.

7. **Semi-somnambulant** (som-năm´byə-lənt): half asleep or half-sleepwalking.

WORDS TO KNOW

pious (pī´əs) *adj.* having or showing reverence for God
sordid (sôr´dĭd) *adj.* wretched; dirty; morally degraded

wretchedly train-sick throughout the journey that she had no recollection of anything but her discomfort, and, to all intents and purposes, there were but a few hours of nightmare between the farm in Red Willow County and my study on Newbury Street. I had planned a little pleasure for her that afternoon, to repay her for some of the glorious moments she had given me when we used to milk together in the straw-thatched cowshed and she, because I was more than usually tired, or because her husband had spoken sharply to me, would tell me of the splendid performance of the *Huguenots*[8] she had seen in Paris, in her youth. At two o'clock the Symphony Orchestra was to give a (Wagner) program, and I intended to take my aunt; though, as I conversed with her, I grew doubtful about her enjoyment of it. Indeed, for her own sake, I could only wish her taste for such things quite dead, and the long struggle mercifully ended at last. I suggested our visiting the Conservatory and the Common[9] before lunch, but she seemed altogether too timid to wish to venture out. She questioned me absently about various changes in the city, but she was chiefly concerned that she had forgotten to leave instructions about feeding half-skimmed milk to a certain weakling calf, "old Maggie's calf, you know, Clark," she explained, evidently having forgotten how long I had been away. She was further troubled because she had neglected to tell her daughter about the freshly-opened kit of mackerel[10] in the cellar, which would spoil if it were not used directly.

I asked her whether she had ever heard any of the Wagnerian operas,[11] and found that she had not, though she was perfectly familiar with their respective situations, and had once possessed the piano score of *The Flying Dutchman*. I began to think it would have been best to get her back to Red Willow County without waking her, and regretted having suggested the concert.

Pause & Reflect

---

8. *Huguenots* (hyōō′gə-nŏts′): an opera by the German composer Giacomo Meyerbeer.
9. **the Common**: Boston Common, a public park.
10. **mackerel**: a fish commonly found in the Altantic Ocean.
11. **Wagnerian operas**: The orchestra will play selections from several operas composed by Wagner, including *The Flying Dutchman, Tannhauser, Tristan and Isolde,* and a cycle of four operas called *The Ring of the Nibelung.*

More About . . .

(WAGNER) Richard Wagner was a German composer who lived during the nineteenth century. He was famous for his operas. His works are dramatic, bold, and complex. Wagner is considered by many to be the greatest composer of German opera.

☑ **Reading Check**
How has Aunt Georgiana changed since leaving Boston?

Pause & Reflect

1. Look at the two passages that you circled as you read. What do they reveal about the kind of person Aunt Georgiana is? (Draw Conclusions About Character)

_____
_____
_____

_____

📖 READ ALOUD   2. Read aloud the boxed passage on page 228. Aunt Georgiana is trying to tell Clark_____

_____

_____

_____.

(Paraphrase)

- Clark and Aunt Georgiana go to the concert.

- The music makes Clark think about his aunt's life in Nebraska.

- Aunt Georgiana is moved by the music.

☑ Reading Check

Why is Clark concerned about what his aunt is wearing?

What Does It Mean?

In the highlighted lines, the narrator compares his aunt to old miners who know that even if they cleaned up and dressed exactly like everyone else, they still would not fit in.

READ ALOUD Lines 176–187

As you read these lines aloud, picture the scene described. What contrast is there between Aunt Georgiana and the other women at the matinee?
(Compare and Contrast)

_____

_____

_____

_____

FOCUS
Clark and his aunt arrive at the concert hall, and the music begins.

✎ MARK IT UP Circle details that tell you something about how Aunt Georgiana reacts to the concert hall and to the music.

160

From the time we entered the concert hall, however, she was a trifle less passive and inert, and for the first time seemed to perceive her surroundings. I had felt some <u>trepidation</u> lest she might become aware of the absurdities of her attire, or might experience some painful embarrassment at stepping suddenly into the world to which she had been dead for a quarter of a century. But, again, I found how <u>superficially</u> I had judged her. She sat looking about her with eyes as impersonal, almost as stony, as those with which the granite Rameses[12] in a museum watches the froth and fret that ebbs and flows[13] about his pedestal—separated from it by the lonely stretch of centuries. I have seen this same

170 aloofness in old miners who drift into the Brown hotel at Denver, their pockets full of bullion,[14] their linen soiled, their haggard faces unshaven; standing in the thronged corridors as solitary as though they were still in a frozen camp on the Yukon,[15] conscious that certain experiences have isolated them from their fellows by a gulf no haberdasher[16] could bridge.

We sat at the extreme left of the first balcony, facing the arc of our own and the balcony above us, veritable hanging gardens, brilliant as tulip beds. The matinée audience was made up chiefly of women. One lost the contour of faces and

180 figures, indeed any effect of line whatever, and there was only the color of bodices past counting, the shimmer of fabrics soft and firm, silky and sheer; red, mauve, pink, blue, lilac, purple, ecru, rose, yellow, cream, and white, all the colors that an impressionist[17] finds in a sunlit landscape, with here and there the dead shadow of a frock coat. My Aunt Georgiana regarded them as though they had been so many daubs of tube-paint on a palette.

---

12. **Rameses** (răm'sēz'): one of the ancient kings of Egypt of that name.

13. **froth . . . flows:** happiness and sadness that comes and goes.

14. **bullion:** gold.

15. **Yukon** (yoo'kŏn'): a river in the Yukon Territory, in northwest Canada.

16. **haberdasher:** someone who sells men's clothing.

17. **impressionist:** member of a movement in French painting that emphasized the play of light and color.

WORDS
TO
KNOW

trepidation (trĕp'ĭ-dā'shən) n. fearful uncertainty or worry
superficially (soo'pər-fĭsh'ə-lē) adv. in a shallow way; concerned with only what is obvious

When the musicians came out and took their places, she gave a little stir of anticipation and looked with quickening interest down over the rail at that invariable grouping, perhaps the first wholly familiar thing that had greeted her eye since she had left old Maggie and her weakling calf. I could feel how all those details sank into her soul, for I had not forgotten how they had sunk into mine when I came fresh from ploughing forever and forever between green aisles of corn, where, as in a treadmill, one might walk from daybreak to dusk without perceiving a shadow of change. The clean profiles of the musicians, the gloss of their linen, the dull black of their coats, the beloved shapes of the instruments, the patches of yellow light thrown by the green shaded lamps on the smooth, varnished bellies of the 'cellos and the bass viols in the rear, the restless, wind-tossed forest of fiddle necks and bows—I recalled how, in the first orchestra I had ever heard, those long bow strokes seemed to draw the heart out of me, as a conjurer's stick reels out yards of paper ribbon from a hat.

The first number was the *Tannhauser* overture. When the horns drew out the first strain of the Pilgrim's chorus, my Aunt Georgiana clutched my coat sleeve. Then it was I first realized that for her this broke a silence of thirty years; the inconceivable silence of the plains. With the battle between the two motives, with the frenzy of the Venusberg theme and its ripping of strings, there came to me an overwhelming sense of the waste and wear we are so powerless to combat; and I saw again the tall, naked house on the prairie, black and grim as a wooden fortress; the black pond where I had learned to swim, its margin pitted with sun-dried cattle tracks; the rain gullied clay banks about the naked house, the four dwarf ash seedlings where the dishcloths were always hung to dry before the kitchen door. The world there was the flat world of the ancients; to the east, a cornfield that stretched to daybreak; to the west, a corral that reached to sunset; between, the conquests of peace, dearer bought than those of war.

The overture closed, my aunt released my coat sleeve, but she said nothing. She sat staring at the orchestra through a dullness of thirty years, through the films made little by little by each of the three hundred and sixty-five days in every one of them. What, I wondered, did she get from it? She had been a good pianist in her day I knew, and her musical education had been broader than that of most music teachers of a

What Does It Mean?
Quickening means "coming to life."

What Does It Mean?
Conjurer's stick refers to a magician's wand.

☑ **Reading Check**

How does Aunt Georgiana react as she listens to the first number?

☆ **Reader Success Strategy**

In this section, notice the contrast between life in Nebraska and life in Boston. As you read, fill in the chart below to compare the two places.

Nebraska	Boston

quarter of a century ago. She had often told me of Mozart's operas and Meyerbeer's, and I could remember hearing her sing, years ago, certain melodies of Verdi's. When I had fallen ill with a fever in her house she used to sit by my cot in the evening—when the cool, night wind blew in through the faded mosquito netting tacked over the window and I lay watching a certain bright star that burned red above the cornfield—and sing "Home to our mountains, O, let us return!" in a way fit to break the heart of a Vermont boy near dead of homesickness already.

Pause & Reflect

240

> **FOCUS**
>
> As the concert goes on, Clark watches his aunt closely.
>
> **MARK IT UP** Underline passages that show Aunt Georgiana's changing responses to the music.

I watched her closely through the prelude to *Tristan and Isolde,* trying vainly to conjecture what that seething turmoil of strings and winds might mean to her, but she sat mutely staring at the violin bows that drove obliquely downward, like the pelting streaks of rain in a summer shower. Had this music any message for her? Had she enough left to at all comprehend this power which had kindled the world since she had left it? I was in a fever of curiosity, but Aunt Georgiana sat silent upon her peak in Darien.[18] She preserved this utter immobility throughout the number from *The Flying Dutchman,* though her fingers worked mechanically upon her black dress, as though, of themselves, they were recalling the piano score they had once played. Poor old hands! They had been stretched and twisted into mere tentacles to hold and lift and knead with; the palms unduly swollen, the fingers bent and knotted—on one of them a thin, worn band that had once been a wedding ring. As I pressed and gently quieted one of those groping hands, I remembered with quivering eyelids their services for me in other days.

---

18. **peak in Darien** (dâr′ē-ĕn′): an allusion to a poem by the English poet John Keats. In the poem Keats describes Spanish explorers on a mountain in Darien, a region that is now Panama. The Spaniards stand silent and amazed as they become the first Europeans to view the Pacific Ocean.

WORDS
TO
KNOW

conjecture (kən-jĕk′chər) *v.* to make a judgment on the basis of uncertain evidence; guess

---

Pause & Reflect

Look back at the details that you circled as you read. What do you think Aunt Georgiana is feeling when she arrives at the concert hall? **(Draw Conclusions About Character)**

_____

_____

_____

_____

As the story ends . . .

- Clark observes his aunt closely throughout the concert.
- Some of the music is familiar to her.
- Aunt Georgiana has strong feelings at the end of the concert.

What Does It Mean?

Strings and winds refers to musical instruments. A violin is an example of a string instrument and a flute is an example of a wind instrument.

Soon after the tenor began the "Prize Song," I heard a quick drawn breath and turned to my aunt. Her eyes were closed, but the tears were glistening on her cheeks, and I think, in a moment more, they were in my eyes as well. It never really died, then—the soul that can suffer so <u>excruciatingly</u> and so interminably; it withers to the outward eye only; like that strange moss which can lie on a dusty shelf half a century and yet, if placed in water, grows green again. She wept so
270 throughout the development and elaboration of the melody.

During the intermission before the second half of the concert, I questioned my aunt and found that the "Prize Song" was not new to her. Some years before there had drifted to the farm in Red Willow County a young German, a tramp cow puncher, who had sung the chorus at Bayreuth,[19] when he was a boy, along with the other peasant boys and girls. Of a Sunday morning he used to sit on his gingham-sheeted bed in the hands' bedroom which opened off the kitchen, cleaning the leather of his boots and saddle, singing
280 the "Prize Song," while my aunt went about her work in the kitchen. She had hovered about him until she had prevailed upon him to join the country church, though his sole fitness for this step, in so far as I could gather, lay in his boyish face and his possession of this divine melody. Shortly afterward he had gone to town on the Fourth of July, been drunk for several days, lost his money at a faro[20] table, ridden a saddled Texas steer on a bet, and disappeared with a fractured collarbone. All this my aunt told me huskily, wanderingly, as though she were talking in the weak lapses of illness.

290 "Well, we have come to better things than the old *Trovatore*[21] at any rate, Aunt Georgie?" I queried, with a well meant effort at jocularity.

Her lip quivered and she hastily put her handkerchief up to her mouth. From behind it she murmured, "And you have been hearing this ever since you left me, Clark?" Her question was the gentlest and saddest of reproaches.

---

19. **Bayreuth** (bī-roit'): the Bayreuth Festival, an annual international music festival in Germany that presents Wagner's operas.

20. **faro**: a gambling game.

21. *Trovatore* (trô'vä-tô're): *Il Trovatore* is an opera by the Italian composer Giuseppe Verdi.

WORDS
TO
KNOW
excruciatingly (ĭk-skrōō'shē-ā'tĭng-lə) *adv.* in a way that causes great pain or distress

☑ **Reading Check**
How is Aunt Georgiana like "that strange moss"?

More About . . .
A cow puncher, or a cowboy, is someone who tends cattle. During this time, some cowboys moved from place to place, looking for work. They were called "tramps" because they had no fixed place to live or specific place to go.

What Does It Mean?
Reproaches means "expressions of disappointment or displeasure." The tone of Aunt Georgiana's question suggests that she is sad, nostalgic, and a little envious.

The second half of the program consisted of four numbers from the *Ring*, and closed with Siegfried's funeral march. My aunt wept quietly, but almost continuously, as a shallow vessel overflows in a rainstorm. From time to time her dim eyes looked up at the lights which studded the ceiling, burning softly under their dull glass globes; doubtless they were stars in truth to her. I was still perplexed as to what measure of musical comprehension was left to her, she who had heard nothing but the singing of Gospel Hymns at Methodist services in the square frame school-house on Section Thirteen for so many years. I was wholly unable to gauge how much of it had been dissolved in soapsuds, or worked into bread, or milked into the bottom of a pail.

The deluge of sound poured on and on; I never knew what she found in the shining current of it; I never knew how far it bore her, or past what happy islands. From the trembling of her face I could well believe that before the last numbers she had been carried out where the myriad graves are, into the grey, nameless burying grounds of the sea; or into some world of death vaster yet, where, from the beginning of the world, hope has lain down with hope and dream with dream and, renouncing,[22] slept.

The concert was over; the people filed out of the hall chattering and laughing, glad to relax and find the living level again, but my kinswoman made no effort to rise. The harpist slipped its green felt cover over his instrument; the flute-players shook the water from their mouthpieces; the men of the orchestra went out one by one, leaving the stage to the chairs and music stands, empty as a winter cornfield.

I spoke to my aunt. She burst into tears and sobbed pleadingly. "I don't want to go, Clark, I don't want to go!"

I understood. For her, just outside the door of the concert hall, lay the black pond with the cattle-tracked bluffs; the tall, unpainted house, with weather-curled boards; naked as a tower, the crook-backed ash seedlings where the dish-cloths hung to dry; the gaunt, molting turkeys picking up refuse about the kitchen door.

Pause & *Reflect*

✔ **Reading Check**

What opportunities to hear music does Aunt Georgiana have in Nebraska?

Pause & *Reflect*

Read aloud the boxed passage on this page. What are Aunt Georgiana's feelings at the end of the concert? **(Draw Conclusions About Character)**

_____

_____

_____

_____

CHALLENGE

In what ways do you think Aunt Georgiana has influenced the behavior and attitudes of the narrator? Review the story and mark passages that support your conclusions. **(Draw Conclusions)**

22. **renouncing:** giving up.

Active Reading SkillBuilder

Drawing Conclusions About Character

Readers **draw conclusions,** or make logical decisions, about what a character is like by combining all the information that they learn about the character while reading the story. When reading this story, pay close attention to details that reveal Aunt Georgiana's personality, including what she says and does and how Cather describes her. Fill in the chart below, explaining what these details reveal about the kind of person Aunt Georgiana is. Later, you will use this evidence to draw conclusions about her. Examples are given.

Observations	What They Reveal
Physical appearance clothes covered with soot and dust	She is not interested in how she looks.
Major decisions	
Actions and reactions helped Clark with his Latin homework and taught him music	She is well-educated and continues to care about learning and music.

Literary Analysis SkillBuilder

Setting

Setting is the time and place of the action of a literary work. The action may occur in a real or an imaginary place in the past, present, or future. In this story, Cather portrays two very different places—a Nebraska farm and the Boston concert hall—that have important effects on Aunt Georgiana. Review the story and use the "houses" below to record details that describe these two contrasting settings. Examples are given.

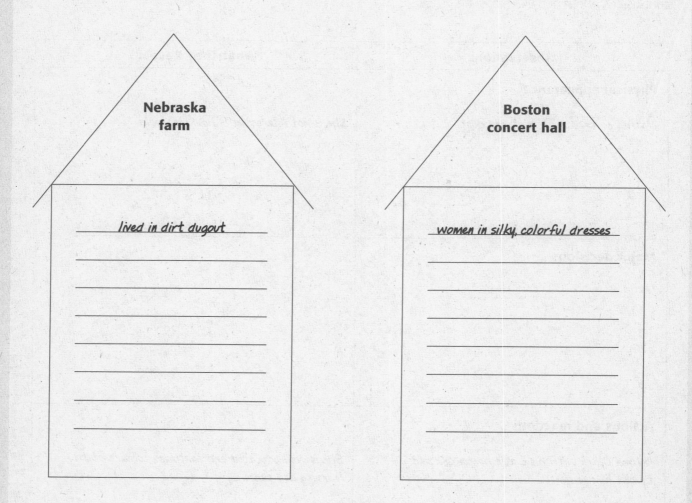

Nebraska farm

lived in dirt dugout

_____

_____

_____

_____

_____

_____

Boston concert hall

women in silky, colorful dresses

_____

_____

_____

_____

_____

_____

Follow Up: Using the details that you listed, sketch each of the settings. Then compare your drawings with those of your classmates.

Words to Know SkillBuilder

Words to Know

callow	excruciatingly	pathetic	reproach	superficially
conjecture	inexplicable	pious	sordid	trepidation

A. Each of the following sentences suggests a word in the word list. The word itself is hidden in the sentence. Underline the hidden word and then write it on the line. An example, using another word from the story, has been done for you.

Example: Between the verses is the familiar section I most like to teach, or   to, back when I had music students.   *chorus*

1. Is the condition of this house the result of laziness, or did you think the filth and trash would disappear by magic?

   _____ (1)

2. Your childish treatment of the topic keeps your report from being properly scientific. Allow me to add my mature wisdom.

   _____ (2)

3. Pa, the ticks are so bad that poor Spot is covered with them. He's miserable, and I'm afraid he'll get sick!

   _____ (3)

4. Appropriate music for church is rarely rock or rap, IOUs are not proper offerings, and swimwear offends the congregation.

   _____ (4)

B. Decide which word from the word list belongs in each numbered blank. Then write the word on the blank line on the right.

The famine's cause was far from evident;
It was an (1) event.

_____ (1)

Your stern look makes me (2)
I'm about to get a lecture.

_____ (2)

When I messed up, the angry coach
Administered a sharp (3).
He couldn't help but blow a gasket.
I'd scored in the opponents' basket.

_____ (3)

A gnat or fly can drive you nuts, by acting irritatingly.
But either's better than a wasp, which stings (4).

_____ (4)

Before a test, I wouldn't call my mood anticipation.
It's quite a bit more accurate to call it (5).

_____ (5)

A lot of my confusion will remain
If you just (6) explain.

_____ (6)

C. Imagine that Aunt Georgiana decides to remain in Boston. Write a letter she might send to her husband explaining her decision. Use at least **five** of the Words to Know.

"Hope" is the thing with feathers

I heard a Fly buzz when I died

Because I could not stop for Death

My life closed twice before its close

Emily Dickinson

Before You Read

Connect to Your Life

What words would you use to describe hope? What words would you use to describe death? Are any of the words the same? Fill in the Venn diagram below with your responses.

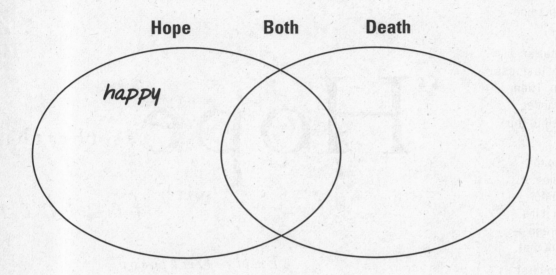

Hope **Both** **Death**

happy

Key to the Poems

WHAT TO LISTEN FOR Emily Dickinson's poems have a rhythm of stressed and unstressed words or syllables. Read aloud the following lines from "My life closed twice before its close." Notice that each stressed word or syllable has been underlined.

My <u>life</u> closed <u>twice</u> be<u>fore</u> its <u>close</u>—

It <u>yet</u> re<u>mains</u> to <u>see</u>

Now read these lines. Underline the stressed words and syllables.

Because I could not stop for Death—

He kindly stopped for me—

Reading Tips

Many readers find Emily Dickinson's poems difficult. She often relies on sugges-tion, and she uses words in unusual ways. She is inven-tive in her capitalization and makes use of many dashes. To make sense of these poems, allow your imagina-tion to run free.

- When you encounter an unusual phrase, try to guess what it might mean. Then see if your guess makes sense when applied to the poem.

- Don't worry if you can't understand every line. Focus on what you do understand—even if it's only one line or phrase—and try to build from that.

- Read each poem several times, and at least once aloud.

As the poem begins . . .

- Like a bird, hope perches.

- Like a bird, hope sings a tune without any words.

What Does It Mean?

This metaphor explains that hope resides deep down in all of us.

PREVIEW Emily Dickinson was a person of contrasts. She lived what appeared to be an extremely quiet and simple life in 19th-century New England. Yet she wrote many poems that are highly original in thought and style. They express strong feelings and ideas, and they often reveal insights in unexpected ways. Although only a few of her poems were published in her lifetime, Dickinson is now considered a major American poet.

"Hope" is the thing with *feathers*

Emily Dickinson

> **FOCUS**
> In this poem, Dickinson compares hope to a bird.
> **MARK IT UP** Underline words and phrases that describe a bird. An example is highlighted.

"Hope" is the thing with feathers—
That perches in the soul—
And sings the tune without the words—
And never stops—at all—

5 And sweetest—in the Gale[1]—is heard—
And sore[2] must be the storm—
That could abash[3] the little Bird
That kept so many warm—

I've heard it in the chillest land—
10 And on the strangest Sea—
Yet, never, in Extremity,[4]
It asked a crumb—of Me.

Pause **&** **Reflect**

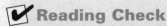

Reading Check

How is the little bird in a storm like hope during troubled times?

Reader Success Strategy

Dickinson used dashes to highlight important words and help break up the singsong rhythm of her poems. To help you understand the poems, try reading them aloud and pausing at each dash.

Pause **&** **Reflect**

1. Look at the words and phrases that you underlined as you read. List the details about the bird that seem important to you. **(Evaluate)**

_____

_____

_____

_____

READ ALOUD **2.** Read aloud the two boxed lines. The bird doesn't ask for a crumb from the speaker, not even when it is in great need. What message about hope do you think the speaker may be expressing here? **(Reading Poetry)**

_____

_____

_____

_____

1. **Gale:** extremely strong wind.
2. **sore:** severe.
3. **abash:** frustrate; baffle
4. **Extremity:** greatest need or peril.

My life closed twice before its close

Emily Dickinson

FOCUS

The speaker describes how it feels to lose someone you love. As you read, look for signs of how great the impact of loss can be.

My life closed twice before its close[1]—
It yet remains to see
If Immortality unveil
A third event to me[2]

5 So huge, so hopeless to conceive
As these that twice befell.[3]
Parting is all we know of heaven,[4]
And all we need of hell.

Pause & Reflect

As the poem begins . . .

- The speaker looks ahead to her own death.
- The speaker states that she has already experienced two events that "closed" her life.

Pause & Reflect

1. What might the two events that closed her life be? **(Infer)**

_____

_____

_____

_____

2 Complete the following sentences:
Parting tells us "all we know of heaven" because _____

_____

_____.

Parting gives us "all we need of hell" because _____

_____

_____.

(Analyze)

---

1. **close:** end; the speaker's death.
2. **If . . . third event:** The speaker is referring to her own death. She wonders if she will experience an afterlife.
3. **befell** (bĭ-fĕl′): happened.
4. **Parting . . . heaven:** When people die, it is often said that they have gone to heaven. Those left behind, of course, do not have any direct experience of heaven.

I heard a Fly buzz when I died

Emily Dickinson

As the poem begins . . .

- The speaker hears a buzzing fly.
- The speaker sees and hears family and friends who stand or sit nearby.
- The sounds and sights fade as death approaches.

FOCUS

The speaker in this poem describes the moments leading up to her death.

MARK IT UP Underline details that tell what the speaker sees and hears as she is dying.

I heard a Fly buzz—when I died—
The Stillness in the Room
Was like the Stillness in the Air—
Between the Heaves[1] of Storm—

5   The Eyes around—had wrung them dry—
And Breaths were gathering firm
For that last Onset—when the King[2]
Be witnessed—in the Room[3]—

I willed my Keepsakes—Signed away
10 What portion of me be
Assignable[4]—and then it was
There interposed[5] a Fly—

More About . . .

STORMS During a *storm*, there are often brief moments of silence and calm between bursts of bad weather. In lines 2–4, the speaker compares the stillness in the room to those quiet moments in a storm.

READ ALOUD   Lines 5–8

Read aloud the boxed lines, paying attention to the capitalized words. In these lines the speaker describes the mourners. What does she observe about their "Eyes" and "Breaths"? **(Clarify)**

_____
_____
_____
_____

What Does It Mean?

Onset means "the moment of death."

---

1. **Heaves:** risings and fallings.
2. **the King:** God.
3. **in the Room:** in the 19th century, people usually died at home in the presence of friends and family.
4. **I willed . . . Assignable:** The speaker seems to be referring to her physical possessions, such as those that might be included in a will. *Assignable* is a legal term referring to things that might be given away.
5. **interposed:** came between

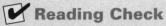

Reading Check

Reread lines 9–11. What does the speaker take care of just before she dies?

Pause & Reflect

1. Reread lines 11–14. What does the speaker sense that the fly has done? What might the fly represent? **(Infer)**

   _____

   _____

   _____

2. Describe, in your own words, what is happening at the very end of the poem. **(Reading Poetry)**

   _____

   _____

   _____

With Blue—uncertain stumbling Buzz—
Between the light—and me—
And then the Windows failed—and then
I could not see to see—

Pause & Reflect

Because I could not stop for Death

Emily Dickinson

FOCUS

In this poem, death is pictured as a carriage driver. The speaker imagines herself riding in death's carriage.

MARK IT UP Underline words and phrases that help you visualize death as a carriage driver.

Because I could not stop for Death—
He kindly stopped for me—
The Carriage held but just Ourselves—
And Immortality.

5   We slowly drove—He knew no haste
And I had put away
My labor and my leisure too,
For His Civility[1]—

We passed the School, where Children strove
10   At Recess—in the Ring—
We passed the Fields of Gazing Grain[2]—
We passed the Setting Sun—

Or rather—He[3] passed Us—
The Dews drew quivering and chill[4]—
15   For only Gossamer,[5] my Gown—
My Tippet[6]—only Tulle[7]—

---

1. **Civility:** politeness.
2. **Gazing Grain:** grain leaning toward the sun.
3. **He:** the sun.
4. **The Dews . . . chill:** It is so cold that even the dew seems to shiver.
5. **Gossamer:** a thin, light cloth.
6. **Tippet:** shawl.
7. **Tulle** (tool): fine netting.

As the poem begins . . .

- Death picks up the speaker in a carriage.
- As the speaker and the driver travel along, they pass many familiar scenes.
- The speaker becomes aware of the setting sun.

☆ Reader Success Strategy

Dickinson uses a device called **personification** in this poem. She makes death a character and gives him human qualities. Read the poem carefully and highlight details about the passengers in the carriage.

What Does It Mean?

Here, *immortality* means "unending life in the world beyond this one."

✔ Reading Check

Why does the speaker feel chilled? What might this mean?

Eternity is time without end. The speaker uses this term to refer to life after death.

Pause & Reflect

1. Read through the words and phrases that you underlined as you read. How would you describe the character of the carriage driver? **(Reading Poetry)**

_____

_____

_____

_____

MARK IT UP **2.** Circle four things the speaker sees during the carriage ride (lines 9–12). **(Clarify)**

READ ALOUD **3.** Read lines 17–20 aloud. What do you think this house represents? **(Reading Poetry)**

_____

_____

_____

CHALLENGE

Three of these poems are concerned with death. In two of them, the speaker is someone who has already died. How do you think Dickinson feels about death? Is she frightened? Angry? Calm? Use the poems to support your opinions. **(Analyze)**

We paused before a House that seemed
A Swelling of the Ground—
The Roof was scarcely visible—
The Cornice[7]—in the Ground—

20

Since then—'tis Centuries—and yet
Feels shorter than the Day
I first surmised[8] the Horses' Heads
Were toward Eternity—

Pause & Reflect

7. **Cornice** (kôr′nĭs): the molding around the top of a building.

8. **surmised** (sər-mīzd′): guessed.

Active Reading SkillBuilder

Strategies for Reading Poetry

The following suggestions can help readers increase their understanding and enjoyment of Dickinson's poetry. Read each poem once for overall impression and once for meaning; then read it aloud to appreciate Dickinson's unique **style, rhythm,** and **imagery;** note the **figurative language** and words that are capitalized for emphasis; pause when you encounter dashes, just as you do when you come to commas or periods in a poem.

Use the chart below to record your questions about any poetic element or device. One example is included.

Poems	Questions
"'Hope' is the thing with feathers—"	*Why is "Gale" capitalized, but not "storm" (lines 5-6)?*
"My life closed twice before its close—"	
"I heard a Fly buzz—when I died—"	
"Because I could not stop for Death—"	

Literary Analysis SkillBuilder

Figurative Language

Figurative language consists of groups of words that express ideas beyond the literal meaning of the words. Dickinson's poetry features such common figures of speech as **similes**—comparisons that use *like* or *as;* **metaphors**—direct comparisons between two unlike things; **extended metaphors**—comparisons of two things at length and in several ways; and **personification**—figurative language that gives human characteristics to an object, animal, or idea. Examples of personification and extended metaphor from Dickinson's poems are given below. In the four poems you have read, find one example of a simile and one example of a metaphor. Then fill in the remaining boxes.

Figures of Speech

Personification	Extended Metaphor
Death is personified as a kind gentleman in "Because I could not stop for Death."	"'Hope' is the thing with feathers" compares hope to a bird.
Simile	**Metaphor**

THE YELLOW WALLPAPER

CHARLOTTE PERKINS GILMAN

Before You Read

Connect to Your Life

Imagine you are forced to spend a few weeks alone in your room. What would you do to entertain yourself in such a situation? List your ideas on the lines below.

What I'd Do

listen to the radio

_____

_____

_____

_____

_____

Key to the Story

WHAT YOU NEED TO KNOW Charlotte Perkins Gilman wrote this story in 1890. At that time, mental illnesses such as depression were not treated medically. Many doctors told patients who suffered from depression to rest and to spend time alone. Patients were not permitted to read, write, or see friends. Such treatments often made the patients' illnesses get worse instead of better.

THE YELLOW WALLPAPER

CHARLOTTE PERKINS GILMAN

PREVIEW This story, set in the 1890s, is narrated by a young married woman whose husband is a doctor. He believes that his wife has a "nervous condition" and tells her to rest and do no work. The husband, John, has rented an old mansion for them for the summer. The narrator, who is never named, spends most of her time in a large top-floor room that has ugly yellow wallpaper. She pays more and more attention to the wallpaper and keeps a secret journal about what she sees and feels. Her journal—the story—lets us inside her mind as her thoughts and behavior become increasingly strange.

FOCUS

In this section, the narrator writes about her husband, the house where they are living, and her mental state.

MARK IT UP Underline words and phrases the narrator uses to describe the wallpaper in her room. Two examples have been highlighted on page 254.

10

It is very seldom that mere ordinary people like John and myself secure ancestral halls for the summer.

A colonial mansion, a hereditary estate, I would say a haunted house, and reach the height of romantic <u>felicity</u>—but that would be asking too much of fate!

Still I will proudly declare that there is something queer about it.

WORDS TO KNOW   **felicity** (fĭ-lĭs'ĭ-tē) *n.* happiness; bliss

Reading Tips

This short story is told by a **first-person narrator.** Because the narrator is becoming mentally ill, her story can be confusing.

- Pay attention to both the narrator's view of her illness and to her husband's view.

- Jot down in the margins any questions that come to mind. Then read on to see if the story gives you the answers.

- Pay attention to changes in the way the narrator describes the wallpaper. Try to figure out what she really sees and what she imagines.

As the story begins . . .

- The narrator and her husband are spending the summer in an old house.

- The narrator's husband is a doctor and he doesn't believe that she is sick.

- The narrator explains that she is forced to stay in a room upstairs that she doesn't like. She finds the wallpaper particularly ugly.

Else, why should it be let[1] so cheaply? And why have stood so long untenanted?

John laughs at me, of course, but one expects that in marriage.

John is practical in the extreme. He has no patience with faith, an intense horror of superstition, and he scoffs openly at any talk of things not to be felt and seen and put down in figures.

20 John is a physician, and *perhaps*—(I would not say it to a living soul, of course, but this is dead paper and a great relief to my *mind*)—*perhaps* that is one reason I do not get well faster.

You see he does not believe I am sick!

And what can one do?

If a physician of high standing, and one's own husband, assures friends and relatives that there is really nothing the matter with one but temporary nervous depression—a slight (hysterical[2]) tendency—what is one to do?

My brother is also a physician, and also of high standing, and he says the same thing.

30 So I take phosphates or phosphites—whichever it is, and tonics, and journeys, and air, and exercise, and am absolutely forbidden to "work" until I am well again.

Personally, I disagree with their ideas.

Personally, I believe that congenial work, with excitement and change, would do me good.

But what is one to do?

I did write for a while in spite of them; but it *does* exhaust me a good deal—having to be so sly about it, or else meet with heavy opposition.

40 I sometimes fancy that in my condition if I had less opposition and more society and stimulus—but John says the very worst thing I can do is to think about my condition, and I confess it always makes me feel bad.

So I will let it alone and talk about the house.

The most beautiful place! It is quite alone, standing well back from the road, quite three miles from the village. It makes me think of English places that you read about, for there are hedges and walls and gates that lock, and lots of separate little houses for the gardeners and people.

---

1. **let:** rented.

2. **hysterical:** Hysteria is the presence of a physical ailment with no underlying physical cause.

There is a *delicious* garden! I never saw such a garden—large and shady, full of box-bordered paths, and lined with long grape-covered arbors with seats under them.

There were greenhouses, too, but they are all broken now.

There was some legal trouble, I believe, something about the heirs and coheirs; anyhow, the place has been empty for years.

That spoils my ghostliness, I am afraid, but I don't care—there is something strange about the house—I can feel it.

I even said so to John one moonlight evening, but he said what I felt was a draft, and shut the window.

I get unreasonably angry with John sometimes. I'm sure I never used to be so sensitive. I think it is due to this nervous condition.

But John says if I feel so, I shall neglect proper self-control; so I take pains to control myself—before him, at least, and that makes me very tired.

I don't like our room a bit. I wanted one downstairs that opened on the piazza and had roses all over the window, and such pretty old-fashioned chintz hangings! but John would not hear of it.

He said there was only one window and not room for two beds, and no near room for him if he took another.

He is very careful and loving, and hardly lets me stir without special direction.

I have a schedule prescription for each hour in the day; he takes all care from me, and so I feel <u>basely</u> ungrateful not to value it more.

He said we came here solely on my account, that I was to have perfect rest and all the air I could get. "Your exercise depends on your strength, my dear," said he, "and your food somewhat on your appetite; but air you can absorb all the time." So we took the nursery at the top of the house.

It is a big, airy room, the whole floor nearly, with windows that look all ways, and air and sunshine galore. It was nursery first and then playroom and gymnasium, I should judge; for the windows are barred for little children, and there are rings and things in the walls.

What Does It Mean?
A *piazza* is a large, covered porch.

✔ **Reading Check**
What makes the narrator angry with her husband?

WORDS
TO
KNOW   **basely** (bās'lē) *adv.* dishonorably; meanly

1. Why is the narrator writing in secret? **(Cause and Effect)**

_____

_____

_____

_____

2. Describe the relationship between the narrator and her husband. **(Infer)**

_____

_____

_____

_____

3. Look at the words and phrases that you underlined as you read. What does the wallpaper look like? **(Visualize)**

_____

_____

_____

_____

As the story continues . . .

- The narrator begins to hate the room where she has been forced to stay.

- The narrator says that her husband doesn't think her illness is serious.

The paint and paper look as if a boys' school had used it. It is stripped off—the paper—in great patches all around the head of my bed, about as far as I can reach, and in a great place on the other side of the room low down. I never saw a worse paper in my life.

One of those sprawling flamboyant patterns committing every artistic sin.

It is dull enough to confuse the eye in following, pronounced enough to constantly irritate and provoke study, and when you follow the lame uncertain curves for a little distance they suddenly commit suicide—plunge off at outrageous angles, destroy themselves in unheard of contradictions.

The color is repellent, almost revolting; a smouldering unclean yellow, strangely faded by the slow-turning sunlight.

It is a dull yet lurid orange in some places, a sickly sulphur tint in others.

No wonder the children hated it! I should hate it myself if I had to live in this room long.

There comes John, and I must put this away, —he hates to have me write a word.

Pause & Reflect

FOCUS

In this section, you will learn more about the narrator and how John treats her.

MARK IT UP As you read, underline details that tell about the narrator's state of mind.

We have been here two weeks, and I haven't felt like writing before, since that first day.

I am sitting by the window now, up in this atrocious nursery, and there is nothing to hinder my writing as much as I please, save lack of strength.

John is away all day, and even some nights when his cases are serious.

I am glad my case is not serious!

But these nervous troubles are dreadfully depressing.

John does not know how much I really suffer. He knows there is no *reason* to suffer, and that satisfies him.

WORDS
TO
KNOW

atrocious (ə-trō′shəs) *adj.* shockingly bad or lacking in taste; awful

Of course it is only nervousness. It does weigh on me so not to do my duty in any way!

I meant to be such a help to John, such a real rest and comfort, and here I am a comparative burden already!

Nobody would believe what an effort it is to do what little I am able,—to dress and entertain, and order things.

It is fortunate Mary is so good with the baby. Such a dear baby!

130 And yet I *cannot* be with him, it makes me so nervous.

I suppose John never was nervous in his life. He laughs at me so about this wallpaper!

At first he meant to repaper the room, but afterwards he said that I was letting it get the better of me, and that nothing was worse for a nervous patient than to give way to such fancies.

He said that after the wallpaper was changed it would be the heavy bedstead, and then the barred windows, and then that gate at the head of the stairs, and so on.

140 "You know the place is doing you good," he said, "and really, dear, I don't care to renovate the house just for a three months' rental."

"Then do let us go downstairs," I said, "there are such pretty rooms there."

Then he took me in his arms and called me a blessed little goose, and said he would go down to the cellar, if I wished, and have it whitewashed into the bargain.

But he is right enough about the beds and windows and things.

150 It is an airy and comfortable room as any one need wish, and, of course, I would not be so silly as to make him uncomfortable just for a whim.

I'm really getting quite fond of the big room, all but that horrid paper.

Out of one window I can see the garden, those mysterious deepshaded arbors, the riotous old-fashioned flowers, and bushes and gnarly trees.

Out of another I get a lovely view of the bay and a little private wharf belonging to the estate. There is a beautiful shaded lane that runs down there from the house. I always 160 fancy I see people walking in these numerous paths and arbors, but John has cautioned me not to give way to fancy in the least. He says that with my imaginative power and habit of story-making, a nervous weakness like mine is sure to lead

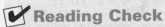

Reading Check

How does the narrator feel about her role in her marriage?

⭐ **Reader Success Strategy**

As you read, pay close attention to the narrator's descriptions of the wallpaper and the way her feelings toward the wallpaper change. Highlight the portions of the text in which she describes the wallpaper. Then, keep track of the way the narrator's feelings toward the wallpaper change in the flow chart below.

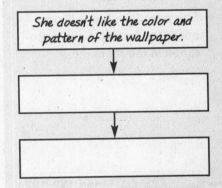

She doesn't like the color and pattern of the wallpaper.

↓

↓

✏️ **MARK IT UP** Lines 140–152

Reread lines 140–152. Circle words or phrases that show John's attitude toward the narrator. **(Analyze)**

What Does It Mean?

In line 161, *fancy* is a verb that means "imagine." In line 162, it is a noun, meaning "imagination."

Pause & Reflect

1. Review the details you underlined as you read. How would
you describe the narrator's
state of mind? **(Infer)**

_____

_____

_____

2. The narrator mentions her
writing several times in this
section. Why do you think
writing is important to her?
(Draw Conclusions)

_____

_____

_____

As the story continues . . .

• The narrator says that the
wallpaper is preventing her
from getting well.

• She describes her feelings
about the furniture and deco-
ration in the room.

READ ALOUD Lines 189–197

How would you describe the
narrator's imagination as a child?
(Infer)

_____

_____

_____

_____

to all manner of excited fancies, and that I ought to use my
will and good sense to check the tendency. So I try.

I think sometimes that if I were only well enough to write a
little it would relieve the press of ideas and rest me.

But I find I get pretty tired when I try.

170 It is so discouraging not to have any advice and
companionship about my work. When I get really well, John
says we will ask Cousin Henry and Julia down for a long visit;
but he says he would as soon put fireworks in my pillowcase
as to let me have those stimulating people about now.

Pause & Reflect

FOCUS

Now the narrator gives
more details about
what she sees in the
wallpaper. She also
describes other parts
of the room. As you
180 read, think about why
the narrator reacts
so strongly to the
wallpaper.

I wish I could get well faster.

But I must not think about that. This
paper looks to me as if it knew what a
vicious influence it had!

There is a recurrent spot where the
pattern lolls like a broken neck and two
bulbous eyes stare at you upside down.

I get positively angry with the
<u>impertinence</u> of it and the everlastingness.

Up and down and sideways they crawl,
and those absurd, unblinking eyes are everywhere. There is one
place where two breadths[3] didn't match, and the eyes go all up
and down the line, one a little higher than the other.

I never saw so much expression in an <u>inanimate</u> thing
before, and we all know how much expression they have! I
190 used to lie awake as a child and get more entertainment and
terror out of blank walls and plain furniture than most
children could find in a toystore.

I remember what a kindly wink the knobs of our big, old
bureau used to have, and there was one chair that always
seemed like a strong friend.

I used to feel that if any of the other things looked too
fierce I could always hop into that chair and be safe.

---

3. **breadths:** strips of wallpaper of equal widths.

WORDS
TO
KNOW

impertinence (ĭm-pûr′tn-əns) _n._ improper boldness;
rudeness

inanimate (ĭn-ăn′ə-mĭt) _adj._ not alive; lifeless

The furniture in this room is no worse than inharmonious, however, for we had to bring it all from downstairs. I suppose when this was used as a playroom they had to take the nursery things out, and no wonder! I never saw such ravages as the children have made here.

The wallpaper, as I said before, is torn off in spots, and it sticketh closer than a brother—they must have had <u>perseverance</u> as well as hatred.

Then the floor is scratched and gouged and splintered, the plaster itself is dug out here and there, and this great heavy bed which is all we found in the room, looks as if it had been through the wars.

But I don't mind it a bit—only the paper.

There comes John's sister. Such a dear girl as she is, and so careful of me! I must not let her find me writing.

She is a perfect and enthusiastic housekeeper, and hopes for no better profession. I verily believe she thinks it is the writing which made me sick!

But I can write when she is out, and see her a long way off from these windows.

There is one that commands the road, a lovely shaded winding road, and one that just looks off over the country. A lovely country, too, full of great elms and velvet meadows.

This wallpaper has a kind of sub-pattern in a different shade, a particularly irritating one, for you can only see it in certain lights, and not clearly then.

But in the places where it isn't faded and where the sun is just so—I can see a strange, provoking, formless sort of figure, that seems to skulk about behind that silly and conspicuous front design.

There's sister on the stairs!

Pause **&** *Reflect*

Pause **&** *Reflect*

1. What does John's sister do in the house? **(Clarify)**

_____

_____

2. Circle three words below that describe the narrator's reactions to the wallpaper. **(Infer)**

peaceful   happy

annoyed   angry

intrigued   uninterested

MARK IT UP   3. The narrator sees something behind the wallpaper. Circle the passage in lines 225–228 that tells what she sees. **(Clarify)**

WORDS
TO
KNOW

perseverance (pûr'sə-vîr'əns) *n.* persistence in the face of difficulty; determination

- The narrator says that she cries most of the time.
- She spends most of her time looking at the wallpaper.

More About . . .

(WEIR MITCHELL) The author of this story consulted Dr. Silas Weir Mitchell when she suffered from depression. He advised her to get plenty of rest and to spend only two hours a day thinking. Gilman recovered from her depression, but only after she decided *not* to follow Dr. Mitchell's advice. She wrote this story to protest the "rest cures" that doctors so often prescribed for women.

230 **FOCUS**

The narrator is spending more time looking at the wallpaper.

MARK IT UP As you read, circle details that help you understand her worsening mental condition.

Well, the Fourth of July is over! The people are all gone and I am tired out. John thought it might do me good to see a little company, so we just had mother and Nellie and the children down for a week.

Of course I didn't do a thing. Jennie sees to everything now.

But it tired me all the same.

John says if I don't pick up faster he shall send me to (Weir) **240** (Mitchell[4]) in the fall.

But I don't want to go there at all. I had a friend who was in his hands once, and she says he is just like John and my brother, only more so!

Besides, it is such an undertaking to go so far.

I don't feel as if it was worth while to turn my hand over for anything, and I'm getting dreadfully fretful and <u>querulous</u>.

I cry at nothing, and cry most of the time.

Of course I don't when John is here, or anybody else, but when I am alone.

250 And I am alone a good deal just now. John is kept in town very often by serious cases, and Jennie is good and lets me alone when I want her to.

So I walk a little in the garden or down that lovely lane, sit on the porch under the roses, and lie down up here a good deal.

I'm getting really fond of the room in spite of the wallpaper. Perhaps *because* of the wallpaper.

It dwells in my mind so!

I lie here on this great immovable bed—it is nailed down, I **260** believe—and follow that pattern about by the hour. It is as good as gymnastics, I assure you. I start, we'll say, at the bottom, down in the corner over there where it has not been touched, and I determine for the thousandth time that I *will* follow that pointless pattern to some sort of a conclusion.

I know a little of the principle of design, and I know this thing was not arranged on any laws of radiation, or

---

4. **Weir Mitchell:** Dr. Silas Weir Mitchell, famous for his "rest cure" for nervous diseases, which is no longer considered effective.

WORDS
TO
KNOW

querulous (kwĕr′ə-ləs) *adj.* given to complaining

alternation, or repetition, or symmetry, or anything else that I ever heard of.

It is repeated, of course, by the breadths, but not otherwise.

270 Looked at in one way each breadth stands alone, the bloated curves and flourishes—a kind of "debased Romanesque"[5] with *delirium tremens*[6]—go waddling up and down in isolated columns of fatuity.[7]

But, on the other hand, they connect diagonally, and the sprawling outlines run off in great slanting waves of optic horror, like a lot of wallowing seaweeds in full chase.

The whole thing goes horizontally, too, at least it seems so, and I exhaust myself in trying to distinguish the order of its going in that direction.

280 They have used a horizontal breadth for a frieze[8], and that adds wonderfully to the confusion.

There is one end of the room where it is almost intact, and there, when the crosslights fade and the low sun shines directly upon it, I can almost fancy radiation after all,—the interminable grotesques seem to form around a common center and rush off in headlong plunges of equal distraction.

It makes me tired to follow it. I will take a nap I guess.

I don't know why I should write this.

I don't want to.

290 I don't feel able.

And I know John would think it absurd. But I *must* say what I feel and think in some way—it is such a relief!

But the effort is getting to be greater than the relief.

Half the time now I am awfully lazy, and lie down ever so much.

John says I mustn't lose my strength, and has me take cod liver oil and lots of tonics and things, to say nothing of ale and wine and rare meat.

Dear John! He loves me very dearly, and hates to have me 300 sick. I tried to have a real earnest reasonable talk with him the other day, and tell him how I wish he would let me go and make a visit to Cousin Henry and Julia.

But he said I wasn't able to go, nor able to stand it after I

---

5. **Romanesque:** an artistic style characterized by simple ornamentation.

6. *delirium tremens* (dĭ-lîr′ē-əm trē′mənz): violent trembling and hallucinations caused by excessive drinking.

7. **fatuity** (fə-tōō′ĭ-tē): foolishness; smug stupidity.

8. **frieze** (frēz): a narrow band of wallpaper placed along the upper edge of a wall.

Reader Success Strategy
Reread the boxed text. Be sure to read the footnotes at the bottom of the page to help you understand the difficult language that the narrator uses here to describe the wallpaper. Try to use these details to visualize the pattern in the wallpaper. Then sketch a design that you think would fit this description.

1. Look at the details that you circled as you read. Put an **X** next to the phrase below that does *not* apply to the narrator's mental condition. **(Clarify)**

____ cries all the time

____ has trouble thinking straight

____ screams at her husband

____ stares at the wallpaper

MARK IT UP **2.** The narrator says that she tries to "have a real earnest reasonable talk" with John (lines 300–302). Underline the lines that describe John's response. **(Cause and Effect)**

READ ALOUD **3.** Read aloud the boxed passage. What does the narrator now see "creeping behind" the wallpaper patterns? **(Visualize)**

_____

_____

_____

_____

As the story continues . . .

• The narrator asks her husband if they can leave the house.

• John says that he thinks the narrator's health is improving and that they must stay in the house for the remaining three weeks of the summer.

got there; and I did not make out a very good case for myself, for I was crying before I had finished.

It is getting to be a great effort for me to think straight. Just this nervous weakness I suppose.

And dear John gathered me up in his arms, and just carried me upstairs and laid me on the bed, and sat by me and read 310 to me till it tired my head.

He said I was his darling and his comfort and all he had, and that I must take care of myself for his sake, and keep well.

He says no one but myself can help me out of it, that I must use my will and self-control and not let any silly fancies run away with me.

There's one comfort, the baby is well and happy, and does not have to occupy this nursery with the horrid wallpaper.

If we had not used it, that blessed child would have! What a fortunate escape! Why, I wouldn't have a child of mine, an 320 impressionable little thing, live in such a room for worlds.

I never thought of it before, but it is lucky that John kept me here after all, I can stand it so much easier than a baby, you see.

Of course I never mention it to them any more—I am too wise,—but I keep watch of it all the same.

There are things in that paper that nobody knows but me, or ever will.

> Behind that outside pattern the dim shapes get clearer every day.
>
> 330 It is always the same shape, only very numerous.
>
> And it is like a woman stooping down and creeping about behind that pattern. I don't like it a bit. I wonder—I begin to think—I wish John would take me away from here!

Pause & Reflect

FOCUS

In this section, the narrator tries again to talk to John.

MARK IT UP As you read, circle passages in which the narrator attempts to speak up for herself.

It is so hard to talk with John about my case, because he is so wise, and because he loves me so.

But I tried it last night.

It was moonlight. The moon shines in all around just as the sun does.

I hate to see it sometimes, it creeps so

slowly, and always comes in by one window or another.

John was asleep and I hated to waken him, so I kept still and watched the moonlight on that <u>undulating</u> wallpaper till I felt creepy.

The faint figure behind seemed to shake the pattern, just as if she wanted to get out.

I got up softly and went to feel and see if the paper *did* move, and when I came back John was awake.

"What is it, little girl?" he said. "Don't go walking about like that—you'll get cold."

I thought it was a good time to talk, so I told him that I really was not gaining here, and that I wished he would take me away.

"Why darling!" said he, "our lease will be up in three weeks, and I can't see how to leave before.

"The repairs are not done at home, and I cannot possibly leave town just now. Of course if you were in any danger, I could and would, but you really are better, dear, whether you can see it or not. I am a doctor, dear, and I know. You are gaining flesh and color, your appetite is better, I feel really much easier about you."

"I don't weigh a bit more," said I, "nor as much; and my appetite may be better in the evening when you are here, but it is worse in the morning when you are away!"

"Bless her little heart!" said he with a big hug, "she shall be as sick as she pleases! But now let's improve the shining hours⁹ by going to sleep, and talk about it in the morning!"

"And you won't go away?" I asked gloomily.

"Why, how can I, dear? It is only three weeks more and then we will take a nice little trip of a few days while Jennie is getting the house ready. Really dear you are better!"

"Better in body perhaps—" I began, and stopped short, for he sat up straight and looked at me with such a stern, reproachful look that I could not say another word.

"My darling," said he, "I beg of you, for my sake and for our child's sake, as well as for your own, that you will never

Reading Check
John tends to treat his wife as if she were just a little girl. What effect does this have on her?

What Does It Mean?
When John says "she shall be as sick as she pleases!" he means that the narrator is making herself sick on purpose or imagining that she is sick.

Reader Success Strategy
Reread the dialogue between the narrator and her husband on this page. Using two different colored markers, highlight the narrator's lines of dialogue in one color and John's lines in another color.

---

9. **improve the shining hours:** make good use of time (an allusion to the poem "Against Idleness and Mischief" by Isaac Watts: "How doth the little busy bee / Improve each shining hour, / And gather honey all the day / From every opening flower!").

WORDS TO KNOW 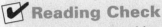 **undulating** (ŭn′jə-lā′tĭng) *adj.* moving with a wavelike motion **undulate** *v.*

Pause & Reflect

In your opinion, is John's treatment of his wife helpful? Why or why not? (**Make Judgments**)

_____

_____

_____

for one instant let that idea enter your mind! There is nothing so dangerous, so fascinating, to a temperament like yours. It is a false and foolish fancy. Can you not trust me as a physician when I tell you so?"

So of course I said no more on that score, and we went to sleep before long. He thought I was asleep first, but I wasn't, and lay there for hours trying to decide whether that front pattern and the back pattern really did move together or separately.

Pause & Reflect

As the story continues...

- The narrator says that the pattern of the wallpaper is very confusing, and she compares it to a bad dream.

- She becomes certain that there is a woman locked inside the pattern.

FOCUS

At this stage, the wallpaper controls the narrator's thoughts and daily activities.

MARK IT UP As you read, circle phrases that suggest the narrator's increasing mental unbalance.

On a pattern like this, by daylight, there is a lack of sequence, a defiance of law, that is a constant irritant to a normal mind.

The color is hideous enough, and unreliable enough, and infuriating enough, but the pattern is torturing.

You think you have mastered it, but just as you get well underway in following, it turns a back-somersault and there you are. It slaps you in the face, knocks you down, and tramples upon you. It is like a bad dream.

The outside pattern is a florid arabesque,[10] reminding one of a fungus. If you can imagine a toadstool in joints, an interminable string of toadstools, budding and sprouting in endless convolutions—why, that is something like it.

That is, sometimes!

There is one marked peculiarity about this paper, a thing nobody seems to notice but myself, and that is that it changes as the light changes.

When the sun shoots in through the east window—I always watch for that first long, straight ray—it changes so quickly that I never can quite believe it.

That is why I watch it always.

By moonlight—the moon shines in all night when there is a moon—I wouldn't know it was the same paper.

At night in any kind of light, in twilight, candle light, lamplight, and worst of all by moonlight, it becomes bars!

What Does It Mean?

Interminable means "unending."

What Does It Mean?

Convolutions are "folds" or "coils."

10. **florid arabesque:** an elaborate interwoven pattern.

The outside pattern I mean, and the woman behind it is as plain as can be.

I didn't realize for a long time what the thing was that showed behind, that dim sub-pattern, but now I am quite sure it is a woman.

By daylight she is subdued, quiet. I fancy it is the pattern that keeps her so still. It is so puzzling. It keeps me quiet by the hour.

I lie down ever so much now. John says it is good for me, and to sleep all I can.

Indeed he started the habit by making me lie down for an hour after each meal.

It is a very bad habit I am convinced, for you see I don't sleep.

And that cultivates deceit, for I don't tell them I'm awake—O no!

The fact is I am getting a little afraid of John.

He seems very queer sometimes, and even Jennie has an inexplicable look.

It strikes me occasionally, just as a scientific hypothesis,—that perhaps it is the paper!

I have watched John when he did not know I was looking, and come into the room suddenly on the most innocent excuses, and I've caught him several times *looking at the paper!* And Jennie too. I caught Jennie with her hand on it once.

She didn't know I was in the room, and when I asked her in a quiet, a very quiet voice, with the most restrained manner possible, what she was doing with the paper—she turned around as if she had been caught stealing, and looked quite angry—asked me why I should frighten her so!

Then she said that the paper stained everything it touched, that she had found yellow smooches[11] on all my clothes and John's, and she wished we would be more careful!

Did not that sound innocent? But I know she was studying that pattern, and I am determined that nobody shall find it out but myself!

Pause & **Reflect**

---

11. **smooches:** dirty marks or spots; smudges.

Reading Check

Reread the highlighted passage. What has Jennie found? What might have caused this thing to occur?

Pause & **Reflect**

1. Review the phrases that you circled as you read. How does the narrator feel about the "woman" she sees in the wallpaper? **(Infer)**

_____

_____

_____

2. Do you think the narrator's interpretation of Jennie's behavior is accurate? *Yes/No,* because _____

_____

_____

(Evaluate)

3. What do you think will happen to the narrator? **(Predict)**

_____

_____

_____

_____

As the story continues...

- The narrator feels that the smell of the wallpaper "creeps all over the house."

- She says that she considered burning down the house to get rid of the smell.

FOCUS

The narrator thinks about nothing but the wallpaper. As you read, notice details that suggest the narrator is losing her mind.

Life is very much more exciting now than it used to be. You see I have something more to expect, to look forward to, to watch. I really do eat better, and am more quiet than I was.

John is so pleased to see me improve! He laughed a little the other day, and said I seemed to be flourishing in spite of my wallpaper.

I turned it off with a laugh. I had no intention of telling him it was *because* of the wallpaper—he would make fun of me. He might even want to take me away.

I don't want to leave now until I have found it out. There is a week more, and I think that will be enough.

I'm feeling ever so much better! I don't sleep much at night, for it is so interesting to watch developments; but I sleep a good deal in the daytime.

In the daytime it is tiresome and perplexing.

There are always new shoots on the fungus, and new shades of yellow all over it. I cannot keep count of them, though I have tried conscientiously.

It is the strangest yellow, that wallpaper! It makes me think of all the yellow things I ever saw—not beautiful ones like buttercups, but old foul, bad yellow things.

But there is something else about that paper—the smell! I noticed it the moment we came into the room, but with so much air and sun it was not bad. Now we have had a week of fog and rain, and whether the windows are open or not, the smell is here.

It creeps all over the house.

I find it hovering in the dining room, skulking in the parlor, hiding in the hall, lying in wait for me on the stairs.

It gets into my hair.

Even when I go to ride, if I turn my head suddenly and surprise it—there is that smell!

Such a peculiar odor, too! I have spent hours in trying to analyze it, to find what it smelled like.

It is not bad—at first, and very gentle, but quite the subtlest, most enduring odor I ever met.

In this damp weather it is awful, I wake up in the night and find it hanging over me.

It used to disturb me at first. I thought seriously of burning the house—to reach the smell.

But now I am used to it. The only thing I can think of that it is like is the *color* of the paper!

A yellow smell.

> There is a very funny mark on this wall, low down, near the mopboard.[12] A streak that runs round the room. It goes behind every piece of furniture, except the bed, a long, straight, even *smooch*, as if it had been rubbed over and over.
>
> I wonder how it was done and who did it, and what they did it for. Round and round and round—round and round and round—it makes me dizzy!

500

I really have discovered something at last.

Through watching so much at night, when it changes so, I have finally found out.

The front pattern *does* move—and no wonder! The woman behind shakes it!

Sometimes I think there are a great many women behind, and sometimes only one, and she crawls around fast, and her crawling shakes it all over.

510

Then in the very bright spots she keeps still, and in the very shady spots she just takes hold of the bars and shakes them hard.

And she is all the time trying to climb through. But nobody could climb through that pattern—it strangles so; I think that is why it has so many heads.

They get through, and then the pattern strangles them off and turns them upside down, and makes their eyes white!

If those heads were covered or taken off it would not be half so bad.

520

I think that woman gets out in the daytime!

And I'll tell you why—privately—I've seen her!

I can see her out of every one of my windows!

It is the same woman, I know, for she is always creeping, and most women do not creep by daylight.

I see her on that long road under the trees, creeping along, and when a carriage comes she hides under the blackberry vines.

Reader Success Strategy

What do you think of when you hear the words "a yellow smell"? Brainstorm a list of words or images that come to mind.

READ ALOUD Lines 496–502

The narrator wonders who made the smooch, or mark, and why. How do you think the mark got on the wall? **(Cause and Effect)**

_____

_____

_____

Reading Check

What has the narrator "discovered" about the wallpaper?

---

12. **mopboard:** baseboard; wooden molding that covers the corner where a floor and a wall are joined.

1. The narrator is going mad. What does she now believe about the wallpaper? Check each statement below that applies. **(Infer)**

It has a foul smell.

A woman is behind the wallpaper.

The pattern moves.

It changes color.

2. What does the woman in the wallpaper do that the narrator also does? Why might the narrator think that she and the woman have this in common? **(Clarify; Infer)**

_____

_____

_____

_____

As the story ends...

- The narrator starts to suspect that John is only pretending to be loving and kind.

- She suspects that John and Jennie are being affected by the wallpaper, too.

I don't blame her a bit. It must be very humiliating to be caught creeping by daylight!

530 I always lock the door when I creep by daylight. I can't do it at night, for I know John would suspect something at once.

And John is so queer now, that I don't want to irritate him. I wish he would take another room! Besides, I don't want anybody to get that woman out at night but myself.

I often wonder if I could see her out of all the windows at once.

But, turn as fast as I can, I can only see out of one at one time.

And though I always see her, she may be able to creep

540 faster than I can turn!

I have watched her sometimes away off in the open country, creeping as fast as a cloud shadow in a high wind.

Pause & Reflect

If only that top pattern could be gotten off from the under one! I mean to try it, little by little.

I have found out another funny thing, but I shan't tell it this time! It does not do to trust people too much.

There are only two more days to get

550 this paper off, and I believe John is beginning to notice. I don't like the look in his eyes.

And I heard him ask Jennie a lot of professional questions about me. She had a very good report to give.

She said I slept a good deal in the daytime.

John knows I don't sleep very well at night, for all I'm so quiet!

He asked me all sorts of questions, too, and pretended to be very loving and kind.

As if I couldn't see through him!

560 Still, I don't wonder he acts so, sleeping under this paper for three months.

It only interests me, but I feel sure John and Jennie are secretly affected by it.

Hurrah! This is the last day,[13] but it is enough. John to stay in town over night, and won't be out until this evening.

Jennie wanted to sleep with me—the sly thing! but I told her I should undoubtedly rest better for a night all alone.

That was clever, for really I wasn't alone a bit! As soon as it was moonlight and that poor thing began to crawl and shake the pattern, I got up and ran to help her.

I pulled and she shook, I shook and she pulled, and before morning we had peeled off yards of that paper.

A strip about as high as my head and half around the room.

And then when the sun came and that awful pattern began to laugh at me, I declared I would finish it today!

We go away tomorrow, and they are moving all my furniture down again to leave things as they were before.

Jennie looked at the wall in amazement, but I told her merrily that I did it out of pure spite at the vicious thing.

She laughed and said she wouldn't mind doing it herself, but I must not get tired.

How she betrayed herself that time!

But I am here, and no person touches this paper but me,—not *alive!*

She tried to get me out of the room—it was too <u>patent</u>! But I said it was so quiet and empty and clean now that I believed I would lie down again and sleep all I could; and not to wake me even for dinner—I would call when I woke.

So now she is gone, and the servants are gone, and the things are gone, and there is nothing left but that great bedstead nailed down, with the canvas mattress we found on it.

We shall sleep downstairs tonight, and take the boat home tomorrow.

I quite enjoy the room, now it is bare again.

How those children did tear about here!

This bedstead is fairly gnawed!

But I must get to work.

---

13. **This . . . last day:** The narrator is actually speaking on the night before the last full day. The word *this* refers to the day that will begin the next morning.

WORDS
TO
KNOW   **patent** (păt′nt) *adj.* obvious; apparent

✔ **Reading Check**

Why doesn't the narrator want Jennie to sleep in the room?

What Does It Mean?

When people act out of *spite*, they do something to "get back" at someone or something that is angering or bothering them. *Vicious* means "fierce and cruel." The narrator is peeling the wallpaper to get back at it for tormenting her.

What Does It Mean?

How she betrayed herself that time means "how she gave herself away." The narrator thinks Jennie has unintentionally revealed that she wanted to tear the paper down herself.

☆ **Reader Success Strategy**

As you read this section, try to determine what is **reality** and what is **fantasy.** Fill in the following chart with details that are real and details that are in the narrator's imagination.

Reality	John is worried about his wife.
Fantasy	John and Jennie are affected by the wallpaper.

600   I have locked the door and thrown the key down into the front path.

I don't want to go out, and I don't want to have anybody come in, till John comes.

I want to astonish him.

I've got a rope up here that even Jennie did not find. If that woman does get out, and tries to get away, I can tie her!

But I forgot I could not reach far without anything to stand on!

This bed will *not* move!

610   I tried to lift and push it until I was lame, and then I got so angry I bit off a little piece at one corner—but it hurt my teeth.

Then I peeled off all the paper I could reach standing on the floor. It sticks horribly and the pattern just enjoys it! All those strangled heads and bulbous eyes and waddling fungus growths just shriek with <u>derision</u>!

I am getting angry enough to do something desperate. To jump out of the window would be admirable exercise, but the bars are too strong even to try.

620   Besides I wouldn't do it. Of course not. I know well enough that a step like that is improper and might be misconstrued.

I don't like to *look* out of the windows even—there are so many of those creeping women, and they creep so fast.

I wonder if they all come out of that wallpaper as I did?

But I am securely fastened now by my well-hidden rope—you don't get *me* out in the road there!

I suppose I shall have to get back behind the pattern when it comes night, and that is hard!

It is so pleasant to be out in this great room and creep **630** around as I please!

I don't want to go outside. I won't, even if Jennie asks me to.

For outside you have to creep on the ground, and everything is green instead of yellow.

But here I can creep smoothly on the floor, and my shoulder just fits in that long smooch around the wall, so I cannot lose my way.

Why there's John at the door!

It is no use, young man, you can't open it!

WORDS TO KNOW

derision (dĭ-rĭzh′ən) *n.* harsh ridicule or mockery; scorn

640 How he does call and pound!

Now he's crying for an axe.

It would be a shame to break down that beautiful door!

"John dear!" said I in the gentlest voice, "the key is down by the front steps, under a plantain leaf!"

That silenced him for a few moments.

Then he said—very quietly indeed, "Open the door, my darling!"

"I can't," said I. "The key is down by the front door under a plantain leaf!"

650 And then I said it again, several times, very gently and slowly, and said it so often that he had to go and see, and he got it of course, and came in. He stopped short by the door.

"What is the matter?" he cried. "What are you doing!"

I kept on creeping just the same, but I looked at him over my shoulder.

"I've got out at last," said I, "in spite of you and Jane.[14] And I've pulled off most of the paper, so you can't put me back!"

Now why should that man have fainted? But he did, and 660 right across my path by the wall, so that I had to creep over him every time!

Pause & Reflect

Pause & Reflect

MARK IT UP **1.** How do you know that the narrator is now mad? Underline details that support your answer. **(Clarify)**

_____

_____

_____

_____

2. The narrator is desperate to peel off all the wallpaper. Why is this so important to her? **(Infer)**

_____

_____

_____

_____

CHALLENGE

Who or what is to blame for the narrator's losing her mind? Mark passages that provide evidence for your conclusions. **(Draw Conclusions)**

14. **in spite of you and Jane:** This reference to a previously unmentioned Jane is a point of debate. It could be an error made by the original printer for the name of the sister-housekeeper Jennie or Cousin Julia. It is also possible, however, that Jane is the narrator. If so, the narrator has freed herself from her wifely "Jane" identity.

Active Reading SkillBuilder

Making Inferences About the Narrator

Inferences are logical guesses based on the details the narrator provides and what you know about life. When reading "The Yellow Wallpaper," try to see things as the narrator does. Use the questions in this sequence chart to figure out what is happening. Two answers are given.

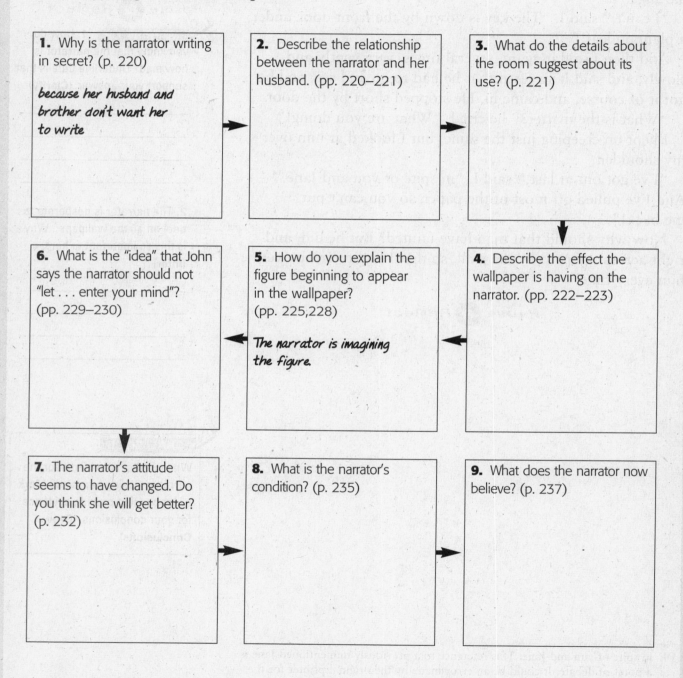

1. Why is the narrator writing in secret? (p. 220)

because her husband and brother don't want her to write

2. Describe the relationship between the narrator and her husband. (pp. 220–221)

3. What do the details about the room suggest about its use? (p. 221)

6. What is the "idea" that John says the narrator should not "let . . . enter your mind"? (pp. 229–230)

5. How do you explain the figure beginning to appear in the wallpaper? (pp. 225,228)

The narrator is imagining the figure.

4. Describe the effect the wallpaper is having on the narrator. (pp. 222–223)

7. The narrator's attitude seems to have changed. Do you think she will get better? (p. 232)

8. What is the narrator's condition? (p. 235)

9. What does the narrator now believe? (p. 237)

Literary Analysis SkillBuilder

First-Person Narrator

The **narrator** relates the story's events to the reader and, in the first-person point of view, is a character in the story. In this story, the first-person narrator begins to see **images** in the wallpaper: bars, bulbous eyes, a creeping woman, and more. If the wallpaper reflects the narrator's mental state, readers can use it as evidence to draw conclusions about her feelings and preoccupations. Use the chart below to list images from the story that describe the wallpaper. Then try to interpret each image, associating it with some aspect of the narrator's life.

Image	Interpretation
pattern that lolls like a broken neck (p. 224)	*The narrator feels like her spirit and creativity are being broken.*

Follow Up: With a small group, discuss conclusions you draw about the narrator's problem. What are the advantages and disadvantages of using a first-person narrator to tell this story, especially in light of the narrator's condition?

Words to Know SkillBuilder

Words to Know

atrocious	derision	impertinence	patent	querulous
basely	felicity	inanimate	perseverance	undulating

A. On each blank line, write the word from the word list that the rhyme describes.

If this is your style, you find things that are wrong.
You whine and complain as you grumble along.

_____ (1)

If something is too clear for you to miss,
You might describe that thing as being this.

_____ (2)

This is what you show when it's a long way to the top,
But, though you are exhausted, you keep on and
    will not stop.

_____ (3)

If this describes the artworks you create,
The comments of the critics won't be "Great!"

_____ (4)

If this describes the ride you choose,
Your cash may not be all you lose.

_____ (5)

This is treating folks with less respect than they deserve,
To which they may respond by saying, "What a
    lot of nerve!"

_____ (6)

This does not describe a daisy or a doctor or a dog.
It does describe a rock, a chair, a sidewalk, and a log.

_____ (7)

Is this the state of mind you're in?
No wonder you can't help but grin.

_____ (8)

This is the reaction other people show to you
When they just laugh in nasty ways at everything
    you do.

_____ (9)

This is how a cheater cheats,
Cowards lie about their feats,
Robbers rob or big kids bully,
Wolves deceive in clothing woolly.

_____ (10)

B. Write a description of the narrator of "The Yellow Wallpaper," from the point of view of her husband. Use at least **four** of the Words to Know.

WE WEAR THE MASK

Paul Laurence Dunbar

Sympathy

Paul Laurence Dunbar

Before You Read

Connect to Your Life

How would you feel if people treated you as though you were not smart or important? Express your thoughts on the lines below.

I would feel _____

_____

because _____

_____

Key to the Poems

WHAT'S THE BIG IDEA? A **symbol** is a person, place, or object that stands for something beyond itself. For example, a dove is a kind of bird. As a symbol, a dove stands for the concept of peace. Each of the poems you are about to read contains a central symbol. In "We Wear the Mask," the central symbol is a mask. In "Sympathy," the central symbol is a bird that is trapped in a cage. Before you read, think about how the poet might use these symbols to express deeper thoughts. Jot down answers to the following questions:

1. For what reasons might people wear masks?

_____

_____

_____

2. What feelings might a bird trapped in a cage have? What might the bird try to do?

_____

_____

_____

PREVIEW Paul Laurence Dunbar, an African–American poet, died young—at the age of 33 in 1906. He did not live to see such **lyric poems** as "We Wear the Mask" and "Sympathy" win him lasting respect. In these poems the speakers comment on the situation of African Americans. At that time, many white Americans stereotyped blacks as grinning and happy-go-lucky. A popular theatrical event was the minstrel show. In it, white entertainers darkened their faces, pretending to be black and performing funny antics. Dunbar's poems express the misery of his people in this climate of racial prejudice.

WE WEAR THE MASK

Paul Laurence Dunbar

Reading Tips

Lyric poems express deep feelings in emotional language. These lyric poems were written in the 1890s. As you read, keep these points in mind:

• Read the poems first silently and then aloud to get a sense of the feelings the poet expresses.

• Check the footnotes for help with difficult words and phrases.

• Remember that if the word order in a line is unusual, you won't find the structure *subject-verb-object*. Instead, look for the subject and the verb after the object or at the end of a line of verse.

As the poem begins . . .

• The speaker explains what feelings the mask hides.

What Does It Mean?

A *debt* is "something owed," or "an obligation."

FOCUS

In this poem the "mask" is a false appearance that hides true feelings. Read to find out about the contrast between the way the mask looks and the feelings it hides.

MARK IT UP As you read, underline words and phrases that help you understand the pain hidden by the mask. An example is highlighted.

We wear the mask that grins and lies,
It hides our cheeks and shades our eyes,—
This debt we pay to human guile;[1]
With torn and bleeding hearts we smile,
5 And mouth[2] with myriad subtleties.[3]

---

1. **guile:** slyness and craftiness in dealing with others.
2. **mouth:** to speak without conviction.
3. **myriad subtleties:** countless misleading statements.

Why should the world be overwise,
In counting all our tears and sighs?
Nay, let them only see us, while
    We wear the mask.

10   We smile, but, O great Christ, our cries
To Thee from tortured souls arise.
We sing, but oh, the clay is vile[4]
Beneath our feet, and long the mile;
But let the world dream otherwise,
15   We wear the mask.

Pause **&** **Reflect**

More About...

RACIAL STEREOTYPES In his poems, Paul Laurence Dunbar was responding to the negative stereotypes that many white people of his era held about black people.

Pause **&** *Reflect*

1. Review the words and phrases you underlined as you read. Then describe the contrast between the way the mask looks and the feelings it hides. **(Compare and Contrast)**

_____
_____
_____
_____

2. Why do the speaker and his people hide their true feelings from the world? **(Infer)**

_____
_____
_____
_____

3. Do you think people gain more or lose more by hiding their true feelings? **(Connect)**

_____
_____
_____
_____

4. **vile:** disgusting or objectionable.

Sympathy

Paul Laurence Dunbar

I know what the caged bird feels, alas!
    When the sun is bright on the upland slopes;
When the wind stirs soft through the springing grass,
And the river flows like a stream of glass;
    When the first bird sings and the first bud opes,[1]
And the faint perfume from its chalice steals[2]—
I know what the caged bird feels!

I know why the caged bird beats his wing
    Till its blood is red on the cruel bars;
For he must fly back to his perch and cling
When he fain[3] would be on the bough a-swing;
    And a pain still throbs in the old, old scars
And they pulse again with a keener sting—
I know why he beats his wing!

---

1. **opes:** opens.
2. **the faint perfume . . . steals:** the lovely smell from the opening bud (**its chalice**) attracts the senses.
3. **fain:** gladly or willingly.

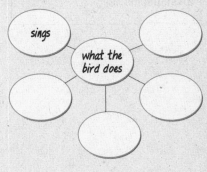

1. Review the details you under-lined as you read. Why does the caged bird struggle so fiercely? **(Infer)**

_____

_____

_____

_____

READ ALOUD 2. Read aloud lines 15–21. What feelings does the caged bird's song express? **(Infer)**

_____

_____

_____

_____

CHALLENGE

Irony is the contrast between appearance and reality. For example, the mask in "We Wear the Mask" appears to "grin" but in fact conceals the reality of "tears and sighs." How would you describe the central irony in "Sympathy"? Mark or high-light lines that support your interpretation. What **theme,** or message, about African Americans does the irony in these poems suggest?

15 I know why the caged bird sings, ah me,
         When his wing is bruised and his bosom sore,—
    When he beats his bars and he would be free;
    It is not a carol⁴ of joy or glee,
         But a prayer that he sends from his heart's deep core,
20 But a plea, that upward to Heaven he flings—
    I know why the caged bird sings!

4. **carol:** song, especially for Christmas.

Active Reading SkillBuilder

Interpreting Symbols

Interpreting symbols involves discovering what they might represent. On a second reading of these poems, use the following strategies to help figure out the symbolic meanings in the poems. Identify a possible symbol; consider the qualities of the symbolic object; note the ideas or feelings the poet associates with the symbol; consider the associations the symbol seems to trigger in you; make a logical guess about what the symbol might represent. Use the chart to organize your thoughts about the symbols. The symbolic objects in each poem are shown.

	Object	Qualities	Symbol of . . .
"We Wear the Mask"	mask		
"Sympathy"	caged bird		

Literary Analysis SkillBuilder

Symbol

A **symbol** is a person, place, or object that represents something beyond itself. Symbols in literature generally have several possible interpretations rather than one precise meaning, and often communicate complex, abstract ideas. Clues to the meaning of a particular symbol are usually found within the work itself. Identify what the mask and the caged bird represent in Dunbar's poems. Then think of other symbols that could represent similar ideas. Write these symbols in the diagrams below. Two examples are given.

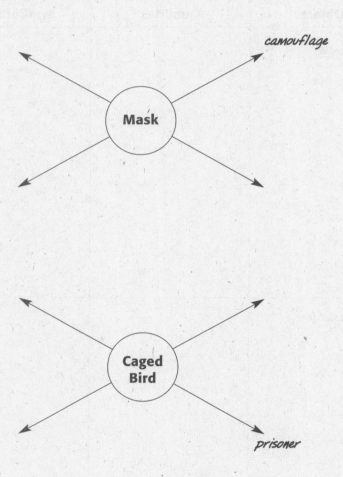

I, Too

Harlem

The Weary Blues

Langston Hughes

Before You Read

Connect to Your Life

When people are faced with serious problems or unfair treatment, they often find strength by focusing on what makes them proud and what they are determined to do in the future.

What qualities do you have that make you proud?

_____

What goals, or dreams, do you have for the future?

_____

Key to the Poems

WHAT TO LISTEN FOR In his poems, Langston Hughes used the patterns of everyday speech and the rhythms of African American music, particularly jazz and the blues. Read each of these excerpts from two of the poems that you are about to read. Then follow the directions below each one.

1. Down on Lenox Avenue the other night
   By the pale dull pallor of an old gas light
       He did a lazy sway. . . .
       He did a lazy sway. . . .

Underline your choice to describe the sound of these lines. Then explain.

I think these lines sound like /everyday speech/music/ because

_____

2. They send me to eat in the kitchen
   When company comes,

Underline your choice to describe the sound of these lines. Then explain.

I think these lines sound like /everyday speech/music/ because

_____

PREVIEW Langston Hughes was an African-American poet who wrote in the early and mid-20th century. In his poems, he used the rhythms of blues music and jazz to create unforgettable pictures of ordinary working people. The three poems you will read express deep feelings. They show the beauties, strengths, and hardships of African-American life.

I, Too

Langston Hughes

FOCUS

In this poem, the speaker uses his own experience to show the painful effects of racial prejudice.

MARK IT UP Put a **P** next to those sentences that describe the present. Put an **F** next to those that describe the future. Examples are given on pages 283 and 284.

P I, too, sing America.

I am the darker brother.
They send me to eat in the kitchen
When company comes,
5 But I laugh,
And eat well,
And grow strong.

Reading Tips

These poems contain some surprises. To get to know the poems well, read each one several times.

- When you read each poem the first time, notice what words, lines, or descriptions grab you. Don't worry about understanding everything.

- Then read each poem aloud, slowly, to get a sense of the **sounds** and **rhythms**. Read each one aloud again once or twice, experimenting with different rhythms.

As the poem begins . . .

- The speaker says he is sent to eat "in the kitchen."

- The speaker says that he is growing strong. He is optimistic about the future.

What Does It Mean?

Darker brother refers to African Americans.

More About . . .

RACIAL SEGREGATION Until the Civil Rights Act of 1964, many states had Jim Crow laws that segregated, or separated, African Americans from white society. For example, many restaurants and lunch counters refused to serve meals to African Americans. Even in many white homes, African American employees were expected to (eat in the kitchen.) In this poem, Langston Hughes uses images of eating in the dining room and eating in the kitchen to protest against such racial segregation.

☑ **Reading Check**

In the speaker's point of view, what will cause the people to include him at the dining room table?

Pause & Reflect

✎ **MARK IT UP** **1.** Reread lines 1–7. Circle the words that help you picture the speaker. **(Visualize)**

2. Look at the lines you marked in the poem. In what way does the speaker expect the future to be different from the present? **(Compare and Contrast)**

_____

_____

_____

_____

F Tomorrow,
I'll be at the table
10 When company comes.
Nobody'll dare
Say to me,
("Eat in the kitchen,")
Then.

15 Besides,
They'll see how beautiful I am
And be ashamed—

I, too, am America.

Pause & Reflect

Harlem

Langston Hughes

FOCUS

This poem begins with a question about a dream deferred, or postponed. Several comparisons follow.

MARK IT UP Number the five comparisons made in lines 2 through 10.

What happens to a dream deferred?

Does it dry up
like a raisin in the sun?
Or fester like a sore—
5 And then run?
Does it stink like rotten meat?
Or crust and sugar over—
like a syrupy sweet?

Maybe it just sags
10 like a heavy load.

Or does it explode?

Pause & *Reflect*

As the poem begins . . .

• The speaker compares a delayed dream to a raisin, drying up in the hot sun.

• Then he compares it to other things, such as an open wound.

What Does It Mean?

A sore, or wound, that *festers* becomes infected or rots. When a wound becomes infected, fluid builds up and eventually *runs*, or leaks, out from the pressure.

Reading Check

What might the speaker mean when he suggests that a delayed dream might explode?

Pause & *Reflect*

1. Look back at the comparisons you numbered. What do the five comparisons have in common? **(Compare and Contrast)**

_____

_____

_____

2. What is it like to have to constantly postpone something you really want to do? **(Connect)**

_____

_____

_____

The Weary Blues

Langston Hughes

As the poem begins . . .

• The speaker describes what he saw and heard on Lenox Avenue one night.

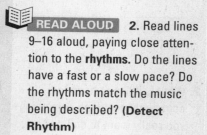

Reader Success Strategy

The speaker uses words and phrases from an everyday African American dialect. In the margins, make a glossary to help you understand and remember the meanings. For example, jot down that *o'* (line 8) means "of."

Pause **&** *Reflect*

MARK IT UP **1.** Look at the passages that you circled. Place a check (√) next to the ones that describe sights. Place a star next to the ones that describe sounds. **(Clarify)**

READ ALOUD **2.** Read lines 9–16 aloud, paying close attention to the **rhythms**. Do the lines have a fast or a slow pace? Do the rhythms match the music being described? **(Detect Rhythm)**

_____

_____

_____

FOCUS

In the first 16 lines of this poem, the poet describes an African-American blues piano player in New York City.

MARK IT UP Circle at least four words, lines, or details that help you imagine the scene.

Droning[1] a drowsy syncopated[2] tune,
Rocking back and forth to a mellow croon,[3]
   I heard a Negro play.
Down on Lenox Avenue the other night
By the pale dull pallor[4] of an old gas light   5
   He did a lazy sway. . . .
   He did a lazy sway. . . .
To the tune o' those Weary Blues.
With his ebony hands on each ivory key
He made that poor piano moan with melody.   10
   O Blues!
Swaying to and fro on his rickety[5] stool
He played that sad raggy tune like a musical fool.
   Sweet Blues!
Coming from a black man's soul.   15
   O Blues!

Pause **&** *Reflect*

---

1. **droning:** The piano player is singing in a low, steady voice.
2. **syncopated** (sĭng'kə-pā'tĭd): characterized by a shifting of stresses from normally strong to normally weak beats.
3. **croon:** a soft humming or singing.
4. **pallor** (păl'ər): lack of color.
5. **rickety** (rĭk'ĭ-tē): likely to break or fall apart.

FOCUS

In the second part of the poem, the poet includes two **stanzas** of the actual blues song the musician is singing.

MARK IT UP Put brackets around the two stanzas of the song.

As the poem ends...

- In the first stanza, the singer expresses loneliness.

- In the second stanza, the singer expresses the type of sadness that is known as "the blues."

In a deep song voice with a melancholy[6] tone
I heard that Negro sing, that old piano moan—
 "Ain't got nobody in all this world,
 Ain't got nobody but ma self.
20 I's gwine to quit ma frownin'
 And put ma troubles on the shelf."
Thump, thump, thump, went his foot on the floor.
He played a few chords then he sang some more—
 "I got the Weary Blues
25 And I can't be satisfied.
 Got the Weary Blues
 And can't be satisfied—
 I ain't happy no mo'
30 And I wish that I had died."
And far into the night he crooned that tune.
The stars went out and so did the moon.
The singer stopped playing and went to bed
While the Weary Blues echoed through his head.
35 He slept like a rock or a man that's dead.

Pause & Reflect

More About...

BLUES Blues is a style of music that evolved from southern African American songs. Blues songs often have a slow, repetitive rhythm and express sadness.

Pause & Reflect

READ ALOUD   **1.** Read the two stanzas of the blues song aloud. What three phrases are repeated? **(Clarify)**

_____

_____

_____

_____

2. Why do you think the blues singer sleeps so soundly? **(Infer)**

_____

_____

_____

_____

CHALLENGE

What do these three poems have in common? Use examples from the poems to support your ideas. **(Compare and Contrast)**

---

6. **melancholy** (mĕl'ən-kŏl'ē): sad or gloomy.

Active Reading SkillBuilder

Detecting Rhythm in Poetry

Inspired by the blues and jazz that he heard in Harlem nightclubs, Hughes tried to write poetry with the distinctive **rhythms** of these types of music. Try to detect the different rhythms that Hughes creates through his arrangement of stressed and unstressed syllables in a line. Read each poem aloud, listen for the rhythm, then tap it out as you read the poem silently. Imagine how the poems would sound recited over a background of blues or jazz music. On the chart below, write down lines in each poem that have a rhythm you particularly like. Mark syllables that you think should be stressed. An example is given.

Poems	Lines with Rhythm I Like
"I, Too"	*"Í am the dárker bróther."*
"Harlem"	
"The Weary Blues"	

Literary Analysis SkillBuilder

Mood

The **mood** of a poem is the emotional feeling or atmosphere that the poet creates
for a reader. Poets create mood through their use of imagery, figurative language,
sound devices, description, and rhythm. Use the chart below to identify the
mood of each of these poems. Then list the various elements that Hughes uses
to develop that mood. Two examples are given.

Poem	Mood of Poem	Elements That Contribute to Mood
"I, Too"	self-confident; proud	word choice—"Nobody'll dare/Say to me,"
"Harlem"		
"The Weary Blues"		

How It Feels to Be Colored Me

ZORA
NEALE
HURSTON

Before You Read

Connect to Your Life

Each person is unique and special. Imagine that you are filling out an application for college or a job. One of the questions asks you to explain what makes you unique and special. On the lines below, list all the qualities that you would use to answer that question.

_____

_____

_____

_____

_____

_____

Key to the Essay

WHAT'S THE BIG IDEA? Zora Neale Hurston grew up in an African American town in Florida in the early 1900s. Because she did not meet many white people during her childhood, she was unaware of racial prejudice until she attended high school in Jacksonville, Florida. By then, her sense of self was strong enough to withstand the discrimination she faced. In 1925, Hurston moved to Harlem, an African American neighborhood in New York City. There, the Harlem Renaissance was thriving. The Harlem Renaissance refers to the flowering of African American art and literature in the 1920s. After graduating from Barnard College in 1928, Hurston became famous as the best African American female writer of her time. Like other writers of the Harlem Renaissance, Hurston strove to write in a very personal voice.

Reading Tips

Hurston uses many types of **figurative language** to create clear pictures in your mind. At first reading, some of her images may be confusing. Don't stop to try to figure out the meaning. You will find it easier to understand Hurston's images after you have read the entire essay.

How It Feels to Be Colored Me

ZORA NEALE HURSTON

PREVIEW In this **essay**, first published in 1928, the author describes her feelings about herself as an African American. She recalls her first 13 years growing up in an African-American town in Florida. She also reflects upon the times in her later life when she was most aware of her race. Finally, she describes what she and all others have in common.

As the essay begins . . .

- Hurston states that everyone in town was curious about the Northern whites who passed through town.
- She says that she liked to perform for them.

More About . . .

EATONVILLE, FLORIDA

Eatonville is an important town in African American history. It is the oldest surviving incorporated African American town in America. Every January, the city celebrates the Zora Neale Hurston Festival.

FOCUS
Read to find out about Hurston's experiences with white people as a child in Eatonville.

MARK IT UP As you read, circle details that tell you how she reacted to the white people traveling through town. An example is highlighted.

I am colored[1] but I offer nothing in the way of <u>extenuating</u> circumstances except the fact that I am the only Negro in the United States whose grandfather on the mother's side was *not* an Indian chief.

I remember the very day that I became colored. Up to my thirteenth year I lived in the little Negro town of Eatonville, Florida. It is exclusively a colored town. The only white people I knew passed through the town going to or coming from Orlando. The native whites rode dusty horses; the Northern tourists chugged down the sandy village road in automobiles. The town knew the Southerners and never stopped cane chewing when they passed. But the Northerners were something else again. They

---

1. **colored:** Hurston uses the term *colored* to refer to herself and to other African Americans. This term was in use in 1928 when Hurston wrote this essay.

WORDS TO KNOW **extenuating** (ĭk-stĕn′yo͞o-ā′tĭng) *adj.* lessening a fault by serving as a partial excuse **extenuate** *v.*

were peered at cautiously from behind curtains by the timid. The more venturesome would come out on the porch to watch them go past and got just as much pleasure out of the tourists **20** as the tourists got out of the village.

The front porch might seem a daring place for the rest of the town, but it was a gallery seat for me. My favorite place was atop the gatepost. Proscenium box[2] for a born first-nighter.[3] Not only did I enjoy the show, but I didn't mind the actors knowing that I liked it. I usually spoke to them in passing. I'd wave at them and when they returned my salute, I would say something like this: "Howdy-do-well-I-thank-you-where-you-goin'?" Usually the automobile or the horse paused at this, and after a queer exchange of compliments, I would **30** probably "go a piece of the way" with them, as we say in farthest Florida. If one of my family happened to come to the front in time to see me, of course negotiations would be rudely broken off. But even so, it is clear that I was the first "welcome-to-our-state" Floridian, and I hope the Miami Chamber of Commerce will please take notice.

During this period, white people differed from colored to me only in that they rode through town and never lived there. They liked to hear me "speak pieces" and sing and wanted to see me dance the parse-me-la, and gave me generously of their **40** small silver for doing these things, which seemed strange to me, for I wanted to do them so much that I needed bribing to stop. Only they didn't know it. The colored people gave no dimes. They <u>deplored</u> any joyful tendencies in me, but I was their Zora nevertheless. I belonged to them, to the nearby hotels, to the county—everybody's Zora.

But changes came in the family when I was thirteen, and I was sent to school in Jacksonville. I left Eatonville, the town of the oleanders,[4] as Zora. When I disembarked from the riverboat at Jacksonville, she was no more. It seemed that I **50** had suffered a sea change.[5] I was not Zora of Orange County

---

2. **proscenium** (prō-sē′nē-əm) **box:** a box seat near the stage.

3. **first-nighter:** a person who attends the opening performance of a play, an opera, or a similar show.

4. **oleanders** (ō′lē-ăn′dərz): evergreen shrubs with fragrant flowers.

5. **sea change:** complete transformation.

WORDS
TO
KNOW

deplore (dĭ-plôr′) v. to feel strong disapproval of or deeply regret

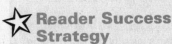

Reader Success Strategy

As you read, highlight any passages that seem confusing. Then, once you have read the entire essay, try to use context clues to figure out the meaning of each difficult passage.

Reading Check

Why did Hurston think it was strange that the white people gave her money when she performed for them?

MARK IT UP WORD POWER

Mark words that you'd like to add to your **Personal Word List.** After reading, you can record the words and their meanings beginning on page 476.

How It Feels to Be . . . **293**

How does Hurston's view of herself change when she leaves home at 13? Write the answer below. Then underline words and phrases on pages 293 and 294 that led you to the answer. **(Main Idea)**

_____

_____

_____

_____

As the essay continues . . .

- Hurston distances herself from African Americans who remain angry about the abuses of slavery.

- She expresses her eager feelings about the future.

What Does It Mean?

Helter-skelter means "disorderly or confused." A *skirmish* is a battle.

What Does It Mean?

In the highlighted lines, the author is comparing the Civil War, the Reconstruction, and her parents' generation to saying "On the line! Get set! Go!" as though it's the start of a race. Now she, Hurston, is *off to a flying start* running the race that goes away from slavery and towards the future.

---

any more, I was now a little colored girl. I found it out in certain ways. In my heart as well as in the mirror, I became a fast brown—warranted not to rub nor run.

Pause & Reflect

FOCUS

The word *tragic* means "doomed or unhappy." Hurston begins this part by stating, "But I am not tragically colored." Read to find out her feelings about her race and about her people's past experience of slavery.

60

But I am not tragically colored. There is no great sorrow dammed up in my soul, nor lurking behind my eyes. I do not mind at all. I do not belong to the sobbing school of Negrohood who hold that nature somehow has given them a lowdown dirty deal and whose feelings are all hurt about it. Even in the helter-skelter skirmish that is my life, I have seen that the world is to the strong regardless of a little pigmentation[6] more or less. No, I do not weep at the world—I am too busy sharpening my oyster knife.[7]

Someone is always at my elbow reminding me that I am the granddaughter of slaves. It fails to register depression with me. Slavery is sixty years in the past. The operation was successful and the patient is doing well, thank you. The

70 terrible struggle that made me an American out of a potential slave said, "On the line!" The Reconstruction said, "Get set!" and the generation before said, "Go!" I am off to a flying start and I must not halt in the stretch to look behind and weep. Slavery is the price I paid for civilization, and the choice was not with me. It is a bully[8] adventure and worth all that I have paid through my ancestors for it. No one on earth ever had a greater chance for glory. The world to be won and nothing to be lost. It is thrilling to think—to know that for any act of mine, I shall get twice as much praise or twice as

80 much blame. It is quite exciting to hold the center of the national stage, with the spectators not knowing whether to laugh or to weep.

---

6. **pigmentation:** darkness of skin coloration.

7. **oyster knife:** a reference to the saying "The world is my oyster," implying that the world contains treasure waiting to be taken, like the pearl in an oyster.

8. **bully:** excellent; splendid.

The position of my white neighbor is much more difficult. No brown <u>specter</u> pulls up a chair beside me when I sit down to eat. No dark ghost thrusts its leg against mine in bed. The game of keeping what one has is never so exciting as the game of getting.

I do not always feel colored. Even now I often achieve the unconscious Zora of Eatonville before the Hegira.[9] I feel most colored when I am thrown against a sharp white background.

For instance at Barnard.[10] "Beside the waters of the Hudson"[11] I feel my race. Among the thousand white persons, I am a dark rock surged upon, and overswept, but through it all, I remain myself. When covered by the waters, I am; and the ebb but reveals me again.

Pause & Reflect

Pause & Reflect

How does Hurston feel about her race? **(Clarify)**

_____

_____

_____

_____

More About . . .

BARNARD Barnard is the women's college affiliated with Columbia University, which at that time admitted only male undergraduates. Like most colleges during that era, Barnard and Columbia had student populations that were almost entirely white.

FOCUS

Hurston describes what she experiences while listening to jazz. **MARK IT UP** As you read, underline the details that help you understand her reaction to this music.

Sometimes it is the other way around. A white person is set down in our midst, but the contrast is just as sharp for me. For instance, when I sit in the drafty basement that is The New World Cabaret with a white person, my color comes. We enter chatting about any little nothing that we have in common and are seated by the jazz waiters. In the abrupt way that jazz orchestras have, this one plunges into a number. It loses no time in circumlocutions,[12] but gets right down to business. It constricts the thorax and splits the heart with its tempo and narcotic harmonies. This orchestra grows rambunctious, rears on its hind legs and attacks the tonal veil with primitive fury, <u>rending</u> it, clawing it until it breaks through to the jungle

As the essay continues . . .

• Hurston begins her description of jazz by saying that it "splits the heart."

• She compares the orchestra to a wild animal of the jungle.

---

9. **Hegira** (hǐ-jī′rə): journey (from the name given to Mohammed's journey from Mecca to Medina in 622).

10. **Barnard:** the college in New York City from which Hurston graduated in 1928.

11. **"Beside the waters of the Hudson":** a reference to the first line of Barnard's school song.

12. **circumlocutions** (sûr′kəm-lō-kyoo′shənz): unnecessary elaboration or "beating around the bush."

WORDS TO KNOW
specter (spěk′tər) *n.* a ghostly vision; phantom
rend (rěnd) *v.* to tear or split apart violently

Pause & Reflect

1. Look at the details you under-lined as you read. Then write a sentence to **summarize** Hurston's reaction to jazz.

_____

_____

_____

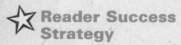 **READ ALOUD** 2. Read aloud the boxed passage on this page. How does Hurston's reaction to jazz differ from her white com-panion's reaction? **(Compare and Contrast)**

_____

_____

_____

_____

beyond. I follow those heathen—follow them exultingly. I dance wildly inside myself; I yell within, I whoop; I shake my assegai[13] above my head, I hurl it true to the mark *yeeeeooww!* I am in the jungle and living in the jungle way. My face is painted red and yellow and my body is painted blue. My pulse is throbbing like a war drum. I want to slaughter something—give pain, give death to what, I do not know. But the piece ends. The men of the orchestra wipe their lips and rest their fingers. I creep back slowly to the <u>veneer</u> we call civilization with the last tone and find the white friend sitting motionless in his seat, smoking calmly.

"Good music they have here," he remarks, drumming the table with his fingertips.

Music. The great blobs of purple and red emotion have not touched him. He has only heard what I felt. He is far away and I see him but dimly across the ocean and the continent that have fallen between us. He is so pale with his whiteness then and I am *so* colored.

Pause & Reflect

As the essay ends . . .

• Hurston states that some-times she feels as if she has no particular race.

• She sees herself as a mix-ture of many qualities and attributes.

⭐ **Reader Success Strategy**

As you read lines 129–139, try to put yourself in Hurston's shoes. Use your own experi-ences to understand how she feels. How would you walk if you wanted the world to look up to you?

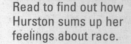 **FOCUS**

Read to find out how Hurston sums up her feelings about race.

At certain times I have no race. I am *me*. When I set my hat at a certain angle and saunter down Seventh Avenue, Harlem City, feeling as snooty as the lions in front of the Forty-Second Street Library, for instance. So far as my feelings are concerned, Peggy Hopkins Joyce on the Boule Mich with her gorgeous raiment, stately carriage,[14] knees knocking together in a most aristocratic manner, has nothing on me. The cosmic[15] Zora emerges. I belong to no race nor time. I am the eternal feminine with its string of beads.

---

13. **assegai** (ăs'ə-gī'): a light spear, especially one with a short shaft and long blade, used in southern Africa.

14. **Peggy Hopkins Joyce . . . carriage:** one of the richest women of Hurston's day, walking along the Boulevard Saint-Michel in Paris, dressed in beautiful clothes, carrying herself like a queen.

15. **cosmic:** of or belonging to the universe.

WORDS TO KNOW   **veneer** (və-nîr') *n.* a thin surface layer that conceals what is below

140   I have no separate feeling about being an American citizen and colored. I am merely a fragment of the Great Soul that surges within the boundaries. My country, right or wrong.

   Sometimes, I feel discriminated against, but it does not make me angry. It merely astonishes me. How *can* any deny themselves the pleasure of my company? It's beyond me.

>   But in the main, I feel like a brown bag of miscellany[16] propped against a wall. Against a wall in company with other bags, white, red, and yellow. Pour out the contents, and there is discovered a jumble of small things priceless and worthless.
> 150 A first-water[17] diamond, an empty spool, bits of broken glass, lengths of string, a key to a door long since crumbled away, a rusty knife blade, old shoes saved for a road that never was and never will be, a nail bent under the weight of things too heavy for any nail, a dried flower or two still a little fragrant. In your hand is the brown bag. On the ground before you is the jumble it held—so much like the jumble in the bags, could they be emptied, that all might be dumped in a single heap and the bags refilled without altering the content of any greatly. A bit of colored glass more or less would not matter.
> 160 Perhaps that is how the Great Stuffer of Bags filled them in the first place—who knows?

Pause & Reflect

---

16. **miscellany** (mĭs′ə-lā′nē): a collection of various parts, items, or ingredients.
17. **first-water**: of the highest quality or purity.

Reading Check

Why is Hurston shocked when she feels that someone has discriminated against her?

Pause & Reflect

READ ALOUD   **1.** Read aloud the last paragraph of this essay. How important does Hurston feel race is in determining the kind of person you are? **(Main Idea)**

_____

_____

_____

_____

2. If you had met Zora Neale Hurston, would you have liked her? Explain. **(Connect)**

_____

_____

_____

_____

CHALLENGE

Tone is the writer's attitude toward his or her subject. When Hurston describes her childhood and how she loved to entertain others, her tone is happy, light, and optimistic. Choose a passage from this essay. What is the tone of that section? **(Analyze)**

Active Reading SkillBuilder

Drawing Conclusions About Author's Purposes

A writer usually writes for one or more **purposes**—to inform, to entertain, to express himself or herself, or to persuade readers to believe or do something. When reading this essay, identify passages from each part that affect you strongly. For each passage, consider the kinds of experiences Hurston relates, descriptive details she provides, and her direct statements and comparisons. Use the following chart to record data about the selected passages. Then use the data to draw conclusions about Hurston's purposes for writing each passage. Record these conclusions on the chart. An example is shown.

Hurston's Essay	
Passages	**Purposes**
1. Childhood in Eatonville *Hurston describes growing up in an African-American town in Florida where she "was everybody's Zora" and enjoyed entertaining Northern white tourists who rode through town.*	
2. Experiencing Live Jazz	
3. Comparison of People to Stuffed Bags	

Literary Analysis SkillBuilder

Autobiographical Essay

An **autobiographical essay** is a short work of nonfiction that focuses on an aspect of the writer's life. One of the challenges for the writer of an autobiographical essay is to combine objective description with the expression of subjective feelings. Use the following chart to analyze Hurston's account of listening to jazz at The New World Cabaret. Identify examples of both objective description and Hurston's expression of subjective feelings. An example is shown.

Objective Description	Subjective Expression
The club is located in a drafty basement.	physical effect of listening to jazz—"constricts the thorax and splits the heart"

Words to Know SkillBuilder

Words to Know

deplore   extenuating   rend   specter   veneer

A. On each blank line, write the word from the word list that the clue describes.

1. This word is most commonly used to modify *circumstances.* A lawyer might use it to explain why a defendant should receive mercy.

_____
(1)

2. To do this is to separate or tear something, but forcefully and destructively. Lightning bolts do it to trees, predators to their prey.

_____
(2)

3. This is the visible form of something not actually present, always mysterious and usually frightening. It is often used figuratively to describe something dreaded, such as war.

_____
(3)

4. To do this is to be very sorry about something or to find a lot of fault with it. People tend to disapprove of rudeness but do this to murder.

_____
(4)

5. This is a surface, and only a surface, appearance. It can be a layer of fine oak on top of plywood or a friendly smile that hides jealousy or hate.

_____
(5)

B. Fill in each blank with the correct word from the word list.

1. Under her _____ of sternness is a soft heart. You could describe her as a cement-covered marshmallow.

2. Are past hardships and injustices _____ conditions for a crime committed in the present? People disagree, to put it mildly.

3. I remain haunted by the _____ of poverty. It looms in my pantry, waiting for me to waste a bite of food.

4. Most people _____ the poverty that large numbers of families live in. How many do something about it?

5. I'll _____ this dress right up the back the first time I bend over. What ever possessed me to buy a garment so much too small?

C. Imagine that you are listening to a piece of music that strongly affects you as the music at The New World Cabaret affects Hurston. Write a description of the music and your reaction to it, similar in nature to how Hurston describes the jazz she listens to. Use at least **two** of the Words to Know.

The DEATH of the HIRED MAN

ROBERT FROST

Before You Read

Connect to Your Life

What words comes to mind when you hear the word *home*? Use this word web to jot down your ideas. One idea has been provided as an example.

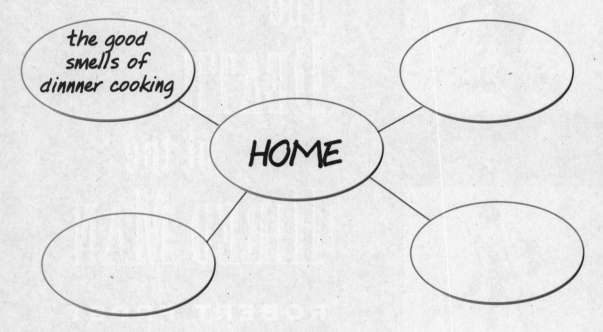

the good smells of dinnner cooking

HOME

Key to the Poem

WHAT TO LISTEN FOR This poem tells a story and contains everyday language. Notice Frost's use of everyday language in the following line.

> He's worn out. He's asleep beside the stove.

Frost also used blank verse rather than rhymed or rhythmic lines. Notice that the following lines do not rhyme, and they contain only the natural rhythms of everyday speech.

> Warren leaned out and took a step or two
> Picked up a little stick, and brought it back
> And broke it in his hand and tossed it by.

The DEATH of the HIRED MAN

ROBERT FROST

PREVIEW "The Death of the Hired Man" is one of Robert Frost's best known poems. It is set on a farm in New England in the early years of the 20th century. At that time, much of the work on a farm had to be done by hand. Farmers needed extra workers at certain times, especially during the fall harvest. The hired man, mentioned in this poem, is a wandering laborer. He works on farms in exchange for room and board. As the poem begins, he has just returned to the farm he left during the last harvest.

FOCUS

Mary waits to tell her husband, Warren, about the return of Silas, the hired man. Read to find out how Warren feels about Silas.

MARK IT UP As you read, circle words or phrases that help you understand Warren's feelings about Silas. An example is highlighted on page 304.

As the poem begins . . .

- Mary and Warren discuss Silas.

Mary sat musing on the lamp-flame[1] at the table,
Waiting for Warren. When she heard his step,
She ran on tiptoe down the darkened passage
To meet him in the doorway with the news
And put him on his guard. "Silas is back."

What Does It Mean?

To *put him on his guard* means "to warn or alert him."

---

1. **musing on the lamp-flame:** looking thoughtfully at the flame of an oil lamp.

SEASONAL WORKERS During harvests, when crops needed to be picked or hay needed to be cut and baled, many farmers hired temporary workers. Often, such workers were not paid. Instead, they received meals and a place to stay.

✔ **Reading Check**

What does Warren mean when he says, "I'm done"?

Pause & **Reflect**

1. Review the words or phrases you circled as you read. Why doesn't Warren want to take Silas back? **(Infer)**

_____

_____

_____

_____

📖 READ ALOUD **2.** Read aloud lines 22–24. In these lines, Warren recalls his last conversation with Silas. In line 24, Silas says the first three words, and Warren says the last six. Why did Silas leave Warren and Mary at haying time? **(Infer)**

_____

_____

_____

_____

She pushed him outward with her through the door
And shut it after her. "Be kind," she said.
She took the market things from Warren's arms
And set them on the porch, then drew him down
10 To sit beside her on the wooden steps.

"When was I ever anything but kind to him?
But I'll not have the fellow back," he said.
"I told him so last haying², didn't I?
If he left then, I said, that ended it.
What good is he? Who else will <u>harbor</u> him
At his age for the little he can do?
What help he is there's no depending on.
Off he goes always when I need him most.
He thinks he ought to earn a little pay,
20 Enough at least to buy tobacco with,
So he won't have to beg and be <u>beholden</u>.
'All right,' I say, 'I can't afford to pay
Any fixed wages,³ though I wish I could.'
'Someone else can.' 'Then someone else will have to.'
I shouldn't mind his bettering himself
If that was what it was. You can be certain,
When he begins like that, there's someone at him
Trying to coax him off with pocket money—
In haying time, when any help is scarce.
30 In winter he comes back to us. I'm done."

Pause & **Reflect**

_____

2. **haying:** the time of the year when hay is cut.

3. **fixed wages:** a specified sum of money given by an employer to a worker.

WORDS TO KNOW	**harbor** (här′bər) *v.* to shelter; protect
	beholden (bǐ hōl′ dən) *adj.* obliged to feel grateful; indebted

Mary describes her impressions of Silas on his return. Her feelings for Silas are different from her husband's.

MARK IT UP As you read, underline words or phrases that suggest her feelings for Silas.

"Sh! not so loud: he'll hear you," Mary said.

"I want him to: he'll have to soon or late."[4]

"He's worn out. He's asleep beside the stove.
When I came up from Rowe's I found him here,
Huddled against the barn door fast asleep,
A miserable sight, and frightening, too—
You needn't smile—I didn't recognize him—
I wasn't looking for him—and he's changed.
Wait till you see."

        "Where did you say he'd been?"

40 "He didn't say. I dragged him to the house,
And gave him tea and tried to make him smoke.
I tried to make him talk about his travels.
Nothing would do: he just kept nodding off."

"What did he say? Did he say anything?"

"But little."

        "Anything? Mary, confess
He said he'd come to ditch the meadow[5] for me."

"Warren!"

        "But did he? I just want to know."

"Of course he did. What would you have him say?
50 Surely you wouldn't grudge the poor old man
Some humble way to save his self-respect.
He added, if you really care to know,
He meant to clear the upper pasture, too.
That sounds like something you have heard before?"

As the poem continues . . .

• Mary says that Silas is very tired.

• When Mary asks Warren to lower his voice so that Silas won't hear him talking, Warren says that he wants Silas to hear what he has to say.

⭐ **Reader Success Strategy**

Pay close attention to the quotation marks in this section. They will help you figure out when Mary speaks and when Warren speaks. Using two different colored markers, highlight Mary's speeches in one color and Warren's speeches in another. Then, with a partner, read the dialogue out loud.

📖 **READ ALOUD** Lines 44–53

Warren suggests that he has often heard Silas's so-called reason for returning to the farm. What does Mary understand about Silas that Warren does not? **(Infer)**

_____

_____

_____

_____

---

4. **soon or late:** sooner or later; eventually.

5. **ditch the meadow:** to dig one or more channels in a field in order to drain off excess water.

Warren, I wish you could have heard the way
He jumbled everything. I stopped to look
Two or three times—he made me feel so queer—
To see if he was talking in his sleep.

Pause & Reflect

As the poem continues . . .

- Mary says that Silas and Harold are different in many ways.

- Mary says that Silas has suggested that he and Harold might make a great team on the farm.

What Does It Mean?

Between them they will lay this farm as smooth means that Silas and Harold Wilson will do an excellent job of haying.

☆ **Reader Success Strategy**

Reread lines 65–77, paying attention to the differences between Silas and Harold. Using the chart below, brainstorm a list of words and phrases that you would use to describe Silas and Harold.

Silas	Harold

FOCUS

Mary recalls Silas's relationship with Harold Wilson. He was a college student who worked on the farm four years ago. Read to find out what Silas thinks of Harold.

He ran on[6] Harold Wilson—you remember—
The boy you had in haying four years since.[7]
He's finished school, and teaching in his college.
Silas declares you'll have to get him back.
He says they two will make a team for work:
Between them they will lay this farm as smooth!
The way he mixed that in with other things.
He thinks young Wilson a likely lad, though daft
On[8] education—you know how they fought
All through July under the blazing sun,
Silas up on the cart to build the load,
Harold along beside to pitch it on."

"Yes, I took care to keep well out of earshot."

"Well, those days trouble Silas like a dream.
You wouldn't think they would. How such things linger!
Harold's young college-boy's <u>assurance</u> piqued[9] him.

---

6. **ran on:** kept talking about.

7. **since:** ago.

8. **daft on:** crazy about; obsessed with.

9. **piqued** (pēkt): aroused resentment in.

WORDS
TO
KNOW

assurance (ə-shŏŏr′əns) *n.* self-confidence

After so many years he still keeps finding
Good arguments he sees he might have used.
I sympathize. I know just how it feels
To think of the right thing to say too late.
Harold's associated in his mind with Latin.[10]
He asked me what I thought of Harold's saying
He studied Latin, like the violin,
Because he liked it—that an argument!
He said he couldn't make the boy believe
He could find water with a hazel prong—[11]
Which showed how much good school had ever done
   him.
He wanted to go over that. But most of all
He thinks if he could have another chance
To teach him how to build a load of hay—"

"I know, that's Silas' one accomplishment.
He bundles every forkful in its place.
And tags and numbers it for future reference,
So he can find and easily dislodge it
In the unloading. Silas does that well.
He takes it out in bunches like big birds' nests.
You never see him standing on the hay
He's trying to lift, straining to lift himself."
"He thinks if he could teach him that, he'd be
Some good perhaps to someone in the world.
He hates to see a boy the fool of books.[12]
Poor Silas, so concerned for other folk,
And nothing to look backward to with pride,
And nothing to look forward to with hope,
So now and never any different."

Pause **&** *Reflect*

---

10. **Harold's associated . . . with Latin:** To Silas, Harold's love of the Latin language stands for all knowledge with no practical use.

11. **find . . . prong:** refers to the practice of dowsing, in which a person uses a forked stick made of hazel wood to try to find underground water.

12. **the fool of books:** a person with much education but no common sense.

Reading Check

What skill does Silas have that Warren respects? Underline the lines in which he expresses positive thoughts and feelings about Silas.

Pause **&** *Reflect*

▲ MARK IT UP **1.** What does Silas think of Harold Wilson? Write the answer below. Then circle details on pages 306 and 307 that led you to your conclusion. (**Draw Conclusions**)

_____

_____

_____

_____

2. Reread lines 88–95. How would you evaluate Silas as a worker? (**Evaluate**)

_____

_____

_____

_____

READ ALOUD **3.** Read aloud lines 99–102. How do these lines make you feel about Silas? (**Connect**)

_____

_____

_____

_____

- Mary explains to Warren why Silas *really* came back to their farm.

- Mary and Warren disagree about the meaning of home.

FOCUS

The narrator describes the moonlight flowing upon Mary. Mary and Warren then tell what home means to each of them.

MARK IT UP As you read, mark Warren's definition of home with a **W.** Mark Mary's definition of home with an **M.**

Part of a moon was falling down the west,
Dragging the whole sky with it to the hills.
Its light poured softly in her lap. She saw it
And spread her apron to it. She put out her hand
Among the harplike morning-glory strings,
<u>Taut</u> with the dew from garden bed to eaves,
As if she played unheard some tenderness
That wrought on[13] him beside her in the night.

"Warren," she said, "he has come home to die:
You needn't be afraid he'll leave you this time."

"Home," he mocked gently.
                              "Yes, what else but home?
It all depends on what you mean by home.
Of course he's nothing to us, any more
Than was the hound that came a stranger to us
Out of the woods, worn out upon the trail."

"Home is the place where, when you have to go there,
They have to take you in."

                              "I should have called it
Something you somehow haven't to deserve."

Pause & Reflect

Pause & Reflect

READ ALOUD **1.** Read aloud lines 103–110. These lines associate Mary with moonlight, flowers, and music. What do these lines suggest about her character? **(Infer)**

_____

_____

_____

_____

2. Review the definitions you marked as you read. Which definition do you prefer? *Warren's/Mary's,* because ____

_____

_____

_____

_____ .

(Compare and Contrast)

13. **wrought** (rôt) **on:** worked on.

WORDS
TO
KNOW

taut (tôt) *adj.* pulled tight; straight

Warren wonders why Silas didn't go to his
brother for help. Read to find out about
Silas's relationship with his brother.

Warren leaned out and took a step or two,
Picked up a little stick, and brought it back
And broke it in his hand and tossed it by.
"Silas has better claim on us you think
Than on his brother? Thirteen little miles
As the road winds would bring him to his door.
Silas has walked that far no doubt today.
Why doesn't he go there? His brother's rich,
A somebody—director in the bank."

130   "He never told us that."

           "We know it, though."

"I think his brother ought to help, of course.
I'll see to that if there is need. He ought of right
To take him in, and might be willing to—
He may be better than appearances.[14]
But have some pity on Silas. Do you think
If he had any pride in claiming kin
Or anything he looked for from his brother,
He'd keep so still about him all this time?"

"I wonder what's between them."

           "I can tell you.
140 Silas is what he is—we wouldn't mind him—
But just the kind that kinsfolk[15] can't abide.
He never did a thing so very bad.
He don't know why he isn't quite as good
As anybody. Worthless though he is,
He won't be made ashamed to please his brother."

Pause & Reflect

14. **better than appearances:** better than he looks.
15. **kinsfolk:** relatives.

WORDS
TO   **abide** (e-bīd´) v. to put up with
KNOW

As the poem continues . . .
• Warren says that Silas' brother
is rich and lives nearby.

• Mary says that Silas has
never mentioned his brother.

⭐ **Reader Success
Strategy**

Read lines 128–145 at least
twice. The first time, read to get
an overall impression of Silas'
relationship with his brother.
Then carefully study what
Warren and Mary say. To make
sure you understand the deep
feelings expressed in this part
of the poem, put each sentence
into your own words.

Pause & Reflect

1. Why does Warren feel that
Silas should go to his brother's
house? **(Clarify)**

_____

_____

_____

_____

✏️ **MARK IT UP** 2. What facts
and feelings have led Mary to
understand why Silas has come
to their farm rather than go to
his brother's house? **(Draw
Conclusions)**

_____

_____

_____

_____

Pause & Reflect

1. Why does Mary ask Warren to go in and see Silas? **(Clarify)**

_____

_____

_____

_____

READ ALOUD **2.** Read aloud lines 164–166. What reactions do you have to the poem's ending? **(Connect)**

_____

_____

_____

_____

CHALLENGE

Frost wanted this poem to teach its readers something. What is the wisdom that the poem teaches you?

FOCUS

Read to find out what happens to the hired man at the end of the poem.

"I can't think Si ever hurt anyone."

"No, but he hurt my heart the way he lay
And rolled his old head on the sharp-edged chair-back.
He wouldn't let me put him on the lounge.[16]
You must go in and see what you can do.
I made the bed up for him there tonight.
You'll be surprised at him—how much he's broken.[17]
His working days are done; I'm sure of it."

"I'd not be in a hurry to say that."

"I haven't been. Go, look, see for yourself.
But, Warren, please remember how it is:
He's come to help you ditch the meadow.
He has a plan. You mustn't laugh at him.
He may not speak of it, and then he may.
I'll sit and see if that small sailing cloud
Will hit or miss the moon."

It hit the moon.
Then there were three there, making a dim row,
The moon, the little silver cloud, and she.

Warren returned—too soon, it seemed to her—
Slipped to her side, caught up her hand and waited.

"Warren?" she questioned.
"Dead," was all he answered.

Pause & Reflect

---

16. **lounge:** couch.
17. **broken:** weakened.

Active Reading SkillBuilder

Understanding Form in Poetry

Form is the placement of a poem's lines on the page and the grouping of those lines into stanzas. The blank-verse form of "The Death of the Hired Man" may make it difficult to keep track of the dialogue. Frost uses several devices to help the reader. Two of these devices are quotation marks and line breaks. A third device is point of view—the narrator always speaks in the third person. On the chart below, record any parts of the poem that cause you to pause to identify the speaker.

Line(s) from Poem	Who I Think Is Speaking	Why I Think So

Literary Analysis SkillBuilder

Blank Verse

"The Death of the Hired Man" is written in **blank verse,** lines of unrhymed iambic pentameter. Well-written blank verse imitates natural rhythms of English speech and sounds very much like the way people talk. A line of blank verse has five iambic feet, each consisting of an unstressed syllable followed by a stressed syllable. In each box below, write a line from the poem that sounds to you like natural speech. Mark the syllables as unstressed (ˇ) or stressed (´). An example is shown.

Line A

"It all depends on what you mean by home." (line 114)

Line B

Line C

Words to Know SkillBuilder

Words to Know

abide   assurance   beholden   harbor   taut

A. Decide which Word to Know is described by each clue. Write the word on the blank line next to the clue.

1. If you hold your head up and act with confidence, people will think you know what you are doing.

   _____ (1)

2. Keep the clothesline pulled tight to keep the clothing from sagging to the ground.

   _____ (2)

3. If you accept that favor, you might feel that you owe something in return.

   _____ (3)

4. My little brother can be an awful pest, but I have to put up with him.

   _____ (4)

5. This term is usually used in connection with ships or boats, but it can be used for people, too.

   _____ (5)

B. Circle the word in each group that is a synonym for the boldfaced word.

1. **abide**   home   endure   brick   leave

2. **assurance**   intelligence   reluctance   confidence   influence

3. **beholden**   indebted   excluded   upset   disinterested

4. **harbor**   exclude   refute   display   protect

5. **taut**   loose   smooth   tight   educated

C. "The Death of the Hired Man" includes a famous definition of *home*. Write your description of an ideal home. Include details about both the physical environment and the people who share this home. Use at least **two** Words to Know in your description.

The End of Something

Ernest Hemingway

Before You Read

Connect to Your Life

In this short story, a young man and a young woman are having trouble in their relationship. Have you ever been in a relationship that started out strong and then ended? Do you know anyone else this happened to? What are some reasons why people fall out of love? List your reasons on the lines below. Then, as you read the story, find out what happens between Nick and Marjorie.

_____

_____

_____

Key to the Story

WHAT YOU NEED TO KNOW In this story, the main character, Nick Adams, represents many soldiers who lived through World War I. Like Hemingway, the war left Nick disillusioned and saddened. He doesn't understand why nothing makes him happy anymore. Marjorie can't understand what happened to Nick. He is not physically hurt, but he is not the same as he was before the war. This theme of **alienation**—a deep feeling of being disconnected from other people—appears often in the literature written after World War I.

Reading Tips

Hemingway's **style**—the way he writes—is direct and matter-of-fact. He doesn't explain a lot about how the **characters** feel. As you read, you will need to make some guesses about what exactly is going on.

- Keep the title in mind.
- Try to picture the details of **setting** and **action** that Hemingway describes.
- Pay close attention to the **dialogue**. Try to figure out what the **main characters** are thinking and feeling from what they say and from what they don't say.

As the story begins . . .

- Nick, a World War I veteran, and his girlfriend, Marjorie, are introduced.
- They are fishing on a lake.

✏️ **MARK IT UP** **KEEP TRACK**

As you read, you can use these marks to keep track of your understanding.

✔ ..... I understand.

? ..... I don't understand this.

! ..... Interesting or surprising idea

The End of Something

Ernest Hemingway

PREVIEW This story takes place in the summer of 1919, after the end of World War I. The two main characters are Nick, a former soldier, and his girlfriend, Marjorie. They are going fishing near the ruins of an old lumber mill on Lake Michigan, a place they know well. Nick is trying to sort out his life now that the war is over. As he and Marjorie fish and talk, a change in their relationship becomes clear.

FOCUS
The story opens with a brief history of the town of Hortons Bay and then introduces the two **main characters**. As you read, look for hints about the kind of relationship the two characters have.

In the old days Hortons Bay was a lumbering town. No one who lived in it was out of sound of the big saws in the mill by the lake. Then one year there were no more logs to make lumber. The lumber schooners came into the bay and were loaded with the cut of the mill that stood stacked in the yard. All the piles of lumber were carried away. The big mill building had all its machinery that

10

was removable taken out and hoisted on board one of the schooners by the men who had worked in the mill. The schooner moved out of the bay toward the open lake carrying the two great saws, the travelling carriage that hurled the logs against the revolving, circular saws and all the rollers, wheels, belts, and iron piled on a hull-deep load of lumber. Its open hold covered with canvas and lashed tight, the sails of the schooner filled and it moved out into the open lake, carrying with it everything that had made the mill a mill and

20 Hortons Bay a town.

The one-story bunk houses, thè eating-house, the company store, the mill offices, and the big mill itself stood deserted in the acres of sawdust that covered the swampy meadow by the shore of the bay.

Ten years later there was nothing of the mill left except the broken white limestone of its foundations showing through the swampy second growth[1] as Nick and Marjorie rowed along the shore. They were trolling[2] along the edge of the channel-bank where the bottom dropped off suddenly from sandy shallows to twelve feet of dark water. They were trolling on their way to the point to set night lines for rainbow trout.

"There's our old ruin, Nick," Marjorie said.

Nick, rowing, looked at the white stone in the green trees.

"There it is," he said.

"Can you remember when it was a mill?" Marjorie asked.

"I can just remember," Nick said.

"It seems more like a castle," Marjorie said.

Nick said nothing. They rowed on out of sight of the mill, following the shore line. Then Nick cut across the bay.

"They aren't striking," he said.

"No," Marjorie said. She was intent on the rod all the time they trolled, even when she talked. She loved to fish. She loved to fish with Nick.

Close beside the boat a big trout broke the surface of the water. Nick pulled hard on one oar so the boat would turn and the bait spinning far behind would pass where the trout was feeding. As the trout's back came up out of the water the minnows jumped wildly. They sprinkled the surface like a handful of shot[3] thrown into the water. Another trout broke water, feeding on the other side of the boat.

"They're feeding," Marjorie said.

"But they won't strike," Nick said.

He rowed the boat around to troll past both the feeding fish, then headed it for the point. Marjorie did not reel in until the boat touched the shore.

---

1. **swampy second growth:** new trees and other plants growing in swampy area surrounding the ruins of the mill.

2. **trolling:** a method of fishing in which a line and baited hook trail along behind a slow-moving boat.

3. **shot:** the tiny metal pellets used as ammunition in a shotgun.

1. What happened to the old
lumber mill in Hortons Bay?
(Clarify)

_____

_____

_____

2. Check two words or phrases
below that you think describe
the relationship between Nick
and Marjorie at this point.
(Infer)

are often together

angry

very romantic

matter-of-fact

talk a lot

As the story continues . . .

• Marjorie senses that something is wrong with Nick.

What Does It Mean?

The fishing rods have clicking devices that will make a sound when a fish takes the bait. Nick is *setting the click* so he and Marjorie will know when they have caught a fish.

They pulled the boat up the beach and Nick lifted out a pail of live perch. The perch swam in the water in the pail. Nick caught three of them with his hands and cut their heads off and skinned them while Marjorie chased with her hands in the bucket, finally caught a perch, cut its head off and skinned it. Nick looked at her fish.

"You don't want to take the ventral fin[4] out," he said. "It'll be all right for bait but it's better with the ventral fin in."

He hooked each of the skinned perch through the tail. There were two hooks attached to a leader[5] on each rod. Then Marjorie rowed the boat out over the channel-bank, holding the line in her teeth, and looking toward Nick, who stood on the shore holding the rod and letting the line run out from the reel.

"That's about right," he called.

"Should I let it drop?" Marjorie called back, holding the line in her hand.

"Sure. Let it go." Marjorie dropped the line overboard and watched the baits go down through the water.

Pause & Reflect

FOCUS
In this part of the story, Nick and Marjorie's relationship is about to go through a major change.
MARK IT UP As you read, underline passages that show what is happening to the relationship. An example is highlighted on page 319.

She came in with the boat and ran the second line out the same way. Each time Nick set a heavy slab of driftwood across the butt of the rod to hold it solid and propped it up at an angle with a small slab. He reeled in the slack line so the line ran taut out to where the bait rested on the sandy floor of the channel and set the click on the reel. When a trout, feeding on the bottom, took the bait it would run with it, taking line out of the reel in a rush and making the reel sing with the click on.

Marjorie rowed up the point a little way so she would not disturb the line. She pulled hard on the oars and the boat

---

4. **ventral fin:** fin on the underside of a fish.
5. **leader:** short length of line by which a hook is fastened to a fishing line.

90 went way up the beach. Little waves came in with it. Marjorie
stepped out of the boat and Nick pulled the boat high up
the beach.

"What's the matter, Nick?" Marjorie asked.

"I don't know," Nick said, getting wood for a fire.

They made a fire with driftwood. Marjorie went to the boat
and brought a blanket. The evening breeze blew the smoke
toward the point, so Marjorie spread the blanket out between
the fire and the lake.

100 Marjorie sat on the blanket with her back to the fire and
waited for Nick. He came over and sat down beside her on
the blanket. In back of them was the close second-growth
timber[6] of the point and in front was the bay with the mouth
of Hortons Creek. It was not quite dark. The fire-light went
as far as the water. They could both see the two steel rods at
an angle over the dark water. The fire glinted on the reels.

Marjorie unpacked the basket of supper.

"I don't feel like eating," said Nick.

"Come on and eat, Nick."

"All right."

110 They ate without talking, and watched the two rods and
the fire-light in the water.

"There's going to be a moon tonight," said Nick. He
looked across the bay to the hills that were beginning to
sharpen against the sky. Beyond the hills he knew the moon
was coming up.

"I know it," Marjorie said happily.

"You know everything," Nick said.

"Oh, Nick, please cut it out! Please, please don't be
that way!"

120 "I can't help it," Nick said. "You do. You know everything.
That's the trouble. You know you do."

Marjorie did not say anything.

"I've taught you everything. You know you do. What don't
you know, anyway?"

"Oh, shut up," Marjorie said. "There comes the moon."

They sat on the blanket without touching each other and
watched the moon rise.

"You don't have to talk silly," Marjorie said. "What's really
the matter?"

---

6. **second-growth timber:** trees that cover an area after the original, "old
growth" trees have been cut or burned.

Reader Success Strategy

In the chart below, fill in the first column with words and phrases that describe Nick. In the second column do the same for Marjorie. You can use your own words or words from the story.

Nick	Marjorie

Reading Check

What do Marjorie and Nick do on the beach?

"I don't know."

"Of course you know."

"No I don't."

"Go on and say it."

Nick looked on at the moon, coming up over the hills.

"It isn't fun any more."

He was afraid to look at Marjorie. Then he looked at her. She sat there with her back toward him. He looked at her back. "It isn't fun any more. Not any of it."

She didn't say anything. He went on. "I feel as though everything was gone to hell inside of me. I don't know, Marge. I don't know what to say."

He looked on at her back.

"Isn't love any fun?" Marjorie said.

"No," Nick said. Marjorie stood up. Nick sat there his head in his hands.

"I'm going to take the boat," Marjorie called to him. "You can walk back around the point."

"All right," Nick said. "I'll push the boat off for you."

"You don't need to," she said. She was afloat in the boat on the water with the moonlight on it. Nick went back and lay down with his face in the blanket by the fire. He could hear Marjorie rowing on the water.

He lay there for a long time. He lay there while he heard Bill come into the clearing walking around through the woods. He felt Bill coming up to the fire. Bill didn't touch him, either.

"Did she go all right?" Bill said.

"Yes," Nick said, lying, his face on the blanket.

"Have a scene?"

"No, there wasn't any scene."

"How do you feel?"

"Oh, go away, Bill! Go away for a while."

Bill selected a sandwich from the lunch basket and walked over to have a look at the rods.

Pause & **Reflect**

Pause & **Reflect**

1. Look back at the passages that you underlined as you read. Describe what happens to Nick and Marjorie's relationship. **(Infer)**

_____

_____

_____

_____

2. Think of one question that you would like to ask about the ending of the story. Write it below. **(Question)**

_____

_____

_____

_____

CHALLENGE

How does the history of Hortons Bay reflect the relationship between Nick and Marjorie? Mark words and phrases in the description of Hortons Bay that relate to what happens to the two characters. **(Evaluate)**

Active Reading SkillBuilder

Making Inferences

The scenes in "The End of Something" are made up almost entirely of dialogue between Nick and Marjorie. As they speak, the narrator gives little direct information about how they feel or think. Hemingway's plain style challenges readers to **make inferences,** or logical guesses, to discover the meanings behind the characters' spoken words. Their remarks give clues about their relationship. On the chart below, record lines of dialogue that seem especially meaningful. Then explain what you think these remarks show. An example has been done for you.

Dialogue Clues	What They Show
Nick's Comments "You know everything."	He is feeling critical of Marjorie.
Marjorie's Comments	

Literary Analysis SkillBuilder

Style

Style is the distinctive way in which a piece of literature is written. "The End of Something" reflects the simple, direct style of a newspaper reporter and journalist. It has short sentences, attention to detail, simple descriptions, clear language, and a matter-of-fact tone. In the chart below, identify an example of each of these characteristics of Hemingway's style. An example has been done for you.

Characteristics of Style	Example
Short Sentences	
Attention to Detail	
Simple Descriptions	*They made a fire with driftwood.*
Clear Language	
Matter-of-Fact Tone	

Follow Up: Work with a small group of classmates to rewrite a passage of the story to include Nick's feelings and thoughts. Discuss differences between Hemingway's style and the style of your rewrite.

The Love Song of J. Alfred Prufrock

T. S. Eliot

Before You Read

Connect to Your Life

The speaker in this poem, J. Alfred Prufrock, is on his way to a party. As he walks, he thinks about what he wants to say to a woman who will be at the party. However, he gets more and more nervous about it. Have you ever been nervous about talking to someone special? How did you feel? What did you do? How did it turn out? Write about your experiences in the chart below.

Situation	
What I did	
How it turned out	

Key to the Poem

WHAT YOU NEED TO KNOW *Stream of consciousness* is a literary technique that shows the flow of seemingly unconnected thoughts, responses, and sensations as they occur in a character's mind. The technique allows the writer to present the innermost thoughts and feelings of a character. In this poem, Eliot uses stream of consciousness to reveal the jumble of images, ideas, feelings, and daydreams that flow through Prufrock's mind.

Reading Tips

This poem goes into the mind of the main character, J. Alfred Prufrock. Because Prufrock's thoughts are often rambling and disconnected, you may be confused at first. The following strategies may help:

- As you read, note places in the poem that seem disconnected. Try to figure out what is going on before and after the break in thought.

- Look for repeated words or lines. They may give you clues to what is happening.

- Use the information in the Guide for Reading to help you with difficult words and passages.

As the poem begins . . .

- The speaker, Prufrock, describes what he sees on his way to the party.

- He wants to ask an "overwhelming question."

MARK IT UP **KEEP TRACK**

As you read, you can use these marks to keep track of your understanding.

✔ ..... I understand.

? ..... I don't understand this.

! ..... Interesting or surprising idea

The Love Song of J. Alfred Prufrock

T. S. Eliot

PREVIEW This poem, written in the early 20th century, follows the inner thoughts and feelings of the speaker, J. Alfred Prufrock. Prufrock is going to a high society party and is worrying about asking a woman an "overwhelming question." The more he thinks about his decision, the more insecure he becomes. Prufrock's thoughts reveal his fears, dreams, and limitations.

FOCUS

Prufrock is walking through city streets on his way to a tea party.

MARK IT UP As you read, underline details that help you picture the streets. Two examples are highlighted.

S'io credessi che mia risposta fosse
a persona che mai tornasse al mondo,
questa fiamma staria senza più scosse.
Ma per ciò che giammai di questo fondo
non tornò vivo alcun, s'i'odo il vero,
senza tema d'infamia ti rispondo.

Let us go then, you and I,
When the evening is spread out against the sky
Like a patient etherized upon a table;
Let us go, through certain half-deserted streets,
The muttering retreats
Of restless nights in one-night cheap hotels
And sawdust restaurants with oyster-shells:

5

Use this guide for help with unfamiliar words and difficult passages.

This is a quotation in Italian from Dante's *Inferno*. One of the people in hell is speaking to a visitor. The speaker says that he will describe his torment only because the visitor cannot return alive to the world to repeat it.

1 you and I: Prufrock may be addressing a companion, the reader, or possibly part of himself.

3 Ether was used to make a patient unconscious during an operation.

7 Cheap seafood restaurants sprinkled sawdust on the floor to absorb moisture. Customers also dropped oyster shells on the floor.

MARK IT UP WORD POWER

Mark words that you'd like to add to your **Personal Word List.** After reading, you can record the words and their meanings beginning on page 476.

More About . . .

DANTE'S *INFERNO* The *Inferno* is one part of a long poem called *The Divine Comedy*. It was written around 1300 by the Italian poet Dante Alighieri. The *Inferno* is about the speaker's journey through Hell. Eliot uses this passage to compare Prufrock with a damned person who is stuck in Hell.

✔ Reading Check

What does the speaker compare the evening to? Why do you think he makes that comparison?

JOT IT DOWN **Reread Lines 4–7**

What do these lines suggest to you about this section of the city? **(Infer)**

_____

_____

_____

Streets that follow like a tedious argument
Of insidious intent
To lead you to an overwhelming question . . .
Oh, do not ask, "What is it?"
Let us go and make our visit.

In the room the women come and go
Talking of Michelangelo.

The yellow fog that rubs its back upon the window-
  panes,
The yellow smoke that rubs its muzzle on the window-
  panes,
Licked its tongue into the corners of the evening,
Lingered upon the pools that stand in drains,
Let fall upon its back the soot that falls from chimneys,
Slipped by the terrace, made a sudden leap,
And seeing that it was a soft October night,
Curled once about the house, and fell asleep.

Pause & Reflect

FOCUS
Read on to learn why Prufrock worries
about the party.
MARK IT UP Underline the words or
phrases that are repeated in these lines.

And indeed there will be time
For the yellow smoke that slides along the street
Rubbing its back upon the window-panes;
There will be time, there will be time
To prepare a face to meet the faces that you meet;
There will be time to murder and create,
And time for all the works and days of hands
That lift and drop a question on your plate;
Time for you and time for me,
And time yet for a hundred indecisions,
And for a hundred visions and revisions,
Before the taking of a toast and tea.

In the room the women come and go
Talking of Michelangelo.

8 tedious (tē′dē-əs): tiresome.

9 insidious (ĭn-sĭd′ē-əs): harmful.

10–12 Prufrock appears reluctant to say what his "overwhelming question" is.

13–14 The women mentioned in these lines may be those at the party Prufrock is going to attend, or they may be women at other parties Prufrock has attended. These lines also appear later in the poem.

14 Michelangelo (mī′kəl-ăn′jə-lō′): a famous 16th-century Italian painter and sculptor.

23–34 This stanza reveals part of Prufrock's problem—he has trouble making up his mind and taking action.

27 This line suggests that Prufrock and the people at the tea party are not sincere or open.

What Does It Mean?

Overwhelming means "overpowering."

JOT IT DOWN Reread Lines 13–14

Do you think this is a serious discussion of the great artist or simply party talk? **(Infer)**

_____

_____

Pause & Reflect

Look at the details you underlined as you read. What do these city streets look like? (Visualize)

_____

_____

_____

As the poem continues . . .

• Prufrock's tension grows as he tries to decide whether to ask the question.

And indeed there will be time
To wonder, "Do I dare?" and, "Do I dare?"
Time to turn back and descend the stair,

40   With a bald spot in the middle of my hair—
(They will say: "How his hair is growing thin!")
My morning coat, my collar mounting firmly to
       the chin,
My necktie rich and modest, but asserted by a
       simple pin—
(They will say: "But how his arms and legs are thin!")

45   Do I dare
Disturb the universe?
In a minute there is time
For decisions and revisions which a minute will reverse.

Pause **&** *Reflect*

FOCUS
Prufrock imagines trying to ask the "overwhelming question." He wonders if he can
do it.
MARK IT UP   As you read, circle the
phrases Prufrock uses to describe himself
and his life.

For I have known them all already, known them all—
50   Have known the evenings, mornings, afternoons,
I have measured out my life with coffee spoons;
I know the voices dying with a dying fall
Beneath the music from a farther room.
       So how should I <u>presume</u>?

55   And I have known the eyes already, known them all—
The eyes that fix you in a formulated phrase,
And when I am formulated, sprawling on a pin,
When I am pinned and wriggling on the wall,
Then how should I begin
60   To spit out all the butt-ends of my days and ways?
       And how should I presume?

WORDS
TO
KNOW

presume (prĭ-zo͞om′) *v.* to act overconfidently; go beyond
       the proper limits; dare

42 morning coat: man's formal dress coat, cut high at the waist and tapering to tails at the back.

51 coffee spoons: small spoons about half the size of teaspoons.

55–58 Prufrock recalls being stared at by women at other parties. The image of himself is one of a live insect that has been classified, labeled, and mounted for display.
56 formulated: reduced to a formula or prepared according to a formula.

Pause **&** **Reflect**

1. Look at the repeated words and phrases that you underlined as you read. What do they tell you about Prufrock's worries? **(Infer)**

_____
_____
_____
_____

2. The question "Do I dare?" suggests that Prufrock wants to do something amazing at the party. What do you think he wants to do? **(Predict)**

_____
_____
_____
_____

MARK IT UP **3.** Prufrock wonders about the impression he will make at the party. Star lines on page 330 in which Prufrock imagines what people will say about him. **(Clarify)**

As the poem continues . . .

• Prufrock imagines asking his question and how it would feel.

What Does It Mean?

In the highlighted line, Prufrock believes he has spent his life in superficial social settings.

READ ALOUD **Lines 49–54**

As you read these lines aloud, listen for the repeated vowel sounds ī, ō, and o̅o̅. They help to express Prufrock's sadness.

And I have known the arms already, known them all—
Arms that are braceleted and white and bare
(But in the lamplight, downed with light brown hair!)
65 Is it perfume from a dress
That makes me so <u>digress</u>?
Arms that lie along a table, or wrap about a shawl.
      And should I then presume?
      And how should I begin?

• • • • •

70 Shall I say, I have gone at dusk through narrow streets
And watched the smoke that rises from the pipes
Of lonely men in shirt-sleeves, leaning out
      of windows? . . .
I should have been a pair of ragged claws
Scuttling across the floors of silent seas.

• • • • •

Pause & Reflect

FOCUS

In lines 75–110, Prufrock considers his
"overwhelming question" further. As you
read, note Prufrock's fears.
MARK IT UP Underline lines that are
repeated in this section, which will help
you identify his fears.

75 And the afternoon, the evening, sleeps so peacefully!
Smoothed by long fingers,
Asleep . . . tired . . . or it <u>malingers</u>,
Stretched on the floor, here beside you and me.
Should I, after tea and cakes and ices,
80 Have the strength to force the moment to its crisis?
But though I have wept and fasted, wept and prayed,
Though I have seen my head (grown slightly bald)
      brought in upon a platter,
I am no prophet—and here's no great matter;

WORDS
TO
KNOW

digress (dī-grĕs′) v. to wander away from the main subject
      in a conversation or in writing; ramble
malinger (mə-lĭng′gər) v. to pretend illness in order to
      avoid duty or work

62–69 Prufrock is talking about the women at the party. He finds them attractive, but he doesn't know how to talk to them.

73–74 Prufrock has presented an image of himself as an insect (lines 57–58) and, here, as a crab or lobster; **scuttling:** running in a hurried way.

75 Note that Prufrock earlier compared the evening to a cat that fell asleep.

81–83 These lines refer to the biblical story of John the Baptist, who is imprisoned by King Herod (Matthew 14; Mark 6). To please his stepdaughter Salome, Herod orders the Baptist's head cut off and brought to him on a platter; **fasted:** for religious reasons, did not eat for a long period; **prophet:** an important religious figure who delivers messages from God.

Pause & Reflect

1. Look at the phrases that you circled as you read. On a scale of 1 to 10 (1 is lowest), how would you rate Prufrock's level of self-confidence? **(Evaluate)**

   _____

2. Why does Prufrock keep saying that he has "known them all" (lines 49, 55, and 62)? Does Prufrock have positive or negative feelings about these people? **(Infer)**

   _____

   _____

   _____

   _____

3. In lines 68 to 74, Prufrock seems on the verge of asking the "overwhelming question." Does he do it? *Yes/No*, because _____

   _____

   _____

   _____ .

   (Infer)

As the poem continues . . .

- Prufrock wonders if he has the strength to ask his question.
- He again imagines asking the question and what it would be like to get the answer.

☆ Reader Success Strategy

With a partner, talk about Prufrock's personality—do you like him or not? What do you think he looks like? Brainstorm a list of words to describe him. Highlight passages that make you feel this way.

I have seen the moment of my greatness flicker,

And I have seen the eternal Footman hold my coat, and
    snicker,

And in short, I was afraid.

And would it have been worth it, after all,

After the cups, the marmalade, the tea,

Among the porcelain, among some talk of you and me,

Would it have been worth while,

To have bitten off the matter with a smile,

To have squeezed the universe into a ball

To roll it towards some overwhelming question,

To say: "I am Lazarus, come from the dead,

Come back to tell you all, I shall tell you all"—

If one, settling a pillow by her head,

    Should say: "That is not what I meant at all.

    That is not it, at all."

And would it have been worth it, after all,

Would it have been worth while,

After the sunsets and the dooryards and the sprinkled
    streets,

After the novels, after the teacups, after the skirts that
    trail along the floor—

And this, and so much more?—

It is impossible to say just what I mean!

But as if a magic lantern threw the nerves in patterns
    on a screen:

Would it have been worth while

If one, settling a pillow or throwing off a shawl,

And turning toward the window, should say:

"That is not it at all,

That is not what I meant, at all."

Pause & Reflect

85 eternal Footman: The image here is of Prufrock being mocked by a servant. The "eternal Footman" may represent Death, who waits for all and knows the hidden weaknesses of each person.

87–110 In these two stanzas, Prufrock rationalizes his failure to ask the "overwhelming question."

89 porcelain: expensive china dishes.

94 Lazarus: In the biblical story (John 11:17–44), Lazarus lay dead in his tomb for four days before Jesus brought him back to life. By comparing himself to Lazarus, Prufrock shows his desire for recognition. He wants other people to think he is important. He also wants to come alive again emotionally.

105 The magic lantern was a forerunner of the slide projector. In this image, the "nerves" may be Prufrock's inner self exposed for all to see.

107 shawl: a large piece of cloth, often woven of wool or silk, that can be worn around the shoulders or used as a light covering.

What Does It Mean?

I have seen the moment of my greatness flicker means that Prufrock was afraid to seize the moment. He lost his courage and kept silent.

✔ Reading Check

How does Prufrock imagine the woman will react to his question?

Pause & Reflect

1. What is the "crisis" Prufrock refers to in line 80? **(Infer)**

_____

2. Look back at the lines you underlined as you read. What is Prufrock afraid of? **(Infer)**

_____

3. Why would Prufrock be like Lazarus if he asked the "overwhelming question"? **(Compare and Contrast)**

_____

FOCUS

At this point, Prufrock gives up on the possibility of asking the question. As you read, think about what Prufrock's life will be like in the future.

No! I am not Prince Hamlet, nor was meant to be;
Am an attendant lord, one that will do
To swell a progress, start a scene or two,
Advise the prince; no doubt, an easy tool,
115   Deferential, glad to be of use,
Politic, cautious, and <u>meticulous</u>;
Full of high sentence, but a bit <u>obtuse</u>;
At times, indeed, almost ridiculous—
Almost, at times, the Fool.

120   I grow old . . . I grow old . . .
I shall wear the bottoms of my trousers rolled.

Shall I part my hair behind? Do I dare to eat a peach?
I shall wear white flannel trousers, and walk upon the
    beach.
I have heard the mermaids singing, each to each.

125   I do not think that they will sing to me.

I have seen them riding seaward on the waves
Combing the white hair of the waves blown back
When the wind blows the water white and black.

We have lingered in the chambers of the sea
130   By sea-girls wreathed with seaweed red and brown
Till human voices wake us, and we drown.

Pause & **Reflect**

WORDS
TO
KNOW

meticulous (mĭ-tĭk′yə-ləs) *adj.* extremely careful and pre-
    cise about details
obtuse (ŏb-tōōs′) *adj.* slow to understand; dull

As the poem ends . . .

- Prufrock seems to accept that he isn't a "star."
- He also seems to give up on the idea of love.

111–119 Notice that Prufrock resigns himself to playing a supporting role rather than a starring one in life.

111 Prince Hamlet: the tragic hero in Shakespeare's drama *Hamlet.*

113 progress: a ceremonial journey made by a king or queen ; to "swell a progress" was to join it and so help increase its size.

115 deferential (dĕf'ə-rĕn'shəl): yielding to someone else's opinion.

116 politic (pŏl'ĭ-tĭk): skillful in dealing with others; diplomatic.

117 high sentence: lofty thoughts and opinions.

124–128 In mythology, mermaids attract men by their beauty and their singing, sometimes allowing men to live with them in the sea.

129–131 Prufrock continues his fantasy of seeing mermaids. However, his fantasy image ends in drowning. The "we" here might refer to different parts of Prufrock himself (see line 1) or to Prufrock and others who, like him, have retreated to a fantasy world.

What Does It Mean?

Rolled trousers were a style that young boys wore. The highlighted sentence expresses Prufrock's desire to be young again.

Pause & Reflect

1. How would you describe Prufrock's attitude about his life? **(Infer)**

_____
_____
_____
_____

2. Prufrock imagines a fantasy world inhabited by mermaids. Circle two phrases below that describe how this fantasy makes him feel. **(Infer)**

separated from other people   sad about his life

hopeful about the future   satisfied with his life

CHALLENGE

This poem is full of **irony**—when what happens is the opposite of what is expected. One of the greatest ironies is in the title. What is ironic about this poem being called a "love song"? **(Analyze)**

Active Reading SkillBuilder

Understanding Stream of Consciousness

Stream of consciousness writing presents the flow of thoughts, responses, and sensations as they occur in a character's mind. Eliot uses this technique to reveal the jumble of images, ideas, feelings, and daydreams that flow through Prufrock's mind. To help you follow Prufrock's random thoughts and feelings, fill in the chart below with key details about a decision that he is trying to make. One example is done for you.

	Details
Part 1: Prufrock's musings about asking the "overwhelming question" (lines 1–83)	*"Oh, do not ask, 'What is it?'"*
Part 2: Prufrock's decision (lines 84–86)	
Part 3: Prufrock's justification for his decision (lines 87–110)	

Literary Analysis SkillBuilder

Imagery

Imagery consists of words and phrases that appeal to any of the five senses. Imagery helps the reader imagine precisely what the writer is describing. In "The Love Song of J. Alfred Prufrock," Eliot uses imagery to describe Prufrock and to picture details of the setting in the poem, such as the city streets and the tea party. On the chart below, list three images that describe Prufrock and three images that give some detail of the setting. Examples are given.

Images That Describe Prufrock	Images That Picture the Setting
1. *his hair is growing thin (line 41)*	1. *yellow smoke that slides along the street (line 24)*
2.	2.
3.	3.
4.	4.

Follow Up: What do the images of Prufrock tell you about him?

Words to Know SkillBuilder

Words to Know

| digress | malinger | meticulous | obtuse | presume |

A. Find familiar words in the puzzle below. Circle all the ones you can find that go from left to right or top to bottom in the puzzle. Write them down to the right of the puzzle or on a separate sheet of paper.

S	U	S	T	F	A	K	E	C
D	O	P	E	U	H	W	O	R
S	N	O	B	S	A	E	F	A
A	C	R	A	S	V	A	F	B
B	U	L	L	Y	E	K	S	O
O	R	U	B	O	L	D	H	U
U	E	M	I	L	A	Z	Y	T

Use five words from the puzzle to fill in the blanks in the following sentences. If you cannot find a word that makes sense and has the correct meaning, look at the puzzle again. Don't use the same word more than once.

1. A meticulous person may seem _____ to other people.

2. You might tell an obtuse person not to be such a _____.

3. When you digress, you say things that are _____ the subject.

4. People who malinger _____ an illness.

5. When you presume, you are being _____.

B. Fill in each blank with the correct word from the word list.

"I hate it when people _____," said my boss. "Half

of the staff have 'stomach aches' today? How _____

do they think I am? I'll fire them! Which reminds me, where are the matches?"

"Don't _____," I said. "The problem has to do with

needing a lunchroom chef who's a little more _____

about sanitary conditions. I didn't eat there yesterday and neither did you, Fred."

"That's Mr. Fritzel to you, young lady. Don't _____."

C. Write a brief stream-of-consciousness narrative that Prufrock might write as an old man looking back on his life. Use at least **three** of the Words to Know.

The JILTING of
Granny Weatherall

Katherine Anne Porter

Before You Read

Connect to Your Life

As the main character in this story nears death, memories of major events in her life keep coming to her mind. Think about memories that replay again and again in your mind. Why do those particular memories keep coming back? Use the following word web to jot down your ideas.

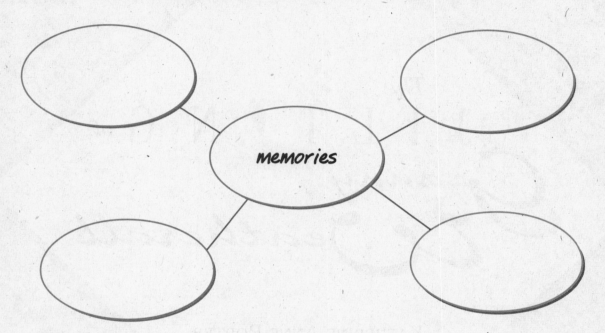

memories

Key to the Story

WHAT YOU NEED TO KNOW As the title implies, the main character of this story, Granny Weatherall, was jilted 60 years before this story takes place. To jilt someone means to end a relationship with a person in a deceitful or abrupt way. Now 80, Granny has survived many other difficult experiences to live a long and happy life. As her name implies, she has *weathered* it *all*. As you read the story, think about the name *Weatherall* and consider whether it is or is not a good name for this character.

The JILTING of Granny Weatherall

Katherine Anne Porter

PREVIEW In her writing, Katherine Anne Porter was able to say little and suggest much. She does exactly that in this **short story**. Its main character, Granny Weatherall, is nearly 80 years old and near death. As she lies in her sickroom, she recalls key moments and relationships in her life. A terrible event still haunts her memory. Sixty years ago, her bridegroom-to-be did not show up for the wedding. This jilting hurt Granny's pride, and time has not healed the wound.

FOCUS
As Granny Weatherall lies in bed, Doctor Harry examines her. The first sentence shows her reaction as he takes her pulse. The second sentence takes you into her mind to reveal her feelings about Doctor Harry.

MARK IT UP As you read, circle details that help you form impressions of Granny. An example is highlighted.

She flicked her wrist neatly out of Doctor Harry's pudgy careful fingers and pulled the sheet up to her chin. The brat ought to be in knee breeches.[1] Doctoring around the country with spectacles on his nose! "Get along now, take your schoolbooks and go. There's nothing wrong with me."

Doctor Harry spread a warm paw like a cushion on her forehead where the forked green vein danced and made her eyelids twitch. "Now, now, be a good girl, and we'll have you up in no time."

"That's no way to speak to a woman nearly eighty years old just because she's down. I'd have you respect your elders, young man."

"Well, Missy, excuse me." Doctor Harry patted her cheek. "But I've got to warn you, haven't I? You're a marvel, but you must be careful or you're going to be good and sorry."

---

1. **knee breeches:** short pants or knickers worn by young boys.

SHORT STORY

Reading Tips
Most of this **short story** takes place in the mind of the **main character.** Her mind wanders from present to past and back again. To take you inside her mind, the author uses a technique called **stream-of-consciousness.** This technique presents the flow of thoughts in a character's mind.

- Be aware that sometimes the main character gets confused about where she is and what is happening.
- As you read each section, try to put the major events in a time **sequence.** Consider whether an event tells about the main character as a young girl, as a wife and mother, or as an old widow.

As the story begins . . .
- The main character, Granny Weatherall, is an older woman who is about to die.

☆ Reader Success Strategy
There are many time jumps in this story. Granny often confuses the past with the present. To help you understand what is happening, highlight the events that took place in the past in one color and the events that are happening in the present in another color.

⭐ **Reader Success Strategy**

To help you keep the characters straight, use a character chart. Before you read, create the chart like the one below. Then, each time a new character is introduced, jot down details about him or her. Pay particular attention to details that will tell you whether or not the character is actually in the room with Granny.

Character	Details
Doctor Harry	
Cornelia	
John	
George	
Hapsy	
Lydia and Jimmy	

20 "Don't tell me what I'm going to be. I'm on my feet now, morally speaking. It's Cornelia. I had to go to bed to get rid of her."

Her bones felt loose, and floated around in her skin, and Doctor Harry floated like a balloon around the foot of the bed. He floated and pulled down his waistcoat and swung his glasses on a cord. "Well, stay where you are, it certainly can't hurt you."

"Get along and doctor your sick," said Granny Weatherall. "Leave a well woman alone. I'll call for you when I want you.

30 . . . Where were you forty years ago when I pulled through milk-leg² and double pneumonia? You weren't even born. Don't let Cornelia lead you on," she shouted, because Doctor Harry appeared to float up to the ceiling and out. "I pay my own bills, and I don't throw my money away on nonsense!"

She meant to wave good-by, but it was too much trouble. Her eyes closed of themselves, it was like a dark curtain drawn around the bed. The pillow rose and floated under her, pleasant as a hammock in a light wind. She listened to the leaves rustling outside the window. No, somebody was

40 swishing newspapers: no, Cornelia and Doctor Harry were whispering together. She leaped broad awake, thinking they whispered in her ear.

"She was never like this, *never* like this!" "Well, what can we expect?" "Yes, eighty years old. . . ."

Well, and what if she was? She still had ears. It was like Cornelia to whisper around doors. She always kept things secret in such a public way. She was always being <u>tactful</u> and kind. Cornelia was dutiful; that was the trouble with her. Dutiful and good: "So good and dutiful," said Granny, "that

50 I'd like to spank her." She saw herself spanking Cornelia and making a fine job of it.

"What'd you say, Mother?"

Granny felt her face tying up in hard knots.

"Can't a body think, I'd like to know?"

"I thought you might want something."

"I do. I want a lot of things. First off, go away and don't whisper."

---

2. **milk-leg:** a painful swelling of the leg experienced by some women after giving birth.

WORDS
TO   **tactful** (tăkt'fəl) *adj.* careful of others' feelings; considerate
KNOW

She lay and drowsed, hoping in her sleep that the children would keep out and let her rest a minute. It had been a long day. Not that she was tired. It was always pleasant to snatch a minute now and then. There was always so much to be done, let me see: tomorrow.

Pause & Reflect

FOCUS
Granny plans for the next day and recalls the time when she thought she was going to die.

MARK IT UP As you read, circle details that help you understand her feelings about death.

Tomorrow was far away and there was nothing to trouble about. Things were finished somehow when the time came; thank God there was always a little margin over for peace: then a person could spread out the plan of life and tuck in the edges orderly. It was good to have everything clean and folded away, with the hair brushes and tonic bottles sitting straight on the white <u>embroidered</u> linen: the day started without fuss and the pantry shelves laid out with rows of jelly glasses and brown jugs and white stone-china jars with blue whirligigs[3] and words painted on them: coffee, tea, sugar, ginger, cinnamon, allspice: and the bronze clock with the lion on top nicely dusted off. The dust that lion could collect in twenty-four hours! The box in the attic with all those letters tied up, well, she'd have to go through that tomorrow. All those letters—George's letters and John's letters and her letters to them both—lying around for the children to find afterwards made her uneasy. Yes, that would be tomorrow's business. No use to let them know how silly she had been once.

While she was <u>rummaging</u> around she found death in her mind and it felt clammy and unfamiliar. She had spent so much time preparing for death there was no need for bringing it up again. Let it take care of itself now. When she was sixty she had felt very old, finished, and went around making farewell trips to see her children and grandchildren, with a secret in her mind: This is the very last of your mother, children! Then she made her will and came down with a long

Pause & Reflect

MARK IT UP What does Granny think of her daughter Cornelia? Write the answer below. Then underline the clues on page 344 that led you to it. **(Infer)**

_____

_____

_____

_____

As the story continues...
• Granny decides she isn't going to worry about her death.

☆ Reader Success Strategy
As you read, fill in the word web below with details that describe Granny Weatherall.

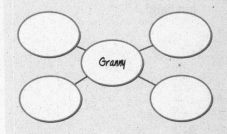

<hr>

3. **stone-china jars with blue whirligigs** (hwûr´lĭ-gĭgz´): jars made of thick pottery with blue spiral designs.

WORDS TO KNOW	**embroidered** (ĕm-broi´dərd) *adj.* decorated with stitched designs **embroider** *v.* **rummage** (rŭm´ĭj) *v.* to search through a confusion of objects

1. Granny does not want her children to read the letters in the box in the attic. What do you suppose those letters contain? (Infer)

_____

_____

_____

_____

2. Review the details you circled as you read. How would you describe Granny's feelings about death? (Infer)

_____

_____

_____

_____

As the story continues...

• Granny thinks about her children and her dead husband.

fever. That was all just a notion like a lot of other things, but it was lucky too, for she had once for all got over the idea of dying for a long time. Now she couldn't be worried. She hoped she had better sense now. Her father had lived to be one hundred and two years old and had drunk a noggin of strong hot toddy[4] on his last birthday. He told the reporters it was his daily habit, and he owed his long life to that. He had made quite a scandal and was very pleased about it. She

100 believed she'd just <u>plague</u> Cornelia a little.

"Cornelia! Cornelia!" No footsteps, but a sudden hand on her cheek. "Bless you, where have you been?"

"Here, Mother."

"Well, Cornelia, I want a noggin of hot toddy."

"Are you cold, darling?"

"I'm chilly, Cornelia. Lying in bed stops the circulation. I must have told you that a thousand times."

Pause & Reflect

110

Well, she could just hear Cornelia telling her husband that Mother was getting a little childish and they'd have to humor her. The thing that most annoyed her was that Cornelia thought she was deaf, dumb, and blind. Little hasty glances and tiny gestures tossed around her and over her head saying, "Don't cross her, let her have her way, she's eighty years old," and she sitting there as if she lived in a thin glass cage. Sometimes Granny almost made up her mind to pack up and move back to her own house where nobody could remind her every minute that she was old. Wait, wait,

120 Cornelia, till your own children whisper behind your back!

In her day she had kept a better house and had got more work done. She wasn't too old yet for Lydia to be driving eighty miles for advice when one of the children jumped the track, and Jimmy still dropped in and talked things over: "Now, Mammy, you've a good business head, I want to know what you think of this? . . ." Old. Cornelia couldn't change

---

4. **noggin of strong hot toddy:** mug of a strong, hot alcoholic drink.

WORDS
TO
KNOW

plague (plāg) *v.* to annoy; harass

the furniture around without asking. Little things, little things!
They had been so sweet when they were little. Granny wished
the old days were back again with the children young and
130 everything to be done over. It had been a hard pull, but not
too much for her. When she thought of all the food she had
cooked, and all the clothes she had cut and sewed, and all the
gardens she had made—well, the children showed it. There
they were, made out of her, and they couldn't get away from
that. Sometimes she wanted to see John again and point to
them and say, Well, I didn't do so badly, did I? But that would
have to wait. That was for tomorrow. She used to think of
him as a man, but now all the children were older than their
father, and he would be a child beside her if she saw him
140 now.[5] It seemed strange and there was something wrong in the
idea. Why, he couldn't possibly recognize her. She had fenced
in a hundred acres once, digging the post holes herself and
clamping the wires with just a negro boy to help. That
changed a woman. John would be looking for a young
woman with the peaked Spanish comb in her hair and the
painted fan. Digging post holes changed a woman. Riding
country roads in the winter when women had their babies was
another thing: sitting up nights with sick horses and sick
negroes and sick children and hardly ever losing one. John, I
150 hardly ever lost one of them! John would see that in a minute,
that would be something he could understand, she wouldn't
have to explain anything!

　　It made her feel like rolling up her sleeves and putting the
whole place to rights again. No matter if Cornelia was
determined to be everywhere at once, there were a great many
things left undone on this place. She would start tomorrow
and do them. It was good to be strong enough for everything,
even if all you made melted and changed and slipped under
your hands, so that by the time you finished you almost
160 forgot what you were working for. What was it I set out to
do? she asked herself <u>intently</u>, but she could not remember. A
fog rose over the valley, she saw it marching across the creek
swallowing the trees and moving up the hill like an army of
ghosts. Soon it would be at the near edge of the orchard, and

---

5. **She used to think of him . . . now:** Granny's husband, John, died at a
　younger age than his children have reached.

WORDS
　TO
KNOW 　　**intently** (ĭn-tĕnt′lē) *adv.* with concentrated attention

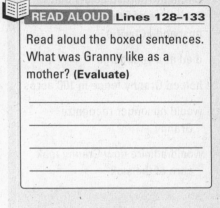
READ ALOUD Lines 128–133

Read aloud the boxed sentences.
What was Granny like as a
mother? **(Evaluate)**

_____

_____

_____

_____

 Reading Check

What hardships has Granny
faced? What do you learn about
Granny from the way she dealt
with her hardships?

Pause & Reflect

Circle the phrase below that is *not* true of Granny's dead husband. **(Clarify)**

died at a young age

helped Granny fence in 100 acres

would no longer recognize Granny

would admire how Granny took care of the sick

then it was time to go in and light the lamps. Come in, children, don't stay out in the night air.

Lighting the lamps had been beautiful. The children huddled up to her and breathed like little calves waiting at the bars in the twilight. Their eyes followed the match and watched the flame rise and settle in a blue curve, then they moved away from her. The lamp was lit, they didn't have to be scared and hang on to mother any more. Never, never, never more. God, for all my life I thank Thee. Without Thee, my God, I could never have done it. Hail, Mary, full of grace.[6]

I want you to pick all the fruit this year and see that nothing is wasted. There's always someone who can use it. Don't let good things rot for want of using. You waste life when you waste good food. Don't let things get lost. It's bitter to lose things. Now, don't let me get to thinking, not when I am tired and taking a little nap before supper. . . .

Pause & Reflect

As the story continues . . .

• Granny says that the jilting seriously hurt her pride.

FOCUS

Granny recalls her jilting by George, the man she was supposed to marry. Read to find out whether or not she has forgiven him.

The pillow rose about her shoulders and pressed against her heart and the memory was being squeezed out of it: oh, push down the pillow, somebody: it would smother her if she tried to hold it. Such a fresh breeze blowing and such a green day with no threats in it. But he had not come, just the same. What does a woman do when she has put on the white veil and set out the white cake for a man and he doesn't come? She tried to remember. No, I swear he never harmed me but in that. He never harmed me but in that. . .and what if he did? There was the day, the day, but a whirl of dark smoke rose and covered it, crept up and over into the bright field where everything was planted so carefully in orderly rows. That was hell, she knew hell when she saw it. For sixty years she had prayed against remembering him and against losing her soul in the deep pit of hell, and now the two things were mingled in one and the thought of him was a smoky cloud from hell that moved and crept in her head when she had just got rid of Doctor Harry and was trying to rest a minute. Wounded vanity,[7] Ellen, said a sharp voice in the top of her mind.

What Does It Mean?

Ellen is Granny's first name.

---

6. **Hail . . . grace:** the beginning of a Roman Catholic prayer to the Virgin Mary.

7. **vanity:** pride.

Don't let your wounded vanity get the upper hand of you. Plenty of girls get jilted. You were jilted, weren't you? Then stand up to it. Her eyelids wavered and let in streamers of blue-gray light like tissue paper over her eyes. She must get up and pull the shades down or she'd never sleep. She was in bed again and the shades were not down. How could that happen? Better turn over, hide from the light, sleeping in the light gave you nightmares. "Mother, how do you feel now?" and a stinging wetness on her forehead. But I don't like having my face washed in cold water!

Hapsy? George? Lydia? Jimmy? No, Cornelia, and her features were swollen and full of little puddles. "They're coming, darling, they'll all be here soon." Go wash your face, child, you look funny.

Instead of obeying, Cornelia knelt down and put her head on the pillow. She seemed to be talking but there was no sound. "Well, are you tongue-tied? Whose birthday is it? Are you going to give a party?"

Cornelia's mouth moved urgently in strange shapes. "Don't do that, you bother me, daughter."

"Oh, no, Mother. Oh, no. . . ."

Nonsense. It was strange about children. They disputed your every word. "No what, Cornelia?"

"Here's Doctor Harry."

"I won't see that boy again. He just left five minutes ago."

"That was this morning, Mother. It's night now. Here's the nurse."

"This is Doctor Harry, Mrs. Weatherall. I never saw you look so young and happy!"

"Ah, I'll never be young again—but I'd be happy if they'd let me lie in peace and get rested."

She thought she spoke up loudly, but no one answered. A warm weight on her forehead, a warm bracelet on her wrist, and a breeze went on whispering, trying to tell her something. A shuffle of leaves in the everlasting hand of God, He blew on them and they danced and rattled. "Mother, don't mind, we're going to give you a little hypodermic."[8] "Look here, daughter, how do ants get in this bed? I saw sugar ants yesterday." Did you send for Hapsy too?

Pause & Reflect

8. **hypodermic** (hī′pə-dûr′mĭk): injection.

What Does It Mean?
Granny asks whose birthday it is because all of the family has gathered around. She doesn't realize they have all come because she is dying.

Pause & Reflect

MARK IT UP **1.** Review the boxed passage on page 348. Do you think Granny has forgiven George for jilting her? Write your answer below. Then circle details in the passage that led you to your conclusion. **(Draw Conclusions)**

_____
_____
_____
_____

2. Do you think people should forgive those who have hurt them deeply? Why or why not? **(Connect)**

_____
_____
_____
_____

- Granny works hard to remember Hapsy.

- Father Connolly arrives.

What Does It Mean?

The highlighted sentence means that Granny has to search back through all her many memories to remember Hapsy.

📖 **READ ALOUD** Lines 261–265

Read aloud the boxed sentences. What do you suppose George took from Granny that she never got back? **(Infer)**

_____

_____

_____

More About . . .

CHILDBIRTH At the time that Granny was giving birth, many women gave birth at home. Home births were particularly common in farm areas, where hospitals were far away. Also, in those days doctors used to go to patients' homes to care for them. Granny knew, from the labor pains, that she was about to have her baby. That is why she told her husband to get the doctor.

FOCUS
Read to find out how Granny feels about Hapsy, her dead daughter, and John, her late husband.

It was Hapsy she really wanted. She had to go a long way back through a great many rooms to find Hapsy standing with a baby on her arm.[9] She seemed to herself to be Hapsy also, and the baby on Hapsy's arm was Hapsy and himself and herself, all at once, and there was no surprise in the meeting. Then Hapsy melted from within and turned flimsy as gray gauze and the baby was a gauzy shadow, and Hapsy
250 came up close and said, "I thought you'd never come," and looked at her very searchingly and said, "You haven't changed a bit!" They leaned forward to kiss, when Cornelia began whispering from a long way off, "Oh, is there anything you want to tell me? Is there anything I can do for you?"

Yes, she had changed her mind after sixty years and she would like to see George. I want you to find George. Find him and be sure to tell him I forgot him. I want him to know I had my husband just the same and my children and my house like any other woman. A good house too and a good
260 husband that I loved and fine children out of him. Better than I hoped for even. Tell him I was given back everything he took away and more. Oh, no, oh, God, no, there was something else besides the house and the man and the children. Oh, surely they were not all? What was it? Something not given back. . . . Her breath crowded down under her ribs and grew into a monstrous frightening shape with cutting edges; it bored up into her head, and the agony was unbelievable: Yes, John, get the Doctor now, no more talk, my time has come.[10]
270 When this one was born it should be the last. The last. It should have been born first, for it was the one she had truly wanted. Everything came in good time. Nothing left out, left over. She was strong, in three days she would be as well as ever. Better. A woman needed milk in her to have her full health.

"Mother, do you hear me?"

---

9. **Hapsy standing with a baby on her arm:** This detail may suggest that Hapsy died in childbirth.

10. **Her breath . . . my time has come:** The memory of George triggers a horrible pain, and Granny relives a moment at the beginning of childbirth, perhaps the birth of Hapsy.

"I've been telling you—"

"Mother, Father Connolly's here."

"I went to Holy Communion only last week. Tell him I'm
not so sinful as all that."

"Father just wants to speak to you."

He could speak as much as he pleased. It was like him to
drop in and inquire about her soul as if it were a teething
baby, and then stay on for a cup of tea and a round of cards
and gossip. He always had a funny story of some sort, usually
about an Irishman who made his little mistakes and confessed
them, and the point lay in some absurd thing he would blurt
out in the confessional showing his struggles between native
piety and original sin. Granny felt easy about her soul.
Cornelia, where are your manners? Give Father Connolly a
chair. She had her secret comfortable understanding with a
few favorite saints who cleared a straight road to God for her.
All as surely signed and sealed as the papers for the new Forty
Acres. Forever. . . . heirs and assigns[11] forever. Since the day
the wedding cake was not cut, but thrown out and wasted.
The whole bottom dropped out of the world, and there she
was blind and sweating with nothing under her feet and the
walls falling away. His hand had caught her under the breast,
she had not fallen, there was the freshly polished floor with
the green rug on it, just as before. He had cursed like a sailor's
parrot and said, "I'll kill him for you." Don't lay a hand on
him, for my sake leave something to God. "Now, Ellen, you
must believe what I tell you. . . ."

Pause & Reflect

FOCUS

Granny slips closer and closer to death. Read to find out what happens to her at the end of the story.

So there was nothing, nothing to worry about any more, except sometimes in the night one of the children screamed in a nightmare, and they both hustled out shaking and hunting for the matches and calling, "There, wait a
minute, here we are!" John, get the doctor now, Hapsy's time
has come. But there was Hapsy standing by the bed in a

---

11. **assigns:** people to whom property is transferred in a will or other legal document.

white cap.[12] "Cornelia, tell Hapsy to take off her cap. I can't see her plain."

Her eyes opened very wide and the room stood out like a picture she had seen somewhere. Dark colors with the shadows rising towards the ceiling in long angles. The tall black dresser gleamed with nothing on it but John's picture, enlarged from a little one, with John's eyes very black when they should have been blue. You never saw him, so how do you know how he looked? But the man insisted the copy was perfect, it was very rich and handsome. For a picture, yes, but it's not my husband. The table by the bed had a linen cover and a candle and a crucifix.[13] The light was blue from Cornelia's silk lampshades. No sort of light at all, just frippery. You had to live forty years with kerosene lamps to appreciate honest electricity. She felt very strong and she saw Doctor Harry with a rosy nimbus[14] around him.

"You look like a saint, Doctor Harry, and I vow that's as near as you'll ever come to it."

"She's saying something."

"I heard you, Cornelia. What's all this carrying-on?"

"Father Connolly's saying—"

Cornelia's voice staggered and bumped like a cart in a bad road. It rounded corners and turned back again and arrived nowhere. Granny stepped up in the cart very lightly and reached for the reins, but a man sat beside her and she knew him by his hands, driving the cart. She did not look in his face, for she knew without seeing, but looked instead down the road where the trees leaned over and bowed to each other and a thousand birds were singing a Mass. She felt like singing too, but she put her hand in the bosom of her dress and pulled out a rosary,[15] and Father Connolly murmured Latin in a very solemn voice and tickled her feet.[16] My God,

320

330

340

---

12. **Hapsy . . . in a white cap:** Granny mistakenly thinks she sees Hapsy in the white cap. She actually sees the nurse whom Cornelia mentioned.

13. **crucifix** (krōō′sə-fĭks′): a cross bearing a sculptured representation of the crucified Christ.

14. **nimbus:** halo of light.

15. **rosary** (rō′zə-rē): a string of beads used by Roman Catholics to count their prayers.

16. **Father Connolly . . . tickled her feet:** Father Connolly puts oil on Granny's feet as part of the ritual for anointing the sick and dying.

What Does It Mean?

Frippery is something that is frivolous or just for show. The light is more decorative than useful.

☑ **Reading Check**

What is Father Connolly doing?

will you stop that nonsense? I'm a married woman. What if
he did run away and leave me to face the priest by myself? I
found another a whole world better. I wouldn't have
exchanged my husband for anybody except St. Michael
himself, and you may tell him that for me with a thank you in
350 the bargain.

Light flashed on her closed eyelids, and a deep roaring
shook her. Cornelia, is that lightning? I hear thunder. There's
going to be a storm. Close all the windows. Call the children
in. . . . "Mother, here we are, all of us." "Is that you,
Hapsy?" "Oh, no, I'm Lydia. We drove as fast as we could."
Their faces drifted above her, drifted away. The rosary fell
out of her hands and Lydia put it back. Jimmy tried to help,
their hands fumbled together, and Granny closed two fingers
around Jimmy's thumb. Beads wouldn't do, it must be
360 something alive. She was so amazed her thoughts ran round
and round. So, my dear Lord, this is my death and I wasn't
even thinking about it. My children have come to see me
die. But I can't, it's not time. Oh, I always hated surprises.
I wanted to give Cornelia the amethyst set—Cornelia, you're
to have the amethyst set, but Hapsy's to wear it when she
wants, and, Doctor Harry, do shut up. Nobody sent for
you. Oh, my dear Lord, do wait a minute. I meant to do
something about the Forty Acres, Jimmy doesn't need it and
Lydia will later on, with that worthless husband of hers. I
370 meant to finish the altar cloth and send six bottles of wine
to Sister Borgia for her dyspepsia.[17] I want to send six bottles
of wine to Sister Borgia, Father Connolly, now don't let
me forget.

Cornelia's voice made short turns and tilted over and
crashed. "Oh, Mother, oh, Mother, oh, Mother . . . ."

"I'm not going, Cornelia. I'm taken by surprise. I can't go."
You'll see Hapsy again. What about her? "I thought
you'd never come." Granny made a long journey outward,
looking for Hapsy. What if I don't find her? What then?
380 Her heart sank down and down, there was no bottom to
death, she couldn't come to the end of it. The blue light
from Cornelia's lampshade drew into a tiny point in the
center of her brain, it flickered and winked like an eye,
quietly it fluttered and dwindled. Granny lay curled down

---

17. dyspepsia (dĭs-pĕp′shə): indigestion.

READ ALOUD Lines 356–363

Granny realizes she is about to
die. She tells herself she "always
hated surprises." On what other
occasion was she given a terrible
surprise? (**Compare and
Contrast**)

_____

_____

_____

_____

What Does It Mean?

The highlighted phrase explains
that before Granny dies, she
begins searching the afterlife
to find Hapsy.

What Does It Mean?

Dwindled means "got weaker"
or "ran out."

Pause & Reflect

READ ALOUD **1.** Read aloud the boxed sentences. Then circle the *two* words below that describe Granny's attitude at the moment of death. **(Infer)**

peaceful   bitter

happy   disappointed

2. What did you find most memorable about Granny? **(Connect)**

_____

_____

_____

_____

CHALLENGE

This story takes place in Granny's mind and from her point of view. Because her eyesight and her hearing are failing and she is getting weaker, we do not see and hear everything that is happening. Why do you think Porter chose to write the story from Granny's point of view? What might have been different if Porter had told the story from the point of view of a narrator who knew everything? **(Analyze)**

within herself, amazed and watchful, staring at the point of light that was herself; her body was now only a deeper mass of shadow in an endless darkness and this darkness would curl around the light and swallow it up. God, give a sign!

390 For the second time there was no sign. Again no bridegroom and the priest in the house. She could not remember any other sorrow because this grief wiped them all away. Oh, no, there's nothing more cruel than this—I'll never forgive it. She stretched herself with a deep breath and blew out the light.

Pause & Reflect

Active Reading SkillBuilder

Sequencing

In this stream-of-consciousness narrative, Porter shuffles the past and the present to show the distorted way that a dying person perceives the **sequence,** or time order, of events. The reader experiences Granny's sense of time as she imaginatively travels backward and forward through her life, re-creating dramatic moments. Complete the time line below, sequencing additional important events in Granny's life in chronological order. An example is shown.

Jilting by George	*Marriage to John*	**Examination by Dr. Harry**

Literary Analysis SkillBuilder

Stream of Consciousness

Stream of consciousness is a literary technique developed by modernist writers to present the flow of a character's unconnected thoughts, responses, and sensations. A stream-of-consciousness narrative is not structured into a coherent, logical presentation of events. Rather, one event triggers thoughts of another. In the chart below, write three events in the story that take place in Granny's sickroom shortly before her death and three events that take place in her mind. An example is shown.

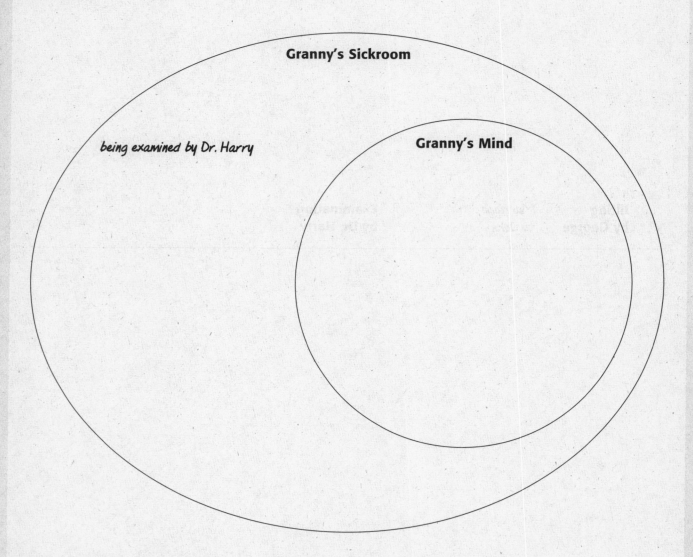

Granny's Sickroom

being examined by Dr. Harry

Granny's Mind

Follow Up: Write a short stream-of-consciousness narrative in which George lies on his deathbed and recalls jilting Granny. Share your narrative with classmates.

Words to Know SkillBuilder

Words to Know

embroidered   intently   plague   rummage   tactful

A. Decide which Word to Know best completes each sentence below. Then write the word on the blank line on the right.

I like to watch Grandma (1) through the contents of her trunk. She pulls out all sorts of knickknacks and letters.

_____ (1)

I am amazed by her (2) pillowcases. The detail in the stitching is wonderful.

_____ (2)

I try not to bother her with constant interruptions. I do not want to (3) her with questions while she is searching.

_____ (3)

She is looking (4) for a particular letter. Her attention never wanders; eventually she finds the letter she has saved for so long.

_____ (4)

I would like to know what the letter says. Maybe if I am (5) and ask in a diplomatic way, she will read the letter to me.

_____ (5)

B. For each phrase in the first column, find the phrase in the second column that is closest in meaning. Write the letter of that phrase in the blank.

1. search in the salvage   A. a tactful trainer

2. fiercely focused   B. plague the policeman

3. a considerate coach   C. rummage in the wreckage

4. beautifully embroidered   D. intently interested

5. annoy the cop   E. stunningly stitched

C. Write a letter that Granny Weatherall might write to George. Use at least **three** Words to Know in your letter.

from **LETTER FROM BIRMINGHAM JAIL**

Martin Luther King, Jr.

APRIL 16, **1963**

Before You Read

Connect to Your Life

What issue do you feel strongly about? How far would you go to support that issue? Would you speak out, write to Congress, march in a demonstration, or take even stronger measures? Write your responses in the space below.

Issue: _____

What I would do: _____

_____

_____

Key to the Letter

WHAT YOU NEED TO KNOW Martin Luther King, Jr. wrote this letter in 1963 from a jail cell in Birmingham, Alabama. He was in jail because he had led a large group of African Americans to demonstrate against the injustices African Americans experienced. The demonstrations—protest marches and gatherings—drew attention to unfair election laws that prevented African Americans from voting and the unfair segregation of such public places as schools, lunch counters, and hotels. *Segregation* is forced legal separation of people. In Birmingham, and other areas in the southern U.S., African Americans were not allowed to go the same schools, restaurants, hotels, or even rest rooms as white people.

Reading Tips

This piece of writing is a **persuasive essay** as well as a **personal letter**. It will be easier to understand if you do the following:

- Pay close attention to the first sentence or two in each paragraph. That's usually where King states his **main idea**.

- Try to identify the major reasons that King gives to support his actions and beliefs.

- For now, don't worry about names or details that are unfamiliar. Keep in mind that you don't have to understand everything to get a general sense of King's meaning.

As the letter begins . . .

- King begins his letter by explaining why he came to Birmingham.

MARK IT UP KEEP TRACK

As you read, you can use these marks to keep track of your understanding.

✔ ..... I understand.

? ..... I don't understand this.

! ..... Interesting or surprising idea

from LETTER FROM BIRMINGHAM JAIL

APRIL 16, 1963

Martin Luther King, Jr.

PREVIEW Martin Luther King, Jr., was put in jail several times when he was campaigning for civil rights in Birmingham, Alabama, in 1963. During one of those imprisonments, eight local white clergymen published a letter in which they criticized King's methods. King responded with a long letter defending his actions. Here he explains why civil disobedience—breaking unjust laws—is necessary in the struggle for justice.

FOCUS
In the first part of his letter, King defends his presence in Birmingham, Alabama.
MARK IT UP Underline the reasons that King gives for being in Birmingham. An example is highlighted on page 361.

My Dear Fellow Clergymen:

While confined here in the Birmingham city jail, I came across your recent statement calling my present activities "unwise and untimely." Seldom do I pause to answer criticism of my work and ideas. If I sought to answer all the criticisms that cross my desk, my secretaries would have little

10 time for anything other than such correspondence in the course of the day, and I would have no time for constructive work. But since I feel that you are men of genuine goodwill and that your criticisms are sincerely set forth, I want to try to answer your statement in what I hope will be patient and reasonable terms.

I think I should indicate why I am here in Birmingham, since you have been influenced by the view which argues against "outsiders coming in." I have the honor of serving as president of the Southern Christian Leadership Conference, an

20 organization operating in every Southern state, with

headquarters in Atlanta, Georgia. We have some eighty-five affiliated organizations across the South, and one of them is the Alabama Christian Movement for Human Rights. Frequently we share staff, educational, and financial resources with our affiliates. Several months ago the affiliate here in Birmingham asked us to be on call to engage in a nonviolent direct-action program if such were deemed necessary. We readily consented, and when the hour came, we lived up to our promise. So I, along with several members of my staff, am

30 here because I was invited here. I am here because I have organizational ties here.

But more basically, I am in Birmingham because injustice is here. Just as the prophets of the eighth century B.C. left their villages and carried their "thus saith the Lord" far beyond the boundaries of their hometowns,[1] and just as the Apostle Paul left his village of Tarsus and carried the gospel of Jesus Christ to the far corners of the Greco-Roman world, so am I compelled to carry the gospel of freedom beyond my own hometown. Like Paul, I must constantly respond to the

40 Macedonian call for aid.[2]

Moreover, I am cognizant of the interrelatedness of all communities and states. I cannot sit idly by in Atlanta and not be concerned about what happens in Birmingham. Injustice anywhere is a threat to justice everywhere. We are caught in an inescapable network of mutuality,[3] tied in a single garment of destiny. Whatever affects one directly, affects all indirectly. Never again can we afford to live with the narrow, provincial "outside agitator" idea. Anyone who lives inside the United States can never be considered an outsider anywhere within its

50 bounds.

Pause & Reflect

---

1. **prophets . . . hometowns:** Hebrew religious figures, including Amos, Hosea, and Micah, who traveled from village to village with messages from God for the Hebrew people.

2. **Macedonian** (măs´ĭ-dō´nē-ən) **call for aid:** According to the Bible (Acts 16), a man appeared to the Apostle Paul in a vision, calling him to preach in Macedonia (at that time a Roman province north of Greece).

3. **inescapable network of mutuality:** King makes the point that people must depend on one another in this world.

WORDS
TO
KNOW

affiliate (ə-fĭl´ē-ĭt) *n.* a person or organization associated with another
cognizant (kŏg´nĭ-zənt) *adj.* aware

Pause & Reflect

1. Look at the passages that you underlined. King is in Birmingham because _____

_____

_____

_____.

(Logical Argument)

2. An agitator is someone who stirs up people to take action. Why was King called an "outside agitator" (line 48) by some people in Birmingham? **(Infer)**

_____

_____

_____

_____

3. How would you feel if you were put in jail for doing what you thought was right? **(Connect)**

_____

_____

_____

_____

- King explains why his group took action and what actions they took.

What Does It Mean?

Deplore means "to show disapproval" or "to condemn."

More About . . .

RACIAL TERMS Throughout this letter, King refers to African Americans as (Negroes) and colored people. When he wrote this letter, those terms were acceptable; however, they are now considered inappropriate.

MARK IT UP Lines 67–75

Underline examples of racial injustice in Birmingham that King mentions in this passage. (Clarify)

More About . . .

(RACIAL SIGNS) Prior to the Civil Rights Act of 1964, which made segregation illegal, business owners in many Southern cities posted signs outside their restaurants, hotels, or stores that said "for whites only." City and town governments also put up signs like these to keep African Americans from using the same water fountains, public benches and picnic tables, and even telephone booths that white people used.

FOCUS
King identifies the four basic steps of a nonviolent protest campaign: (1) gathering facts, (2) negotiation, (3) self-purification, and (4) direct action.

MARK IT UP As you read, look for the passages that deal with each step of the campaign in Birmingham. In the margin, number the steps 1, 2, 3, and 4.

You the demonstrations taking place in Birmingham. But your statement, I am sorry to say, fails to express a similar concern for the conditions that brought about the demonstrations. I am sure that none of you would want to rest content with the superficial kind of social analysis that deals merely with effects and does not grapple with underlying causes. It is unfortunate that demonstrations are taking place in Birmingham, but it is even more unfortunate that the city's white power structure left the (Negro) community with no alternative.

In any nonviolent campaign there are four basic steps: collection of the facts to determine whether injustices exist; negotiation; self-purification; and direct action. We have gone through all these steps in Birmingham. There can be no gainsaying[4] the fact that racial injustice engulfs this community. Birmingham is probably the most thoroughly segregated city in the United States. Its ugly record of brutality is widely known. Negroes have experienced grossly unjust treatment in the courts. There have been more unsolved bombings of Negro homes and churches in Birmingham than in any other city in the nation. These are the hard, brutal facts of the case. On the basis of these conditions, Negro leaders sought to negotiate with the city fathers. But the latter consistently refused to engage in good-faith negotiations.

Then, last September, came the opportunity to talk with leaders of Birmingham's economic community. In the course of the negotiations, certain promises were made by the merchants—for example, to remove the stores' humiliating racial signs.[5] On the basis of these promises, The Reverend Fred Shuttlesworth and the leaders of the Alabama Christian Movement for Human Rights agreed to a moratorium[6] on all demonstrations. As the weeks and months went by, we

---

4. **gainsaying:** denying.

5. **racial signs:** signs marking segregated buildings and other facilities.

6. **moratorium** (môr′ə-tôr′ē-əm): temporary stoppage.

WORDS
TO
KNOW
segregated (sĕg′rĭ-gā′tĭd) *adj.* separated according to race
segregate v.

realized that we were the victims of a broken promise. A few signs, briefly removed, returned; the others remained.

As in so many past experiences, our hopes had been blasted, and the shadow of deep disappointment settled upon us. We had no alternative except to prepare for direct action, whereby we would present our very bodies as a means of laying our case before the conscience of the local and the national community. Mindful of the difficulties involved, we decided to undertake a process of self-purification. We began a series of workshops on nonviolence, and we repeatedly asked ourselves: "Are you able to accept blows without <u>retaliating</u>?" "Are you able to endure the ordeal of jail?" We decided to schedule our direct-action program for the Easter season, realizing that except for Christmas, this is the main shopping period of the year. Knowing that a strong economic-withdrawal program[7] would be the by-product of direct action, we felt that this would be the best time to bring pressure to bear on the merchants for the needed change.

Then it occurred to us that Birmingham's mayoral election was coming up in March, and we speedily decided to postpone action until after election day. When we discovered that the Commissioner of Public Safety, Eugene "Bull" Connor, had piled up enough votes to be in the runoff, we decided again to postpone action until the day after the runoff so that the demonstrations could not be used to cloud the issues. Like many others, we waited to see Mr. Connor defeated, and to this end we endured postponement after postponement. Having aided in this community need, we felt that our direct-action program could be delayed no longer.

You may well ask: "Why direct action? Why sit-ins,[8] marches, and so forth? Isn't negotiation a better path?" You are quite right in calling for negotiation. Indeed, this is the very purpose of direct action. Nonviolent direct action seeks to create such a crisis and foster such a tension that a community which has constantly refused to negotiate is forced to confront the issue. It seeks so to dramatize the issue that it

---

7. **a strong economic-withdrawal program:** King knew that demonstrations would result in fewer customers for the merchants.

8. **sit-ins:** peaceful demonstrations in which protesters occupied, and refused to leave, seats in segregated lunch counters and other places of business.

WORDS
TO
KNOW

retaliating (rĭ-tăl′ē-ā′tĭng) *n.* taking revenge **retaliate** *v.*

What Does It Mean?
A *runoff* election is held when two candidates in an election get the same, or nearly the same, number of votes. The results of the runoff election determine the winner.

More About . . .
SIT-INS Typically, at the sit-ins that King describes, African Americans sat in all the seats at a "whites-only" restaurant and refused to leave. The restaurant owner had two choices: serve African Americans or do no business at all. Most restaurant owners still refused to serve the protestors, who were carried out and arrested for breaking the law.

1. According to King, the purpose of direct action, such as sit-ins and marches, is to _____
_____
_____
_____ .
(Clarify)

2. Review the four steps of the Birmingham campaign that you numbered. Do you think the campaign was justified? *Yes/No,* because _____
_____
_____
_____ .
(Evaluate)

can no longer be ignored. My citing the creation of tension as part of the work of the nonviolent-resister may sound rather shocking. But I must confess that I am not afraid of the word "tension." I have earnestly opposed violent tension, but there is a type of constructive, nonviolent tension which is necessary for growth. Just as Socrates[9] felt that it was necessary to create a tension in the mind so that individuals could rise

130 from the bondage of myths and half-truths to the unfettered realm of creative analysis and objective <u>appraisal</u>, so must we see the need for nonviolent gadflies[10] to create the kind of tension in society that will help men rise from the dark depths of prejudice and racism to the majestic heights of understanding and brotherhood.[11]

The purpose of our direct-action program is to create a situation so crisis-packed that it will inevitably open the door to negotiation. I therefore concur with you in your call for negotiation. Too long has our beloved Southland been bogged

140 down in a tragic effort to live in monologue rather than dialogue.

Pause & Reflect

As the letter continues . . .

- King points out that those in power never think it's a good time for a movement such as his.

FOCUS

King now responds to the criticism that his demonstrations are "untimely." He explains why he thinks action cannot be delayed.

MARK IT UP As you read, look for passages that support King's position. Mark the
150 passages with an *S.*

One of the basic points in your statement is that the action that I and my associates have taken in Birmingham is untimely. Some have asked: "Why didn't you give the new city administration time to act?" The only answer that I can give to this query is that the new Birmingham administration must be prodded about as much as the outgoing one before it will act. . . . My friends, I

9. **Socrates** (sŏk′rə-tēz′): a Greek philosopher of the fifth century B.C.—one of the major influences in the development of Western thought. Socrates taught people through the use of questions. He made people uncomfortable so that they could discover truth for themselves.

10. **gadflies:** critics.

11. King compares the civil-rights protesters to Socrates. They must create tension so that people can be led to new ways of thinking and living.

WORDS
TO
KNOW **appraisal** (ə-prā′zəl) *n.* evaluation

must say to you that we have not made a single gain in civil rights without determined legal and nonviolent pressure. Lamentably, it is a historical fact that privileged groups seldom give up their privileges voluntarily. Individuals may see the moral light and voluntarily give up their unjust posture; but, as Reinhold Niebuhr[12] has reminded us, groups tend to be more immoral than individuals.

We know through painful experience that freedom is never voluntarily given by the oppressor; it must be demanded by the oppressed. Frankly, I have yet to engage in a direct-action campaign that was "well-timed" in the view of those who have not suffered unduly from the disease of segregation. For years now I have heard the word "Wait!" It rings in the ear of every Negro with piercing familiarity. This "Wait" has almost always meant "Never." We must come to see, with one of our distinguished jurists,[13] that "justice too long delayed is justice denied."

We have waited for more than 340 years for our constitutional and God-given rights. The nations of Asia and Africa are moving with jetlike speed toward gaining political independence, but we still creep at horse-and-buggy pace toward gaining a cup of coffee at a lunch counter. Perhaps it is easy for those who have never felt the stinging darts of segregation to say, "Wait." But when you have seen vicious mobs lynch your mothers and fathers at will and drown your sisters and brothers at whim; when you have seen hate-filled policemen curse, kick, and even kill your black brothers and sisters; when you see the vast majority of your twenty million Negro brothers smothering in an airtight cage of poverty in the midst of an affluent society; when you suddenly find your tongue twisted and your speech stammering as you seek to explain to your six-year-old daughter why she can't go to the public amusement park that has just been advertised on television, and see tears welling up in her eyes when she is told that Funtown is closed to colored children, and see ominous[14] clouds of inferiority beginning to form in her little mental sky, and see her beginning to distort her personality by developing an unconscious bitterness toward white people;

12. **Reinhold Niebuhr** (rĭn'hōld' nē'boor'): a 20th-century American theologian whose writings deal mainly with moral and social problems.

13. **distinguished jurists:** outstanding judges or legal scholars.

14. **ominous** (ŏm'ə-nəs): threatening.

What Does It Mean?
Lamentably means "sadly."

⭐ **Reader Success Strategy**

When you come across a difficult or new word, use the context—the surrounding words and sentences—to help you figure out the word's meaning. Often, clues to a word's meaning are in the next few words or even the next sentence.

READ ALOUD Lines 163–166

Read aloud the boxed passage. Why does King say "Wait!" almost always means "Never" for African Americans? **(Paraphrase)**

_____

_____

_____

_____

What Does It Mean?
Lynch means "execute, usually by hanging, without a trial."

（190） when you have to concoct an answer for a five-year-old son who is asking: "Daddy, why do white people treat colored people so mean?"; when you take a cross-country drive and find it necessary to sleep night after night in the uncomfortable corners of your automobile because no motel will accept you; when you are humiliated day in and day out by nagging signs reading "white" and "colored"; when your first name becomes "nigger," your middle name becomes "boy" (however old you are) and your last name becomes "John," and your wife and mother are never given the respected title "Mrs."; when you are

（200） harried by day and haunted by night by the fact that you are a Negro, living constantly at tiptoe stance, never quite knowing what to expect next, and are plagued with inner fears and outer resentments; when you are forever fighting a degenerating sense of "nobodiness"—then you will understand why we find it difficult to wait. There comes a time when the cup of endurance runs over, and men are no longer willing to be plunged into the abyss of despair. I hope, sirs, you can understand our legitimate and unavoidable impatience.

Pause & Reflect

What Does It Mean?

Harried means "harassed." *At tiptoe stance* means "cautiously." *Degenerating* means "sinking" or "worsening."

Pause & Reflect

✎ **MARK IT UP** Look back at the passages that you marked with an *S.* Star the passage that you find most convincing. **(Evaluate)**

As the letter continues . . .

• King refers to many well-respected figures from history to support his beliefs.

FOCUS

（210） King now talks about just and unjust laws. He explains the differences between these kinds of laws.

✎ **MARK IT UP** As you read, underline the qualities of a just law.

You express a great deal of anxiety over our willingness to break laws. This is certainly a legitimate concern. Since we so <u>diligently</u> urge people to obey the Supreme Court's decision of 1954 outlawing segregation in the public schools,[15] at first glance it may seem rather paradoxical[16] for us consciously to break laws. One may well ask: "How can you advocate breaking some laws and obeying others?" The answer lies in the fact that there are two types of laws: just and unjust. I would be

（220） the first to advocate obeying just laws. One has not only a legal

---

15. **the Supreme Court's . . . public schools:** the U.S. Supreme Court's decision in the case *Brown* v. *Board of Education of Topeka, Kansas.*

16. **paradoxical** (păr′ə-dŏk′sĭ-kəl): self-contradictory.

WORDS TO KNOW
diligently (dĭl′ə-jənt-lē) *adv.* in a persevering, painstaking manner

but a moral responsibility to obey just laws. Conversely, one has a moral responsibility to disobey unjust laws. I would agree with St. Augustine[17] that "an unjust law is no law at all."

Now, what is the difference between the two? How does one determine whether a law is just or unjust? A just law is a man-made code that squares with the moral law or the law of God. An unjust law is a code that is out of harmony with the moral law. To put it in the terms of St. Thomas Aquinas:[18] An unjust law is a human law that is not rooted in eternal law and natural law. Any law that uplifts human personality is **230** just. Any law that degrades human personality is unjust. All segregation <u>statutes</u> are unjust because segregation distorts the soul and damages the personality. It gives the segregator a false sense of superiority and the segregated a false sense of inferiority. Segregation, to use the terminology of the Jewish philosopher Martin Buber,[19] substitutes an "I-it" relationship for an "I-thou" relationship and ends up relegating persons to the status of things. Hence segregation is not only politically, economically, and sociologically unsound, it is morally wrong **240** and sinful. Paul Tillich[20] has said that sin is separation. Is not segregation an existential[21] expression of man's tragic separation, his awful <u>estrangement</u>, his terrible sinfulness? Thus it is that I can urge men to obey the 1954 decision of the Supreme Court, for it is morally right; and I can urge them to disobey segregation ordinances, for they are morally wrong.

Let us consider a more concrete example of just and unjust laws. An unjust law is a code that a numerical or power majority group compels a minority group to obey but does not make binding on itself. This is *difference* made legal. By **250** the same token, a just law is a code that a majority compels a minority to follow and that it is willing to follow itself. This is *sameness* made legal.

---

17. **St. Augustine** (ô′gə-stēn′): a North African bishop, whose writings have influenced the history of Christianity.
18. **St. Thomas Aquinas** (ə-kwī′nəs): a noted philosopher and theologian in the Middle Ages.
19. **Martin Buber** (bōō′bər): an influential 20th-century Jewish philosopher.
20. **Paul Tillich** (tĭl′ĭk): a German-born American theologian of the 20th century.
21. **existential** (ĕg′zĭ-stĕn′shəl): existing in the real world.

READ ALOUD Lines 231–235

Read aloud the boxed passage. What type of laws relating to African Americans does King give as an example of unjust laws? **(Clarify)**

_____

_____

What Does It Mean?

Here, King is pointing out that a majority isn't always the group with the most members; it can also be the group that has the most power.

Reading Check

According to King, what is the difference between an unjust law and a just law?

More About . . .

THE (FIRST AMENDMENT) This
refers to the First Amendment
in the Bill of Rights, which are
part of the U.S. Constitution.
The First Amendment protects
some of the most important
rights in a free society: freedom
to assemble, or gather together;
freedom of religion, of speech,
and of the press; and the right
to petition the government.

What Does It Mean?

A *rabid segregationist* is an
extremist who strongly believes
in keeping blacks and whites
separate.

 READ ALOUD Lines 274–279

As you read this passage aloud,
notice the respect that King
shows for the law.

What Does It Mean?

Here, *sublimely* means "in a
way that is spiritually, morally,
or intellectually worthy."

What Does It Mean?

Academic freedom means
"the right of academics, such
as college professors and
students, to speak and write
about whatever they feel is
important, without fear of
punishment."

Let me give another explanation. A law is unjust if it is
inflicted on a minority that, as a result of being denied the
right to vote, had no part in enacting or devising the law.
Who can say that the legislature of Alabama which set up that
state's segregation laws was democratically elected?
Throughout Alabama all sorts of devious[22] methods are used
to prevent Negroes from becoming registered voters, and there
260 are some counties in which, even though Negroes constitute a
majority of the population, not a single Negro is registered.
Can any law enacted under such circumstances be considered
democratically structured?

Sometimes a law is just on its face and unjust in its
application. For instance, I have been arrested on a charge of
parading without a permit. Now, there is nothing wrong in
having an ordinance which requires a permit for a parade. But
such an ordinance becomes unjust when it is used to maintain
segregation and to deny citizens the (First Amendment) privilege
270 of peaceful assembly and protest.

I hope you are able to see the distinction I am trying to
point out. In no sense do I advocate evading or defying the
law, as would the rabid segregationist. That would lead to
anarchy.[23] One who breaks an unjust law must do so openly,
lovingly, and with a willingness to accept the penalty. I submit
that an individual who breaks a law that conscience tells him is
unjust, and who willingly accepts the penalty of imprisonment
in order to arouse the conscience of the community over its
injustice, is in reality expressing the highest respect for law.

280 Of course, there is nothing new about this kind of civil
disobedience. It was evidenced sublimely in the refusal of
Shadrach, Meshach, and Abednego to obey the laws of
Nebuchadnezzar,[24] on the ground that a higher moral law was
at stake. It was practiced superbly by the early Christians,
who were willing to face hungry lions and the excruciating
pain of chopping blocks rather than submit to certain unjust
laws of the Roman Empire. To a degree, academic freedom is
a reality today because Socrates practiced civil disobedience.

---

22. **devious:** tricky; indirect.

23. **anarchy** (ăn′ər-kē): an absence of law and order in a society.

24. **the refusal . . . Nebuchadnezzar** (nĕb′ə-kəd-nĕz′ər): In the Bible (Daniel 3),
 Shadrach (shăd′răk), Meshach (mē′shăk), and Abednego (ə-bĕd′nĭ-gō′) are
 three Hebrews condemned to death for refusing to worship an idol set up
 by Nebuchadnezzar, king of Babylon. When cast into a fiery furnace, they
 are miraculously protected from the fire and emerge unharmed.

In our own nation, the Boston Tea Party represented a
290 massive act of civil disobedience.

We should never forget that everything Adolf Hitler did in
Germany was "legal" and everything the Hungarian freedom
fighters[25] did in Hungary was "illegal." It was "illegal" to aid
and comfort a Jew in Hitler's Germany. Even so, I am sure
that, had I lived in Germany at the time, I would have aided
and comforted my Jewish brothers. If today I lived in a
Communist country where certain principles dear to the
Christian faith are suppressed, I would openly advocate
disobeying that country's antireligious laws.

Pause & Reflect

300 **FOCUS**
Read to find out why
King is disappointed
with "white moderates"
who criticize his
nonviolent direct
action.

I must make two honest confessions to
you, my Christian and Jewish brothers.
First, I must confess that over the past
few years I have been gravely
disappointed with the white moderate. I
have almost reached the regrettable
conclusion that the Negro's great
stumbling block in his stride toward freedom is not the White
Citizen's Counciler or the Ku Klux Klanner,[26] but the white
moderate, who is more devoted to "order" than to justice;
310 who prefers a negative peace which is the absence of tension
to a positive peace which is the presence of justice; who
constantly says: "I agree with you in the goal you seek, but I
cannot agree with your methods of direct action"; who
paternalistically[27] believes he can set the timetable for another
man's freedom; who lives by a mythical concept of time and
who constantly advises the Negro to wait for a "more
convenient season." Shallow understanding from people of
goodwill is more frustrating than absolute misunderstanding
from people of ill will. Lukewarm acceptance is much more
320 bewildering than outright rejection.

---

25. **Hungarian freedom fighters:** Hungarians who participated in a 1956
rebellion against the Communist government of their homeland. (The
uprising was crushed by troops sent into Hungary by the Soviet Union.)

26. **the White . . . Klanner:** a member of either of two hate groups which claim
that white people are superior to African Americans and other minorities.

27. **paternalistically** (pə-tûr′nə-lĭs′tĭ-klē): in a manner that suggests the way a
father deals with his children.

Pause & Reflect

1. Review what you underlined
about the qualities of a just law.
Star the quotes below from
King's letter that apply to a just
law. **(Clarify)**

"moral responsibility to obey"

"uplifts human personality"

"*sameness* made legal"

"out of harmony with the moral
law"

MARK IT UP 2. Review
the examples that King gives
of breaking the law for a just
cause (lines 280–299). What are
King's most powerful examples?
Circle them. **(Evaluate)**

As the letter continues . . .

• King explains that African
Americans have been victim-
ized and then criticized for
fighting back.

What Does It Mean?

Mythical concept of time refers
to King's belief that white moderates had an unrealistic
expectation that, after centuries
of oppression, African Americans would be content to wait
even longer for equality.

What Does It Mean?
Plight means "bad situation."

☑ **Reading Check**
What does King say he is doing to the tension in the South?

☑ **Reading Check**
Reread the boxed paragraph on this page. Circle the sentence below that best expresses the main idea of this passage.

   Condemning peaceful protests is like treating the victims of crimes as though they had caused the crimes.

   Peaceful protests should be condemned because they lead to violence.

What Does It Mean?
Manifests means "appears" or "shows."

I had hoped that the white moderate would understand that law and order exist for the purpose of establishing justice and that when they fail in this purpose, they become the dangerously structured dams that block the flow of social progress. I had hoped that the white moderate would understand that the present tension in the South is a necessary phase of the transition from an obnoxious negative peace, in which the Negro passively accepted his unjust plight, to a substantive and positive peace, in which all men will respect the dignity and worth of human personality. Actually, we who engage in nonviolent direct action are not the creators of tension. We merely bring to the surface the hidden tension that is already alive. We bring it out in the open, where it can be seen and dealt with. Like a boil that can never be cured so long as it is covered up but must be opened with all its ugliness to the natural medicines of air and light, injustice must be exposed, with all the tension its exposure creates, to the light of human conscience and the air of national opinion before it can be cured.

In your statement you assert that our actions, even though peaceful, must be condemned because they precipitate violence. But is this a logical assertion? Isn't this like condemning a robbed man because his possession of money precipitated[28] the evil act of robbery? Isn't this like condemning Socrates because his unswerving commitment to truth and his philosophical inquiries precipitated the act by the misguided populace in which they made him drink hemlock?[29] Isn't this like condemning Jesus because his unique God-consciousness and never-ceasing devotion to God's will precipitated the evil act of crucifixion? We must come to see that, as the federal courts have consistently affirmed, it is wrong to urge an individual to cease his efforts to gain his basic constitutional rights because the quest may precipitate violence. Society must protect the robbed and punish the robber. . . .

Oppressed people cannot remain oppressed forever. The yearning for freedom eventually manifests itself, and that is what has happened to the American Negro. Something within has reminded him of his birthright of freedom, and something

---

28. **precipitated** (prĭ-sĭp′ĭ-tā′tĭd): brought about; caused.

29. **Socrates . . . hemlock:** Socrates was tried for ruining the minds of the youth of Athens. He was condemned to die by drinking hemlock, a poison.

360 without has reminded him that it can be gained. Consciously or unconsciously, he has been caught up by the *Zeitgeist*,[30] and with his black brothers of Africa and his brown and yellow brothers of Asia, South America, and the Caribbean, the United States Negro is moving with a sense of great urgency toward the promised land of racial justice. If one recognizes this vital urge that has engulfed the Negro community, one should readily understand why public demonstrations are taking place. The Negro has many pent-up resentments and <u>latent</u> frustrations, and he must release them. 370 So let him march; let him make prayer pilgrimages to the city hall; let him go on ⬭freedom rides⬭—and try to understand why he must do so. If his repressed emotions are not released in nonviolent ways, they will seek expression through violence; this is not a threat but a fact of history. So I have not said to my people: "Get rid of your discontent." Rather, I have tried to say that this normal and healthy discontent can be channeled into the creative outlet of nonviolent direct action. And now this approach is being termed extremist.

Pause & Reflect

FOCUS
380 King answers those who call him an extremist. Then he goes on to point out the "real heroes" of the South.

MARK IT UP Circle some of the names King gives as examples of extremists.

But though I was initially disappointed at being categorized as an extremist, as I continued to think about the matter, I gradually gained a measure of satisfaction from the label. Was not Jesus an extremist for love: "Love your enemies, bless them that curse you, do good to them that hate you, and pray for them which despitefully use you, and persecute you." Was not Amos[31] an

---

30. *Zeitgeist* (tsīt′gīst′) *German:* spirit of the time—the beliefs and attitudes shared by most of the people living in a particular period.

31. **Amos:** a Hebrew prophet whose words are recorded in the Old Testament book bearing his name.

WORDS
TO
KNOW
latent (lāt′nt) *adj.* existing in a hidden form

More About . . .

FREEDOM RIDES were organized trips that civil rights protestors took on buses and trains. The purpose was to protest segregation on interstate bus and train routes and in stations.

Pause & Reflect

King regards the white moderates as "the Negro's great stumbling block in his stride toward freedom" (lines 306–307). Star the phrases below that identify reasons King gives for his opinion. **(Logical Argument)**

more interested in "order" than in justice

don't approve of direct action

openly reject African Americans

prefer an absence of tension to the presence of justice

As the letter continues . . .

• King talks about the term *extremist* and what it means to him.

✔ **Reading Check**

Why does King say that he "gained satisfaction" from being called an extremist?

extremist for justice: "Let justice roll down like waters and righteousness like an ever-flowing stream." Was not Paul an extremist for the Christian gospel: "I bear in my body the marks of the Lord Jesus." Was not Martin Luther[32] an extremist: "Here I stand; I cannot do otherwise, so help me God." And John Bunyan:[33] "I will stay in jail to the end of my days before I make a butchery of my conscience." And Abraham Lincoln: "This nation cannot survive half slave and half free." And Thomas Jefferson: "We hold these truths to be self-evident, that all men are created equal. . . ." So the question is not whether we will be extremists, but what kind of extremists we will be. Will we be extremists for hate or for love? Will we be extremists for the preservation of injustice or for the extension of justice? In that dramatic scene on Calvary's hill[34] three men were crucified. We must never forget that all three were crucified for the same crime—the crime of extremism. Two were extremists for immorality, and thus fell below their environment. The other, Jesus Christ, was an extremist for love, truth, and goodness, and thereby rose above his environment. Perhaps the South, the nation and the world are in dire need of creative extremists. . . .

I wish you had commended the Negro sit-inners and demonstrators of Birmingham for their sublime courage, their willingness to suffer, and their amazing discipline in the midst of great <u>provocation</u>. One day the South will recognize its real heroes. They will be the James Merediths,[35] with the noble sense of purpose that enables them to face jeering and hostile mobs, and with the agonizing loneliness that characterizes the life of the pioneer.

Reading Check

Who are some of the extremists King identifies? Why do you think he refers to them?

---

32. **Martin Luther:** a German monk who started the Protestant Reformation. Luther condemned the wealth and corruption of the 16th-century Roman Catholic Church.

33. **John Bunyan:** a 17th-century English preacher and author of the famous religious work *The Pilgrim's Progress*. He was twice imprisoned for preaching without a license.

34. **Calvary's hill:** the site of Jesus's crucifixion.

35. **James Merediths:** people like James Meredith, who endured violent opposition from whites to become the first African American to attend the University of Mississippi.

WORDS TO KNOW

provocation (prŏv′ə-kā′shən) *n.* something that arouses anger

They will be old, oppressed, battered Negro women,
symbolized in a seventy-two-year-old woman in
Montgomery, Alabama, who rose up with a sense of dignity
and with her people decided not to ride segregated buses,
and who responded with ungrammatical profundity to one
who inquired about her weariness: "My feets is tired,
but my soul is at rest." They will be the young high
school and college students, the young ministers of the
gospel and a host of their elders, courageously and
nonviolently sitting in at lunch counters and willingly
going to jail for conscience' sake. One day the South will
know that when these disinherited children of God sat
down at lunch counters, they were in reality standing
up for what is best in the American dream and for the
most sacred values in our Judaeo-Christian heritage,
thereby bringing our nation back to those great wells
of democracy which were dug deep by the founding
fathers in their formulation of the Constitution and the
Declaration of Independence.

Pause & Reflect

FOCUS
The ending of the letter
returns to a more
personal tone. Read to
find out about King's
feelings and hopes.

Never before have I written so long a
letter. I'm afraid it is much too long
to take your precious time. I can
assure you that it would have been
much shorter if I had been writing
from a comfortable desk, but what
else can one do when he is alone in a narrow jail cell,
other than write long letters, think long thoughts, and
pray long prayers?

If I have said anything in this letter that overstates the
truth and indicates an unreasonable impatience, I beg you
to forgive me. If I have said anything that understates the
truth and indicates my having a patience that allows me
to settle for anything less than brotherhood, I beg God to
forgive me.

READ ALOUD Lines 419–425
As you read these lines aloud,
listen to what the elderly woman
says about herself.

What Does It Mean?
Ungrammatical profundity
means "a comment that is not
in standard English, but that has
deep meaning."

Pause & Reflect

King identifies several groups
of people as the "real heroes"
of the South (lines 411–437). Do
you agree with King that these
people are heroic? *Yes/No*,
because _____

_____

_____ .

(Evaluate)

As the letter ends . . .

• King apologizes for the length
of his letter.

• He expresses hope for the
future.

✔ Reading Check
Why would King beg God to
forgive him if he has been too
patient?

1. King expresses his hopes in the final paragraph of his letter. What is his goal? **(Infer)**

_____

_____

_____

2. Based on this letter, what is your impression of King? **(Connect)**

_____

_____

_____

_____

CHALLENGE

How would you describe King's attitude toward the eight clergy-men he is writing to? Mark words and phrases in the letter that tell something about his attitudes. **(Recognizing Tone)**

I hope this letter finds you strong in the faith. I also hope that circumstances will soon make it possible for me to meet each of you, not as an integrationist or a civil-rights leader but as a fellow clergyman and a Christian brother. Let us all hope that the dark clouds of racial prejudice will soon pass away and the deep fog of misunderstanding will be lifted from our fear-drenched communities, and in some 460 not too distant tomorrow the radiant stars of love and brotherhood will shine over our great nation with all their scintillating[36] beauty.

Yours for the cause of Peace and Brotherhood,

Martin Luther King, Jr.

Pause **&** Reflect

36. **scintillating** (sĭn′tl-āt′ĭng): sparkling.

Active Reading SkillBuilder

Logical Argument: Induction and Deduction

Writers often use different processes of reasoning in one nonfiction work. **Induction** is a process of reasoning in which a writer begins with specific facts and then reaches a general conclusion based on these facts. **Deduction** is a process of reasoning in which a writer begins with a general statement and then infers specific statements from it. Read King's letter, then use the diagram below to analyze a passage that appeals to you. One example is given.

Passage: ___pages 360–361, lines 16–31___

General Statements	Specific Statements and Facts
"I am here because I have organizational ties here."	King is president of Southern Christian Leadership Conference.
	SCLC is associated with the Alabama Christian Movement for Human Rights.
	SCLC shares resources with the Alabama organization.
Reasoning Process: *induction*	

←→

Passage: _____

General Statements	Specific Statements and Facts
Reasoning Process:	

Literary Analysis SkillBuilder

Allusion

An **allusion** is a reference to a historical or literary person, place, or event with which the reader is assumed to be familiar. By using allusions, writers draw upon associations already in the reader's mind. On the chart below, list allusions to people, places, or events that King makes in this selection. Then explain the meaning that each allusion suggests to you. Briefly explain why you think King includes the allusion in his argument. An example has been done for you.

Allusion	Possible Meaning	Why Included
Apostle Paul	religious leader who traveled far to spread his message	King believes he must carry his "gospel of freedom" wherever there is injustice.

Words to Know SkillBuilder

Words to Know

affiliate	cognizant	estrangement	provocation	segregated
appraisal	diligently	latent	retaliating	statute

A. Fill in each blank with the correct Word to Know.

1. During the early 1960s there was more than one _____ that enforced segregation.

2. The _____ between the races led to misunderstanding and violence.

3. The civil rights movement made many more people _____ of the evils of racism.

4. Dr. King discouraged his supporters from _____ when pro-voked.

5. We can all benefit from a frequent _____ of the status of civil rights in this country.

B. Write the Word to Know that best completes each of the following analogies.

1. threat : intimidation : : insult : _____

2. acceptance : rejection : : integrated : _____

3. walk : purposefully : : labor : _____

4. obvious : overt : : hidden : _____

5. teacher : instructor : : associate : _____

C. Write a letter to Martin Luther King, Jr. Describe two or three things about the sta-tus of African Americans in 1963 that you learned from his writings. Use at least **three** of the Words to Know in your letter.

MEXICANS BEGIN JOGGING

Gary Soto

LEGAL ALIEN

Pat Mora

Before You Read

Connect to Your Life

Both of the poems that you are about to read deal with the speaker's feelings about being "prejudged." The word *prejudged* has the same roots as the word *prejudice*—the unfair, negative feelings a person of one group may feel about another group. Have you ever felt prejudged? Did someone ever decide things about you before they even knew anything about you? Write about your experience.

_____

_____

_____

_____

Key to the Poems

WHAT'S THE BIG IDEA? Both of the poems in this selection deal with alienation. Alienation is feeling separate from or different than the people around you. Complete the word web below with situations in which one might feel alienated.

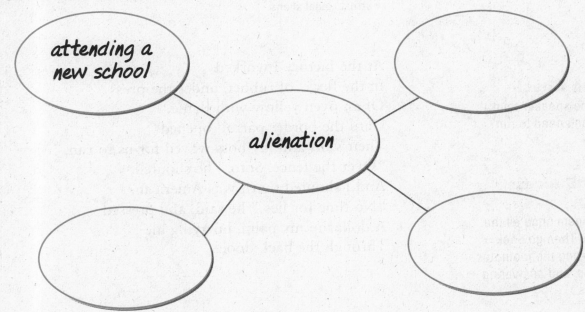

attending a
new school

alienation

Reading Tips

- Read "Mexicans Begin Jogging" and "Legal Alien" silently and then aloud to get a sense of what these poems are about. Hearing the sounds of a poem makes the meaning clearer and may add to your enjoyment.

- As you read each poem, try to imagine each situation that is described. Put your-self in the speaker's situa-tion and try to relate to his or her feelings.

- After reading each poem a few times, zero in on the **figurative language,** or imaginative comparisons. For each comparison, identify the things com-pared and think about how they are alike.

As the poem begins . . .

- The speaker is mistaken for an illegal alien.

PREVIEW Gary Soto and Pat Mora are Mexican-American poets who are widely read. The poems "Mexicans Begin Jogging" and "Legal Alien" explore what happens when someone is prejudged or is treated differently because of his or her ethnic background. The speaker in "Mexicans Begin Jogging" is a United States citizen who is mistaken for an "illegal alien"— an immigrant who has unlawfully entered the country. "Legal Alien" is a term applied to an immigrant who, though not a U. S. citizen, is allowed to live in the United States.

MEXICANS BEGIN JOGGING

Gary Soto

FOCUS
The speaker of this poem works in a factory. Read to find out what happens to the speaker when the police arrive to arrest illegal aliens.

✔ Reading Check

Why does the speaker think that he doesn't need to run?

☆ Reader Success Strategy

Read each poem once all the way through. Then go back and read it using the footnotes, sidebar notes, and answering the questions.

At the factory I worked
In the fleck[1] of rubber, under the press
Of an oven yellow with flame,
Until the border patrol[2] opened
5   Their vans and my boss waved for us to run.
"Over the fence, Soto," he shouted,
And I shouted that I was American.
"No time for lies," he said, and pressed
A dollar in my palm, hurrying me
10   Through the back door.

---

1. **fleck:** a small bit or flake.
2. **border patrol:** a group of guards who watch the border between Mexico and the United States and arrest illegal aliens.

Since I was on his time, I ran
And became the wag to a short tail of Mexicans—
Ran past the amazed crowds that lined
The street and blurred like photographs, in rain.
I ran from that industrial road to the soft
Houses where people paled at the turn of an
    autumn sky.
What could I do but yell *vivas*[3]
To baseball, milkshakes, and those sociologists[4]
Who would clock me
As I jog into the next century
On the power of a great, silly grin.

Pause & Reflect

What Does It Mean?

The highlighted phrase means "at the end of the line, like the wagging tail of a dog."

Pause & Reflect

1. What happens to the speaker in this poem? (**Summarize**)

_____

_____

_____

2. How would you feel if you were in the speaker's situation? (**Connect**)

_____

_____

_____

_____

READ ALOUD   3. Read aloud lines 17–21. Cross out the sentence below that does *not* apply to the speaker. (**Clarify**)

He cheers American culture, as if to prove that he belongs.

He no longer wants to live in the United States.

He feels that his actions are being watched.

---

3. *vivas* (vē′väs): *Spanish:* cheers.
4. **sociologists** (sō′sē-ŏl′ə-jists): people who study group behavior.

LEGAL ALIEN
Pat Mora

As the poem begins . . .

• The speaker describes how she is treated by Mexicans and Americans.

What Does It Mean?

Bi-lingual means "able to speak two languages." *Bi-cultural* means "belonging to two cultures."

More About . . .

(ANGLOS) *Anglo* is a Spanish term that means any English-speaking, white person.

Pause & Reflect

✎ **MARK IT UP** How does the speaker feel about her situation? Write the answer below. Then circle details in the poem that led you to your conclusion. **(Infer)**

_____

_____

_____

_____

CHALLENGE

In the first poem, the speaker uses "a great, silly grin" to protect himself from the challenges he faces. In the second poem, the speaker uses a smile to "mask" the pain of being pre-judged. In your opinion, why do they rely on smiles? **(Connect)**

FOCUS
The speaker of this poem is Mexican-American. She knows Spanish and English and is a blend of two cultures. Read to find out about her situation.

Bi-lingual, Bi-cultural,
able to slip from "How's life?"
to *"Me'stan volviendo loca,"*[1]
able to sit in a paneled office
5 drafting memos in smooth English,
able to order in fluent Spanish
at a Mexican restaurant,
American but hyphenated,[2]
viewed by (Anglos) as perhaps exotic,[3]
10 perhaps inferior, definitely different,
viewed by Mexicans as alien,
(their eyes say, "You may speak
Spanish but you're not like me")
an American to Mexicans
15 a Mexican to Americans
a handy token
sliding back and forth
between the fringes of both worlds
by smiling
20 by masking the discomfort
of being pre-judged
Bi-laterally.[4]

Pause & Reflect

1. *"Me'stan volviendo loca"* (mĕ-stän′ vôl-vē-ĕn′dô lô′kä) *Spanish:* "They're making me crazy."
2. **American but hyphenated:** viewed as a Mexican-American, rather than just an American.
3. **exotic:** foreign; strange.
4. **Bi-laterally:** in a way that is undertaken by two sides equally.

Active Reading SkillBuilder

Comparing Writers' Attitudes

Tone is a **writer's attitude** toward the subject that he or she is writing about. Read "Mexicans Begin Jogging," and then identify on the chart below Soto's attitude toward being prejudged. Copy down a word, phrase, or line from Soto's poem that suggests his tone to you. When reading "Legal Alien," compare or contrast its tone with that of the first poem. Identify Mora's tone on the chart, then copy onto the chart a word, phrase, or line in the poem that you think conveys this tone.

"Mexicans Begin Jogging"

Tone: _____

_____

_____

Suggested by: _____

_____

_____

"Legal Alien"

Tone: _____

_____

_____

Suggested by: _____

_____

_____

Literary Analysis SkillBuilder

Tone

Tone is a writer's attitude toward the subject that he or she is writing about. In these two poems, the poets convey their attitudes toward being prejudged through their diction—their choice of words—their direct statements of their positions, and their use of imagery. On the chart below, list specific words, statements, and images that you think convey Soto's tone in "Mexicans Begin Jogging," and Mora's tone in "Legal Alien." Examples are shown.

	Diction	Direct Statements	Imagery
"Mexicans Begin Jogging"	*wag*	*"I shouted that I was American."*	
"Legal Alien"			

Straw into Gold:

The Metamorphosis of the Everyday

Sandra Cisneros

Before You Read

Connect to Your Life

In this essay, Sandra Cisneros describes people and events that shaped her life. What people, events, or experiences have shaped or changed your life? Use this chart to list them.

PEOPLE	EVENTS	EXPERIENCES

Key to the Essay

WHAT'S THE BIG IDEA? In this essay, Cisneros describes some of her accomplishments, many of which she didn't expect to achieve. She feels that she has been able to take what life has given her and spin it into gold—or make a happy life as a successful writer. Read the selection to learn how Cisneros turned her "straw" into "gold."

Straw into Gold:
The Metamorphosis of the Everyday

Sandra Cisneros

PREVIEW Sandra Cisneros is a Mexican-American writer who has earned many awards. One of her famous works is *The House on Mango Street.* It tells about a young girl's coming of age in inner-city Chicago. In this essay Cisneros relates some of her own recollections of growing up. The title "Straw into Gold" refers to the incredible task faced by the heroine of the folk tale "Rumpelstiltskin." She had to spin gold out of straw or be put to death. The word *metamorphosis* (mĕt´ə-môr′fə-sĭs) in the subtitle means "a change in form."

Reading Tips

The author's style in this **essay** is personal, informal, and conversational. You might feel as though she is speaking directly to you. As you read, keep these points in mind:

- Look for the places where the author refers to the **title** of this essay. How does the title help you to understand the **main idea** of the essay?

- Remember the author's situation as a girl growing up in a Mexican-American family. Her culture had strong beliefs about the proper roles of females. She was expected to get married and devote herself to her home and family.

As the essay begins . . .

- Cisneros describes a time when she was expected to do something that she didn't know how to do.

FOCUS

Cisneros begins her essay with an anecdote, or a brief story. Read to find out what happens when she is asked to cook at a dinner party in France.

When I was living in an artists' colony in the south of France, some fellow Latin-Americans who taught at the university in Aix-en-Provence invited me to share a home-cooked meal with them. I had been living abroad almost a year then on an NEA[1] grant, subsisting mainly on French bread and lentils so that my money could last longer. So when the invitation to dinner arrived, I accepted without hesitation. Especially since they had promised Mexican food.

What I didn't realize when they made this invitation was that I was supposed to be involved in preparing the meal. I guess they assumed I knew how to cook Mexican food because I am Mexican. They wanted specifically tortillas, though I'd never made a tortilla[2] in my life.

MARK IT UP KEEP TRACK

As you read, you can use these marks to keep track of your understanding.

✔ ..... I understand.

? ..... I don't understand this.

! ..... Interesting or surprising idea

---

1. **NEA:** National Endowment for the Arts—a federal agency that funds artistic projects of organizations and individuals.
2. **tortilla** (tôr-tē′yə): A flat thin disk of bread made from corn meal or flour.

✔ **Reading Check**

Why do Cisneros's friends think she can make tortillas?

Pause & **Reflect**

1. Why did making corn tortillas seem to be an impossible task to Cisneros? **(Main Idea)**

_____

_____

_____

_____

2. Cisneros compares making corn tortillas to writing a critical essay. What does she find similar about these challenges? **(Compare and Contrast)**

_____

_____

_____

_____

It's true I had witnessed my mother rolling the little armies of dough into perfect circles, but my mother's family is from Guanajuato; they are *provincianos,* country folk. They only know how to make flour tortillas. My father's family, on the other hand, is *chilango*[3] from Mexico City. We ate corn tortillas but we didn't make them. Someone was sent to the corner tortilleria to buy some. I'd never seen anybody make corn tortillas. Ever.

Somehow my Latino hosts had gotten a hold of a packet of corn flour, and this is what they tossed my way with orders to produce tortillas. *Así como sea.* Any ol' way, they said and went back to their cooking.

Why did I feel like the woman in the fairy tale who was locked in a room and ordered to spin straw into gold? I had the same sick feeling when I was required to write my critical essay for the MFA[4] exam—the only piece of noncreative writing necessary in order to get my graduate degree. How was I to start? There were rules involved here, unlike writing a poem or story, which I did intuitively. There was a step by step process needed and I had better know it. I felt as if making tortillas—or writing a critical paper, for that matter—were tasks so impossible I wanted to break down into tears.

Somehow though, I managed to make tortillas—crooked and burnt, but edible nonetheless. My hosts were absolutely ignorant when it came to Mexican food; they thought my tortillas were delicious. (I'm glad my mama wasn't there.) Thinking back and looking at an old photograph documenting the three of us consuming those lopsided circles I am amazed. Just as I am amazed I could finish my MFA exam.

Pause & **Reflect**

---

3. **chilango** (chē-län′gō): *Mexican slang:* native to Mexico City.

4. **MFA:** master of fine arts (an academic degree).

WORDS TO KNOW	**intuitively** (ĭn-tōō′ĭ-tĭv-lē) *adv.* without thinking; instinctively
	edible (ĕd′ə-bəl) *adj.* fit to eat

FOCUS

Read to find out what Cisneros's father and mother were like.

MARK IT UP As you read, circle details that tell you about her parents. An example is highlighted.

I've managed to do a lot of things in my life I didn't think I was capable of and which many others didn't think I was capable of either. Especially because I am a woman, a Latina,[5] an only daughter in a family of six men. My father would've liked to have seen me married long ago. In our culture men and women don't leave their father's house except by way of marriage. I crossed my father's threshold with nothing carrying me but my own two feet. A woman whom no one came for and no one chased away.

To make matters worse, I left before any of my six brothers had <u>ventured</u> away from home. I broke a terrible taboo.[6] Somehow, looking back at photos of myself as a child, I wonder if I was aware of having begun already my own quiet war.

I like to think that somehow my family, my Mexicanness, my poverty, all had something to do with shaping me into a writer. I like to think my parents were preparing me all along for my life as an artist even though they didn't know it. From my father I inherited a love of wandering. He was born in Mexico City but as a young man he traveled into the U.S. vagabonding. He eventually was drafted and thus became a citizen. Some of the stories he has told about his first months in the U.S. with little or no English surface in my stories in *The House on Mango Street* as well as others I have in mind to write in the future. From him I inherited a sappy heart. (He still cries when he watches Mexican soaps—especially if they deal with children who have forsaken their parents.)

My mother was born like me—in Chicago but of Mexican descent. It would be her tough street-wise voice that would haunt all my stories and poems. An amazing woman who loves to draw and read books and can sing an opera. A smart cookie.

When I was a little girl we traveled to Mexico City so much I thought my grandparents' house on La Fortuna, number 12,

As the essay continues . . .
• Cisneros talks about the importance of her family.

What Does It Mean?
Vagabonding means "traveling in a carefree, wandering way."

MARK IT UP WORD POWER

Mark words that you'd like to add to your **Personal Word List**. After reading, you can record the words and their meanings beginning on page 476.

---

5. **Latina:** a woman or girl from a Spanish-speaking culture.
6. **taboo:** a strict cultural rule forbidding something.

WORDS TO KNOW

venture (věn′chər) *v.* to dare to go

1. What cultural taboo, or rule, did Cisneros break? **(Clarify)**

_____

_____

_____

_____

2. Review the details you circled as you read. What two traits did Cisneros get from her father? **(Clarify)**

_____

_____

_____

_____

As the essay continues . . .

• Cisneros describes what kind of student she was.

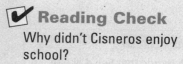

Reading Check

Why didn't Cisneros enjoy school?

---

was home. It was the only constant in our nomadic[7] ramblings from one Chicago flat to another. The house on Destiny Street, number 12, in the colonia Tepeyac would be perhaps the only home I knew, and that nostalgia[8] for a home would be a theme that would obsess me.

My brothers also figured greatly in my art. Especially the older two; I grew up in their shadows. Henry, the second oldest and my favorite, appears often in poems I have written and in stories which at times only borrow his nickname, Kiki. He played a major role in my childhood. We were bunk-bed mates. We were co-conspirators. We were pals. Until my oldest brother came back from studying in Mexico and left me odd woman out for always.

Pause & Reflect

FOCUS

Read to find out about Cisneros's struggles as a child and her triumphs as an adult.

What would my teachers say if they knew I was a writer now? Who would've guessed it? I wasn't a very bright student. I didn't much like school because we moved so much and I was always new and funny looking. In my fifth-grade report card I have nothing but an <u>avalanche</u> of C's and D's, but I don't remember being that stupid. I was good at art and I read plenty of library books and Kiki laughed at all my jokes. At home I was fine, but at school I never opened my mouth except when the teacher called on me.

When I think of how I see myself it would have to be at age eleven. I know I'm thirty-two on the outside, but inside I'm eleven. I'm the girl in the picture with skinny arms and a crumpled skirt and crooked hair. I didn't like school because all they saw was the outside me. School was lots of rules and sitting with your hands folded and being very afraid all the time. I liked looking out the window and thinking. I liked staring at the girl across the way writing her name over and over again in red ink. I wondered why the boy with the dirty

---

7. **nomadic:** moving from home to home; wandering.

8. **nostalgia** (nŏ-stăl′jə): a longing for things or people in the past.

WORDS TO KNOW   **avalanche** (ăv′ə-lănch′) _n._ an overwhelming amount

collar in front of me didn't have a mama who took better care of him.

I think my mama and papa did the best they could to keep us warm and clean and never hungry. We had birthday and graduation parties and things like that, but there was another hunger that had to be fed. There was a hunger I didn't even have a name for. Was this when I began writing?

In 1966 we moved into a house, a real one, our first real home. This meant we didn't have to change schools and be the new kids on the block every couple of years. We could make friends and not be afraid we'd have to say goodbye to them and start all over. My brothers and the flock of boys they brought home would become important characters eventually for my stories—Louie and his cousins, Meme Ortiz and his dog with two names, one in English and one in Spanish.

My mother flourished in her own home. She took books out of the library and taught herself to garden—to grow flowers so envied we had to put a lock on the gate to keep out the midnight flower thieves. My mother has never quit gardening.

This was the period in my life, that slippery age when you are both child and woman and neither, I was to record in *The House on Mango Street*. I was still shy. I was a girl who couldn't come out of her shell.

How was I to know I would be recording and <u>documenting</u> the women who sat their sadness on an elbow and stared out a window? It would be the city streets of Chicago I would later record, as seen through a child's eyes.

I've done all kinds of things I didn't think I could do since then. I've gone to a prestigious[9] university, studied with famous writers, and taken an MFA degree. I've taught poetry in schools in Illinois and Texas. I've gotten an NEA grant and run away with it as far as my courage would take me. I've seen the bleached and bitter mountains of the Peloponnesus.[10]

---

9. **prestigious** (prĕ-stē′jəs): respected.

10. **Peloponnesus** (pĕl′ə-pə-nē′səs): the peninsula forming the southern part of mainland Greece.

Reader Success Strategy

Fill in the web below with the things that helped Cisneros become a writer.

Helped Cisneros Become a Writer

Reading Check

How did the move to the new house change Cisneros's life?

READ ALOUD Lines 142–145

As you read these lines aloud, imagine yourself in Cisneros's place, observing people in your new neighborhood. What questions might you ask about the women "who sat their sadness on an elbow"? **(Connect)**

_____

_____

_____

_____

What Does It Mean?

Promenaders means "people who promenade, or stroll in public."

More About . . .

Polaroid-blue refers to the deep blue of a Polaroid photograph.

Pause & Reflect

✎ **MARK IT UP** Cisneros faced many struggles as a child. Underline details on pages 390 and 391 that tell you about them. In your opinion, what was her greatest challenge? **(Evaluate)**

_____

_____

_____

_____

✎ **CHALLENGE**

The **theme** is the main idea or opinion that the writer wants the reader to understand. Mark details or passages in this essay that reveal or hint at the writer's main idea or opinion. How would you state the theme of this essay? **(Analyze)**

I've lived on an island. I've been to Venice twice. I've lived in Yugoslavia. I've been to the famous Nice[11] flower market behind the opera house. I've lived in a village in the pre-Alps and witnessed the daily parade of promenaders.

I've moved since Europe to the strange and wonderful country of Texas, land of polaroid-blue skies and big bugs. I met a mayor with my last name. I met famous Chicana and Chicano artists and writers and *políticos*.[12]

160   Texas is another chapter in my life. It brought with it the Dobie-Paisano Fellowship, a six-month residency on a 265-acre ranch. But most important, Texas brought Mexico back to me.

In the days when I would sit at my favorite people-watching spot, the snakey Woolworth's counter across the street from the Alamo[13] (the Woolworth's which has since been torn down to make way for progress), I couldn't think of anything else I'd rather be than a writer. I've traveled and lectured from Cape Cod to San Francisco, to Spain,
170 Yugoslavia, Greece, Mexico, France, Italy, and now today to Texas. Along the way there has been straw for the taking. With a little imagination, it can be spun into gold.

Pause & Reflect

---

11. **Nice** (nēs): a port city in southern France.

12. *políticos* (pô-lē′tē-kôs): *Spanish*: politicians.

13. **Alamo**: a mission chapel in San Antonio, Texas—site of a famous battle in Texas's war for independence from Mexico.

Active Reading SkillBuilder

Analyzing Structure

The **structure** of an essay—the way in which its parts are arranged—is related to its purpose. For example, Cisneros's purpose in her essay is to share some of her formative experiences. Her essay, organized around recollections of growing up, begins with a story about making tortillas. In the first box below, write a summary of this opening anecdote. Write summaries of Cisneros's other recollections in the second box. On the lines between the boxes, write connections between the anecdote and the rest of the essay. An example is shown.

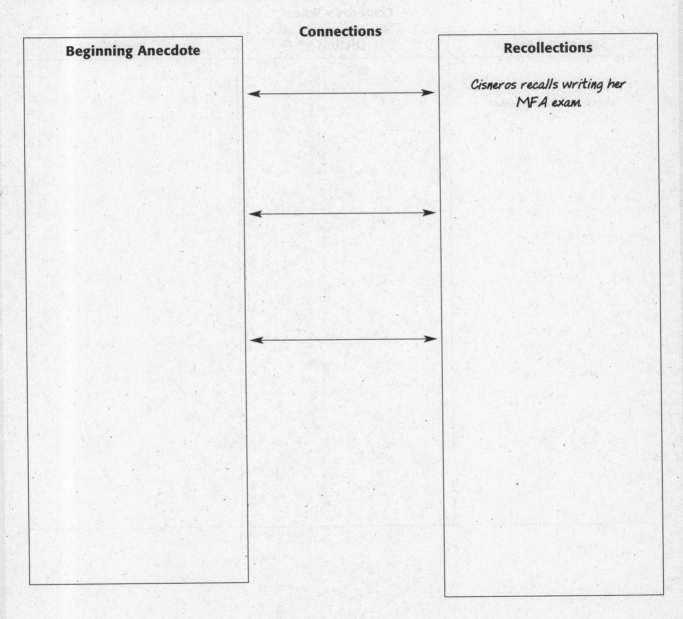

Connections

Beginning Anecdote		**Recollections**
		Cisneros recalls writing her MFA exam.

Literary Analysis SkillBuilder

Voice

Voice refers to a writer's unique use of language that allows a reader to "hear" a human personality in his or her writing. The elements that work together to create a writer's voice include sentence structure, diction, and tone. Use the following chart to analyze Cisneros's anecdote about making tortillas. Record information about sentence length, diction, and the writer's attitude toward her subject. An example is shown.

Cisneros's Voice

Sentence Length	Diction	Tone
short, simple sentences		

Words to Know SkillBuilder

Words to Know

avalanche   document   edible   intuitively   venture

A. Fill in each blank with the correct Word to Know.

1. Cisneros broke a terrible taboo when she decided to

   _____ away from home before any of her brothers did.

2. In her writing, Cisneros tries to _____ the lives of the
   people with whom she grew up.

3. Sometimes Cisneros can write a poem or story _____,
   almost without thinking.

4. In school Cisneros earned so many C's and D's that it seemed like an

   _____ in the Alps.

5. Cisneros was relieved when the tortillas she made turned out to be

   _____ .

B. Write the Word to Know that best complete each book title.

1. An _____ in the Mountains

2. A Childhood to Remember: My Attempt to _____ the Past

3. Speaking _____ : How to Communicate Quickly and Insightfully

4. All Things _____ : An All-Purpose Cookbook

5. My _____ into Freedom: A Daring Escapade

C. Write an anecdote about a time in your life when you succeeded at something
that you thought you could not do. Use at least **three** of the Words to Know in
your anecdote.

Academic and Informational Reading

In this section, you'll find strategies to help you read all kinds of informational materials. The examples here range from magazines you read for fun to textbooks and maps you read for information. Applying these simple and effective techniques will help you become a more successful reader of the many texts you encounter every day.

Reading a Magazine Article

A magazine article is designed to catch and hold your interest. Learning how to recognize the items on a magazine page will help you read even the most complicated articles. Look at the sample magazine article as you read each strategy below.

A Read the **title** and any other **headings** to get an idea of what the article is about. Frequently, the title presents the article's main topic.

B Study **visuals**—photos, pictures, or maps. Visuals help bring the topic to life and also help you understand the article.

C Notice any **quotations.** Who is quoted? Evaluate whether the person is a reliable authority on the subject.

D Stop and think about the author's **questions** while reading. These questions are used to introduce important topics.

E Look for **special features,** such as charts, tables, or graphs, that provide more detailed information on the topic.

MARK IT UP ▷ Use the sample magazine page at right and the tips above to help you answer the following questions.

1. What is the article's main topic? _____

_____

_____

2. How is the quotation related to the title of the article? _____

_____

3. Put check marks beside the two quotations. Why is the first speaker a reliable authority on the subject? _____

_____

4. Circle the question used to introduce the story of how windshield wipers were invented.

5. What information appears in the shaded box? _____

_____

A Shouldn't We Know Who Invented the Windshield Wiper?

by James T. Terry

We know the famous ones—the Thomas Edisons and the Alexander Graham Bells— but what about the less famous inventors? What about the people who invented the traffic light and the windshield wiper? Shouldn't we know who they are?

Joan McLean thinks so. In fact, McLean, a professor of physics at Mountain University in Range, Colorado, feels so strongly about this matter that she's developed a course on the topic. In addition to learning "who" invented "what," however, McLean also likes her students to learn the answers to the "why" and "how" questions. According to McLean, "When students learn the answers to these questions, they are better prepared to recognize opportunities for inventing and more motivated to give inventing a try."

Her students agree. One young man with a patent pending for an unbreakable umbrella is walking proof of McLean's statement. "If I had not heard the story of the windshield wiper's invention," said Tommy Lee, a senior physics major, "I never would have dreamed of turning my frustration during a rainstorm into something so constructive." Lee is currently negotiating to sell his patent to an umbrella manufacturer once it is approved.

So, just what is the story behind the windshield wiper? Well, Mary Anderson came up with the idea in 1902 after a visit to New York City. The day was cold and blustery, but Anderson still wanted to see the sights, so she hopped aboard a streetcar. Noticing that the driver was struggling to see through the sleet and snow covering the windshield, she found herself wondering why there couldn't be a built-in device for cleaning the window. Still wondering about this when she returned home to Birmingham, Alabama, Anderson started sketching out solutions. One of her ideas, a lever on the inside of a vehicle that would control an arm on the outside, became the first windshield wiper.

Today we benefit from countless inventions and innovations. It's hard to imagine getting by without Garrett A. Morgan's traffic light. It's equally impossible to picture a world without Katherine J. Blodgett's innovation that makes glass invisible. Can you picture life without transparent windows and eyeglasses?

As I think about stories like these, I am convinced that they will help untold numbers of inventors. So, only one question nags: how did we ever manage to give rise to so many inventors before McLean invented this class?

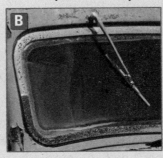

C "When students learn the answers to these questions, they are better prepared to recognize opportunities for inventing...."

E Someone Also Invented . . .

Dishwashers	Josephine Cochran
Disposable Diapers	Marion Donovan
Fire Escapes	Anna Connelly
Peanut Butter	George Washington Carver

Reading a Textbook

The first page of a textbook lesson introduces you to a particular topic. The page also provides important information that will guide you through the rest of the lesson. Look at the sample textbook page as you read each strategy below.

A Preview the **title** and other **headings** to find out the lesson's main topic and related subtopics.

B Look for a list of terms or **vocabulary words.** These words will be identified and defined throughout the lesson.

C Read the **main idea, objectives,** or **focus.** These items summarize the lesson and establish a purpose for your reading.

D Find words set in special type, such as **italics** or **boldface.** Look for definitions or explanations before or after these terms.

E Notice any **special features** such as extended quotations or text placed in a tinted or colored box. For example, a **primary source** such as a **direct quotation** from a diary or interview is often used to provide firsthand information on a historical topic.

F Examine **visuals,** such as photos and drawings, and their captions. Visuals help bring the topic to life and enrich the text.

║ MARK IT UP ▷ Use the sample textbook page and the strategies above to help you answer the following questions.

1. What is the main topic of this lesson? _____

   _____

2. Circle the vocabulary term that is used on this page.

3. Draw a box around the lesson's main idea.

4. Put a check mark beside the quotation. Who is being quoted? _____

   _____

5. In the picture, who is observing the fighting? _____

   _____

SECTION 2

A The Civil War Begins

C MAIN IDEA	WHY IT MATTERS NOW	B Terms & Names
Shortly after the nation's Southern states seceded from the Union, war began between the North and South.	The nation's identity was forged in part by the Civil War. Sectional divisions remain very strong today.	•Fort Sumter •Bull Run •Stonewall Jackson •Ulysses S. Grant •Robert E. Lee •Antietam •Emancipation Proclamation •conscription •Clara Barton •income tax

One American's Story

On April 18, 1861, Major Robert Anderson was traveling by ship from Charleston, South Carolina, to New York City. That day, Anderson wrote a report to the secretary of war in which he described his most recent command.

▲ Major Robert Anderson observes the firing at Fort Sumter in 1861.

E **A PERSONAL VOICE** ROBERT ANDERSON

" Having defended Fort Sumter for thirty-four hours, until the quarters were entirely burned, the main gates destroyed by fire, . . . the magazine surrounded by flames, . . . four barrels and three cartridges of powder only being available, and no provisions but pork remaining, I accepted terms of evacuation . . . and marched out of the fort . . . with colors flying and drums beating . . . and saluting my flag with fifty guns. "

—quoted in *Fifty Basic Civil War Documents*

D Months earlier, as soon as the Confederacy was formed, Confederate soldiers in each secessionist state began seizing federal installations—especially forts. By the time of Lincoln's inauguration on March 4, 1861, only four Southern forts remained in Union hands. The most important was **Fort Sumter,** on an island in Charleston harbor.

Lincoln decided to neither abandon Fort Sumter nor reinforce it. He would merely send in "food for hungry men." At 4:30 A.M. on April 12, Confederate batteries began thundering away to the cheers of Charleston's citizens. The deadly struggle between North and South was under way.

A Union and Confederate Forces Clash

News of Fort Sumter's fall united the North. When Lincoln called for volunteers, the response throughout the Northern states was overwhelming. However, Lincoln's call for troops provoked a very different reaction in the states of the

Reading a Chart

Pie charts can be used to show how parts relate to a whole and to each other. These tips can help you read a pie chart quickly and accurately. Look at the example as you read each strategy in this list.

A Read the **title** to find out the subject of the pie chart.

B Study the **labels** placed around the pie chart to identify the different parts of the total, or whole.

C Examine the **number** next to each label. Each number can be represented as a fraction of the total.

D Examine each part, or **sector,** of the pie chart. Each sector represents a fraction of the total.

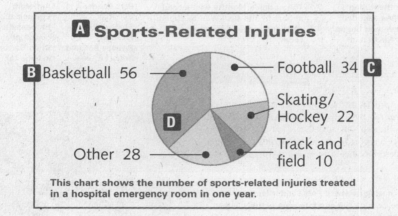

A Sports-Related Injuries

B Basketball 56

Football 34 **C**

Skating/ Hockey 22

Track and field 10

Other 28

D

This chart shows the number of sports-related injuries treated in a hospital emergency room in one year.

MARK IT UP Use the pie chart to answer the following questions.

1. What is the purpose of this pie chart? _____

_____

2. Which sport is associated with the greatest number of injuries? Circle the label on the pie chart.

3. Which sport is associated with the least number of injuries? Draw a line under the label on the pie chart.

4. Which sport is associated with approximately one third of all sports-related injuries? Place a check mark in this sector of the pie chart.

Reading a Map

To read a map correctly, you have to identify and understand its elements. Look at the map below as you read each strategy in this list.

A Scan the **title** to understand the content of the map.

B Study the **legend,** or **key,** to find out what the symbols and colors on the map stand for.

C Study **geographic labels** to identify specific places on the map.

D Look at the **pointer,** or **compass rose,** to determine direction.

E Examine the **scale** to find out what each unit of measurement on the map is equal to in real-world distance.

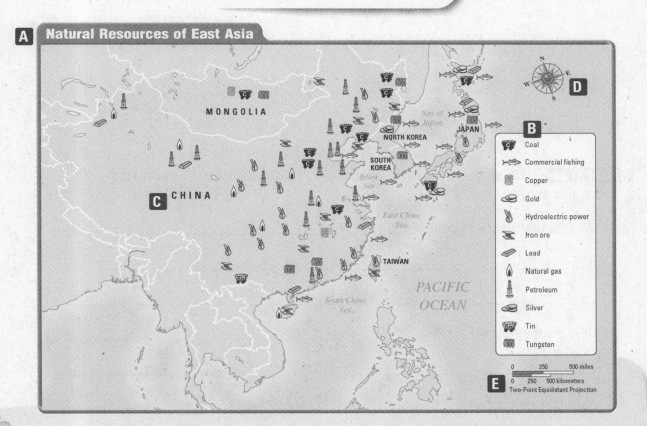

A Natural Resources of East Asia

B Legend:
- Coal
- Commercial fishing
- Copper
- Gold
- Hydroelectric power
- Iron ore
- Lead
- Natural gas
- Petroleum
- Silver
- Tin
- Tungsten

E 0 250 500 miles
0 250 500 kilometers
Two-Point Equidistant Projection

MARK IT UP Use the map to answer the following questions.

1. What is the purpose of this map? _____

2. Place a check mark next to the country with the most resources in East Asia.

3. What are the main resources of the island of Taiwan? _____

4. Circle the name of the large body of water that borders the coast of all of East Asia.

Reading a Diagram

Diagrams combine pictures with a few words to provide a lot of information. Look at the example on the opposite page as you read each of the following strategies.

A Look at the **title** to get a quick idea of what the diagram is about.

B Study the **images** closely to understand each part of the diagram.

C Look at the **captions** and the **labels** for more information.

MARK IT UP Study the diagram, then answer the following questions using the strategies above.

1. What is this diagram about? _____

_____

_____

2. How did the Mississippi River form? _____

_____

3. Approximately when did the Great Lakes first fill with water? _____

_____

4. Draw a circle around the river that carries water from the Great Lakes to the Atlantic Ocean.

5. What is the time span covered in this diagram? _____

_____

Formation of the Great Lakes

14,000 YEARS AGO Meltwater pools in front of the melting ice sheets. Rivers form, draining meltwater to the south into what will become the Mississippi. **C**

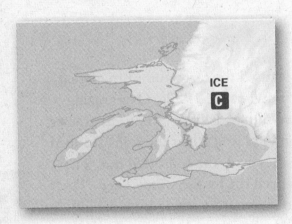

7,000 YEARS AGO As the ice sheet melts and recedes, meltwater fills the lakes and drains westward to the Atlantic through the St. Lawrence River valley.

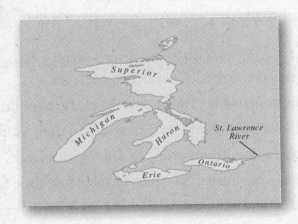

TODAY The Great Lakes drain into the Atlantic Ocean through the St. Lawrence River.

Main Idea and Supporting Details

The *main idea* in a paragraph is its most important point. *Details* in the paragraph support the main idea. Identifying the main idea will help you focus on the main message the writer wants to communicate. Use the following strategies to help you identify a paragraph's main idea and supporting details.

- Look for the **main idea,** which is often the first sentence in a paragraph.

- Use the main idea to help you **summarize** the point of the paragraph.

- Identify specific **details,** including facts and examples, that **support** the main idea.

The Dust Bowl

Main idea — More than one factor caused the farmland of the Great Plains to become a dust bowl in the 1930s. Overgrazing and overplowing stripped the fields bare of natural grasses whose roots kept the soil in place. When the rains stopped

Details — coming as frequently as they had, the soil dried out. The dry topsoil was easily carried off by the wind. Then blowing clouds of dirt made matters worse by blocking out sunlight, burying gardens and chicken coops, and covering train tracks and roads.

MARK IT UP > Read the following paragraph. Circle its main idea. Then underline three of the paragraph's supporting details, numbering each one.

During the 1930s, the Great Plains became a dust bowl. As a result, many Midwestern farmers lost, sold, or simply abandoned their land. After all, producing crops was nearly impossible, and without crops to sell, most farmers could not afford to make their mortgage payments. So either farmers lost their farms when banks foreclosed on overdue mortgages, or they sold their land at ridiculously low prices. Other farmers abandoned their land to seek better lives elsewhere.

Problem and Solution

Does the proposed solution to a problem make sense? In order to decide, you need to look at each part of the text. Use the following strategies to read the text below.

- Look at the beginning or middle of a paragraph to find the **statement of the problem.**

- Find **details** that explain the problem and tell why it is important.

- Look for the **proposed solution.**

- Identify the **supporting details** for the proposed solution.

- Think about whether the solution is a good one.

Let's Hear from the Experts *by Chang Lee*

Statement of problem

In school, we study about famous painters, musicians, and writers of the past but learn little about artists in our own community today. Students in our high school want to learn more about the arts from the real experts—artists themselves.

Explanation of problem

Currently, we learn little about the types of work artists do. Because many of us will pursue careers in the arts, we can learn information about the issues and challenges that artists face—topics that are relevant to us. Also, all students find it more interesting to study current topics that relate directly to their lives.

For these reasons, a group of us have formed a committee to propose a visiting artists program. Our committee researched ten other schools in the state that run successful programs. We put this information in a proposal and presented it to school administrators. There is also a petition that is being circulated in the school. We are asking all students in the school to support our proposal and sign the petition today!

MARK IT UP Read the text above. Then answer these questions.

1. Underline the proposed solution in the third paragraph.

2. Circle at least one detail that supports the solution.

3. Do you think the solution is a good one? Explain why or why not. _____

_____

Sequence

It's important to understand the *sequence,* or order of events, in what you read. It helps you know what happens and why. Read the tips below to make sure a sequence is clear to you. Then look at the example on the opposite page.

- Read through the passage and think about what its **main steps,** or stages, are.

- Look for **words and phrases that signal time:** *today, in 1612, Friday, that morning, later,* or *at 3 o'clock.*

- Look for **words and phrases that signal order:** *first, second, now, during, after that,* or *finally.*

∥ MARK IT UP ⟩ Read the article on the next page that describes the work of Alexander Graham Bell. Use the information from the article and the tips above to answer the questions.

1. Circle words or phrases in the article that signal time.

2. Underline the phrases in the article that signal order.

3. A flow chart can help you understand a sequence of events. Use the information from the article to complete this flow chart.

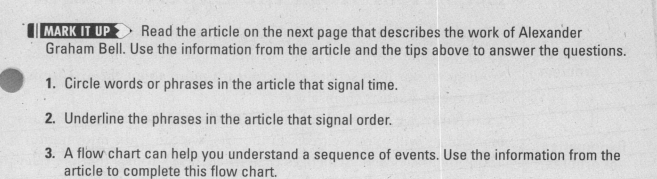

1. Bell moves to Boston.

In 1871, Bell was asked to

_____ in Boston.

2. Bell meets Watson.

The two men worked to create a

_____ to transmit sound

using electricity.

3. Bell and Watson invent the telephone.

The first two words spoken on the

transmitter were _____

_____ .

The Work of Alexander Graham Bell

In 1871, Alexander Graham Bell came to Boston for a few weeks to lecture on his father's system of teaching speech to the deaf. What he didn't know was that this brief trip would have a dramatic impact on his life. Bell's lectures amazed audiences. The Scottish-born teacher and scientist received so many invitations to speak that he decided to stay in the city.

Alexander Graham Bell with a centennial telephone

Soon after, Bell opened a school in Boston for training teachers of the deaf. He also began teaching at Boston University. During this period, Bell met Thomas Watson, a young repair mechanic and model maker. For the next two years, the men worked together to create a machine for transmitting sound by electricity.

Finally, on April 6, 1875, Bell acquired a patent for a multiple telegraph, and a little less than a year later the two men created the first telephone. During the first "telephonic communication," Bell called to his partner over the new transmitter he was trying out. The first words he spoke were "Mr. Watson! Come here! I want you!" and Mr. Watson heard him. By 1915, coast-to-coast telephone communication was a reality.

Also by then, the two had succeeded in inventing many other useful devices. Although Bell is best known for inventing the telephone, he was also the father of many other equally amazing devices and scientific advancements. For example, Bell and others invented the "hydrodome," a hydrofoil boat that traveled above the water at high speeds.

Cause and Effect

A *cause* is an event that brings about another event. An *effect* is something that happens as a result of the first event. Identifying causes and effects helps you understand how events are related. The tips below can help you find causes and effects in any reading.

- Look for an action or event that answers the question "What happened?" This is the **effect.**

- Look for an action or event that answers the question "Why did it happen?" This is the **cause.**

- Identify words or phrases that **signal** causes and effects, such as *because, as a result, therefore, thus, consequently, since,* and *led to.*

MARK IT UP Read the cause-and-effect passage on the next page. Then answer the following questions. Notice that the first cause and effect in the passage are labeled.

1. Circle words in the passage that signal causes and effects. The first one is done for you.

2. Because Congress was concerned about the effects of looters on the parks, what did it do? _____

   _____

   _____

3. Use two of the causes and effects in the first paragraph to complete the following diagram.

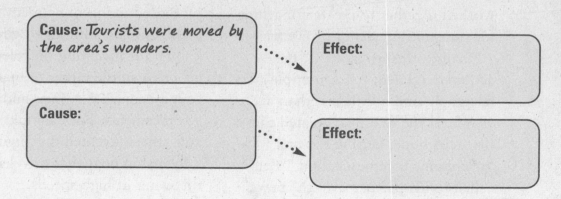

Cause: *Tourists were moved by the area's wonders.*

Effect:

Cause:

Effect:

The First National Parks

In 1872, a group of tourists was awestruck by the deep canyons, dense pine forests, and refreshing rivers and waterfalls of Yellowstone, Montana. Because the visitors were so moved by the area's natural wonders, they immediately wanted to protect them. So they trooped off to Washington, D.C., to demand that Yellowstone lands be set aside for public use. There, before Congress, with the help of breathtaking paintings and photographs by artists who had ventured to Yellowstone with government land surveyors, these passionate preservationists presented their case. Dazzled, Congress responded to their pleas by creating the first national park, Yellowstone National Park.

The next several national parks owe their establishment primarily to the enthusiasm and persuasive abilities of one nature lover, John Muir. Muir took influential friends such as Ralph Waldo Emerson and Theodore Roosevelt on spectacular hikes through the Sierras. While on these hikes, he expressed his love of nature in passionate arguments for its preservation. In 1890, largely as a result of Muir's efforts, Yosemite, Sequoia, and General Grant national parks were established.

Yosemite National Park

Interestingly, however, about 25 percent of today's national parks owe their preservation to looters—or rather, to a Congress roused into action by looters. In 1906, because Congress was concerned that widespread plundering of precious Southwestern archaeological sites was destroying important artifacts, it enacted a law to prevent such plundering. This law, called the Antiquities Act, authorized the president to set aside as national monuments extremely precious or threatened lands. Consequently, by calling on the powers granted to him under the law, President Theodore Roosevelt was able to put under government protection many sites that might otherwise have been destroyed. These sites would eventually earn national-park status.

Comparison and Contrast

Comparing two things means showing how they are the same. *Contrasting* two things means showing how they are different. Comparisons and contrasts are often used in science and history books to make a subject clearer. Use these tips to help you understand comparison and contrast in reading assignments, such as the article on the opposite page.

- Look for **direct statements** of comparison and contrast: "These things are similar because ..." or "One major difference is ...."

- Pay attention to **words and phrases that signal comparisons,** such as *also, both, is the same as,* and *in the same way.*

- Notice **words and phrases that signal contrasts.** Some of these are *however, still, but,* and *on the other hand.*

MARK IT UP ➤ Read the essay on the opposite page. Then use the information from the article and the tips above to answer the questions.

1. Circle the words and phrases that signal comparisons. A sample has been done for you.

2. Underline the words and phrases that signal contrasts. A sample has been done for you.

3. A Venn diagram shows how two subjects are similar and how they are different. Complete this diagram, which uses information from the essay to compare and contrast Booker T. Washington and W.E.B. Du Bois. Add at least one similarity to the middle part of the diagram. Add at least one difference in each outer circle.

BOOKER T. WASHINGTON

believed in vocational training for African Americans

BOTH

promoted equality for African Americans

W.E.B. DU BOIS

believed in college education for African Americans

Less Than Allies

Booker T. Washington and W.E.B. Du Bois were alike in many ways. Both were devoted to helping their fellow African Americans attain equal rights. Both were educated black men with university teaching positions. Both also worked passionately toward their goal at the beginning of the 20th century. Nevertheless, they were not allies. Why? They had very different ideas about how blacks should go about attaining equal rights.

W.E.B. Du Bois

Booker T. Washington

Washington believed that for black people to achieve equal status and power as citizens, they needed to focus on learning crafts, farming, and industrial skills. He argued that by gaining vocational skills and the economic security that would surely follow, black people would naturally earn the respect and acceptance of the white community. In Washington's opinion, however, to earn an education and economic security, black people would need to let go temporarily of the fight for civil rights and political power.

In contrast to Washington, W.E.B. Du Bois said that social change would come by developing a small group of college-educated blacks he called the "Talented Tenth," those best and brightest 10 percent who would guide the black community. Du Bois also believed that black people could not afford to stop fighting for civil rights and political power. In his opinion, only agitation and protest would achieve social change. According to Du Bois, in the climate of extreme racism that existed in America at the time, Washington's approach would merely cause blacks to suffer even more oppression.

So although these two African American contemporaries had the same goal, their different approaches to achieving this goal made them adversaries rather than allies.

Argument

An *argument* is an opinion backed up with reasons and facts.
Examining an opinion and the reasons and facts that back it up will
help you decide if the opinion makes sense. Look at the argument on
the right as you read each of these tips.

- Look for words that **signal an opinion:** *I believe, I think, in my view,
they claim, argue,* or *disagree.*

- Look for reasons, facts, or expert opinions that **support** the
argument.

- Ask yourself if the argument and reasons **make sense.**

- Look for overgeneralizations or other **errors in reasoning** that may
affect the argument.

MARK IT UP Read the argument on the next page, and then answer the questions below.

1. Circle any words that signal an opinion.

2. Underline the words or phrases that give the writer's opinion.

3. The writer presents both sides of the argument. Fill in the chart below to show the two
sides. One reason has been provided for you.

Reasons for	Reasons Against
1. Students become aware of others' needs.	

A Fair Compromise

By Jorge Romero

The requirements for high school graduation have just changed in my community. As a result, all students must complete sixty hours of service learning, or they will not receive a diploma. Service learning is academic learning that also helps the community. Examples of service learning include cleaning up a polluted river, working in a soup kitchen, or tutoring a student. During a service experience, students must keep a journal and then write a report about what they have learned.

Supporters claim that there are many benefits of service learning. Perhaps most important, students are forced to think beyond their own interests and become aware of the needs of others. Students are also able to learn real-life skills that include responsibility, problem-solving, and working as part of a team. Finally, students can explore possible careers through service learning. For example, if a student wonders what teaching is like, he or she can choose to work in an elementary school classroom a few afternoons each month.

While there are many benefits, opponents point out problems with the new requirement. First, they argue that the main reason students go to school is to learn core subjects and skills. Because service learning is time-consuming, students spend less time studying the core subjects. Second, they believe that forcing students to work without pay goes against the Thirteenth Amendment, which protects people from forced servitude, or slavery. By requiring service, the school takes away an individual's freedom to choose.

In my view, service learning is a great way to contribute to the community, learn new skills, and explore different careers. However, I don't believe you should force people to help others—the desire to help must come from the heart. I think the best solution is one that gives students choices: a student should be able to choose sixty hours of independent study or sixty hours of service. Choice encourages both freedom and responsibility, and as young adults we must learn to handle both wisely.

Social Studies

Social studies class becomes easier when you understand how your textbook's words, pictures, and maps work together to give you information. Following these tips can make you a better reader of social studies lessons. As you read the tips, look at the sample lesson on the right-hand page.

A First, look at any **headings** or **subheads** on the page. These give you an idea of what each section covers.

B Make sure you know the meaning of any boldfaced or underlined **vocabulary terms.** These terms often appear on tests.

C Carefully read the text and think about **ways the information is organized.** Social studies books are often organized by chronological order, cause and effect, comparison and contrast, and geographic location.

D Look closely at **visuals** and **captions.** Think about how they relate to the text.

E Notice any **special features** such as extended quotations, sidebar questions, or text in a tinted box. For example, a **primary source** such as a **direct quotation** from a diary or interview is often used to provide information on a historical topic.

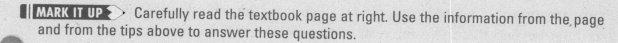 **MARK IT UP** Carefully read the textbook page at right. Use the information from the page and from the tips above to answer these questions.

1. What is the main subject addressed on this page? _____

_____

2. Circle the two vocabulary terms in the article. Then underline the parts of the text that define those terms.

3. Place boxes around two major effects of World War I.

4. Place a check mark next to the quotation.

5. Who is both the speaker in the quotation and the subject of the photograph?

_____

_____

Americans Struggle with Postwar Issues

MAIN IDEA	WHY IT MATTERS NOW	Terms & Names	**B**
A desire for normality after the war and a fear of communism and "foreigners" led to postwar isolationism.	Americans today continue to debate political isolationism and immigration policy.	• nativism • isolationism • communism • anarchists	• Sacco and Vanzetti • quota system • John L. Lewis	

One American's Story

During the 1920s and 1930s, Irving Fajans, a department store sales clerk in New York City, tried to persuade fellow workers to join the Department Store Employees Union. He described some of the techniques union organizers used.

E **A PERSONAL VOICE** IRVING FAJANS

" If you were caught distributing . . . union literature around the job you were instantly fired. We thought up ways of passing leaflets without the boss being able to pin anybody down. . . . We . . . swiped the key to the toilet paper dispensers in the washroom, took out the paper and substituted printed slips of just the right size! We got a lot of new members that way—It appealed to their sense of humor. "

—quoted in *The Jewish Americans*

Irving Fajans **D** organized department store workers in their efforts to gain better pay and working conditions during the 1920s.

During the war, workers' rights had been suppressed. In 1919, workers began to cry out for fair pay and better working conditions. Tensions arose between labor and management, and a rash of labor strikes broke out across the country. The public, however, was not supportive of striking workers. Many citizens longed to get back to normal, peaceful living—they felt resentful of anyone who caused unrest.

Postwar Trends

C World War I had left much of the American public exhausted. The debate over the League of Nations had deeply divided America. Further, the Progressive Era had caused numerous wrenching changes in American life. The economy, too, was in a difficult state of adjustment. Returning soldiers faced unemployment or took their old jobs away from women and minorities. Also, the cost of living had doubled. Farmers and factory workers suffered as wartime orders diminished.

Many Americans responded to the stressful conditions by becoming fearful of outsiders. A wave of **nativism**, or prejudice against foreign-born people, swept the nation. So, too, did a belief in **isolationism**, a policy of pulling away from involvement in world affairs. **B**

Science

Reading in the Content Areas

Reading a science textbook becomes easier when you understand how the explanations, drawings, and special terms work together. Use the strategies below to help you better understand your science textbook. Look at the examples on the opposite page as you read each strategy in this list.

A Preview the **title** and **headings** on the page to see what scientific concepts will be addressed.

B Read the **key idea, objectives,** or **focus.** These items summarize the lesson purpose and establish a focus for your reading.

C Look for **boldfaced** and **italicized** words that appear in the text. Look for **definitions** of those words.

D Carefully examine any **pictures, diagrams,** or **charts.** Read the **titles** and **captions** and evaluate how the graphics help to illustrate and explain the text.

E · science textbooks discuss **scientific concepts** in terms of **everyday events** or **experiences.** Look for these places and consider how they improve your understanding.

MARK IT UP > Use the sample science page and the tips above to help you answer the following questions.

1. What important concept will be addressed in the lesson? Where on the page did you find this information? _____

   _____

2. Draw a circle around the main objective of the article.

3. Place a star next to an important question that is emphasized in italics.

4. What is the relative mass of a proton? _____

   _____

5. What is the purpose of the paper-cutting activity? _____

   _____

422 The InterActive Reader PLUS With Additional Support

3.6 Introduction to the Modern Concept of Atomic Structure

Objective: *To describe some important features of subatomic particles.*

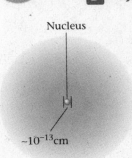

Nucleus

~10^{-13}cm

~10^{-8}cm

Figure 3.9
A nuclear atom viewed in cross section. (The symbol ~ means approximately.) This drawing does not show the actual scale. The nucleus is actually much smaller compared with the size of an atom.

CHEMISTRY

In this model the atom is called a nuclear atom because the positive charge is localized in a small, compact structure (the nucleus) and not spread out uniformly, as in the plum pudding view.

CHEMISTRY

The *chemistry* of an atom arises from its electrons.

WHAT IF?

The average diameter of an atom is 1.3×10^{-10} m.

What if the average diameter of an atom were 1 cm? How tall would you be?

In the years since Thomson and Rutherford, a great deal has been learned about atomic structure. The simplest view of the atom is that it consists of a tiny nucleus (about 10^{-13} cm in diameter) and electrons that move about the nucleus at an average distance of about 10^{-8} cm from it **(Figure 3.9)**. To visualize how small the nucleus is compared with the size of the atom, consider that if the nucleus were the size of a grape, the electrons would be about one *mile* away on average. The nucleus contains protons, which have a positive charge equal in magnitude to the electrons' negative charge, and neutrons, which have almost the same mass as protons but no charge. The neutrons' function in the nucleus is not obvious. They may help hold the protons (which repel each other) together to form the nucleus, but we will not be concerned with that here. The relative masses and charges of the electron, proton, and neutron are shown in **Table 3.4.**

TABLE 3.4

The Mass and Charge of the Electron, Proton, and Neutron

Particle	Relative Mass*	Relative Charge
electron	1	1 −
proton	1836	1 +
neutron	1839	none

*The electron is arbitrarily assigned a mass of 1 for comparison.

An important question arises at this point: *If all atoms are composed of these same components, why do different atoms have different chemical properties?* The answer lies in the number and arrangement of the electrons. The space in which the electrons move accounts for most of the atomic volume. The electrons are the parts of atoms that "intermingle" when atoms combine to form molecules. Therefore, the number of electrons a given atom possesses greatly affects the way it can interact with other atoms. As a result, atoms of different elements, which have different numbers of electrons, show different chemical behavior. Although the atoms of different elements also differ in their numbers of protons, it is the number of electrons that really determines chemical behavior. We will discuss how this happens in later chapters.

CHEMISTRY in ACTION

How Big Is an Atom?

1. Get a strip of paper 11″ by 1″.
2. Cut the paper in half. Discard one piece.
3. Repeat step 2 until you can no longer cut the paper. How many times could you cut it?
4. How many times would you need to cut the paper to have a piece of paper remaining that is the same width as an atom? (Average atom diameter = 1.3×10^{-10} m.)

Mathematics

Reading in mathematics is different from reading in history, literature, or science. Use the strategies below to help you better understand your mathematics textbook. Look at the examples on the opposite page as you read each strategy in the list.

A Preview the **title** and **headings** on the page to see what math concepts will be covered.

B Find and read the **goals** or **objectives** for the lesson. These will tell you the most important points to know.

C Read **explanations** of the central concept carefully. Sometimes a concept is explained in more than one way to make sure you understand it.

D Study any **worked-out solutions** to sample problems. These are the key to understanding how to do the homework assignment.

MARK IT UP 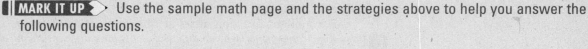 Use the sample math page and the strategies above to help you answer the following questions.

1. Underline the title of the lesson.

2. Place a check mark next to the first learning goal you should have for this lesson.

3. Circle the explanation of how to write an equation for a line when given different types of information.

4. What does the sample problem show you how to do? _____

_____

5. How can the formula for writing an equation of a line be applied to a real-life situation?

_____

_____

2.4

A Writing Equations of Lines

What you should learn

GOAL ① Write linear equations.

GOAL ② Write direct variation equations, as applied in **Example 7**.

Why you should learn it

▼ To model real-life quantities, such as the number of calories you burn while dancing in **Ex. 64**.

B GOAL 1 WRITING LINEAR EQUATIONS

In Lesson 2.3 you learned to find the slope and y-intercept of a line whose equation is given. In this lesson you will study the reverse process. That is, you will learn to write an equation of a line using one of the following: the slope and y-intercept of the line, the slope and a point on the line, or two points on the line.

C CONCEPT SUMMARY WRITING AN EQUATION OF A LINE

SLOPE-INTERCEPT FORM Given the slope m and the y-intercept b, use this equation:

$$y = mx + b$$

POINT-SLOPE FORM Given the slope m and a point (x_1, y_1), use this equation:

$$y - y_1 = m(x - x_1)$$

TWO POINTS Given two points (x_1, y_1) and (x_2, y_2), use the formula

$$m = \frac{y_2 - y_1}{x_2 - x_1}$$

to find the slope m. Then use the point-slope form with this slope and either of the given points to write an equation of the line.

Every nonvertical line has only one slope and one y-intercept, so the slope-intercept form is unique. The point-slope form, however, depends on the point that is used. Therefore, in this book equations of lines will be simplified to slope-intercept form so a unique solution may be given.

D EXAMPLE 1 *Writing an Equation Given the Slope and the y-intercept*

Write an equation of the line shown.

SOLUTION

From the graph you can see that the slope is $m = \frac{3}{2}$. You can also see that the line intersects the y-axis at the point $(0, -1)$, so the y-intercept is $b = -1$.

Because you know the slope and the y-intercept, you should use the slope-intercept form to write an equation of the line.

$y = mx + b$ Use slope-intercept form.

$y = \frac{3}{2}x - 1$ Substitute $\frac{3}{2}$ for m and -1 for b.

▶ An equation of the line is $y = \frac{3}{2}x - 1$.

Reading an Application

Reading and understanding an application will help you fill it out correctly and avoid mistakes. Use the following strategies to help you understand any application. Look at the example on the next page as you read each strategy.

A **Begin at the top.** Scan the application to understand the different sections.

B Look for special **instructions for filling out** the application.

C Notice any **request for materials** that must be attached to the application.

D Watch for **sections you don't have to fill in** or **questions you don't have to answer.**

E Look for difficult or confusing words and abbreviations. Look them up in a dictionary or ask someone what they mean.

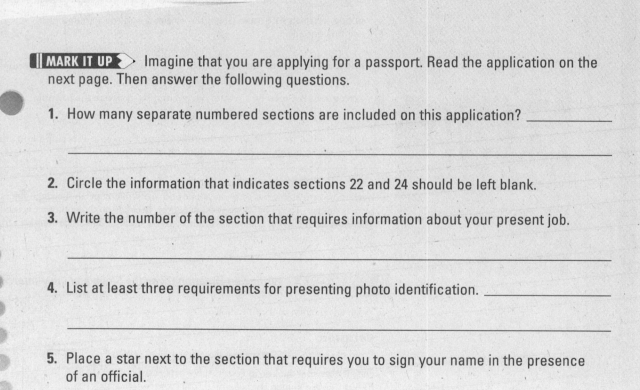

MARK IT UP Imagine that you are applying for a passport. Read the application on the next page. Then answer the following questions.

1. How many separate numbered sections are included on this application? _____

   _____

2. Circle the information that indicates sections 22 and 24 should be left blank.

3. Write the number of the section that requires information about your present job.

   _____

4. List at least three requirements for presenting photo identification. _____

   _____

5. Place a star next to the section that requires you to sign your name in the presence of an official.

6. **ASSESSMENT PRACTICE** Circle the letter of the correct answer.
   What information should be written in section 2 of the application?
   A. birthplace
   B. mailing address
   C. name
   D. social security number

A UNITED STATES DEPARTMENT OF STATE
APPLICATION FOR ☐ PASSPORT ☐ REGISTRATION
(Type or print all capital letters in blue or black ink in white areas only)

1. NAME (First and Middle)

LAST

2. MAIL PASSPORT TO: STREET / RFD # OR P.O. BOX APT. #

CITY STATE

ZIP CODE COUNTRY / IN CARE OF (if applicable)

3. SEX ☐ M ☐ F   **4. PLACE OF BIRTH (City & State or City & Country)**   **5. DATE OF BIRTH** Month Day Year   **6. SOCIAL SECURITY NUMBER** (SEE FEDERAL TAX LAW NOTICE ON PAGE 2)

7. HEIGHT Feet Inches   **8. HAIR COLOR**   **9. EYE COLOR**   **10. HOME TELEPHONE** ( )   **11. BUSINESS TELEPHONE** ( )   **12. OCCUPATION**

13. PERMANENT ADDRESS (DO NOT LIST P.O. BOX) STREET/RFD # CITY STATE ZIP CODE

14. FATHER'S FULL NAME Last First   BIRTHPLACE   BIRTHDATE   U.S. CITIZEN ☐ Yes ☐ No   **15. MOTHER'S FULL MAIDEN NAME** Last First   BIRTHPLACE   BIRTHDATE   U.S. CITIZEN ☐ Yes ☐ No

16. HAVE YOU EVER BEEN MARRIED? ☐ Yes ☐ No   SPOUSE'S OR FORMER SPOUSE'S FULL NAME AT BIRTH Last First   BIRTHPLACE   BIRTHDATE   U.S. CITIZEN ☐ Yes ☐ No

DATE OF MOST RECENT MARRIAGE Month Day Year   WIDOWED/DIVORCED? ☐ Yes Give Date ☐ No Month Day Year   **17. OTHER NAMES YOU HAVE USED** (1) (2)

18. HAVE YOU EVER BEEN ISSUED A U.S. PASSPORT? ☐ Yes ☐ No IF YES, COMPLETE NEXT LINE AND SUBMIT PASSPORT IF AVAILABLE.   DISPOSITION ☐ Submitted ☐ Stolen
NAME IN WHICH ISSUED   MOST RECENT PASSPORT NUMBER   APPROXIMATE ISSUE DATE Month Day Year   ☐ Lost ☐ Other _____ **E**

It is necessary to submit a statement with an application for a new passport when a previous valid or potentially valid passport cannot be presented. The statement must set forth in detail why the previous passport cannot be presented. Use Form DSP-64.

C STAPLE 1" TO 1–3/8" 2" x 2" STAPLE
SUBMIT TWO RECENT IDENTICAL PHOTOS   **B**

19. EMERGENCY CONTACT. If you wish, you may supply the name, address and telephone number of a person not traveling with you to be contacted in case of emergency.
NAME
STREET
CITY   STATE   ZIP CODE
TELEPHONE ( )   RELATIONSHIP

20. TRAVEL PLANS (not mandatory) Month Day Year
Date of Trip
Length of Trip
COUNTRIES TO BE VISITED

21. STOP. DO NOT SIGN APPLICATION UNTIL REQUESTED TO DO SO BY PERSON ADMINISTERING OATH. I have not, since acquiring United States citizenship, performed any of the acts listed under "Acts or Conditions" on the reverse of this application form (unless explanatory statement is attached). I solemnly swear (or affirm) that the statements made on this application are true and the photograph attached is a true likeness of me.

X _____ Parent's/Legal Guardian's Signature if identifying minor child   X _____ Applicant's Signature - age 13 or older

22. FOR ACCEPTANCE AGENT'S USE
Subscribed and sworn to (affirmed) before me   Month Day Year   (SEAL)
☐ Clerk of Court: Location _____
☐ PASSPORT Agent
☐ Postal Employee
(Signature of person authorized to accept application)   ☐ (Vice) Consul USA

23. APPLICANT'S IDENTIFYING DOCUMENTS
☐ DRIVER'S LICENSE   ISSUE DATE: Month Day Year   EXPIRATION DATE: Month Day Year   ID No. _____
☐ PASSPORT
☐ OTHER (Specify) _____ PLACE OF ISSUE: _____ ISSUED IN THE NAME OF: _____

24. FOR ISSUING OFFICE USE ONLY (Applicant's evidence of citizenship)   **D**
☐ Birth Certificate   SR   CR   City   Filed/Issued:
☐ Passport   Bearer's Name:
☐ Report of Birth
☐ Naturalization/Citizenship Cert.   No.:   Issued:
☐ Other:
☐ Seen & Returned
☐ Attached

APPLICATION APPROVAL

25.
FEE _____ EXEC. _____ EF _____ OTHER _____

FORM DSP-11 (12-97)   (SEE INSTRUCTIONS ON PAGE 2)
Page 1
Form Approved OMB No. 1405-0004 (Exp. 5/31/2001) Estimated Burden - 20 Minutes*

Reading a Public Notice

Public notices can tell you about events in your community and give you valuable information about safety. When you read a public notice, follow these tips. Each tip relates to a specific part of the notice on the opposite page.

A Read the notice's **title,** if it has one. The title often gives the main idea or purpose of the notice.

B See if there is a logo, credit, or other way of telling **who created the notice.**

C Search for information that explains **who should read the notice.**

D Look for **instructions**—things the notice is asking or telling you to do.

E See if there are details that tell you how you can **find out more** about the topic.

‖ MARK IT UP ⟩ The notice on the opposite page is from a county government agency. Read it carefully and answer the questions below.

1. Who is the notice from? _____

   _____

2. Who is the notice for? _____

   _____

3. Circle the special abilities that are required for entry into the program.

4. Underline the text that explains how to register for the program.

5. **ASSESSMENT PRACTICE** Circle the letter of the correct answer.
   According to the notice, the Ocean Safety Bureau will only award certificates to those participants who
   A. can run and swim 100 yards nonstop.
   B. complete a 20-hour course.
   C. can do CPR.
   D. meet entry requirements and complete a 20-hour course.

A *FOR IMMEDIATE RELEASE – JUNIOR LIFEGUARD PROGRAM AVAILABLE STARTING IN JUNE*

COUNTY OF KALAI
KALAI FIRE DEPARTMENT

May 9, 2002

B KALAI The Ocean Safety Bureau of the Kalai Fire Department will be conducting its *Junior Lifeguard Program* at various sites between June 17 and July 20, 2002.

C Boys and girls between the ages of 13 and 18 are encouraged to participate in the program, which will teach lifesaving skills, including CPR, and provide extensive training in water safety. In order to participate, you must be able to run and swim 100 yards nonstop.

"Lifeguarding requires many skills that everyone should learn and practice," says County Lifeguard Elaine Ruates. "Knowing what to do, staying calm, and quickly and efficiently administering aid is the basis for successful lifesaving."

To receive a certificate, the participants must complete a 20-hour course at one of the following locations:

Salt Marsh	June 17–21
Papua	June 24–28
Kalai	July 1–5
Anaholo	July 8–12
Hanale	July 15–19

D Classes are conducted Monday through Friday from 10:00 a.m. to 2:30 p.m. Participants should provide their own lunch and equipment (if available). There will be a final competition among the participants on Saturday, July 20, at Kalai Beach.

E To register, call Renee Yamaguchi at 555-5962 or Roger Amato at 555-7381.

Reading a Web Page

If you need information for a report, project, or hobby, the World Wide Web can probably help you. The tips below will help you understand the Web pages you read. As you look at the tips, notice where they match up to the sample Web page on the right.

A Notice the page's **Web address,** or **URL.** You may want to write it down in case you need to access the same page at another time.

B Look for **menu bars** along the top, bottom, or side of the page. These guide you to other parts of the site that may be useful.

C Look for **links** to other parts of the site or to related pages. Links are often shown as underlined words.

D Use a **search** feature to quickly find out whether a certain kind of information is contained anywhere on the site.

E Many sites have a link that allows you to **contact** the creators with questions or feedback.

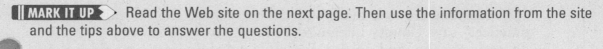

MARK IT UP Read the Web site on the next page. Then use the information from the site and the tips above to answer the questions.

1. Circle the Web address.

2. If you wanted to know whether the American Memory site contained any information about Henry David Thoreau, how could you go about finding out? _____

   _____

3. Place a box around the link that would direct you to historical events that occurred on today's date one hundred years ago.

4. If you were unable to find information at this site using the search feature, what link would allow you to ask for help? _____

   _____

5. **ASSESSMENT PRACTICE** Circle the letter of the correct answer.
   Choose the sentence that best summarizes the American Memory Web site.
   The Web site
   A. describes the history of music in America.
   B. contains the answers to frequently asked questions about the Civil War.
   C. is a gateway to primary source materials relating to United States history and culture.
   D. none of the above

L-Net ⊟ ⊞

| Back | Forward | Reload | Home | Images | Print | Security | Stop |

Location: http://memory.loc.gov/ **A**

The Library of Congress

American Memory

Historical Collections
for the National Digital Library

Collection Finder
Select collections to search

D **Search**
Search for items across all collections

Learning Page
Teaching and learning with American Memory

Today in History
September 5, 2001

What's New

FAQs

American Memory is a gateway to rich primary source materials relating to the history and culture of the United States. The site offers more than 7 million digital items from more than 100 historical collections.

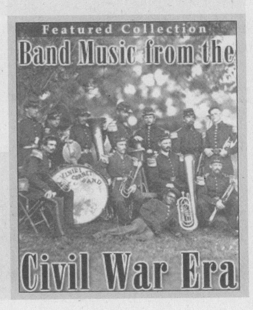

Featured Collection
Band Music from the Civil War Era

C How To View

Copyright & Restrictions

Technical Information

Future Collections

Search example of the day: expedition

C **International Horizons**
Digital Collections from around the world

Sponsors
See who is helping to bring a virtual library to all Americans for the 21st century

America's Library
For kids and families, featuring content from American Memory and other Library of Congress sites

B Library of Congress Home | Collections & Services | Search the Catalog | Help & FAQs
Exhibitions | The Library Today | U.S. Copyright Office |
THOMAS (Legislative Information) | America's Story | Search our Site | Site Map

Library of Congress
Questions: American Memory Help Desk **E**

Please Read Our
LEGAL NOTICES

Aug-24-01

Reading Technical Directions

Reading technical directions will help you understand how to use the products you buy. Use the following tips to help you read a variety of technical directions.

A Scan the **title** and other important **headings** to gain an understanding of the topic to be explained. **Read all the directions** carefully at least once before using the product.

B Look carefully at any **diagrams** or **other images** of the product.

C Note important **labels** or **captions** that identify important parts of the diagram or image.

D Look for **numbers** or **letters** that give the steps in sequence.

MARK IT UP Use the above tips and the technical directions on the next page to help you answer the following questions.

1. What is the main subject of this page in the manual? _____

_____

2. Circle both the numbered step in the sequence of instructions and the diagram label that indicate how to turn the radio on and off.

3. How many steps must you follow to preset a station? _____

_____

4. What is happening when the radio is turned on but the stereo indicator light is off?

_____

5. **ASSESSMENT PRACTICE** Circle the letter of the correct answer.
   Which of the following is NOT a required step when changing a preset station?
   A. Select FM or AM.
   B. Use manual tuning or scan-tuning to choose the station.
   C. Press the automatic tuning button to activate scan-tuning.
   D. Press and hold the preset station selector buttons until you hear a beep.

A How to Operate the Radio

The following diagram of your factory-installed radio shows the locations of its various features.

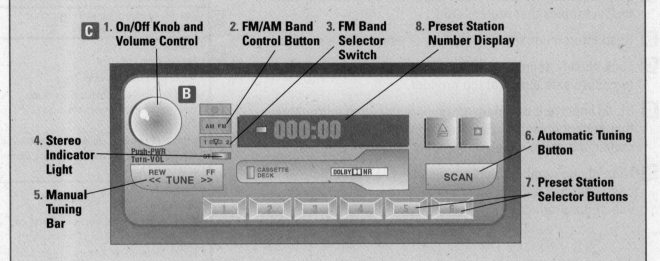

C
1. **On/Off Knob and Volume Control**
2. **FM/AM Band Control Button**
3. **FM Band Selector Switch**
8. **Preset Station Number Display**
4. **Stereo Indicator Light**
5. **Manual Tuning Bar**
6. **Automatic Tuning Button**
7. **Preset Station Selector Buttons**

D

1. On/Off Knob and Volume Control
Push this knob to turn the radio on or off.

2. FM/AM Band Control Button
Press this button to select the AM band and a red light appears. Press this button a second time to deselect the AM band and tune in FM stations.

3. FM Band Selector Switch
Move this switch left to select FM band 1 or right to select FM band 2. *Note: This is inoperative when the AM band is selected.*

4. Stereo Indicator Light (ST)
When the radio receives an FM signal clear enough to produce in stereo, it does so and the light comes on.

5. Manual Tuning Bar
Press the left side of the button to select stations in descending order of frequency. Press the right side to select stations in ascending order.

6. Automatic Tuning Button
Press this button for less than 2 seconds to jump up to the next available frequency. Press this button for longer than 2 seconds to activate scan-tuning.

In scan-tuning mode, the radio jumps to the next station, remains there for 5 seconds, then jumps to the next station, remains there for 5 seconds, and so on, until the button is briefly pressed again.

7. Preset Station Selector Buttons
Use these buttons to preset 18 of your favorite radio stations (12 FM and 6 AM) by following these steps:

1. Select FM or AM with the FM/AM Band Control Button.

2. Select the station using manual tuning or scan-tuning.

3. Press and hold one of the preset station selector buttons until you hear a beep (about 3 seconds).

To change a preset station, repeat the steps above.

8. Preset Station Number Display

When a station or frequency is being broadcast, its number is displayed on this panel.

Product Information: Directions for Use

Companies are required by law to offer instructions and warnings about the safe use of their products. Learning to read and follow product guidelines is important for your own safety. Look at the sample product information as you read each strategy below.

A Scan **headings** to understand important directions and other product topics that are covered.

B Read information on the **purpose,** or **uses,** for the product.

C Look closely at important **directions** and **recommendations** to ensure safe usage of the product.

D Study important **warnings** or other highlighted information that describe specific dangers, side effects, or important conditions under which the product must be taken.

E Note **phone numbers** that are listed in the event that the consumer has a question or concern regarding the safe use of the product.

A | **CALOSMOOTH LOTION**

Active Ingredient	Purpose
Pramoxine HCl 1.01%	External analgesic
Zinc acetate 0.1%	Skin protectant

B **Uses** Relieves itching and discomfort associated with poison ivy

D **Warnings**
- For external use only
- Avoid contact with eyes
- Stop use and ask doctor if condition worsens or itching persists more than 7 days

Keep out of reach of children. If swallowed, get medical help or contact a Poison Control Center right away.

C **Directions**
- Shake well
- Apply over affected area and blend into skin no more than 3 to 4 times daily
- For children under 2 years of age: ask a doctor

Storage 59°–77° F.

Inactive Ingredients Alcohol USP, camphor, citric acid, diazolidinyl, urea, glycerin, fragrance, polysorbate 40, propylparaban, purified water

E **Questions** Call *1–800–555–1234* Monday–Friday, 9AM–5PM EST

MARK IT UP Read the product guidelines to help you answer the following questions.

1. Why would someone purchase this product?

_____

2. Circle the words that warn the customer not to swallow the product.

3. What are the product recommendations for treating a one-year-old child with poison ivy?

_____

4. Underline the number to call if you have a question about how to use the product.

5. **ASSESSMENT PRACTICE** Circle the letter of the correct answer.
   At what temperature should you store this product?
   A. above 59 degrees and below 77 degrees Fahrenheit
   B. 59–77 degrees Celsius
   C. 59–77 degrees Fahrenheit
   D. both A and C

Reading a Recreation Schedule

Knowing how to read a schedule accurately will help you plan events and organize your time wisely. Look at the example as you read each strategy on this list.

A Scan the **title** and important **headings** to know what the schedule covers.

B Note the specific **locations** where different activities will occur.

C Look for **expressions of time** in terms of **dates** or **days of the week** and specific **hours and minutes** to help you understand how the weekly or daily schedule works.

D Look at specific **activities** to determine which ones occur at a given time and place.

TFA Community Recreation Schedule: September 25–December 8		
Exterior doors to building close one-half hour prior to closing time.		
Facility	**Days and Times**	**Activities**
Eno Family Sports Center 555–4531 Rosen Athletic Hall Lockers and Showers Varsity Weight Room	M–S 10 AM–4 PM, Sun closed M–S 9 AM–5 PM, Sun closed Sat/Sun noon–4 PM	Weight Training Weight Training

Banks Recreation Pool 555–0721
Swimming, studying, etc., are not allowed in the facility during non-rec hours.
	M–F 10 AM–2 PM, 6–7:30 PM
	   (Wed–Fri, 9/25–9/27 noon–2 PM only)
	Sat/Sun 1–5 PM
		Adult Rec Swim
		   (must be over 16)
		Family swim—children OK

Ford Center 555–3240	M–F 9 AM–7 PM, Sat/Sun, 1–5 PM M/W/F 9 AM–2 PM, Sat 5–8 PM T/Th 11 AM–3 PM M/W/F 11 AM–3 PM, Sat noon–5 PM Sun noon–2 PM	Exercise Machines Basketball Rec Basketball Rec Badminton Rec Open Rec

■ MARK IT UP ▷ Answer the following questions using the recreation schedule and the strategies on this page.

1. What time span is covered by this schedule? _____

2. What specific sports are played in the Ford Center? _____

3. If you are in weight training, on which day must you plan to shower at home? _____

4. **ASSESSMENT PRACTICE** What hours can adults swim if they go to the pool on the last Friday in September?
   A. 10 AM–2 PM and 6–7:30 PM   **B.** noon–2 PM   **C.** 1–5 PM   **D.** none of the above

Test Preparation Strategies

In this section, you'll find strategies and practice to help you with many different kinds of standardized tests. The strategies apply to questions based on long and short readings as well as questions about charts, graphs, and product labels. You'll also find examples and practice for revising-and-editing tests and writing tests. Applying the strategies to the practice materials and thinking through the answers will help you succeed in many formal testing situations.

Test Preparation Strategies

You can prepare for tests in several ways. First, study and understand the content that will be on the test. Second, learn as many test-taking techniques as you can. These techniques will help you better understand the questions and how to answer them. Following are some general suggestions for preparing for and taking tests. In the next parts, you'll find more detailed suggestions, together with test-taking practice.

Successful Test Taking

 Study Content Throughout the Year

1. **Master the content of your language arts class.** The best way to study for tests is to read, understand, and review the content of your language arts class. Read your daily assignments carefully. Study the notes that you have taken in class. Participate in class discussions. Work with classmates in small groups to help one another learn. You might trade writing assignments and comment on your classmates' work.

2. **Use your textbook for practice.** Your textbook includes many different types of questions. Some may ask you to talk about a story you just read. Others may ask you to figure out what's wrong with a sentence or how to make a paragraph sound better. Try answering these questions out loud and in writing. This type of practice can make taking a test much easier.

3. **Learn how to understand the information in charts, maps, and graphic organizers.** One type of test question may ask you to look at a graphic organizer, such as a spider map, and explain something about the information you see there. Another type of question may ask you to look at a map to find a particular place. You'll find charts, maps, and graphic organizers to study in your literature textbook. You'll also find charts, maps, and graphs in your science, mathematics, and social studies textbooks. When you look at these, ask yourself, What information is being presented and why is it important?

4. **Practice taking tests.** Use copies of tests you have taken in the past or in other classes for practice. Every test has a time limit, so set a timer for 15 or 20 minutes and then begin your practice. Try to finish the test in the time you've given yourself.

✔ Reading Check

In what practical way can your textbooks help you prepare for a test?

5. **Talk about test-taking experiences.** After you've taken a classroom test or quiz, talk about it with your teacher and classmates. Which types of questions were the hardest to understand? What made them difficult? Which questions seemed easiest, and why? When you share test-taking techniques with your classmates, everyone can become a successful test taker.

 ## Use Strategies During the Test

1. **Read the directions carefully.** You can't be a successful test taker unless you know exactly what you are expected to do. Look for key words and phrases, such as *circle the best answer, write a paragraph,* or *choose the word that best completes each sentence.*

2. **Learn how to read test questions.** Test questions can sometimes be difficult to figure out. They may include unfamiliar language or be written in an unfamiliar way. Try rephrasing the question in a simpler way using words you understand. Always ask yourself, What type of information does this question want me to provide?

3. **Pay special attention when using a separate answer sheet.** If you accidentally skip a line on an answer sheet, all the rest of your answers may be wrong! Try one or more of the following techniques:

   - Use a ruler on the answer sheet to make sure you are placing your answers on the correct line.

   - After every five answers, check to make sure you're on the right line.

   - Each time you turn a page of the test booklet, check to make sure the number of the question is the same as the number of the answer line on the answer sheet.

   - If the answer sheet has circles, fill them in neatly. A stray pencil mark might cause the scoring machine to count the answer as incorrect.

4. **If you're not sure of the answer, make your best guess.** Unless you've been told that there is a penalty for guessing, choose the answer that you think is likeliest to be correct.

5. **Keep track of the time.** Answering all the questions on a test usually results in a better score. That's why finishing the test is important. Keep track of the time you have left. At the beginning of the test, figure out how many questions you will have to answer by the halfway point in order to finish in the time given.

✔ **Reading Check**
What are at least two good ways to avoid skipping lines on an answer sheet?

Understand Types of Test Questions

Most tests include two types of questions: multiple choice and open-ended. Specific strategies will help you understand and correctly answer each type of question.

A multiple-choice question has two parts. The first part is the question itself, called the stem. The second part is a series of possible answers. Usually four possible answers are provided, and only one of them is correct. Your task is to choose the correct answer. Here are some strategies to help you do just that.

✔ Reading Check

What words in a multiple-choice question probably signal a wrong answer?

1. Read and think about each question carefully before looking at the possible answers.

2. Pay close attention to key words in the question. For example, look for the word *not,* as in "Which of the following is not a cause of the conflict in this story?"

3. Read and think about all of the possible answers before making your choice.

4. Reduce the number of choices by eliminating any answers you know are incorrect. Then, think about why some of the remaining choices might also be incorrect.

   - If two of the choices are pretty much the same, both are probably wrong.

   - Answers that contain any of the following words are usually incorrect: *always, never, none, all,* and *only.*

5. If you're still unsure about an answer, see if any of the following applies:

   - When one choice is longer and more detailed than the others, it is often the correct answer.

   - When a choice repeats a word that is in the question, it may be the correct answer.

   - When two choices are direct opposites, one of them is likely the correct answer.

   - When one choice includes one or more of the other choices, it is often the correct answer.

   - When a choice includes the word *some* or *often,* it may well be the correct answer.

- If one of the choices is *All of the above,* make sure that at least two of the other choices seem correct.

- If one of the choices is *None of the above,* make sure that none of the other choices seems correct.

An **open-ended test item** can take many forms. It might ask you to write a word or phrase to complete a sentence. You might be asked to create a chart, draw a map, or fill in a graphic organizer. Sometimes, you will be asked to write one or more paragraphs in response to a writing prompt. Use the following strategies when reading and answering open-ended items:

1. If the item includes directions, read them carefully. Take note of any steps required.

2. Look for key words and phrases in the item as you plan how you will respond. Does the item ask you to identify a cause-and-effect relationship or to compare and contrast two or more things? Are you supposed to provide a sequence of events or make a generalization? Does the item ask you to write an essay in which you state your point of view and then try to persuade others that your view is correct?

3. If you're going to be writing a paragraph or more, plan your answer. Jot down notes and a brief outline of what you want to say before you begin writing.

4. Focus your answer. Don't include everything you can think of, but be sure to include everything the item asks for.

5. If you're creating a chart or drawing a map, make sure your work is as clear as possible.

☑ **Reading Check**
What are at least three key strategies for answering an open-ended question?

Reading Test Model
LONG SELECTIONS

DIRECTIONS Here is a selection titled "Listening to the Body," by Tracey E. Fern. Read the selection carefully. The notes in the side columns will help you prepare for the kinds of questions that are likely to follow readings like this. You might want to preview the questions on pages 441 and 442 before you begin reading.

"Listening to the Body"
by Tracey E. Fern

The woman was rushed to Necker Hospital in Paris. Her face was pale and sweaty as she gasped for breath and clutched her chest. Young doctor René Laënnec raced to her bedside. Laënnec saw that this patient was desperately ill, perhaps ill enough to die. But what was the cause of her symptoms?

In 1816 there were no x-ray machines or ultrasounds—no tools at all to help Laënnec diagnose internal illnesses. Like all doctors of his day, Laënnec could only rely on what his patients told him about their symptoms and what he could observe with his own eyes. But this patient was too sick to be of much help. And of course Laënnec couldn't see inside her body. He turned to the only other tools that he had available—his ears.

Doctors have been eavesdropping on the body's sounds for more than two thousand years. The ancient Greek doctor Hippocrates pressed his ear to a patient's chest and heard a "sound like fermenting vinegar" and a "creak like new leather." These were just a few of the strange sounds that whispered from inside the human body. Other doctors heard clicks, coos, high-pitched whines, and a cacophony of other odd sounds. But the importance of these muffled noises remained a mystery for centuries.

Leopold Auenbrugger, a successful Austrian doctor who practiced medicine in the mid-1700s, was the first person to try to decode the sounds of the body. As a young boy Auenbrugger used to tag along with his father, who was an innkeeper. Auenbrugger watched as his father thumped on wine barrels to gauge how much liquid was left inside. An echo meant that

Reading Strategies for Assessment

Analyze the problem. Underline the main problem described in the first two paragraphs.

Notice patterns of organization. Paragraphs 3–7 describe the early use of listening as a tool for diagnosing patients. How are these paragraphs organized?

the barrel was empty where his father tapped, while a muffled *thwump* meant that it was full.

Auenbrugger decided to try this tap-and-listen technique on the human body. It worked. He found that the sounds painted a picture of the internal organs. Auenbrugger trained his ears to hear how these organs were positioned, whether there was fluid in the lungs, or if an abnormal growth was present in the body. Auenbrugger published his findings in 1761, calling his new technique *percussion*.

Auenbrugger was certain that percussion would revolutionize medicine. Instead the few doctors that learned about percussion thought it was ridiculous. Most doctors still believed in the ancient idea that illness was caused by an imbalance in invisible body fluids called humors, but percussion was based on the idea that illness is caused by real structural or mechanical problems in the body. It wasn't until the 1800s that the idea of humors gradually faded away. Unfortunately Auenbrugger was now an old man. Percussion seemed doomed to become a lost art.

Then French physician Jean Nicolas Corvisart discovered a copy of Auenbrugger's book. Corvisart decided to give the strange technique a try. Amazed at his ability to diagnose illness from the sound of a tap, Corvisart was soon using this method on all of his patients. He pronounced percussion a "beautiful invention" that he wanted to "recall to life." He did just that by teaching the technique to hundreds of young doctors.

One of those doctors was René Laënnec. Laënnec remembered the lessons he had learned from Corvisart and decided to try them on his newest patient. He carefully tapped on her chest, just as he had been taught, but heard absolutely nothing. The sounds were completely muffled because the patient was overweight. Percussion could do nothing to help his patient. Time was running out.

Laënnec took a stroll to clear his mind. As he walked through a park, he saw some boys clustered around one end of a long board. They were listening to the sounds made by a boy who was scratching the other end of the wood with a pin. Suddenly Laënnec had a brainstorm. He raced back to his office.

Snatching some papers from his desk, Laënnec rolled them into a tight cylinder. He pressed one end of this makeshift

Look for cause-and-effect relationships. Circle the cause of Laënnec's breakthrough.

tube to his ear and the other end to his patient's chest. The soft swish of the lungs, the drum of the heart— Laënnec listened in amazement to the loud and clear sounds of her body. By applying a familiar technique in an unconventional way, Laënnec had invented a tool that, he explained, let him "hear the beating of the heart with much greater clearness and distinctness than I had ever done before by direct application of my ear." The sounds were unmistakable; his patient had a serious heart condition.

Laënnec knew that his new listening tool could help many other patients, too. But first he had to solve a practical problem. His flimsy paper tube fell apart after only a few uses. Laënnec began to tinker with a wooden version of his tool. He christened his device a stethoscope from the Greek words *stethos,* meaning "chest," and *skopein,* meaning "to examine."

Use context clues. Given clues in the surrounding sentences, what do you think *myriad* means?

Next Laënnec began to decipher the meaning of the myriad sounds that he heard with the stethoscope. Little by little, Laënnec carefully recorded how each sound he heard related to a different illness.

Laënnec published his observations in 1819. They met with jeers. Many doctors feared that the stethoscope would put them out of a job. If it was so accurate and easy to use, then wouldn't even untrained people be able to treat patients? Who would still come to see a doctor? ... Some doctors were so embarrassed to be seen with a stethoscope that they hid it in their top hats. Oliver Wendell Holmes even wrote a song about a misguided doctor who used a stethoscope to diagnose some very sick patients.

Draw conclusions. What can you conclude about the challenges of being a scientist and an inventor?

The stethoscope also helped doctors see themselves as self-reliant scientists. And because listening to the body's sounds required training and practice, doctors began to view the stethoscope as a helpful tool rather than as a threat to their profession. The "medical trumpet" soon became the symbol of the modern doctor.

Today, doctors are still listening to the sounds of our bodies. The steady, rhythmic song of thumps and clicks, the irregular jangle of rattles and whistles—all of these sounds give them important clues about our health.

Now answer questions 1 through 6. Base your answers on the selection "Listening to the Body." Then check yourself by reading through the side column notes.

1 What problem is described in the first two paragraphs of the passage?

   A. In 1816, there were no x-ray machines.

   B. Patients were too sick to help.

   C. Doctors had no tools for analyzing an internal illness.

   D. There were few doctors who could diagnose a patient's illness.

2 What is the author's purpose for describing the early work of Hippocrates, Auenbrugger, and Corvisart?

   E. to provide a historical overview of early medical developments

   F. to highlight differences between ancient and modern medicine

   G. to foreshadow future medical developments

   H. to critique the use of certain medical techniques

3 What event caused the development of the first stethoscope?

   A. the publishing of Auenbrugger's book

   B. Corvisart's lecture on the percussion technique

   C. an idea triggered by observing boys playing the park

   D. Laënnec's experiment with percussion

4 Based on this sentence, what does *myriad* mean?

   Next Laënnec began to decipher the meaning of the myriad sounds that he heard with the stethoscope.

   E. interesting

   F. a huge number

   G. gentle

   H. loud

5 From this selection, what can you conclude about new inventions?

   A. New inventions may not be accepted immediately.

   B. New inventions cause more trouble than they are worth.

   C. New inventions often come to inventors in dreams.

   D. New inventions are often created by teams of scientists.

Answer Strategies

Find the Problem. This question tells you where to find the answer. Quickly scan paragraphs 1–2 to identify the main problem.

Notice patterns of organization. In paragraphs 3–7, the work of these three men is described briefly *in chronological order.* Why?

Identify cause-and-effect relationships. Key words and phrases such as *because, as a result,* and *so* often signal cause-and-effect relationships. However, in this example, the effect directly follows the cause in the passage.

Use context clues. Try out each answer choice in the sentence and choose the one that makes the most sense.

Draw conclusions. Eliminate answers that don't make sense. Choice B implies that all new inventions are worthless! Choices C and D are not even mentioned in the selection.

Answers: 1.C, 2.E, 3.C, 4.F, 5.A

Plan your response. Look at what the question asks and plan how to proceed. For this question, you have to first identify the details in the selection that support the author's statement. Then you have to either restate those details in your own words or quote from the selection.

6 In this selection, the author shows how inventors develop new ideas based upon the previous insights of others. What information does the author use to make this point? Use details from the text to support your conclusion.

Sample short response for question 6:

    The author clearly shows how the invention of the stethoscope was based upon the work of men who learned from one another. First, Auenbrugger created the "percussion" technique and published his work. Next, Corvisart read about this method and taught it to Laënnec. Laënnec then created the first stethoscope. The author explains that "Eventually other physicians improved the stethoscope." This account leads the reader to conclude that an invention is the end product of many individuals' contributions.

Study the response. Notice how the response includes details and a quotation from the selection.

Reading Test Practice
LONG SELECTIONS

DIRECTIONS Now it's time to practice what you've learned about reading test items and choosing the best answers. Read the following selection, "Wild Everest: Over the Top!" Use the side columns to make notes about the important parts of this selection: main ideas, cause and effect, comparisons and contrasts, difficult vocabulary, supporting details, and so on.

from "Wild Everest: Over the Top!"

By Maria L. Chang

It's the ultimate natural wonder of the world. The rugged mountain peak of rock and ice is the planet's highest point of ground where earth and sky collide. Winds whip at 161 kilometers (100 miles) per hour; windchills plunge to 96 degrees Celsius (140°F) below zero. But for thrill-driven mountain climbers, reaching the summit of wild Mount Everest is adventure's grand prize, the ultimate dream.

Almost six miles high, Mount Everest soars 8,848 meters (29,028 ft) above sea level—the tallest mountain on Earth in the world's highest and wildest mountain range, the Himalayas, which form the border between China and Nepal.

Climbers who dare to take on Everest face a rash of dangers: frostbite from severe cold, sunburn from glaring sun, snow-blindness from the sun's blaze reflected off ice. Breathing the frigid air can cause such violent coughing that ribs crack like dry sticks. Add to that Everest's constant peril—shifting ice, deep chasms, brutal storms—and the prize seems hardly worth the murderous risk.

Yet since the first recorded European expedition in the early 1920s, nearly 600 mountaineers have made it to the top. Still, for every 30 people who seek to scale Everest, one dies. About 150 climbers have lost their lives on the mountain.

A Climber's Goal

This spring, mountain climber Tom Whittaker hopes to join the rank of victors. If his dream comes true, he'll be the first disabled climber to reach Everest's summit.

After a car accident in 1979, doctors *amputated,* or cut off, Whittaker's right foot. But that didn't shatter his goal to become a world-class mountain climber. Born in Wales, Whittaker, 48, now trains future professional mountain guides in Prescott, Arizona.

With the help of a *prosthesis,* an artificial device replacing his missing foot, Whittaker continued scaling mountains after his accident. But what would inspire him to tackle the world's most daring climb? "Why does anyone run a marathon or play football? It's pitting yourself against something that is big—and you don't know if you can do it," Whittaker told *SW* [*Science World*].

In 1989, Whittaker reached 7,300 m (24,000 ft) high up Everest but was forced back to Base Camp after a violent storm blew in. In 1995, he tried again—this time mounting Everest's North Face up to 8,382 m (27,500 ft). But his body caved to the rigors of climbing at dizzying altitudes, and he became too ill to continue. This will be Whittaker's third attempt to wrestle Everest.

Breathing Lessons

How does Everest take its terrible toll on the human body? "Very few people can stay indefinitely at altitudes above 5,500 m (18,000 ft) and thrive," says Robert Schoene, a high-altitude physiologist at the University of Washington. The main obstacle: the amount of oxygen available for breathing. Oxygen is the gas nearly all organisms depend on to survive. Living things use oxygen to *metabolize,* or burn food for fuel and energy.

Whether at sea level, where most people live, or at Everest's peak, Earth's air contains 21 percent oxygen. But at such lofty altitudes as Everest's, less oxygen enters the lungs with every breath.

The amount of oxygen usable for breathing is determined by *atmospheric pressure*—pressure caused by air's weight.

The greater the atmospheric pressure, the more closely oxygen molecules are jammed together. At sea level, where air weighs down heavily, living things inhale oxygen-rich air. But at higher altitudes, atmospheric pressure decreases, and air molecules are more spread out. Result: There's less available oxygen for a climber to inhale.

As a result, a mountaineer can easily suffer *hypoxia*—lack of oxygen. To compensate, the body initiates a series of "struggle responses." First, a climber will begin to breathe harder, or *hyperventilate*, as lungs try to draw in more oxygen. Hyperventilating makes the heart beat faster and pump more blood per beat. (Blood carries oxygen to different parts of the body.) The *bone marrow*—the body's blood factory—also produces more new blood cells to circulate oxygen in the body.

All these responses protect the body from hypoxia, but only to a point. Sometimes the bone marrow produces so many blood cells that a person's blood becomes as thick as motor oil, Schoene explains. Then blood can't flow properly or deliver the body's oxygen efficiently.

Mountain Sickness

In about 25 percent of climbers, the oxygen deficit results in *acute mountain sickness* (AMS). As the body strives to circulate more blood and oxygen to the brain, the extra blood can cause the brain to swell, leading to headaches, nausea, weakness, and shortness of breath. Drinking plenty of water and getting rest can relieve AMS.

But far more serious forms of mountain sickness attack climbers at altitudes above 3,660 m (12,000 ft). *High-Altitude Cerebral Edema* (HACE) occurs when the brain swells severely. The sufferer has trouble walking or using his hands, and may start to hallucinate. When fluids accumulate in the lungs, *High-Altitude Pulmonary Edema* (HAPE) can, in effect, drown a person. Both HACE and HAPE may result in death.

Interestingly, Sherpas (pronounced SHUR-puhs), native Himalayans who often guide climbers up Everest, rarely suffer from altitude-caused illness. Some scientists suggest the natives carry a *gene*—chemical instructions passed from parent to offspring—that lets them use oxygen more efficiently.

What are the best strategies for climbers like Whittaker to avoid altitude sickness? He should climb slowly so his body can adjust to the increasing altitude. Experts also recommend that mountaineers ascend no more than 300 to 400 m (1,000 to 2,000 ft) a day. Bottled oxygen also helps, especially above 7,300 m (24,000 ft).

Most important, says Schoene, the best way to tackle Everest is to practice scaling high mountains for 10 to 15 years. "People who climb 4,300-m (14,000-ft) peaks or hike up the Rockies have no real experience how to survive the brutal weather or high altitudes of the Himalayas."

What does Whittaker think of so many obstacles? "They're not as tough as getting through grade school," he jokes. But he admits this is the last time he'll try to tackle Everest's summit. "Most normal people would have said twice is enough. But somebody told me three is a charm, so I'm going back to try it one more time."

Tom Whittaker succeeded in his third attempt to climb Everest.

Now answer questions 1 through 7. Base your answers on the selection "Wild Everest: Over the Top!"

1 What is the author's purpose for writing about Mount Everest?

   A. to explain how foolish many climbers are

   B. to describe the challenges faced by climbers of Mount Everest

   C. to describe Mount Everest

   D. to provide a scientific explanation for various forms of mountain sickness

2 Read this sentence from the selection.

> Add to that Everest's constant peril—shifting ice, deep chasms, brutal storms—and the prize seems hardly worth the murderous risk.

Which of these is an antonym for *peril*?

   E. variety

   F. safety

   G. warmth

   H. wildness

3 The author includes parts of an interview with a high-altitude physiologist. Such information is likely to be

   A. too far removed from the real world to be believable.

   B. invalid because it comes from only one authority.

   C. reliable because it comes from an expert on how organisms function at high altitudes.

   D. reliable because it comes from an expert on human diseases.

4 What is the cause of acute mountain sickness?

   E. insufficient oxygen

   F. lack of rest

   G. atmospheric pressure

   H. weak lungs

5 What is the main point of the section titled "Breathing Lessons?"

    A. to explain the importance of breathing lessons for aspiring mountain climbers

    B. to describe the dangers that climbers like Whittaker face

    C. to describe the interview with Robert Schoene

    D. to explain the symptoms of hypoxia

6 Thickened blood, one of the effects of hypoxia, is compared with

    E. molasses.

    F. motor oil.

    G. shortness of breath.

    H. a silt-filled river.

7 How is Tom Whittaker's character portrayed by the author? Use details from the selection to support your answer.

_____

_____

_____

_____

_____

_____

_____

_____

_____

_____

_____

_____

_____

THINKING IT THROUGH

The notes in the side columns will help you think through your answers. See the key at the bottom of the page.

1 What is the author's purpose for writing about Mount Everest?

A. to explain how foolish many climbers are

B. to describe the challenges climbers of Mount Everest face

C. to describe Mount Everest

D. to provide a scientific explanation for various forms of mountain sickness

> Often the author's purpose can be inferred from the title of the work and the first and last paragraphs. Skim these sections to find the answer.

2 Read this sentence from the selection.

Add to that Everest's constant peril—shifting ice, deep chasms, brutal storms—and the prize seems hardly worth the murderous risk.

Which of these is an antonym for peril?

E. variety

F. safety

G. warmth

H. wildness

> Use context clues in the sentence to figure out the meaning of *peril*. Next, choose the word that is opposite in meaning. Which word means the opposite of *brutal* or *murderous risk*?

3 The author includes parts of an interview with a high-altitude physiologist. Such information is likely to be

A. too far removed from the real world to be believable.

B. invalid because it comes from only one authority.

C. reliable because it comes from an expert on how organisms function at high altitudes.

D. reliable because it comes from an expert on human diseases.

> You can infer that a *high-altitude physiologist* is probably an expert just from the sound of the title. This narrows the choices to C or D. Since C refers to high altitudes—a term in the question stem—it is probably the answer.

4 What is the cause of acute mountain sickness?

E. insufficient oxygen

F. lack of rest

G. atmospheric pressure

H. weak lungs

> Skim the reading looking for the key words *acute mountain sickness*. Reread that section closely to get the answer.

5 What is the main point of the section titled "Breathing Lessons?"

A. to explain the importance of breathing lessons for aspiring mountain climbers

B. to describe the dangers that climbers like Whittaker face

C. to describe the interview with Robert Schoene

D. to explain the symptoms of hypoxia

6 Thickened blood, one of the effects of hypoxia, is compared with

E. molasses.

F. motor oil.

G. shortness of breath.

H. a silt-filled river.

7 How is Tom Whittaker's character portrayed by the author? Use details from the selection to support your answer.

> Tom Whittaker is portrayed as a very determined man who overcame many obstacles to reach his goal. The author first explains how Whittaker confronted a major obstacle—the loss of his right foot. She explains that this experience "...didn't shatter his goal to become a world-class mountain climber." The author also portrays him as a determined man by describing his repeated attempts to climb Mount Everest. He eventually succeeded on his third try. Only a very determined man would repeatedly take such risks.

Reading Test Model
SHORT SELECTIONS

DIRECTIONS This reading selection is just two paragraphs long. The strategies you have just used can also help you with this shorter selection. As you read the selection, respond to the notes in the side column.

When you've finished reading, you'll find two multiple-choice questions. Again, use the side column notes to help you understand what each question is asking for and why each answer is the correct one.

An Innovative Doctor

When a cholera outbreak hit the Soho section of London in 1854, a young doctor named John Snow began to suspect its causes. Snow went into the field and carefully mapped the location of every case of cholera, noting where the victim fell sick. A pattern revealed an unmistakable cluster of fatalities in the area around the Broad Street pump. The conclusion was obvious to Snow: the water from that pump was infecting people. Snow convinced local authorities to remove the handle from the pump, and the epidemic ceased soon afterward.

Snow's detailed observations and standardized methods for recording and analyzing raw data transformed epidemiology from an eccentric activity to a respected science. Every microbe hunter now begins with methods that Snow established in 1854.

1. Based on the information in the passage, you can infer that epidemiology is

   A. an eccentric activity.
   B. the study of how water affects people.
   C. the study of diseases in populations.
   D. the evaluation of pioneering thinking.

2. What is the author's purpose for writing this passage?

   E. to entertain readers by describing a true-life tragedy
   F. to inform readers about an important scientific advance
   G. to persuade readers that Snow was a pioneer
   H. to inform readers about the problem of water contamination

Reading Strategies for Assessment

Find the main idea and supporting details. Circle the main idea, and underline two supporting details.

Use context clues. To understand the meaning of *epidemiology,* look at the words and phrases around it. What is an epidemiologist?

Answer Strategies

Use context clues. To infer the meaning of *epidemiology,* look at the context clues. In the last sentence, an epidemiologist is referred to as a *microbe hunter.*

Analyze style. To figure out whether the author has written to entertain, persuade, or inform, examine the style and content of the writing. Does the writer tell an anecdote? Give an opinion? Provide information?

Answers: 1.C, 2.F

The Eagle
by Alfred Tennyson

He clasps the crag with crooked hands;
Close to the sun in lonely lands,
Ringed with the azure world, he stands.

The wrinkled sea beneath him crawls;
He watches from his mountain walls,
And like a thunderbolt he falls.

3 Which words BEST describe the author's view of the eagle?

   A. a sorrowful and lonely creature
   B. a powerful and majestic creature
   C. an evil and cruel creature
   D. an old and frail creature

4 Which line from the passage shows the BEST example of alliteration?

   E. *He clasps the crag with crooked hands;*
   F. *Ringed with the azure world, he stands.*
   G. *The wrinkled sea beneath him crawls;*
   H. *And like a thunderbolt he falls.*

5 The author uses a simile to compare which two things?

   A. crooked hands and a crag
   B. the sea and a wrinkled face
   C. mountain walls and a thunderbolt
   D. a falling eagle and a thunderbolt

Reading Test Practice
SHORT SELECTIONS

DIRECTIONS Use the following to practice your skills. Read "Cultures in Conflict" and circle the key ideas. Then answer the multiple-choice questions that follow.

Cultures in Conflict

During the 1500s, Montezuma II ruled the empire of the Aztecs, which extended from coast to coast across the central part of Mexico. The Aztecs were wealthy and powerful and scientifically advanced. They had already developed the sciences of mathematics and astronomy.

Meanwhile, the Spanish explorer Hernándo Cortés set out to look for gold in the part of Mexico called the Yucatán. With eleven ships and five hundred men, he landed on the east coast of the Yucatán. Marching inland, the Spanish army easily conquered the Indians they encountered. Many Indians disliked their Aztec rulers and joined Cortés to fight the Aztecs. In 1519, the army entered the Aztec capital, Tenochtitlan, and took Montezuma II prisoner. In 1520, however, the Aztecs rallied against the Spanish, and the Spanish were forced to retreat. Six months later, Cortés returned with a new army of Spanish troops and Indians and completely destroyed the Aztec capital. Renamed Mexico City, it became the center of a new civilization and culture.

1 Why didn't the Indians resist the Spanish army as the troops marched inland?

    A. The Indians were afraid of the Spanish army's guns.

    B. The Indians wanted to live in peace with their neighbors.

    C. The Indians wanted to fight the Aztecs.

    D. The Indians were outnumbered.

2 Which is closest in meaning to the word *rallied?*

    E. teased

    F. came together

    G. shouted

    H. ran away from

DIRECTIONS Use the poem to answer questions 3, 4, and 5.

The Courage That My Mother Had

by Edna St. Vincent Millay

The courage that my mother had
Went with her, and is with her still;
Rock from New England quarried;
Now granite in a granite hill.

⑤ The golden brooch my mother wore
She left behind for me to wear;
I have no thing I treasure more;
Yet, it is something I could spare.

Oh, if instead she'd left to me
⑩ The thing she took into the grave!—
That courage like a rock, which she
Has no more need of, and I have.

3 Which word BEST describes the feelings expressed by the author?

A. anger
B. grief
C. boredom
D. impatience

4 The author uses a simile to compare which two things?

E. courage and a golden brooch
F. a treasure and her mother
G. a treasure and a golden brooch
H. courage and a rock

5 Which two lines do not rhyme?

A. lines 2 and 4
B. lines 5 and 7
C. lines 9 and 11
D. lines 10 and 12

THINKING IT THROUGH

The notes in the side columns will help you think through your answers. Check the key at the bottom of the page. How well did you do?

1 Why didn't the Indians resist the Spanish army as the troops marched inland?

A. The Indians were afraid of the Spanish army's guns.
B. The Indians wanted to live in peace with their neighbors.
C. The Indians wanted to fight the Aztecs.
D. The Indians were outnumbered.

> Locate details using key words and phrases. Search the text for *Spanish army* and *troops marched inland.* Reread this section and then choose the best answer.

2 Which is closest in meaning to the word *rallied?*

E. teased
F. came together
G. shouted
H. ran away from

> To infer the meaning of *rallied,* look at context clues in the sentence. Why were the Spanish forced to retreat?

3 Which word BEST describes the feelings expressed by the author?

A. anger
B. grief
C. boredom
D. impatience

> The author's word choices provide clues to this answer. What feelings are most closely related to words such as *need, left behind,* and *grave?*

4 The author uses a simile to compare which two things?

E. courage and a golden brooch
F. a treasure and her mother
G. a treasure and a golden brooch
H. courage and a rock

> Remember, key words that signal the use of a simile are *like* or *as.*

5 Which two lines do not rhyme?

A. lines 2 and 4
B. lines 5 and 7
C. lines 9 and 11
D. lines 10 and 12

> Use the process of elimination to identify the pair of lines that do not rhyme. Why do you think the author chose to break the pattern of rhyme at the end of the poem?

Answers: 1.C, 2.F, 3.B, 4.H, 5.D

Functional Reading Test Model

DIRECTIONS Study the following information from a tire maintenance manual. Then answer the questions that follow.

GUIDE TO TIRE INFLATION

Always keep the vehicle manufacturer's recommended cold air pressure in all your tires.

Safety Warning Too little air pressure, or *underinflation,* can lead to sudden tire failure due to overheating. Serious injury or death could result. Underinflation may also adversely affect vehicle handling, reduce tire life, and increase fuel consumption.

Safety Warning Too much air, or *overinflation,* is also dangerous. The tires are more likely to be cut, punctured, or broken by sudden impact. Serious injury or death could result.

Tips for Safe Tire Inflation
- Check the tire pressure, including the spare, once a week. Use an accurate pressure gauge.
- Check the tires when they are cold (driven less than 1 mile or stopped for at least 3 hours).
- If you must add air when tires are hot, add 4 pounds per square inch (psi) (28 kPa) above the recommended cold air pressure.
- If tires lose more than 2 psi (14 kPa) per month, the tire, the valve, or the wheel may be damaged. You should have it inspected by a trained mechanic.

Reading Strategies for Assessment

Examine the structure. Circle the four headings used in this manual.

Examine key words. Study the words in boldfaced print and italics.

Answer Strategies

> The key word to consider is *similar.* Compare the description of overinflated tires and underinflated tires and find what they have in common.

1 How are overinflation and underinflation similar?

   A. Both require inspection by a trained mechanic.
   B. Both can lead to serious injury or death.
   C. Both are the result of adding air to overheated tires.
   D. Both require 4 psi above the recommended cold air pressure.

> Skim the text for specific details. The key phrase is *If tires lose more than 2 psi (14 kPa) per month.*

2 According to the manual, if a tire loses 2 psi of air each month, what should be done?

   E. Nothing; the tire is probably normal.
   F. The tire should be replaced.
   G. The tire should be inspected by a mechanic.
   H. The tire has a leak and should be replaced.

> This is a two-step problem. First, figure out whether the tires are considered cold or hot. What do you do when tires are hot and underinflated?

3 If you have driven for the last two hours and your tires are underinflated, what should you do?

   A. Add 4 psi of air.
   B. Have the tire inspected by a trained mechanic.
   C. Add 4 psi of air above the recommended cold air pressure.
   D. Patch the damaged tire.

Answers: 1.B, 2.E, 3.C

Functional Reading Test Practice

DIRECTIONS Study the parking ticket below. Circle the information you think is the most important. Answer the multiple-choice questions that follow.

PARKING VIOLATION
FOR THE CITY OF NELSON

Date: 09/17/02	**Time:** 11:24 A.M.	**State:** Michigan
Vehicle Make: Honda	**Vehicle Color:** BLK	**Route:** 065
Location: 22 Hill St.	**Officer:** Barron	**Badge:** 214
Violation Description: Permit Parking	**Amount Due:** $15.00	**Comments:** No resident parking permit sticker

You may request a hearing to appeal, with supporting documents; *or* make check or money order payable to the Nelson Parking Clerk, place in envelope, and mail within 21 days. Walk-in payments can be made at the Traffic and Parking Dept., 133 Holt St., Nelson, MI, between 9:00 A.M. and 4:00 P.M. Monday through Friday. Tel. (800) 555-1212 Ext. 21 for information. If payment is made after 21 days, this fine is increased. *DO NOT SEND CASH.*

NOTICE TO OFFENDERS
Failure to obey this notice within 21 days may result in the addition of a $5.00 penalty. Failure to obey this notice until the parking clerk has reported to the registrar may result in the addition of a $20.00 penalty.

This violation notice may be returned by mail personally or by an authorized person. A hearing may be obtained upon written request of the registered owner.

FAILURE TO OBEY THIS NOTICE WITHIN TWENTY-ONE DAYS MAY RESULT IN THE NONRENEWAL OF THE LICENSE AND REGISTRATION OF THE REGISTERED OWNER.

---

1 What is the cause of this parking violation?

    A. The car owner had no resident parking permit sticker.

    B. The car owner forgot to put money in the meter.

    C. The car owner did not obey the posted notice.

    D. The car owner neglected to pay the fine in under 21 days.

2 If one chooses not to schedule a hearing, what are the possible effects of not paying the fine within 21 days?

   E. The car owner must pay an additional $5.00.

   F. The car owner must pay an additional fine and may not be able to renew his or her license and registration.

   G. The car owner must return in person to pay the fine and risk being reported to the registrar.

   H. The car owner may be arrested and fined an additional fee.

3 What is closest in meaning to the word *appeal*?

   A. to report a violation of personal rights

   B. to provide evidence regarding the violation

   C. to support the decision

   D. to apply for reconsideration of a legal decision

4 For the person wishing to pay the fine, what are the correct procedures?

   E. return the violation notice and $15.00 cash within 21 days

   F. return the violation notice in person after 21 days

   G. return the violation notice and a check or money order for $15.00 within 21 days

   H. return the violation notice and a check for $20.00 within 21 days

THINKING IT THROUGH

The notes in the side columns will help you think through your answers. Check the key at the bottom of the page. How well did you do?

1 What is the cause of this parking violation?

A. The car owner did not have a resident parking permit sticker.

B. The car owner forgot to put money in the meter.

C. The car owner did not obey the posted notice.

D. The car owner neglected to pay the fine.

> Skim the headings in the top portion of the ticket for information that is specific to this violation.

2 What are the possible effects of not paying the fine within 21 days?

E. The car owner must pay an additional $5.00.

F. The car owner must pay an additional fine and may not be able to renew his or her license and registration.

G. The car owner must return in person to pay the fine and risk being reported to the registrar.

H. The car owner may be arrested and fined an additional fee.

> Do not confuse a true answer with a correct answer. Letter E is true; however, there is a more complete answer.

3 What is closest in meaning to the word *appeal*?

A. to report a violation of personal rights

B. to provide evidence regarding the violation

C. to support the decision

D. to apply for reconsideration of a legal decision

> Use context clues in the sentence to figure out the meaning of *appeal*. Why might someone request a hearing?

4 For the person wishing to pay the fine, what are the correct procedures?

E. return the violation notice and $15.00 cash within 21 days

F. return the violation notice in person after 21 days

G. return the violation notice and a check or money order for $15.00 within 21 days

H. return the violation notice and a check for $20.00 within 21 days

> Reread for specific details. Words spelled out in capital letters emphasize important information.

Answers: 1.A, 2.F, 3.D, 4.G

Revising-and-Editing Test Model

DIRECTIONS Read the following paragraph carefully. Then answer the multiple-choice questions that follow. After answering the questions, read the material in the side column to check your answer strategies.

¹The Silk Road was a network of trails that formed one of the importantest trade routes of the ancient world. ²This route got it's name because camel caravans carried loads of silk from China westward to central Asia and Rome. ³The market for silk—and the Silk Road—grew with the rise of the roman empire during the first and second centuries A.D. ⁴Silk was prized for being beautiful, it was strong, and lightweight. ⁵The cocoons of over 2,000 silkworms, to produce a pound of silk, had to be soaked and unraveled. ⁶The effort was worth it each pound of silk was worth a pound of gold. ⁷However making silk was a difficult process.

Answer Strategies

Regular Comparisons All regular three-syllable modifiers use the superlative form *most*.
For help, see Pupil Edition, p. 1313*
Grammar, Usage, and Mechanics Book, p. 130

1 What change should be made in sentence 1?

A. Change *that formed* to *forming*.

B. Change *Road* to *road*.

C. Change *importantest* to *most important*.

D. Change *ancient* to *Ancient*.

Possessive Pronouns Try to memorize the difference between the possessive pronoun *its* and the contraction *it's*, which means *it is*.
For help, see Pupil Edition, p. 1307
Grammar, Usage, and Mechanics Book, p. 109

2 What change, if any, should be made to sentence 2?

E. Change *it's* to *its*.

F. Insert a semicolon after *because*.

G. Change *westward* to *Westward*.

H. No change is necessary.

Capitalization Capitalize proper nouns—nouns that name specific persons, places, and things.
For help, see Pupil Edition, p. 1329
Grammar, Usage, and Mechanics Book, p. 142

3 What change, if any, should be made to sentence 3?

A. Insert a comma after *grew*.

B. Change *roman empire* to *Roman Empire*.

C. Change *centuries* to *century's*.

D. No change is necessary.

*Pages listed are for the Grammar Handbook in *The Language of Literature* Pupil Edition and the *Grammar, Usage, and Mechanics Book.*

The InterActive Reader PLUS
464 With Additional Support

4 What is the most effective way to rewrite sentence 4?

    E. Silk was prized for being beautiful—it was strong—and lightweight.

    F. Silk was prized for being beautiful: it was strong and lightweight.

    G. Silk was prized for being beautiful, strong, and lightweight.

    H. Silk was prized for being beautiful; strong and lightweight.

Items in a Series Separate items in a series with commas, and make sure all elements are written in parallel form.
For help, see Pupil Edition, p. 1327. Grammar, Usage, and Mechanics Book, p. 157

5 Which sentence clarifies the meaning of sentence 5?

    A. To produce a pound of silk, the cocoons of over 2,000 silkworms had to be soaked and unraveled.

    B. Over 2,000 silkworms had to be soaked and unraveled, producing a pound of silk.

    C. The cocoons of over 2,000 silkworms, soaked and unraveled, produce a pound of silk.

    D. To produce a pound of silk, 2,000 silkworms had to be soaked and unraveled.

Misplaced Modifiers To clarify the meaning, the infinitive phrase *to produce a pound of silk* should be placed near the word that it modifies.
For help, see Pupil Edition, p. 1314. Grammar, Usage, and Mechanics Book, p. 136

6 What change, if any, should be made in sentence 6?

    E. Place a comma after *it*.

    F. Place a period after *it* and change *each* to *Each*.

    G. Place a semicolon after *it* and add *however,*

    H. No change is necessary.

Kinds of Sentences Separate two complete thoughts with a period. This is a run-on sentence. Can you identify two complete thoughts and separate them?
For help, see Pupil Edition, p. 1323. Grammar, Usage, and Mechanics Book, p. 67

7 What change, if any, should be made in sentence 7?

    A. Place a comma after *However*.

    B. Change *However* to *Consequently*.

    C. Change *was* to *is*.

    D. No change is necessary.

Transitional Words A comma should be used to set off transitional words such as *however, in contrast,* and *as a result.*
For help, see Pupil Edition, p. 1327. Grammar, Usage, and Mechanics Book, p. 157

8 What is the most effective way to improve the organization of the paragraph?

    E. Delete sentence 3.

    F. Place sentence 7 after sentence 4.

    G. Place sentence 5 after sentence 7.

    H. Delete sentence 4.

Paragraph Organization This transitional sentence can be used effectively to link the description of silk with the description of silk-making.

Answers:
1.C, 2.E, 3.B, 4.G, 5.A, 6.F, 7.A, 8.F

Revising-and-Editing Test Practice

DIRECTIONS Read the following paragraph carefully. As you read, circle each error you find and identify the error in the side column— for example, you might write *misspelled word* or *not a complete sentence*. When you have finished, circle the letter of the correct choice for each question that follows.

¹Krakatoa is, one of many, Indonesian volcanoes. ²It towers more than 6,000 feet above the sea. ³In 1883, the island was shook by a series of powerful eruptions. ⁴Increasing in frequency, the summer of 1883 was a period when volcanic eruptions continued to occur. ⁵On August 26, Krakatoa preceded to erupt violently. ⁶The volcanos steam and ash blew 17 miles into the air. ⁷On August 27, another climactic explosion occurred and the blast was heard 2,000 miles away in Australia.

1 What change should be made in sentence 1?

A. Delete the comma after *many*.

B. Delete *is*.

C. Change *one of many* to *one of the many*.

D. Delete the commas after *is* and *many*.

2 What change, if any, should be made in sentence 2?

E. Change *it* to *Krakatoa*.

F. Change *feet* to *ft*.

G. Change *towers* to *towered*.

H. No change is necessary.

3 Which of the following is the correct way to write the first part of sentence 3?

A. In 1883, the island was shaked

B. In 1883, the island was shaken

C. In 1883, the island shook

D. In 1883, the island shaked

4 What is the most effective way to write sentence 4?

   E. Increasing in frequency, volcanic eruptions continued to occur during the summer of 1883.

   F. During the summer of 1883, increasing in frequency, a period occurred when volcanic eruptions continued.

   G. A period when volcanic eruptions continued to occur, increased in frequency during the summer of 1883.

   H. Increasing in frequency in the summer of 1883, there was a period when volcanic eruptions continued to occur.

5 What change, if any, should be made in sentence 5?

   A. Change *violently* to *more violently*.

   B. Change *erupt* to *discharge*.

   C. Change *preceded* to *proceeded*.

   D. No change is necessary.

6 What change should be made in sentence 6?

   E. Change *volcanos* to *volcanoes*.

   F. Change *volcanos* to *volcano's*.

   G. Change *volcanos* to *volcanoes'*.

   H. Change *volcanos* to *volcanos'*.

7 What change should be made in sentence 7?

   A. Place a comma after *occurred*.

   B. Delete *and the blast was heard*.

   C. Place a period after *occurred* and change *and* to *And*.

   D. Change *heard* to *herd*.

THINKING IT THROUGH

DIRECTIONS Use the notes in the side column to help you understand why some answers are correct and others are not. See the answer key on the next page. How well did you do?

Because *one of many* is an essential phrase (without it the sentence will not make sense), it should not be set off by commas.
For help, see Pupil Edition, p. 1327.
Grammar, Usage, and Mechanics
Book, p. 58*

1 What change should be made in sentence 1?

  A. Delete the comma after *many*.

  B. Delete *is*.

  C. Change *one of many* to *one of the many*.

  D. Delete the commas after *is* and *many*.

Examine each word for accuracy and sense.

2 What change, if any, should be made in sentence 2?

  E. Change *it* to *Krakatoa*.

  F. Change *feet* to *ft*.

  G. Change *towers* to *towered*.

  H. No change is necessary.

The past participle form of verbs is always preceded by a form of *be* or *have*. In addition, *shake* is an irregular verb that does not add *-d* or *-ed* to the present form.
*For help, see Pupil Edition, p. 1311.
Grammar, Usage, and Mechanics
Book, p. 82*

3 Which of the following is the correct way to write the first part of sentence 3?

  A. In 1883, the Island was shaked

  B. In 1883, the island was shaken

  C. In 1883, the island shook

  D. In 1883, the island shaked

As written, the sentence is confusing. The phrase *increasing in frequency* must be placed close to the word it modifies.
*For help, see Pupil Edition, p. 1314.
Grammar, Usage, and Mechanics
Book, p. 136*

4 What is the most effective way to write sentence 4?

  E. Increasing in frequency, volcanic eruptions continued to occur during the summer of 1883.

  F. During the summer of 1883, increasing in frequency, a period occurred when volcanic eruptions continued.

  G. A period when volcanic eruptions continued to occur, increased in frequency during the summer of 1883.

  H. Increasing in frequency in the summer of 1883, there was a period when volcanic eruptions continued to occur.

*Pages listed are for the Grammar Handbook in *The Language of Literature* Pupil Edition and the *Grammar, Usage, and Mechanics Book*.

5 What change, if any, should be made in sentence 5?

    A. Change *violently* to *more violently*.

    B. Change *erupt* to *discharge*.

    C. Change *preceded* to *proceeded*.

    D. No change is necessary.

> *Precede* and *proceed* are commonly confused words. Choose the one that makes the most sense in the sentence.
> *For help, see Pupil Edition, p. 1334*

6 What change should be made in sentence 6?

    E. Change *volcanos* to *volcanoes*.

    F. Change *volcanos* to *volcano's*.

    G. Change *volcanos* to *volcanoes'*.

    H. Change *volcanos* to *volcanos'*.

> The phrase *volcanos steam* indicates possession. Try to recall the basic rule for forming singular possessives.
> *For help, see Pupil Edition, p. 1306. Grammar, Usage, and Mechanics Book, p. 109*

7 What change should be made in sentence 7?

    A. Place a comma after *occurred*.

    B. Delete *and the blast was heard*.

    C. Place a period after *occurred* and change *and* to *And*.

    D. Change *heard* to *herd*.

> This sentence contains two complete thoughts. In a sentence with two independent clauses, some form of punctuation must be used to separate them.
> *For help, see Pupil Edition, p. 1322. Grammar, Usage, and Mechanics Book, p. 55*

Answers:
1.D, 2.H, 3.B, 4.E, 5.C, 6.F, 7.A

Writing Test Model

DIRECTIONS Many tests ask you to write an essay in response to a writing prompt. A writing prompt is a brief statement that describes a writing situation. Some writing prompts ask you to explain what, why, or how. Others ask you to convince someone about something.

As you analyze the following writing prompts, read and respond to the notes in the side column. Then look at the response to each prompt. The notes in the side column will help you understand why each response is considered strong.

Prompt A

You have just learned that the Board of Education is considering adding another class period to your high school day to provide additional classes for students.

Think about the advantages and disadvantages of an additional class period in the school day. Write to the Board of Education either supporting or disagreeing with the proposed change.

Strong Response

    Our high school should support the proposal to add an additional class period to the school day. Even students who are reluctant to take an additional class will see that the proposed policy has many advantages for both students and school staff.

    The most important advantage is that students will be able to enroll in an additional course of their choice. For instance, students can take a class like Yearbook or Student Leadership that is enjoyable and enables them to get involved in school activities.

    Another advantage of the extra period is that it will give many students a better opportunity to prepare for college by taking electives and more advanced classes. Students will also be able to take required classes, such

Analyzing the Prompt

Understand what's expected of you. What is the purpose of your response? Who is your audience? What must you include?

Clearly describe your position. This writer uses the first paragraph to clearly state his position regarding the proposed policy change.

Answer Strategies

Develop your argument using specific reasons that support your position. This writer describes many benefits of the proposed change.

as Basic Health and Physical Education classes they—might have put off until their junior or senior years.

An extra period will also have many benefits for the school and teachers. Because students will not have time to roam the halls during their shortened lunch hour, the noise and litter in the halls will be reduced. This will obviously benefit the teachers who are trying to conduct classes. Also, because fewer seniors will leave the building to go out for lunch, there will be fewer car accidents.

Some students and teachers believe that an extra period will be wasted. They state that under the current policy, students are exhausted and struggle to concentrate during the last period of the day. Shortening the lunch period, they explain, will only increase this problem. However, if students are learning about a subject of personal interest, they will be more inclined to stay engaged and seek to learn.

Adopting the policy to add an additional period is clearly a good idea. The proposed change will lead not only to more opportunities for students to learn about the subjects that are of interest to them, but also to a school that is cleaner, quieter, and safer. Finally, the new policy will better prepare students for college. The benefits insure a better school and a brighter future for students.

Acknowledge opposing views. This writer includes an opposing viewpoint and then points out the weakness of the argument.

Restate your position. This writer restates his position again and summarizes the reasons to support the proposed policy.

Analyzing the Prompt

Find the main idea. What is the topic of this writing prompt? Restate it in your own words.

Understand what's expected of you. What form will your response take? In addition to stating your opinion, what else must you do?

Answer Strategies

Clearly state your opinion in the first paragraph. This writer believes that sports figures and entertainers should serve as role models.

Develop your argument with strong reasons and specific details. The writer provides good examples to support his point.

Include effective transitional words and phrases. Words such as *the first reason, another important point is, in contrast to,* and *finally* help the reader follow the writer's reasoning.

Don't ignore opposing views. The writer addresses the views of those who disagree with his ideas.

Restate your position in the conclusion. The writer restates his major point in the last paragraph.

Prompt B

Do you believe that athletes and entertainers should serve as role models? Write a letter to the editor of your community newspaper stating your opinion. Be sure to provide support for your argument.

Strong Response

Today, athletes and entertainers are always in the public eye. While there are certainly some who act as public role models, others pursue their own private interests, good or bad. I believe that public figures should not have the luxury to choose: they should accept and live up to their status as role models.

The first reason why athletes and entertainers should act as role models is that children seek to imitate them. Consequently, when athletes and entertainers take drugs, some children will explore this destructive behavior.

Another important point is that athletes and entertainers can make activities such as volunteerism more popular with the public. If, through their own modeling of community involvement, athletes and entertainers increase the number of people who seek to volunteer, imagine how our society would benefit!

Some argue that there will never be consensus on the characteristics of a good role model. While the public may not agree on all the characteristics, there are many upon which the majority of us can agree. For example, I believe few would challenge the importance of honesty, compassion, or generosity.

For these reasons, we need our athletes and entertainers to serve as role models. They have the power to inspire each of us to help create a better society.

Writing Test Practice

DIRECTIONS Read the following writing prompt. Using the strategies you've learned in this Test Preparation Guide, analyze the prompt, plan your response, and then write an essay explaining your position.

Prompt C

The superintendent has proposed a plan to reduce the fine arts budget for the public schools in order to fund a new football field. As a result, art and music classes will no longer be offered. Some adults in the community who support this plan emphasize that team sports foster community spirit and teach students valuable cooperative skills. Those who oppose it assert that students develop creativity and imagination through the study of art and music.

Write an article for your school newspaper in which you examine the positive and negative effects of such a plan, and then express your opinion. Include at least three ideas that support your position.

Scoring Rubrics

DIRECTIONS Use the following checklist to see whether you have written a strong persuasive essay. You will have succeeded if you can check nearly all of the items.

The Prompt

☐ My response meets all the requirements stated in the prompt. I have stated my position clearly and supported it with details. I raised and responded to opposing arguments.

☐ I addressed the audience appropriately.

☐ My essay fits the type of writing suggested in the prompt (letter to the editor, article for the school paper, and so on).

Reasons

☐ The reasons I offer really support my position.

☐ My audience will find the reasons convincing.

☐ I have stated my reasons clearly.

☐ I have given at least three reasons.

☐ I have supported my reasons with sufficient facts, examples, quotations, and other details.

☐ I have presented and responded to opposing arguments.

☐ My reasoning is sound. I have avoided faulty logic.

Order and Arrangement

☐ I have included a strong introduction.

☐ I have included a strong conclusion.

☐ The reasons are arranged in a logical order.

Word Choice

☐ The language of my essay is appropriate for my audience.

☐ I have used precise, vivid words and persuasive language.

Fluency

☐ I have used sentences of varying lengths and structures.

☐ I have connected ideas with transitions and other devices.

☐ I have used correct spelling, punctuation, and grammar.

Personal Word List

Use these pages to build your personal vocabulary. As you read the selections, take time to mark unfamiliar words. These should be words that seem interesting or important enough to add to your permanent vocabulary. After reading, look up the meanings of these words and record the information below. For each word, write a sentence that shows its correct use.

Review your list from time to time. Try to put these words into use in your writing and conversation.

Word: _____

Selection: _____

Page/Line: _____ / _____

Part of Speech: _____

Definition: _____

_____

_____

Sentence: _____

_____

Word: _____

Selection: _____

Page/Line: _____ / _____

Part of Speech: _____

Definition: _____

_____

_____

Sentence: _____

_____

Word: _____

Selection: _____

Page/Line: _____ / _____

Part of Speech: _____

Definition: _____

_____

_____

Sentence: _____

_____

Word: _____

Selection: _____

Page/Line: _____ / _____

Part of Speech: _____

Definition: _____

_____

_____

Sentence: _____

_____

Word: _____

Selection: _____

Page/Line: _____ / _____

Part of Speech: _____

Definition: _____

_____

_____

Sentence: _____

_____

Word: _____

Selection: _____

Page/Line: _____ / _____

Part of Speech: _____

Definition: _____

_____

_____

Sentence: _____

_____

Word:_____

Selection: _____

Page/Line: _____ / _____

Part of Speech: _____

Definition: _____

_____

_____

Sentence: _____

_____

Word:_____

Selection: _____

Page/Line: _____ / _____

Part of Speech: _____

Definition: _____

_____

_____

Sentence: _____

_____

Word:_____

Selection: _____

Page/Line: _____ / _____

Part of Speech: _____

Definition: _____

_____

_____

Sentence: _____

_____

Word:_____

Selection: _____

Page/Line: _____ / _____

Part of Speech: _____

Definition: _____

_____

_____

Sentence: _____

_____

Word:_____

Selection: _____

Page/Line: _____ / _____

Part of Speech: _____

Definition: _____

_____

_____

Sentence: _____

_____

Word:_____

Selection: _____

Page/Line: _____ / _____

Part of Speech: _____

Definition: _____

_____

_____

Sentence: _____

_____

Word:_____

Selection: _____

Page/Line: _____ / _____

Part of Speech: _____

Definition: _____

_____

_____

Sentence: _____

_____

Word:_____

Selection: _____

Page/Line: _____ / _____

Part of Speech: _____

Definition: _____

_____

_____

_____

Sentence: _____

_____

Personal Word List (continued)

Word: _____

Selection: _____

Page/Line: _____ / _____

Part of Speech: _____

Definition: _____

_____

_____

Sentence: _____

_____

Word: _____

Selection: _____

Page/Line: _____ / _____

Part of Speech: _____

Definition: _____

_____

_____

Sentence: _____

_____

Word: _____

Selection: _____

Page/Line: _____ / _____

Part of Speech: _____

Definition: _____

_____

_____

Sentence: _____

_____

Word: _____

Selection: _____

Page/Line: _____ / _____

Part of Speech: _____

Definition: _____

_____

_____

Sentence: _____

_____

Word: _____

Selection: _____

Page/Line: _____ / _____

Part of Speech: _____

Definition: _____

_____

_____

Sentence: _____

_____

Word: _____

Selection: _____

Page/Line: _____ / _____

Part of Speech: _____

Definition: _____

_____

_____

Sentence: _____

_____

Word: _____

Selection: _____

Page/Line: _____ / _____

Part of Speech: _____

Definition: _____

_____

_____

Sentence: _____

_____

Word: _____

Selection: _____

Page/Line: _____ / _____

Part of Speech: _____

Definition: _____

_____

_____

Sentence: _____

_____

Word:_____

Selection: _____

Page/Line: _____ / _____

Part of Speech: _____

Definition: _____

_____

_____

Sentence: _____

_____

Word:_____

Selection: _____

Page/Line: _____ / _____

Part of Speech: _____

Definition: _____

_____

_____

Sentence: _____

_____

Word:_____

Selection: _____

Page/Line: _____ / _____

Part of Speech: _____

Definition: _____

_____

_____

Sentence: _____

_____

Word:_____

Selection: _____

Page/Line: _____ / _____

Part of Speech: _____

Definition: _____

_____

_____

Sentence: _____

_____

Word:_____

Selection: _____

Page/Line: _____ / _____

Part of Speech: _____

Definition: _____

_____

_____

Sentence: _____

_____

Word:_____

Selection: _____

Page/Line: _____ / _____

Part of Speech: _____

Definition: _____

_____

_____

Sentence: _____

_____

Word:_____

Selection: _____

Page/Line: _____ / _____

Part of Speech: _____

Definition: _____

_____

_____

Sentence: _____

_____

Word:_____

Selection: _____

Page/Line: _____ / _____

Part of Speech: _____

Definition: _____

_____

_____

Sentence: _____

_____

Personal Word List (continued)

Word:_____

Selection: _____

Page/Line: _____ / _____

Part of Speech: _____

Definition: _____
_____
_____

Sentence: _____
_____

Word:_____

Selection: _____

Page/Line: _____ / _____

Part of Speech: _____

Definition: _____
_____
_____

Sentence: _____
_____

Word:_____

Selection: _____

Page/Line: _____ / _____

Part of Speech: _____

Definition: _____
_____
_____

Sentence: _____
_____

Word:_____

Selection: _____

Page/Line: _____ / _____

Part of Speech: _____

Definition: _____
_____
_____

Sentence: _____
_____

Word:_____

Selection: _____

Page/Line: _____ / _____

Part of Speech: _____

Definition: _____
_____
_____

Sentence: _____
_____

Word:_____

Selection: _____

Page/Line: _____ / _____

Part of Speech: _____

Definition: _____
_____
_____

Sentence: _____
_____

Word:_____

Selection: _____

Page/Line: _____ / _____

Part of Speech: _____

Definition: _____
_____
_____

Sentence: _____
_____

Word:_____

Selection: _____

Page/Line: _____ / _____

Part of Speech: _____

Definition: _____
_____
_____

Sentence: _____
_____

Word:_____

Selection: _____

Page/Line: _____ / _____

Part of Speech: _____

Definition: _____

_____

_____

Sentence: _____

_____

Word:_____

Selection: _____

Page/Line: _____ / _____

Part of Speech: _____

Definition: _____

_____

_____

Sentence: _____

_____

Word:_____

Selection: _____

Page/Line: _____ / _____

Part of Speech: _____

Definition: _____

_____

_____

Sentence: _____

_____

Word:_____

Selection: _____

Page/Line: _____ / _____

Part of Speech: _____

Definition: _____

_____

_____

Sentence: _____

Word:_____

Selection: _____

Page/Line: _____ / _____

Part of Speech: _____

Definition: _____

_____

_____

Sentence: _____

_____

Word:_____

Selection: _____

Page/Line: _____ / _____

Part of Speech: _____

Definition: _____

_____

_____

Sentence: _____

_____

Word:_____

Selection: _____

Page/Line: _____ / _____

Part of Speech: _____

Definition: _____

_____

_____

Sentence: _____

_____

Word:_____

Selection: _____

Page/Line: _____ / _____

Part of Speech: _____

Definition: _____

_____

_____

Sentence: _____

_____

Personal Word List (continued)

Word: _____

Selection: _____

Page/Line: _____ / _____

Part of Speech: _____

Definition: _____

_____

_____

Sentence: _____

_____

Word: _____

Selection: _____

Page/Line: _____ / _____

Part of Speech: _____

Definition: _____

_____

_____

Sentence: _____

_____

Word: _____

Selection: _____

Page/Line: _____ / _____

Part of Speech: _____

Definition: _____

_____

_____

Sentence: _____

_____

Word: _____

Selection: _____

Page/Line: _____ / _____

Part of Speech: _____

Definition: _____

_____

_____

Sentence: _____

_____

Word: _____

Selection: _____

Page/Line: _____ / _____

Part of Speech: _____

Definition: _____

_____

_____

Sentence: _____

_____

Word: _____

Selection: _____

Page/Line: _____ / _____

Part of Speech: _____

Definition: _____

_____

_____

Sentence: _____

_____

Word: _____

Selection: _____

Page/Line: _____ / _____

Part of Speech: _____

Definition: _____

_____

_____

Sentence: _____

_____

Word: _____

Selection: _____

Page/Line: _____ / _____

Part of Speech: _____

Definition: _____

_____

_____

Sentence: _____

_____

Word:_____

Selection: _____

Page/Line: _____ / _____

Part of Speech: _____

Definition: _____

_____

_____

Sentence: _____

_____

Word:_____

Selection: _____

Page/Line: _____ / _____

Part of Speech: _____

Definition: _____

_____

_____

Sentence: _____

_____

Word:_____

Selection: _____

Page/Line: _____ / _____

Part of Speech: _____

Definition: _____

_____

_____

Sentence: _____

_____

Word:_____

Selection: _____

Page/Line: _____ / _____

Part of Speech: _____

Definition: _____

_____

_____

Sentence: _____

_____

Word:_____

Selection: _____

Page/Line: _____ / _____

Part of Speech: _____

Definition: _____

_____

_____

Sentence: _____

_____

Word:_____

Selection: _____

Page/Line: _____ / _____

Part of Speech: _____

Definition: _____

_____

_____

Sentence: _____

_____

Word:_____

Selection: _____

Page/Line: _____ / _____

Part of Speech: _____

Definition: _____

_____

_____

Sentence: _____

_____

Word:_____

Selection: _____

Page/Line: _____ / _____

Part of Speech: _____

Definition: _____

_____

_____

Sentence: _____

_____

Personal Word List (continued)

Word: _____
Selection: _____
Page/Line: _____ / _____
Part of Speech: _____
Definition: _____
_____
_____
Sentence: _____
_____

Word: _____
Selection: _____
Page/Line: _____ / _____
Part of Speech: _____
Definition: _____
_____
_____
Sentence: _____
_____

Word: _____
Selection: _____
Page/Line: _____ / _____
Part of Speech: _____
Definition: _____
_____
_____
Sentence: _____
_____

Word: _____
Selection: _____
Page/Line: _____ / _____
Part of Speech: _____
Definition: _____
_____
_____
Sentence: _____
_____

Word: _____
Selection: _____
Page/Line: _____ / _____
Part of Speech: _____
Definition: _____
_____
_____
Sentence: _____
_____

Word: _____
Selection: _____
Page/Line: _____ / _____
Part of Speech: _____
Definition: _____
_____
_____
Sentence: _____
_____

Word: _____
Selection: _____
Page/Line: _____ / _____
Part of Speech: _____
Definition: _____
_____
_____
Sentence: _____
_____

Word: _____
Selection: _____
Page/Line: _____ / _____
Part of Speech: _____
Definition: _____
_____
_____
Sentence: _____
_____

Word:_____

Selection: _____

Page/Line: _____ / _____

Part of Speech: _____

Definition: _____

_____

_____

Sentence: _____

_____

Word:_____

Selection: _____

Page/Line: _____ / _____

Part of Speech: _____

Definition: _____

_____

_____

Sentence: _____

_____

Word:_____

Selection: _____

Page/Line: _____ / _____

Part of Speech: _____

Definition: _____

_____

_____

Sentence: _____

_____

Word:_____

Selection: _____

Page/Line: _____ / _____

Part of Speech: _____

Definition: _____

_____

_____

Sentence: _____

_____

Word:_____

Selection: _____

Page/Line: _____ / _____

Part of Speech: _____

Definition: _____

_____

_____

Sentence: _____

_____

Word:_____

Selection: _____

Page/Line: _____ / _____

Part of Speech: _____

Definition: _____

_____

_____

Sentence: _____

_____

Word:_____

Selection: _____

Page/Line: _____ / _____

Part of Speech: _____

Definition: _____

_____

_____

Sentence: _____

_____

Word:_____

Selection: _____

Page/Line: _____ / _____

Part of Speech: _____

Definition: _____

_____

_____

Sentence: _____

_____

Personal Word List (continued)

Word:_____

Selection: _____

Page/Line: _____ / _____

Part of Speech: _____

Definition: _____

_____

_____

Sentence: _____

_____

Word:_____

Selection: _____

Page/Line: _____ / _____

Part of Speech: _____

Definition: _____

_____

_____

Sentence: _____

_____

Word:_____

Selection: _____

Page/Line: _____ / _____

Part of Speech: _____

Definition: _____

_____

_____

Sentence: _____

_____

Word:_____

Selection: _____

Page/Line: _____ / _____

Part of Speech: _____

Definition: _____

_____

_____

Sentence: _____

_____

Word:_____

Selection: _____

Page/Line: _____ / _____

Part of Speech: _____

Definition: _____

_____

_____

Sentence: _____

_____

Word:_____

Selection: _____

Page/Line: _____ / _____

Part of Speech: _____

Definition: _____

_____

_____

Sentence: _____

_____

Word:_____

Selection: _____

Page/Line: _____ / _____

Part of Speech: _____

Definition: _____

_____

_____

Sentence: _____

_____

Word:_____

Selection: _____

Page/Line: _____ / _____

Part of Speech: _____

Definition: _____

_____

_____

Sentence: _____

_____

Word:_____

Selection: _____

Page/Line: _____ / _____

Part of Speech: _____

Definition: _____

_____

_____

Sentence: _____

_____

Word:_____

Selection: _____

Page/Line: _____ / _____

Part of Speech: _____

Definition: _____

_____

_____

Sentence: _____

_____

Word:_____

Selection: _____

Page/Line: _____ / _____

Part of Speech: _____

Definition: _____

_____

_____

Sentence: _____

_____

Word:_____

Selection: _____

Page/Line: _____ / _____

Part of Speech: _____

Definition: _____

_____

_____

Sentence: _____

_____

Word:_____

Selection: _____

Page/Line: _____ / _____

Part of Speech: _____

Definition: _____

_____

_____

Sentence: _____

_____

Word:_____

Selection: _____

Page/Line: _____ / _____

Part of Speech: _____

Definition: _____

_____

_____

Sentence: _____

_____

Word:_____

Selection: _____

Page/Line: _____ / _____

Part of Speech: _____

Definition: _____

_____

_____

Sentence: _____

_____

Word:_____

Selection: _____

Page/Line: _____ / _____

Part of Speech: _____

Definition: _____

_____

_____

Sentence: _____

_____

Personal Word List (continued)

Word:_____

Selection: _____

Page/Line: _____ / _____

Part of Speech: _____

Definition: _____

_____

_____

Sentence: _____

_____

Word:_____

Selection: _____

Page/Line: _____ / _____

Part of Speech: _____

Definition: _____

_____

_____

Sentence: _____

_____

Word:_____

Selection: _____

Page/Line: _____ / _____

Part of Speech: _____

Definition: _____

_____

_____

Sentence: _____

_____

Word:_____

Selection: _____

Page/Line: _____ / _____

Part of Speech: _____

Definition: _____

_____

_____

Sentence: _____

_____

Word:_____

Selection: _____

Page/Line: _____ / _____

Part of Speech: _____

Definition: _____

_____

_____

Sentence: _____

_____

Word:_____

Selection: _____

Page/Line: _____ / _____

Part of Speech: _____

Definition: _____

_____

_____

Sentence: _____

_____

Word:_____

Selection: _____

Page/Line: _____ / _____

Part of Speech: _____

Definition: _____

_____

_____

Sentence: _____

_____

Word:_____

Selection: _____

Page/Line: _____ / _____

Part of Speech: _____

Definition: _____

_____

_____

Sentence: _____

_____

Word: _____

Selection: _____

Page/Line: _____ / _____

Part of Speech: _____

Definition: _____

_____

_____

Sentence: _____

_____

Word: _____

Selection: _____

Page/Line: _____ / _____

Part of Speech: _____

Definition: _____

_____

_____

Sentence: _____

_____

Word: _____

Selection: _____

Page/Line: _____ / _____

Part of Speech: _____

Definition: _____

_____

_____

Sentence: _____

_____

Word: _____

Selection: _____

Page/Line: _____ / _____

Part of Speech: _____

Definition: _____

_____

_____

Sentence: _____

Word: _____

Selection: _____

Page/Line: _____ / _____

Part of Speech: _____

Definition: _____

_____

_____

Sentence: _____

_____

Word: _____

Selection: _____

Page/Line: _____ / _____

Part of Speech: _____

Definition: _____

_____

_____

Sentence: _____

_____

Word: _____

Selection: _____

Page/Line: _____ / _____

Part of Speech: _____

Definition: _____

_____

_____

Sentence: _____

_____

Word: _____

Selection: _____

Page/Line: _____ / _____

Part of Speech: _____

Definition: _____

_____

_____

Sentence: _____

Personal Word List (continued)

Word: _____
Selection: _____
Page/Line: _____ / _____
Part of Speech: _____
Definition: _____
_____
_____
Sentence: _____
_____

Word: _____
Selection: _____
Page/Line: _____ / _____
Part of Speech: _____
Definition: _____
_____
_____
Sentence: _____
_____

Word: _____
Selection: _____
Page/Line: _____ / _____
Part of Speech: _____
Definition: _____
_____
_____
Sentence: _____
_____

Word: _____
Selection: _____
Page/Line: _____ / _____
Part of Speech: _____
Definition: _____
_____
_____
Sentence: _____
_____

Word: _____
Selection: _____
Page/Line: _____ / _____
Part of Speech: _____
Definition: _____
_____
_____
Sentence: _____
_____

Word: _____
Selection: _____
Page/Line: _____ / _____
Part of Speech: _____
Definition: _____
_____
_____
Sentence: _____
_____

Word: _____
Selection: _____
Page/Line: _____ / _____
Part of Speech: _____
Definition: _____
_____
_____
Sentence: _____
_____

Word: _____
Selection: _____
Page/Line: _____ / _____
Part of Speech: _____
Definition: _____
_____
_____
Sentence: _____
_____

Word: _____

Selection: _____

Page/Line: _____ / _____

Part of Speech: _____

Definition: _____

_____

_____

Sentence: _____

_____

Word: _____

Selection: _____

Page/Line: _____ / _____

Part of Speech: _____

Definition: _____

_____

_____

Sentence: _____

_____

Word: _____

Selection: _____

Page/Line: _____ / _____

Part of Speech: _____

Definition: _____

_____

_____

Sentence: _____

_____

Word: _____

Selection: _____

Page/Line: _____ / _____

Part of Speech: _____

Definition: _____

_____

_____

Sentence: _____

_____

Word: _____

Selection: _____

Page/Line: _____ / _____

Part of Speech: _____

Definition: _____

_____

_____

Sentence: _____

_____

Word: _____

Selection: _____

Page/Line: _____ / _____

Part of Speech: _____

Definition: _____

_____

_____

Sentence: _____

_____

Word: _____

Selection: _____

Page/Line: _____ / _____

Part of Speech: _____

Definition: _____

_____

_____

Sentence: _____

_____

Word: _____

Selection: _____

Page/Line: _____ / _____

Part of Speech: _____

Definition: _____

_____

_____

Sentence: _____

_____

Personal Word List (continued)

Word:_____
Selection: _____
Page/Line: _____ / _____
Part of Speech: _____
Definition: _____
_____
_____
Sentence: _____
_____

Word:_____
Selection: _____
Page/Line: _____ / _____
Part of Speech: _____
Definition: _____
_____
_____
Sentence: _____
_____

Word:_____
Selection: _____
Page/Line: _____ / _____
Part of Speech: _____
Definition: _____
_____
_____
Sentence: _____
_____

Word:_____
Selection: _____
Page/Line: _____ / _____
Part of Speech: _____
Definition: _____
_____
_____
Sentence: _____
_____

Word:_____
Selection: _____
Page/Line: _____ / _____
Part of Speech: _____
Definition: _____
_____
_____
Sentence: _____
_____

Word:_____
Selection: _____
Page/Line: _____ / _____
Part of Speech: _____
Definition: _____
_____
_____
Sentence: _____
_____

Word:_____
Selection: _____
Page/Line: _____ / _____
Part of Speech: _____
Definition: _____
_____
_____
Sentence: _____
_____

Word:_____
Selection: _____
Page/Line: _____ / _____
Part of Speech: _____
Definition: _____
_____
_____
Sentence: _____
_____

Word:_____

Selection: _____

Page/Line: _____ / _____

Part of Speech: _____

Definition: _____

_____

_____

Sentence: _____

_____

Word:_____

Selection: _____

Page/Line: _____ / _____

Part of Speech: _____

Definition: _____

_____

_____

Sentence: _____

_____

Word:_____

Selection: _____

Page/Line: _____ / _____

Part of Speech: _____

Definition: _____

_____

_____

Sentence: _____

_____

Word:_____

Selection: _____

Page/Line: _____ / _____

Part of Speech: _____

Definition: _____

_____

_____

Sentence: _____

_____

Word:_____

Selection: _____

Page/Line: _____ / _____

Part of Speech: _____

Definition: _____

_____

_____

Sentence: _____

_____

Word:_____

Selection: _____

Page/Line: _____ / _____

Part of Speech: _____

Definition: _____

_____

_____

Sentence: _____

_____

Word:_____

Selection: _____

Page/Line: _____ / _____

Part of Speech: _____

Definition: _____

_____

_____

Sentence: _____

_____

Word:_____

Selection: _____

Page/Line: _____ / _____

Part of Speech: _____

Definition: _____

_____

_____

Sentence: _____

_____

Acknowledgments

Arte Público Press: "Legal Alien," from *Chants* by Pat Mora (Houston: Arte Público Press—University of Houston, 1985). Copyright © 1985 by Pat Mora. Reprinted by permission of the publisher.

Susan Bergholz Literary Services: "Straw into Gold: The Metamorphosis of the Everyday" by Sandra Cisneros. First published in *The Texas Observer,* 25 September 1987. Copyright © 1987 by Sandra Cisneros. Reprinted by permission of Susan Bergholz Literary Services, New York. All rights reserved.

Chronicle Books: "Mexicans Begin Jogging," from *New and Selected Poems* by Gary Soto. Copyright © 1995 by Gary Soto. Published by Chronicle Books LLC, San Francisco. Used by permission. Visit http://www.chroniclebooks.com.

Cricket Magazine Group: "Listening to the Body" by Tracey E. Fern, *Cricket,* February 2001, Vol. 28, No. 6, pages 47–51. Reprinted by permission of CRICKET magazine.

Enslow Publishers: "John Snow and the Broad Street Pump," from *Plague and Pestilence: A History of Infectious Disease* by Linda Jacobs Altman. Copyright © 1998 by Linda Jacobs Altman. Reprinted by permission of Enslow Publishers, Inc.

Faber and Faber: "The Love Song of J. Alfred Prufrock," from *Collected Poems, 1909–1962* by T. S. Eliot. Reprinted by permission of Faber and Faber Ltd.

Harcourt: "The Jilting of Granny Weatherall," from *Flowering Judas and Other Stories* by Katherine Anne Porter. Copyright 1930 and renewed 1958 by Katherine Anne Porter. Reprinted by permission of Harcourt, Inc.

Henry Holt and Company: "The Death of the Hired Man" by Robert Frost, from *The Poetry of Robert Frost,* edited by Edward Connery Lathem. Copyright © 1958 by Robert Frost, copyright © 1967 by Lesley Frost Ballantine. Copyright 1930, 1939, © 1969 by Henry Holt and Company. Reprinted by permission of Henry Holt and Company, LLC.

Alfred A. Knopf: Excerpts from *Of Plymouth Plantation, 1620–1647* by William Bradford, edited by Samuel Eliot Morison. Copyright © 1952 by Samuel Eliot Morison, renewed 1980 by Emily M. Beck.

"I, Too," "Dream Deferred" ("Harlem") and "The Weary Blues," from *The Collected Poems of Langston Hughes* by Langston Hughes. Copyright © 1994 by The Estate of Langston Hughes. Used by permission of Alfred A. Knopf, a division of Random House, Inc.

Random House: "A Rose for Emily," from *Collected Stories of William Faulkner* by William Faulkner. Copyright © 1930 and renewed 1958 by William Faulkner. Used by permission of Random House, Inc.

Victoria Sandars Associates: "How It Feels to Be Colored Me" by Zora Neale Hurston, from *I Love Myself When I Am Laughing: A Zora Neale Hurston Reader,* edited by Alice Walker. Reprinted by permission of Victoria Sandars Associates on behalf of the Estate of Zora Neale Hurston.

Scholastic: "Wild Everest: Over the Top" by Maria L. Chang, from *Science World,* February 23, 1998. Copyright © 1998 by Scholastic Inc. Reprinted by permission of Scholastic Inc.

Scribner: "The End of Something," from *In Our Time* by Ernest Hemingway. Copyright 1925 by Charles Scribner's Sons, copyright renewed 1953 by Ernest Hemingway. Reprinted with the permission of Scribner, a division of Simon & Schuster.

Viking Penguin: Excerpt from *The Crucible* by Arthur Miller. Copyright © 1952, 1953, 1954, renewed © 1980, 1981, 1982 by Arthur Miller. Used by permission of Viking Penguin, a division of Penguin Putnam Inc.

Writers House: Excerpts from "Letter from Birmingham Jail" by Martin Luther King, Jr. Copyright © 1963 by Martin Luther King, Jr., renewed 1991 by the Estate of Martin Luther King. Reprinted by arrangement with the Heirs to the Estate of Martin Luther King, Jr., c/o Writers House, LLC, as agent for the proprietor.

Cover

Illustration copyright © 1998 Michael Steirnagle.

Art Credits

2–3 *background* Copyright © D. Bowen/Westlight; **15–16** *background* PhotoDisc/Getty Images; **76–77** *background* PhotoDisc/Getty Images; **88** Copyright © Bettmann/Corbis; **88–89** *background* Copyright © Bettmann/Corbis; **150–151** *background* Photograph by Sharon Hoogstraten; **177–178** *background* Photograph by Sharon Hoogstraten; **194** From the Collections of the Library of Congress; **211–212** *background* PhotoDisc/Getty Images; **223–224** *background* Judith DuFour Love; **314** D. J. McKay; **358** Copyright © Bettmann/Corbis; **378–379** *background* AP/Wide World Photos; **406, 409** Copyright © Bettmann/Corbis; **411** PhotoDisc/Getty Images; **413** all Copyright © Bettmann/Corbis; **415** Copyright © Mug Shots/Corbis.